Distributed Algorithms

A Verbose Tour

Fourré Sigs

ISBN: 9781795464420

To the incorrigible disposition of a lazy bum: thanks for being my worst critic and best pal

Table of contents

Preface

Introduction

We live in an age where distributed computing environments are everywhere. They have become absolutely and incontrovertibly all-pervasive in the technical infrastructures that aid and manage just about every facet of our daily lives. It will soon be impossible, if not already, to point out an effective service implementation that handles non-trivial load while being implemented in a monolithic fashion. The focus of this book is the study of algorithms designed to be executed in a distributed environment; i.e. the study of distributed algorithms. The intention of this preface to the book is broadly two-fold: describe the target audience of the book and shed some light on the structure and style adopted for the book's content. Indeed, we will be expounding on two highly interrelated subjects where each determines the other to a good extent.

A note on intended audience

The twenty chapters of this book cover a wide range of material - starting with an introduction to distributed systems, we describe, analyse, and prove scores of distributed algorithms and impossibility results that vary from the simplest to the complex, including several ground-breaking works in the field of distributed computing. The book does not restrict itself to a beginner's guide, though it does take elaborate care to present the various topics in a highly newbie-friendly manner. One specific aim of the book is to function as a smooth, easy, and illuminating read while also being useful as a quick reference for a hands-on professional. Whether you are a seasoned system designer or a programmer with many years of experience in distributed computing, or a student, or someone new to the industry, or an experienced professional who has spent many years on monolithic systems and now planning to make a quick transition to the distributed way of doing things, you are a part of the target audience for this book. Following up on that last statement, please note a critical differentiator: while the contents of the book are varied enough that they cater to all mentioned classes of readers, the style of presentation is expressly chosen with the last three in mind. The next sections will cover this topic in further detail.

Structure and style of presentation

Let us talk about structure first. The book adopts a similar structure as many popular publications on the topic of distributed algorithms: network algorithms and shared memory ones are handled in separate parts of the book. As a result, multiple problem contexts are revisited in the final part of the book which is dedicated to shared memory algorithms. However, we choose not to assign individual parts or sections to synchronous and asynchronous algorithms - the intention is to allow readers to better contrast the behaviours of the synchronous and asynchronous variants of an algorithm by having them rather 'close by' to each other. The first part of the book is the briefest of all three and is used to provide a quick orientation on distributed systems in general and some of their key properties in particular. The second part is dedicated to network algorithms and is the longest of the three by a stretch.

Let us consider the presentation style next. In brief, the style is anything but terse. Indeed, this is hinted at in a rather broad manner by the subtitle of the book: *a verbose tour*. There is a constant effort throughout the book to avoid an excess of mathematical language and notations altogether whenever possible and be kept to a minimum when a total avoidance might take something away from the proof or analysis at hand. Let us also note here, then, that we do give up something when we deviate from a terse manner of description: a terse style does reduce the chances of ambiguity. A verbose approach on the other hand, while lending a quality of light reading, can at times leave itself vulnerable to multiple interpretations - the imbibed meaning at times even dependent on the reader's state of mind, mental makeup, or any preconceptions on the topic being addressed. The book attempts to find a suitable balance by backing up its expansive style with a plenitude of examples, flowcharts, and diagrammatic representations. In short, the verbose nature of presentation is aimed at readability while any consequent ambiguity is resolved by following up the presentation and analysis of a topic with examples and visual representations. Now, this does bring us to the topic of examples.

Good examples need to tread a fine line when it comes to handling complexity. How do we rationalise that statement? To begin with, we can safely assume that an example becomes necessary only when the subject matter at hand approaches a certain level of complexity. The very idea of an example is to present a story that is similar to the topic being exemplified while at the same time existing at a lower level of complexity. Now, an example that is too simple will lose too many details as to deviate significantly from the subject matter. Next, consider the other extreme: an example that (too) closely resembles the topic being exemplified will exist at a similar level of (undesirable) complexity, thus defeating its purpose. Indeed, a fine balance is needed. In this book, when faced with a choice the effort always is to err on the side of simplicity. As a result, a few examples do take creative liberties while opting to maintain a loose connection with the topic at hand. The idea in such cases is to let the example provide only a sharp hint or two in the right direction; the reader is trusted to work out the rest of the details once the correct direction of comprehension is pointed out.

To conclude, a quick note on how to approach reading this book: the first four chapters of the book are oriented towards beginners on the subject, so others might prefer to skip them and refer back later in case of a specific need. From the fifth chapter onwards, the complexity of the contents (algorithms in particular) start stepping up – all the way to a few industrial-strength protocols being analysed in a rather detailed fashion towards the end of the second part of the book. Up until that point, no familiarity with computer programming is assumed. The last and third part of the book, however, does presuppose a basic level of programming experience or knowledge. There is a certain abundance of code (and pseudo code) in the chapters on shared memory algorithms; readers who are not particularly interested in code are still encouraged to make use of the accompanying descriptions and treatment, because the overall style remains the same as elsewhere in the book - fairly verbose and voluble.

PART 1: INTRODUCTION AND FUNDAMENTALS

Chapter 1. Introduction

Welcome to the introductory chapter of this book on *Distributed Algorithms*. The layout or plan associated with this chapter is rather simple: our focus will lie firmly on the underlying platform rather than the algorithms which run on top. We attempt to get a grip on how we can formally define distributed systems, identify certain key attributes or characteristics associated with such frameworks, and finally we look at some of the advantages as well as challenges associated with building, running, and maintaining distributed computing environments.

1.1 Definitions of Distributed Systems

Before we get started with *distributed algorithms*, let us ask ourselves the following question:

Just what is a *distributed system* or *distributed computing environment*?

While that is probably one of the easier questions we will address in this book, *easy* need not imply a single straightforward answer. One can come up with a lot of definitions and descriptions that will portray a distributed system from various angles with varying degrees of accuracy. Consider the following descriptions by Leslie Lamport, for instance:

- *A distributed system consists of a collection of distinct processes which are spatially separated, and which communicate with one another by exchanging messages*

- *A system is distributed if the message transmission delay is not negligible compared to the time between events in a single process*

How about the following one by Andrew S. Tanenbaum:

- *A distributed system is a collection of independent computers that appears to its users as a single coherent system*

Another one from Lamport, with a touch of humour for good measure:

- *You know you have one when the crash of a computer you've never heard of stops you from getting any work done*

We have probably made our point by now with this motley list of descriptions and definitions. However, we still need to get started somewhere; so, we shall eschew technical jargon for now and start from scratch with a very informal attitude.

1.1.1 A quick and informal example

Let us consider adopting the following definition for a distributed system:

A scenario involving a set of players working together to achieve a specific goal.

Now, the above description just might bring to one's mind the concept of a *sports team*. How about a football team, then? Hardly surprising, once we consider a football team in action: a set of players, or *entities*, each with a certain capability and role, working and communicating with each other, executing specific *plans*, striving together towards a specific *goal*.

Let us take a closer look at this *system* and identify its primary characteristics:

Multiple entities that *work* together, and *communicate* with each other, to *execute* well-defined *strategies* (or *algorithms*), for achieving a specific *objective*.

So far so good.

The notion of a football team serves us well to set up an informal, yet reasonably accurate, definition of a distributed system. Let us use this model to understand a few more aspects of distributed systems before moving on to a more formal and useful representation.

How does a good football team operate?

In highly simplified terms:

The team's coach devices an effective strategy or algorithm which is then executed by the team as a whole.

As we look closer at that particular picture, various details begin to emerge:

- Each *entity* or player performs a certain amount of work:
    - accept a pass
    - make progress with the ball
    - make a pass
    - try and score if there is a chance
    - etc
- Players *communicate* with each other, in terms of passing the ball as well as conveying signals and information
- *Timing* and *synchronisation* between players are extremely important; not all players 'operate' at the same speed (or skill), yet the team has to make it work as a whole
- *Faults* or *errors* can happen: a player can make a faulty pass, a perfectly good pass can get intercepted, and so on
- An entity can *go down*: players can get injured, receive a red card, etc - sometimes such an invalid entity is replaced; sometimes not

Interestingly, our analogy of a football team seems to be accurate enough that several of the above characteristics are key elements used in the formal research and study of distributed systems. Having said that, let us leave football for now and move on to a more formal analysis of distributed computing environments - while holding on to the keywords and key characteristics which our football analogy provided us with.

1.1.2 A more formal approach

Let us go with the following description and see where it takes us:

Multiple compute nodes that work and communicate with each other, with a given amount of tolerance to failures and a given amount of timing or synchronisation, to execute a well-defined algorithm in order to solve a specific problem.

Interestingly, multiple parameters that surfaced at various points during our informal analysis till now fit rather neatly into our formal version as well:

- *Multiple*
- *Work*
- *Failure*
- *Timing* or *synchronisation*
- *Algorithm*
- *Communicate*
- *Problem*

Now, this is particularly useful because we have just confirmed what we observed earlier: that we have indeed identified several key attributes that are widely used to analyse and classify distributed frameworks. We shall go ahead and select a few key parameters from this lot for a closer look. Obviously, one of them is *Algorithm* - which is the topic of this book, after all. A close familiarity with a few others will serve us well along the way, because we will be depending directly on them to classify algorithms and to analyse and measure their various properties.

1.2 Attributes of Distributed Systems

1.2.1 Communication

Remember that we have loosely used the term *compute nodes* to describe the entities in a distributed system. That is a broad enough term which could represent anything from a *CPU*, to a physical box running a specific software, to a specific process running in an operating system, or even a virtual machine among many running on top of a virtualisation platform. Whichever the case, they need to *communicate* with each other to get the job done.
We can imagine multiple processes using some form of *IPC* (Inter Process Communication), or physical machines using an ethernet, or a wireless network, or multiple *CPUs* working together using shared memory, and so on. Broadly speaking, our interest will be held by two types of systems differentiated by their means of communication: *message passing* (networked) systems

and *shared memory* systems. In popular usage, a message passing system is referred to as a distributed computing system, while a shared memory one is known as a parallel computing system. Indeed, this is pure nomenclature; one is just a loosely (or tightly) coupled version of the other. The second part of this book deals with the former, while the third part is dedicated to the latter.

1.2.2 Synchronisation

Consider the exact words we used earlier: *a certain amount of timing or synchronisation.* Indeed, *certain* in this context could mean *none*, *some*, or *complete*. How will the system look like in each case?

Consider a Chess match. Or a Tennis (singles) match. There are two entities involved in either case, but the striking aspect in this context is how they operate in *lock-step*. One player makes a move, then the opponent gets to make one. In other words, there is perfect synchronisation in either scenario - such that we have two good examples of a *synchronous distributed system.* The two entities work together, never breaking step, to achieve the final outcome (of the match). So, what about the other extreme, which would be an *asynchronous distributed system*?

Let us go back to the football analogy. Passes get intercepted, nobody gets waited on, players get tackled, yellow cards, red cards, one set of players operating with a stated primary aim of disrupting the rhythm of the other set...we seem to be faced with a maelstrom of semi-controlled chaos here. Is there anything *synchronous* happening here, once we look at the match as a whole? One team might operate at a speed that is completely at odds with the second team. In fact, let us hold that thought for now. We will come back to this conundrum in the next section on *failures* in distributed systems.

So, what about a more definite example of an asynchronous distributed system? How about two chess aficionados, widely separated geographically, using the postal mail system to play chess? X makes a move by writing it down on paper and posting it to Y, and then gets on with other businesses of life. Y receives X's move in due course and responds similarly. X does not exactly wait on Y's reply; whenever the *event* (reply) occurs, X *reacts* to the same. It should be immediately obvious that one defining property of asynchronous systems is *unbounded communication delay*. While this is not a bad example, let us consider another one that will illustrate a different aspect of asynchronous systems, albeit in a more subtle or refined manner.

Consider Jack being in a room, empty except for another person, Lisa. The former has absolutely nothing to do; thoroughly bored. Nobody is a stranger to said affliction where one is acutely aware of each passing second. In fact, we shall adopt a certain rigid formality for an instant and assign the unit of time for Jack to be one second. In other words, for Jack, time flows in units of seconds, each of which Jack is painfully aware of. In contrast, Lisa is practically in another world. Lisa is utterly and totally involved in some mental task - maybe a puzzle, perhaps just daydreaming - that takes up all, every bit, of her attention. For Lisa, seconds and even minutes pass by without realisation. Maybe the unit of time for her is more like 30 minutes, or maybe even an hour - because that is the shortest interval of time which she is aware of. Once again, this is a condition which very few people are unfamiliar with.

Having set the context, we shall consider the scenario of Jack attempting to communicate with Lisa. Most likely, yet another familiar situation for most; attempting to make conversation with someone who is lost in thought. Jack ventures a question,

'Lisa, what is your plan for next week?'

We can intuitively imagine what follows; if Jack is lucky, Lisa might respond ever so subtly, without even lifting her head, sometime in the next one minute or so, with a,

'hmm?'

Which is simply a vague indication along the lines of,

'Ok I received your message. Let me process it and get back to you, right now I'm a bit busy'

Or Lisa might just stay silent. The message is not lost by any means; she is operating at a different clock speed altogether. At some point in the future, maybe after a few minutes, maybe more, she will (might) snap out of her reverie and blurt out,

'What were you saying? oh, next week? yeah, no, actually no plans for next week'

And dive right back into what was occupying her all this while. Next, imagine a roomful of such people, each person in a different 'state of tune', and everyone needing to communicate and arrive at a certain consensus on a topic of some description: we end up with a (very) rough idea of how an asynchronous system goes about doing what it does.

1.2.3 Failure model

As promised previously, we shall go right back to the football analogy. Let us think of a football team in the following manner: we have a group of entities, passing a primary message (the ball) among each other. The problem they attempt to solve is to get the message to a specific destination address (the other goal post) while actively preventing the message ending up at another specific address (their own goal post). Additionally, each player has an address, and a pass from one player to another can be thought of as a message being sent to a specific address along a particular *message channel*.

Next, let us step back a bit: looking at a football match in its entirety, rather than a single team. We have a whole group of entities working together to produce an outcome (of the match). Now, we will transform and reduce this system a bit: where there are two distinct teams operating, replace one of the teams with an appropriate *failure model*. Let one team magically transform to invisible ghosts, so to speak. In other words, now we have only one set of entities passing along a message to each other on its way, *hopefully*, to a final destination address. Why *hopefully*?

Because, we now allow the *message channels* at their disposal to be so unpredictably error prone that a message can be delivered to a totally different or wrong address, including the very address at which they do not want the message to end up (their own goal post). This is the exact representation of a pass being intercepted, ball possession returning firmly to the other team, thus leading directly to them scoring a goal.

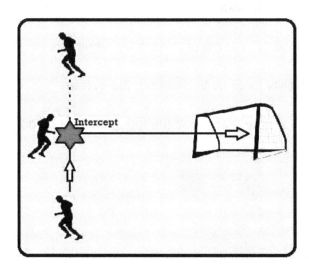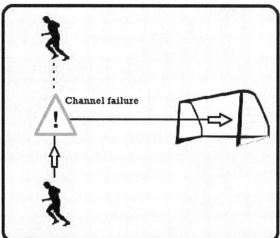

With such a representation or transformation, a football match begins to resemble a synchronous distributed system in action - albeit one whose failure model appears to possess a particularly disruptive nature, to the point of being downright malicious.

1.2.4 Algorithm

To state the obvious, an algorithm is a strategy, a set of steps, a process, designed to solve a specific problem - and a distributed algorithm is one that is designed for a computing environment which is of a distributed nature. The bulk of this book is all about the analysis of various distributed algorithms. We will discuss and study various distributed algorithms in the context of different distributed systems which they are designed for: in terms of the first two attributes that we discussed previously, i.e. the timing model and the communication mechanism.

1.3 Advantages of Distributed Systems

Distributed systems exist for a reason - obviously. In this section, let us try to list some of those, i.e. some of the key reasons why we tend to gravitate towards distributed systems rather than monolithic ones. In the next section, we will take a different perspective and visit the complications introduced by these same aspects. The general model we will adopt is as follows: we have a problem to solve, and once we solve it, we can provide the solution as a service which in turn will find users. So: why a distributed system and not a monolithic one as the platform for the service? Let us consider some possible answers:

1. The solution cannot be implemented on a monolithic system

2. The solution lends itself to a high degree of parallelisation that a monolithic system cannot provide
3. The scalability required from the solution cannot be satisfied by a monolithic system
4. The geographic spread of potential users forces us to distribute the solution geographically
5. Regional restrictions in terms of required resources (like power, etc) force us to distribute the system geographically
6. The *SLA* (Service Level Agreement) requirements in terms of availability require us to distribute the system
7. The *SLA* requirements in terms of data durability force us to distribute the system

Clearly, we benefit across multiple areas; but what if we had to choose the top three? Let us go with:

- Availability
- Scalability
- Performance

So, we are talking about a resultant system that is more available, lends itself to expansion, and finally, one that responds quicker and works faster.

Even if we somehow get hold of a totally failure-proof otherworldly-fast wonder machine - one that cannot go down and will handle unlimited load - the resultant monolithic system will still be exposed to limitations such as availability issues due to a regional outage (how about a meteor strike?), and latency issues due to geographical spread of users. No matter how great the futuristic machine performs in terms of raw output and scalability, availability and performance will still remain as open issues. Even if we fire-proof and bomb-proof and meteor-proof the data center which hosts our wonder machine, distant users will face latency issues - at least till we figure out how to change the properties of light.

Next, let us look at the cost that we (usually) end up paying for all what we accomplish using distributed systems.

1.4 Challenges of Distributed Systems

The technical challenges start with the problem of ensuring that core functionality is retained in an unaffected fashion while distributing an algorithm across multiple processing units. If this hurdle is stumbled upon, all that should follow - availability, scalability, performance et al - lose their purpose and meaning. Once the first step is accomplished, at least in theory if not in practice, some of the subsequent challenges are rather obvious items such as:

- The financial and logistic costs associated with the infrastructure and personnel that is distributed geographically
- The problem of monitoring, maintaining, and administering the distributed framework

- Setting up sensible load balancing schemes and failover policies to ensure optimum performance and fault tolerance
- Etc

Upon starting with a monolithic arrangement consisting of a single machine and building a distributed infrastructure from there, if everything goes well, we would end up with a final configuration that matches Tanenbaum's definition - a collection of independent computers that appears to its users as a single coherent system - one which, ideally, would convince a user that nothing short of a 'super machine' is at the other end. Let us note here that a single machine, for all its inadequacies, has one thing going for it: *consistency*. Such a system is essentially a single point of contact, so the experience you receive is always consistent. If a user from Glasgow makes an update in the system, a user query from Boston will pick it up - right away. On the other hand, a distributed system is a far more complex affair, having multiple data centers with data replicated across numerous databases across the region or even the world. How do you ensure consistency in this scenario?

As an example, consider a file sharing service that lets users upload, download, and modify files. Broadly, we have a system that allows reads and writes. If a user from Houston does a write - i.e. uploads or modifies a file - will those changes be visible to a user from Singapore right away? If not, what is the delay involved? More likely that not, these two users will be talking to different servers and databases located far apart. Obviously, we will need an algorithm in place that implements a suitable replication protocol as per our operational requirements. In other words, the generic solution here is to rely on consistency protocols. Now, such protocols and algorithms clearly will depend on the internal network which provides connectivity between the various 'components' of the system. What will be the result if there is an internal network outage? Note that an external user will (should) remain oblivious to incidents internal to the system. How should an internal outage (be allowed to) affect the user experience of an external entity? There seems to be a point emerging here, which indicates a rather strong relation between system availability, consistency and internal connectivity. Let us use the next chapter to take a close look at this phenomenon before moving on from the topic of distributed systems to that of distributed algorithms.

1.5 Conclusion

To round up, we came up with an informal definition first, and a formal one next, for distributed computing environments. The informal definition was useful enough to highlight the various attributes of such systems, which we confirmed and validated using a similar analysis of the more formal model. Next, we identified certain key attributes of distributed systems that will hold our attention in the coming chapters. Lastly, we listed and described the advantages provided, and the corresponding costs extracted, by the process of converting a monolithic system or service to a distributed one.

1.6 What's next?

We ended section *1.5* with an unanswered question. We follow that up in the next chapter using a couple of examples that highlight an important limitation of distributed systems in general and *distributed data stores* in particular. In a way, the constraint property which we come up against in the next chapter will function as a gentle introduction to similar (and more complex) impossibility statements that later chapters will cover.

Chapter 2. Warming up with CAP theorem

In this chapter, we consider two scenarios to illustrate the mechanics of the *CAP* theorem. One is of a technical disposition, where the players are the some of the key components of the internet. The second involves actual human beings, with a bit of political and military intrigue thrown in for good measure.

2.1 The CAP theorem: Introduction

Also known as *Brewer's theorem*, the relatively simple sounding proposition describes a fundamental trade-off between *Consistency*, *Availability*, and *Partition-tolerance* in any networked data store: *a distributed system cannot simultaneously be consistent, available, and partition-tolerant.*

2.2 A proxy affair

Consider a *proxy server*, located somewhere in the internet. To the uninitiated, a proxy server can be thought of as the combination of two components; a *browser* and a *web server*. This analogy makes sense once you adopt the following line of thought: a web server accepts requests and serves them, while a browser sends requests and accepts their responses. The web server component of a proxy forms the client-facing side, which accepts requests from a (remote) user. Once a request is accepted, it is passed to the second component - the browser component - which sends the request to the intended destination, collects the response, and passes it back to the web server component which, in turn, sends it back to the user.

2.2.1 Adding a web cache

Next, imagine a cache module being plonked on to the client-facing web server component. Upon receiving a request, the cache-equipped web server module will not blindly pass it to the browser component because the required response might be found in the cache. If the cache indeed has a matching entry, the request is served without needing to contact the remote destination. Otherwise, the request is forwarded to the browser component and the response is fetched from the remote server to be forwarded to the user. In such cases, a copy of the response is stored in the cache (if possible).

2.2.2 Using the cache

Now, one ought to be careful with cached entries. We do not want requests to be served with aged or stale responses, so cache entries usually have an 'age' parameter associated with them which indicates whether they have been sitting in the cache for too long or not. What happens if the proxy receives a request and the corresponding response is found in the cache as a stale or aged entry? The proxy will not immediately use it to serve the request, but instead, opts to check with the remote server by passing on the request to the browser subsystem. The request that is subsequently issued to the remote server (by the browser module of the proxy) will contain a subtle question:

I have a cached copy of the response and it is XYZ seconds old; can you please let me know if the cached copy is stale or not?

If the document at the remote server has not changed in the last *XYZ* seconds, the server will respond in a terse fashion:

Your copy is up-to-date. Use it.

If the document had changed in the last *XYZ* seconds, the remote server will issue a 'full' response containing the latest copy of the document. The proxy server will receive and forward the response, while possibly also updating the cached copy with the latest version.

What we just described is an efficient mechanism to fully exploit the potential of a web cache. Even if a cached item might appear stale, the owner of the cache will use it if the upstream server confirms that the item is up-to-date. Note that such a confirmation response is much shorter than a response that returns the entire document. In other words, we end up with considerable savings on network bandwidth.

2.2.3 To be available or consistent

Imagine a request arriving at the proxy server. As usual, the cache is checked. A matching entry is found in the cache, which however is aged - the proxy server is configured with a cache age limit of 120 seconds, and this particular entry is 150 seconds old. The only option at this point is to talk to the remote server. However, the upstream link is down and there is no way to talk to the remote destination. What are the proxy server's options at this point?

1. Ignore the staleness factor of 30 seconds, and use the cached entry to serve the request
2. Wait till the upstream link comes up before serving the request
3. Send a 'destination unavailable' response to the client

What are the consequences of each? The user will see a response in the first case, but the response need not be a correct or consistent one (if the target document at the destination has been modified meanwhile). The second option will see the user experiencing a form of unavailability. The third option has a similar consequence, too. We shall summarise:

- The first option sacrifices consistency for availability.
- The second and third options go the other way, giving up availability for the sake of ensuring consistency
- The fundamental cause of this outcome? a network outage that partitioned the proxy from the remote server.

Next, let us consider a less (much less) technical scenario where a similar choice is presented. In fact, let us go back in time a bit.

2.3 A Game of Spies

So, we are in the 1960s. The fearsome height of the cold war; plenty of geopolitical tension between Eastern bloc nations and the Western bloc ones.

Murdock is known as one of the quieter chaps in a quiet neighbourhood. In fact, his neighbours consider him remarkably unremarkable. There is nothing loud or colorful about him or his routine: he wakes up at 6am like clockwork, goes for a short jog around the neighborhood, leaves for his job which he describes to neighbours as 'paper pushing for the government', comes back by evening, and turns in by 10.

In truth, there is more to Murdock than he's prepared to let slip. Murdock works for the *CIA*; he is a spymaster, a runner of spies in the soviet camp. To clarify, a spy in this context is typically a soviet citizen, typically in a position of power/responsibility, who is willing to pass on classified information - in return for favors, monetary or otherwise. Murdock collects information from the spies he run and pass it to his *CIA* bosses, who constantly and relentlessly bombard him for priceless information on the state of military readiness of the USSR, among other things.

Now, Murdock is not one to micromanage and so he has done the right amount of delegation. He no longer deals with spies directly. There are junior *CIA* officers working in the USSR, ostensibly for the US embassy, and they do the grunt work of physically obtaining information from spies. They set up clandestine meets, service drop locations, all those hollywood stuff and more, process the raw information, and finally pass it to Murdock, who sits in his nice and cosy office in langley, reviews and collates the incoming information, and finally watches reverently as his bosses gleefully lap it all up. Once in a while, Murdock almost feels that he's making a difference in the cold war.

2.3.1 A Breakthrough

Suddenly Murdock's star has started to rise, and how. The reason is simple: two highly placed soviet military officers - Sergei and Yurchik - independently approached the local US embassy and offered their services (technically, such cases are known as walk-ins) in return for money. Their 'product' is priceless, the sort of inside information which Murdock or his bosses never had access to before. The two new spies have indeed started giving away classified information of the highest degree. However, the extremely sensitive nature of the information has made Murdock even more cautious because there is a flipside: major decisions are made based on such information and one cannot afford to be wrong. Everything has to be cross checked. This is the sort of thing that can make or break his career.

So, he comes up with the following arrangement. Murdock assigns a dedicated 'handler' to each spy. The handler, a junior *CIA* operative, is responsible for communicating with his (or her) assigned 'ward' using whichever way he (or she) feels best. So now, we have Sergei handled by Hank and Yurchik handled by Quinn. Needless to say, Sergei is unaware of Yurchik and vice versa.

At this point, let us sum up: Murdock has a *system* in place with a very specific purpose. The system is obviously not monolithic but distributed, with more than one node. Perhaps it is time to claim that it is a distributed system.

2.3.2 How does all this work?

All of which leads to the question...how does this distributed system, work, if at all? Let us take a closer look.

Let us suppose that Murdock's pointy haired boss wakes him up at 2am with a shrill and specific demand for information, such as,

'How many tanks have the russians deployed near the North German Plain?'

Murdock gets to work and sends a coded message, question enclosed, to Hank's desk at the US embassy in Moscow. How Hank deals with the resultant situation will be a reflection of the *CAP* theorem that we are currently dealing with in this chapter.

Before proceeding further, let us pause for a minute to grab some more background. Why did Murdock contact Hank rather than Quinn?

As it turns out, Quinn is much more of a field guy than Hank and prefers to live a rather dangerous life. He tends to go off contact for days as part of his job, trying to spot 'talent' (potential spies), developing new sources, cultivating existing ones, planting bugs, etc. In other words, an unpredictable maverick who keeps his job only because he is extremely effective at what he does. Further, Quinn is best suited for handling Yurchik, simply because Yurchik is (or claims to be) very highly placed in the Soviet establishment. Due to his high ranking, Yurchik is considerably harder to contact than Sergei. So, Quinn's tactics are a perfect fit when it comes to communicating with a delicate source like Yurchik.

Let us get back to Hank. The first step for Hank should be obvious: he passes on the question to Sergei. We will assume that Sergei gets his act together rapidly and responds with,

'There are no less than 1400 T-54A tanks near the North German Plain as of August 2nd'

It would be simple enough for Hank to pass on the newly received information (*'no less than 1400 T-54A'*) to Murdock. But that is where Hank's training kicks in: his next priority is to double check this information. So, what does he do? Hank will try to contact Quinn. In an Ideal world, everything goes as per plan: Hank succeeds in contacting Quinn, passes on the question, which in turn gets passed on to Yurchik, who in turn responds with information that fairly matches the number (1400) and type (*T-54A*) claimed by Sergei.

But the real world is anything but ideal.

2.3.3 The suboptimal and nonideal real world

Hank placed a message for Quinn, but there is no reply. Quinn seems to be out of contact. Maybe Quinn did receive the message but is finding it hard to contact Yurchik. Let us consider this a state of *network partition* being in effect.

What are Hank's options in this situation?

Hank can throw caution to the wind and forward Murdock what Sergei produced: *no less than 1400 T-54A.* But this could be potentially out-dated information. Maybe if Yurchik *had* been contacted, he *might* have come up with more up-to-date information: such as,

'At least 2000 T-54A and 1300 T-62 as of August 14th'

How would Hank know? How does Hank evaluate the risk of triggering a chain of events that might potentially result in a very bad military decision by his country?

2.3.4 Sacrifice Consistency?

Maybe finally Hank does decide to gamble and pass on that (unverified) information to Murdock. Here, the 'system' has decided to sacrifice consistency while remaining partition-tolerant and prioritising availability. Well, good luck to all then. Perhaps Sergei was a soviet 'plant' or maybe a 'triple agent' who's feeding damaging information to Hank. Or maybe Sergei had simply exaggerated his own position and has access to nothing beyond second-hand information or vague rumour. The effectiveness of those decisions that Murdock's bosses make on said information will decide the progress and longevity of his career.

2.3.5 Sacrifice Availability?

Should Hank stay put and wait for Quinn to come up with his reply? In which case, Murdock will see no reply from Hank: a lack of availability. In other words, the 'system' has decided to sacrifice availability while remaining partition-tolerant and prioritising consistency. Personally, Murdock does not find this situation to be particularly pleasant: he sits and squirms in his office while demands of instant enlightenment keep raining on his head from impatient and important folks sitting 'upstairs'.

2.3.6 Sacrifice Partition-tolerance?

In fact, Hank is not exactly out of options. The moment Quinn appears to be out-of-contact, Hank could send Murdock a coded message: *sorry sir, this service is currently down.* In other words, the 'system' does not tolerate a state where *network partitions* exist. More briefly, the system is not *partition-tolerant.*

At this juncture, one might be excused for the following thought: *how does such an outcome indicate anything other than a lack of availability?* The counterpoint being, a partition-tolerant behavior would have at least considered a choice between consistency and availability.

Hopefully, as an effective spymaster, Murdock has trained Hank to take the right call depending on the immediate situation, political climate, available data, criticality of the required information, and so on. In other words, hopefully Murdock has designed an effective system that dynamically makes decisions to sacrifice one from the triplet of partition-tolerance, availability, and consistency. In the real world, one can argue that it is all about a choice between availability and consistency. Partition-intolerance is really not an option because it is indeed hard to distinguish a partition-intolerant system's behavior from that of an unavailable system!

2.4 Eventual consistency

Let us look at the concept of *eventual consistency*, next. We consider both example scenarios that we have discussed so far.

2.4.1 The proxy cache

Consider an alternate option for the proxy server when faced with a cached response that is stale and an unreachable remote destination: use the cached copy to serve the request, while triggering off an asynchronous mechanism to update the cached entry.

Let us break down what we just stated. The first step of the proxy server is to serve the response using the stale cached copy. The response will contain a disclaimer: that the contents might quite possibly be stale. This serves as a useful warning not just for the user, but any downstream intermediaries as well.

Once this is done, the proxy starts a 'background' thread or process. The job of the newly formed entity is simple: keep checking constantly for a revival of upstream network connectivity, contact the remote server once the upstream connectivity is up, and update the stale cached entry. While the user is served with a possibly inconsistent response, the contents of the cache will *eventually* be consistent - thus ensuring that future requests served from the cache will see consistent responses.

2.4.2 A new strategy by Murdock

After a bit of experience with running his new and highly productive spy ring, Murdock decides to make a few minor corrections to the procedures involved. First of all, he conducts a detailed meeting with his bosses and extracts from them a simple promise: all queries from them will be labelled as either *critical* or *non-critical*.

So, how is *that* going to help?

Simple. All critical queries will be handled by Hank with consistency as the priority. In other words, in the event of Quinn being unreachable, Hank will sacrifice either partition-tolerance or availability. No risk, period.

How about non-critical queries?

In such cases, Hank is free to go ahead and sacrifice consistency. Murdock will receive an answer quick enough - the one Hank received from Sergei and possibly unverified with Yurchik via Quinn, and hence one which need not be the most consistent with reality. However, Quinn *might* eventually touch base with Hank. Hence, Murdock checks with Hank more than once over a few days (or maybe Hank gets back to Murdock once Quinn checks in) and eventually one ends up with the most consistent data that one can realistically hope to have.

2.5 Conclusion

We presented the *CAP theorem*, a fundamental trade-off between consistency, availability, and partition-tolerance in distributed systems. Afterwards, we considered a couple of examples and used them as representations for a simple distributed data store, which in turn served as a stage to demonstrate the *CAP* theorem.

2.6 What's next?

This chapter, along with the previous one, provided an introductory or refresher exercise on the general topic of distributed systems. From now onwards, we switch focus to our core topic of interest - which is the study of algorithms that execute in a distributed environment. We will start with algorithms applicable to the *message passing* model, and proceed to look at some of the primitives, the basic operations, the building blocks that are used to implement more complex algorithms.

PART 2: THE MESSAGE PASSING MODEL

Chapter 3. Building blocks: Unicast

We shall start looking at some of the more primitive operations in a distributed network that will help us implement more complex ones. We begin with the mechanism of unicast communication.

3.1 Unicast: an introduction

Unicast quite simply is a one-to-one transmission in a network of two or more entities: one party sending a message to another. This assumes that both parties hold unique addresses.

An example would be A ringing B up to pass a message, or A writing down a message and sending it to B over the postal network. These analogies cannot possibly get any simpler but start comparing them to each other and suddenly we have a fair bit to analyse further.

We have already touched upon the latter example elsewhere, noting its asynchronous nature. It follows fairly clearly, then, that the former is a synchronous method of message passing. Rather than wallow in theory, let us look at a few major distinctions between them in a practical sense.

3.2 Synchronisation

A phone call is synchronous, while messaging over the postal service is asynchronous. In the former, both parties are in lock-step and follow synchronised steps to get the message delivery done. In the latter, one party initiates the *send* operation and reverts to handle other affairs. The other party, possibly in the middle of unrelated matters, notices an *event* (delivery of the message by mail) and *reacts* (reads the message and possibly replies) accordingly.

3.3 Message delay

There is really no room for debate on the relative speeds of the two methods of communication: telephony is real-time while the postal mechanism is anything but. In more technical terms, we are talking about *bounded* and *unbounded* delays. The telephony example actually conveys more. Once we dial a number and start hearing the ringtone through the earpiece, we assume the phone (at the other end) to be ringing at the same time; in other words, we assume both parties to have a *common or global clock*. Clearly, this is predicated on a communication mechanism that provides near-instantaneous speed.

3.4 Message ordering

Synchronous communication is guaranteed to preserve *message ordering*. If A picks up the phone and goes "*Hello, how are you*", B is going to receive exactly that - and not, say "*How, you are hello*". However, if A writes those 4 words in 4 different envelopes and posts them separately, in correct order but say a few hours apart, there is no guarantee that they will reach B in the same order.

3.5 An example

An example might help to differentiate between the synchronous and asynchronous variants of unicast, as far as technical capability and nomenclature is concerned. Let us again bring in a pointy haired boss who comes over to Murdock with a crisp instruction:

'Hey, inform Max that he should cut short his vacation and be back a week early'

Well, Max is on vacation - a vacation which is about to be ruined because apparently his 'customer' insisted on an earlier delivery date than what was originally planned. It is Murdock's job now to inform Max of the good news.

We shall first assume modern times - internet and telephony is at hand. Murdock rings up Max and destroys his happiness. Next day, Murdock's boss saunters over:

'Well then, did you inform Max?'

Murdock's answer is simple and to the point:

'Yes, I talked to him and passed on the message'

Now, how about if this scenario predated the internet and email and all that? Let us also assume that Murdock tried ringing up Max with no luck. So, he sent the message to Max by postal mail. Murdock's boss checks up with him the next day:

'Well then, did you inform Max?'

Murdock's reply is a bit different in this case:

'Umm...well, I sent him the message by post'

So, the *'yes'* in the first scenario is replaced by a far less assertive *'umm well'* in the second one.

Let us derive a technical statement out of this: an entity in a synchronous distributed system can be said to have a *deliver* capability while one in an asynchronous distributed system can be said to have a *send* capability. The former comes with several guarantees which the latter does not provide.

3.6 Conclusion

We had a quick look at one of the simplest primitives in the operation of a distributed computing environment, looked at two of its major variants, and analysed some of their attributes.

3.7 What's next?

Having dealt with *unicast*, let us move on to a more complex operation which builds on what we saw here.

Chapter 4. Building blocks: broadcast

4.1 Broadcast: an introduction

We are all comfortably familiar with the concept of a *broadcast*: a term whose wide usage far predates the modern information technology era. Yet we will set up a formal definition to get things moving: *broadcast is the transmission of a message to all entities in a network or distributed system.* In other words, we are talking about a *one-to-all* association. Let us analyse this concept a bit further using a couple of examples.

4.2 Broadcast-capable network

Person X is in a room with five people. If X needs to broadcast a piece of information to those five folks, all X needs to do is to get their attention and raise his or her voice. The information or *message* is sent as sound waves, and the medium of travel of the message is, of course, air. In this specific case, all concerned entities are *immersed* in the medium and receive the message from X (more or less simultaneously).

A simple point emerges: this particular network medium *supports* broadcast, or has *broadcast capability*, as far as X's choice of communication method is concerned. Of course, if X's choice of communication was notes written on pieces of paper, then the aforementioned medium cannot help with broadcasts. We look at a variation of this problem in the next section.

4.3 Implementing broadcast: a simple algorithm

Next, let us spatially distribute these five folks across five different locations, say five different rooms with a telephone installed in each. X happens to have the phone number of one among them, who in turn has a phone number of another (or more), and so on to ensure total *connectivity*. To use technical jargon, our network resembles a *connected graph*. The following diagram represents the mentioned arrangement.

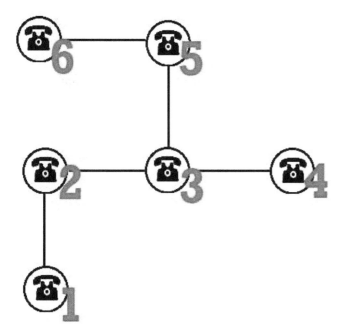

Let us suppose that X is stationed at node 1. How will X perform a broadcast in this situation?

Simple enough, X dials that one number which he or she has - of node 2 - and delivers the message. The recipient at node 2 does the same upon receiving the message: he or she dials all the numbers at his or her disposal and delivers the message, and this continues.

It seems we have a broadcast algorithm, albeit a very simple and possibly inefficient one:

The initiating entity passes the broadcast message to its neighbours, and each recipient does the same.

Let us analyse this trivial algorithm a bit further.

4.4 Simple broadcast algorithm: termination

X set off a sequence of steps once X made that single phone call to that one number X had with him or her, but how and when does that sequence end? By the definition we have so far, it is never going to end. That person (whom X called) will call the two numbers (one of those two might even be X's own number) known to him or her and pass on the message, leading to those two people doing the same, and so on - forever.

Let us adopt a more realistic outlook and assume a possibility that we tentatively suggested earlier ('*one of those two might even be X's own number*'). X called node 2 and passed the message. Now, node 5 knows two numbers, and one of them is X's number. Soon after X made that first call, X gets a ring from node 2 passing X the same message. Since X is not a robot, X takes no further action. In other words, since X already has the message, X does not follow the latter part of the algorithm ('*each recipient does the same*'). So, we have enough grounds to modify our broadcast algorithm in a subtle manner:

The initiating entity passes the broadcast message to its neighbours, and each recipient not already in possession of the message does the same.

Here's a pictorial representation of the updated situation.

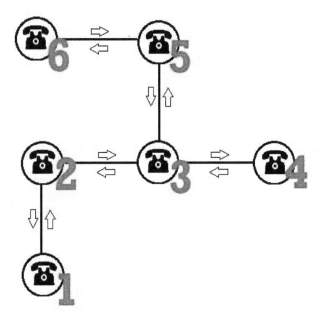

Each arrow indicates one delivery of the message in a particular direction. So, our algorithm gets the job done, but at what cost? And what do we mean by *cost*? Let us go with the following definition:

How many times did the message have to be delivered to achieve broadcast?

The answer is fairly simple: each arrow indicates the message being delivered once, and there are 10 arrows, two for each *connection* in the network. In other words, the message goes through each connection twice - once in each direction - and hence the cost in terms of the total number of times the message had to be delivered to achieve broadcast is a number that is equal to twice the number of connections in the network.

Can we optimise this further?

4.5 Simple broadcast algorithm: an optimisation

How about this: so, X delivered a message to node 2, and assuming the person stationed at node 2 is not a robot, there is no reason for node 2 to deliver the message back to X, the person who was the source of the message in the first place. This is applicable to each node in the network. With this understanding in place, the new arrangement would look like the following diagram.

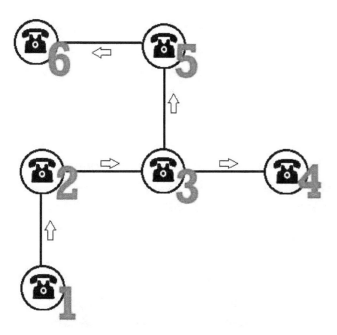

The broadcast cost has now dropped from 10 messages deliveries to just 5. It is time, then, to refine the formal broadcast algorithm further:

The initiating entity passes the broadcast message to its neighbours, and each recipient not already in possession of the message passes on the message to each neighbour except the one who delivered the message.

How do we formally define the new cost? Before we applied this optimisation, the cost was equal to twice the number of connections. What changed once we brought in the optimisation? Each entity receiving a message will no longer echo the message back to the source (who delivered the message to said entity in the first place). In other words, a saving of one message delivery for each entity (except the initiator, who is never a message recipient).

So, the new and optimised cost is simply: *twice the number of connections (which was the cost prior to the optimisation), minus the number of entities minus one (the optimisation does not affect the initiator).*

In mathematical terms,

$$C = (2 \times E) - (N - 1)$$

Where

- C is the cost
- E is the number of *edges* or connections
- N is the number of entities in the network

4.6 Cost: an alternate interpretation

So far, we have been fixated on cost in terms of the number of messages being delivered. How about a different interpretation for cost, one in terms of *time*? Obviously, the time required for broadcast completion would be decided by the entity furthest from the initiator. What we are interested in, actually, is the *worst case scenario* in terms of time.

It might be helpful at this point to note what the *diameter* of a network is: *the shortest distance between the two most distant (separated) nodes in the network*. The worst case scenario for our broadcast algorithm's cost (in terms of time) immediately follows: *when the initiator is one of the two most distant nodes in the network*. In other words, the worst case *time-cost* for our broadcast algorithm is determined by the diameter of the network.

A football analogy might help again. Let us assume that the team is practicing. The ball is to be kicked off from a specific point in the field and passed to the closest player, to be passed further on till it reaches the foremost forward player stationed near the opposite goal post. If the player doing the kickoff is the one who is closest to the foremost forward, the process will be over in the quickest fashion - a single pass is all that is needed. This is the best case scenario. The worst case scenario immediately follows: when the kickoff is done by the goalkeeper, who is furthest from the forward player.

4.7 Conclusion

We came up with a formal definition for broadcast in a network, after which we developed a simple algorithm that uses unicast message delivery as a building block to achieve broadcast in a connected network. Next, we identified and fixed a 'bug' in the algorithm to make sure that it terminates correctly. We then switched our attention to the concept of an algorithm's cost and calculated the cost of our broadcast algorithm. Lastly, we identified room for improvement in terms of cost, applied two performance 'fixes', and succeeded in reducing the algorithm's cost by a fair amount.

4.8 What's next?

Since we have a seemingly efficient broadcast algorithm, we should 'field test' it a bit - so we will get on with that. We will try using our algorithm on more complicated network topologies to see how it performs. We will also be interested in any possibilities for custom optimisations.

Chapter 5. Broadcast algorithms in cubes

5.1 Introduction

As a warmup, let us apply our broadcast algorithm to a simple network which is shaped like a two dimensional cube. Consider the following diagram:

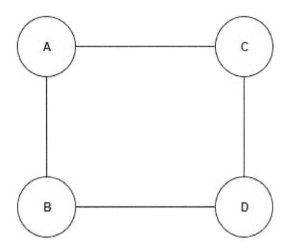

Let A be the broadcast initiator. Our broadcast algorithm reads as:

The initiating entity passes the broadcast message to its neighbours, and each recipient not already in possession of the message passes on the message to each neighbour except the one who delivered the message.

So, A sends to B and C, both of which sends to D because both has D as a neighbour. Now, depending on which message (the one from B or C) arrives first at D, we have the following two possibilities:

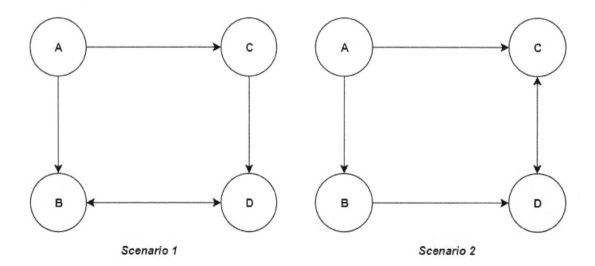

Scenario 1   *Scenario 2*

The distinction should be obvious: if D sees the message from B first, D would deliver the same to C because C forms the set of '*D's neighbours minus the message source*'. By similar reasoning, if it is the message from C that arrives first, D would deliver the same to B. In either case, we have a broadcast cost of *5 messages*.

So, the next question naturally is, can we optimise this any further? For that purpose, let us closely scrutinise the shape traversed by our network topology, i.e a cube.

5.2 Understanding Cubes

To begin with, let us consider a single node.

Now that, right there, is a zero dimensional cube. You cannot move along the cube in any direction. There is a single node, period. If node A has a message, there is nothing more to do because...there is nobody else to deliver the message to. Broadcast cost? Zilch.

How about a one dimensional cube?

The one dimensional cube in the diagram above has but a single dimension, the X axis, along which two nodes lie connected. What we are *really* interested in is the fact that a one dimensional cube can be thought of as being built by joining (the corresponding nodes of) 2 zero dimensional cubes. A similar thought applies for a two dimensional cube as well:

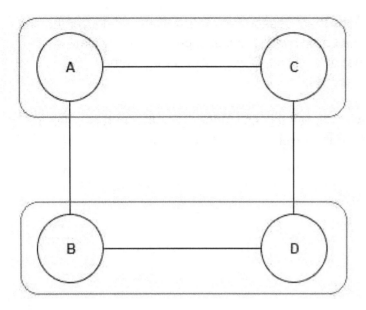

The two dimensional cube in the above diagram can be thought of as a 'parent' cube built from 2 one dimensional cubes which are 'siblings' to each other - one formed by nodes A and C, and the other by nodes B and D.

So, what about a 'proper' cube, i.e. a three dimensional cube, and what about *hypercubes* of higher orders? The exact same reasoning applies. Consider the next diagram where a three dimensional cube is assumed to be built from 2 sibling cubes - both two dimensional - one composed of nodes A, B, C, D, and the other composed of nodes E, F, G, H.

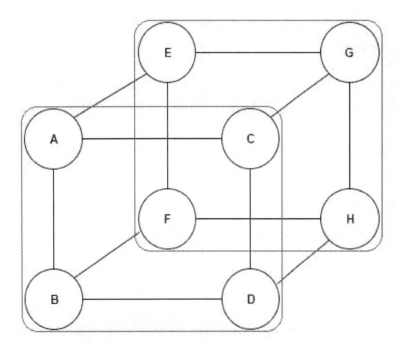

We can take this reasoning to any higher level, building *hypercubes* as we go along. Now, let us try to use this foundation to build a refined broadcast algorithm that is custom-tweaked for cube networks.

We will state the algorithm outright, check the cost out, and then reason out a proof for the same.

5.3 Optimising our broadcast algorithm for cube topologies

Without any more delay, we will propose the modified algorithm:

1. *The broadcast-initiating node delivers the message to all of its neighbours*
2. *A recipient node in a cube will assume the role of an initiator in its cube by delivering the message to all neighbours (in its cube) if the message source is a node belonging to a sibling or parent cube*

The first part should be clear enough, because it is unchanged from the original algorithm that we started off with. The second part deals with the behavior of a node that is the 'message entry point' for a cube. To understand the second part better, and to verify the algorithm in its entirety, let us back up to the case of a simple one dimensional cube and start from there.

5.3.1 One dimensional cube

So, considering the above arrangement, node A and node C form a simple one dimensional cube. Also, let us not forget that A can be considered as a zero dimensional cube, and that the same applies to C. Let us assume that A sends a message to C; this can be viewed as C (who is part of a zero dimensional cube) receiving a message from a node belonging to a sibling cube (another zero dimensional cube). As per the algorithm, C needs to deliver the message to all neighbours *in its cube*. Since C forms a zero dimensional cube, C is sole member - so nothing more to do, and the broadcast is considered finished once A delivers the message to C.

How about a two dimensional cube, then? Let us take a look.

5.3.2 Two dimensional cube

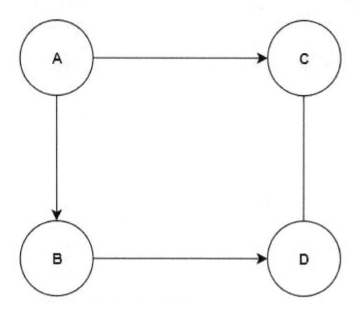

To initiate the broadcast, A delivers the message to C and B. Let us consider C's perspective first. Assuming A and C to form a one dimensional cube, C has received a message from a node in its own cube - not from a node in a parent or sibling node. One can even assume that a sibling node (the zero dimensional cube formed by A) sent the message to C; either way, C has no action to take and hence will not generate any message deliveries.

What about B? Assuming B and D to form a one dimensional cube, B has just received a message from a sibling cube (a one dimensional cube - the other of the pair forming a two dimensional cube) so B must act as an initiator in its own cube and deliver to all of its neighbours - i.e. B will deliver the message to its sole neighbour who is D. That rounds up the broadcast and let us note that the broadcast cost has dropped from 5 messages to *3 messages*. Note that D takes no action upon receipt of the message.

It should be apparent that one can take one's pick when it comes to pairing nodes to form two dimensional cubes - it need not be A and C joined to B and D to form a 2 dimensional cube; A and B combined with C and D will work just as fine, as long as consistency is maintained throughout.

5.3.3 Three dimensional cube

Let us now move on to inspect a three dimensional cube:

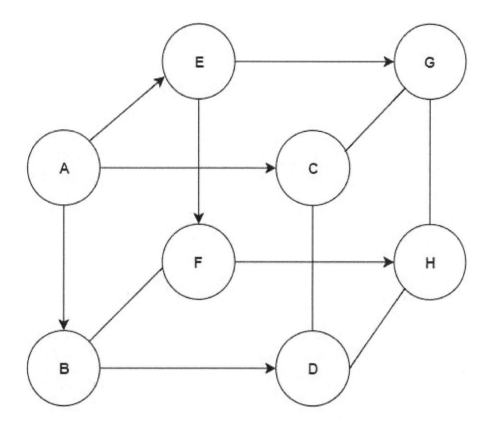

Once again, A is our broadcast initiator. The algorithm works unchanged to the previous scenario as far as the two dimensional cube ACBD is concerned; A also passes on the message to the EGFH cube (which is a sibling to the ACBD one), and E obliges by acting as an initiator in the EGFH cube - E delivers the message to all its neighbours in EGFH, i.e. G and F. As with ACBD, the algorithm works unchanged in the EGFH two dimensional cube, with F passing on the message to H, thus completing the broadcast with a total cost of *7 messages*.

5.4 Informally proving our broadcast algorithm for cube topologies

The algorithm hinges on certain nodes taking no action upon receipt of a message; that is precisely how we gain a performance optimisation. Specifically, we are talking about nodes that receive a message from another node who is a member of the same cube. What grounds do such nodes have to avoid any further action?

It is rather simple, in a way. Consider the two dimensional cube which we visited earlier:

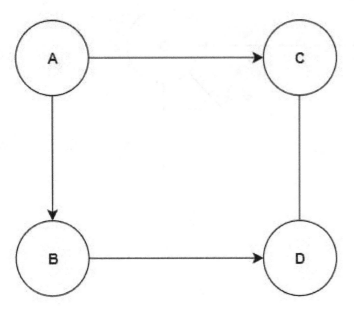

Now C has received a message from its partner in a one dimensional cube, i.e. A. Now, as per the algorithm, C should stay put and *not* send the message to D. Why?

We know that C received the message from A. So, A is either a true initiator, or acting as one (upon receipt of a message from a sibling or parent cube). In either case, D would have received the message from B (B either being or acting as an initiator and passing the message to A and D, or B receiving the message from initiator A and passing it on to D).

5.4.1 Theory of inaction

A simpler way of looking at this is: unless a node N is a message initiator (true or delegated), N needs to take no action upon receiving a message. You may notice that this essentially is a theory of inaction.

Conversely, we can come up with an equivalent theory of action which provides the exact same results.

5.4.2 Theory of action

Let us assume that N is a recipient node. In other words, another node sent a message to N. Now, imagine N, the recipient node, and the source node being part of two different albeit sibling cubes (of the same dimension) that combine to form a cube of the next higher dimension. The next step from N is simple: act as an initiator in the cube which N just identified itself to be part of (i.e. the sibling cube to the one which N just identified the message source to be part of). Note how this (correctly) allows the recipient node in a one dimensional cube network to take no action.

5.5 Hypercube

Let us begin to round things up with a quick pictorial representation of broadcast in a four dimensional cube:

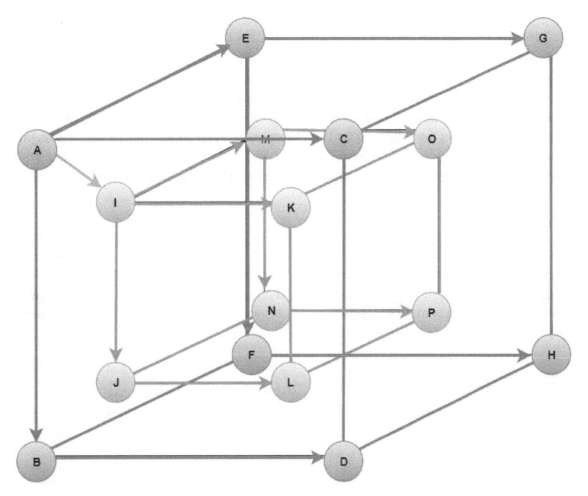

It should be immediately obvious that the exact same treatment applies here: *A* belongs to the 'outer' three dimensional cube and is the initiator who passes the message to all its neighbours, including its counterpart (*I*) in the 'inner' three dimensional cube, thus resulting in the broadcast algorithm taking effect in both sibling three dimensional cubes (that form the four dimensional one). The message cost, as indicated by the number of arrows in the diagram, is 15.

5.6 Mathematical perspective

If you carefully go through section *5.2*, including all its subsections, that describe the optimised broadcast algorithm in a rather prolix fashion, the corresponding terse and mathematical translation will intuitively begin to take shape. To start with, assign increasing integer values to each axis, i.e. *x = 1, y= 2, z = 3*, and so on. That done, there is only one simple rule: *any entity or node receiving a message along a particular axis will forward the message only along a lower one*. The initiator, as always, propagates the message to all of its neighbours, while each recipient follows the aforementioned precept.

The reason why the aforementioned rule applies is, of course: *an n dimensional cube is built by joining together, using links along the nth dimension, two n - 1 dimensional cubes.*

Finally, it should be apparent that the message complexity or cost is given by *n - 1* where *n* is the number of nodes in the relevant cube (*n* is equal to 2^d where *d* is the cube's dimension). This can be easily proved by induction. Consider a two dimensional cube which will require 3 messages for broadcast completion (since there are a total of 3 + 1 = 4 edges). Next, consider a three dimensional cube made out of 2 such two dimensional cubes. The message cost for this three dimensional cube is the total cost for both two dimensional cubes, plus a single message cost of transferring the message from one two dimensional cube to the other, i.e. 3 + 3 + 1 = 7. We can continue along this line of reasoning for cubes of higher dimensions.

5.7 Conclusion

The aim of this chapter was a field test of our broadcast algorithm on cube networks, while also looking out for any potential customisations that will improve its performance. We succeeded on both counts. While we might have ended up being a bit unduly verbose at several points, we did also manage to come up with a simple and terse formula for our broadcast algorithm's message cost in cube networks.

5.8 What's next?

We have looked at a few primitives or building blocks, so now we move on to more complex algorithms. The next chapter is the first of two that are dedicated to the problem of electing a leader from a set of participants.

Chapter 6. Leader election in rings

In distributed computing, *leader election* is the process of selecting one process or node as the controller or leader of a task that is distributed among multiple nodes. As usual, we will rely on an example scenario to get the ball rolling.

6.1 Introduction: showdown in Warzonia

There is a country called *warzonia*. Nothing much has been happening there except war. Why? Because warzonia has been torn across feuding warlords, fighting each other over all sorts of matters big and small, since as far back as anyone can care to remember. In fact, the good folks at warzonia have a bigger problem now - a threat of warzonia being invaded by even fiercer barbarian hordes. It has begun to appear that a semblance of unity is required across this bellicose pack of warlords if they have to stand any chance of holding off the forthcoming invasion.

So, the infighting finally subsides in a hesitant fashion, as each warlord appointed a wise man to confer with each other and come up with a solution. A few days pass, while the wise men formed a council and initiated discussions. Finally, each wise man returned to his own master and presented a plan which they came up with together. The objective of the plan is to elect a leader from among all the warlords, who will then lead the defense against the potential invaders.

6.2 Leader election: a basic plan

The plan, each wise man explained to his warlord, is fairly simple: to begin with, all the warlords will camp out in a neutral territory, a few miles from each other, in approximate ring formation.

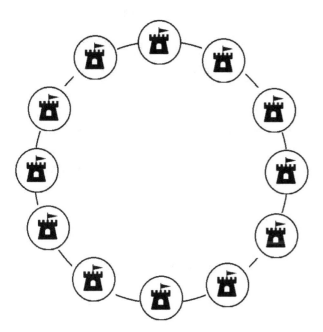

Each icon in the above diagram represents a fortified camp occupied by one warlord. While this might look like a buildup to a wild-west style showdown, that really is not the intention: the warlords cannot afford to lose any more military personnel and equipment if they need to give themselves any chance of resisting an invasion. This settlement has to be a peaceful one, or at least as peaceful as it can realistically get with a bunch of disagreeing warlords.

6.2.1 How it works

The wise men had clearly agreed among themselves on certain aspects:

- Each warlord has a sense of *clockwise and anticlockwise*
- Each warlord has multiple emissaries at his disposal
- Emissaries are selected such that they always tell the truth
- Emissaries are no good at fighting, but the paths they travel are fortunately unvisited by robbers and other similar dangers
- Each warlord has a unique name
- Each warlord has a unique military capability, in terms of weapons and personnel

As per the plan, each warlord will send out an emissary in a clockwise direction, towards his immediate neighbour. In other words, each emissary will traverse the circle, visiting other warlords' camps as they appear in his path.

Upon reaching a warlord's (let us use the term *local warlord*) camp, the emissary will announce his master's (let us use the term *remote warlord*) name and will subsequently be shown in to meet one of the local warlord's ministers. It is the emissary's duty to provide honest and accurate details of the remote warlord's military strength.

The minister naturally is fully aware of the local warlord's military capabilities. After listening to the emissary's report, the minister orders a course of action that aligns with the following:

- *If the remote warlord turns out to be more powerful than the local one, the emissary is allowed to continue his journey to the fortress of the next warlord. The local warlord withdraws from the leader election with immediate effect*
- *If the local warlord turns out to be stronger in military terms, the emissary is promptly imprisoned, and the local warlord stays 'in the running' for the position of leader*
- *A warlord who has withdrawn from the leader election will continue to facilitate the ongoing election by treating visiting emissaries exactly as earlier (imprisonment or safe passage)*

So, the eventual outcome immediately becomes clear:

- *Only one emissary will travel the full circle and return to his master - the emissary of that one warlord with the strongest military resources among the lot*
- *Every other emissary gets imprisoned at the camp of the first warlord he comes across who is better armed than his master*

- *The one warlord who finds his emissary returning, will send out a special emissary to each other warlord with news of him being elected as the leader*

6.2.2 How fast does it work?

Apparently, the plan or algorithm works. The warlords are happy for the moment, but they are an impatient lot. Each of them orders a resident mathematician to figure out the speed of the proposed process and give a thumbs-up or thumbs-down based on the calculated performance. It is not long before the mathematicians work out the details, focusing primarily on the worst case scenario.

6.2.2.1 Worst case scenario

Obviously, the emissary who travels the most is the one belonging to the elected warlord. Assuming the individual camps are separated by a mile each, and that there are *n* such camps (i.e. there are *n* warlords), the winning warlord's emissary has to travel *n* miles.

How about the runner-up? Let us assume that the runner-up was the winner's immediate neighbour, up the road in a clockwise direction. So, the runner-up's emissary will go through every other warlord before coming to the winning warlord's camp - which means, he would have travelled a total distance of *n - 1* miles.

This sequence continues all the way to the weakest warlord of the lot, whose emissary travels a solitary mile before coming across a more powerful warlord's camp where he gets imprisoned in no time.

So, the total distance travelled by all emissaries, quite simply, is:

n + (n - 1) + (n - 2) +...+ 2 + 1

To arrive at a simpler expression, let us first add the series to itself:

```
n + (n - 1) + (n - 2) + ... +      2    +      1
        1  +     2 + ... +  (n - 2)   +  (n - 1) + n
-----------------------------------------------------------
n +  n    +   n  +... +   n       +   n     + n              = n(n + 1)
-----------------------------------------------------------
```

Divide the result by 2 to compensate for the doubling trick that we did, and we have a final result of *n(n + 1)/2*. It is apparent that the result is not linear to the number of the warlords but is decided by *the square of the number of warlords* (n^2). It should also be readily obvious that the worst case scenario relies squarely on a happenstance of the warlords being positioned clockwise in descending order of their military strength.

6.2.2.2 Best case scenario

The best case scenario would arrive if all the warlords were stationed such that each (losing) emissary would find a more powerful warlord at the first camp that he arrives at. In other words, if it so happened that the warlords were stationed in ascending order of military strength, clockwise. Let us also note that the most powerful warlord's emissary is a special case who would still travel *n* miles irrespective of which warlord is stationed where. Every other emissary would travel only a single mile each: for a grand total of *n + (n - 1)* miles.

6.2.3 Does it work fast enough?

The mathematicians are not happy with the worst case result, and if the mathematicians are not happy, the warlords are not happy. Not surprisingly, the wise men and mathematicians are ordered to work together to come up with a faster solution.

6.3 Speeding up the basic election algorithm

As it turns out, several mathematicians point out that the worst case formation (warlords camped out in descending order of military strength, clockwise) would possibly have a milder effect on performance if each camp sends out two emissaries, one in each direction. A specific example is provided in the form of the runner-up who is stationed right after the leader; if he had sent an emissary in the anti-clockwise direction, the leader's camp would appear as the first stop.

The proposed strategy makes sense, but referring to the example: can the runner-up warlord somehow realise within a short span of time that the emissary who traveled anti-clockwise has been imprisoned, and react accordingly? If not, the whole exercise is meaningless.

The mathematicians also point out that the runner-up, shortly after dispatching his emissaries, would receive an emissary from his more powerful neighbour, the eventual leader; thus, realising that he's out of contention, and too late to do anything about his own emissary traveling pointlessly in the clockwise direction, all the way till the eventual leader's camp. This waste of effort is repeated in decreasing amount by every other warlord except the eventual winner. Obviously, two changes are needed:

- Emissaries need to be sent in both directions
- An emissary must be given a proper travel-plan, rather than ploughing on mindlessly

What if both emissaries have been instructed thus: go visit the first camp on your trail, and then come back; If either or both emissaries are not back within a certain reasonable amount of expected time, the warlord knows that his emissaries have been imprisoned, and thus, he is no longer in contention for the position of leader.

It seems that the mathematicians have latched on to a *probe-based* strategy, more or less. The basic idea is for each camp to probe the neighbourhood, in either direction, in a series of steps or *rounds*, with the probe distance increasing with each round. Soon, the final form of the refined algorithm is announced:

- *The election process will proceed in rounds*
- *In any round, each warlord (who is still in contention) will send out two emissaries in either direction (clockwise and anti-clockwise)*
- *In the first round, the emissaries will be instructed to turn back (if possible) after visiting the first camp on their trail*
- *In the second round, the emissaries will be instructed to turn back (if possible) after visiting the second camp on their trail*
- *In the third round, the emissaries will be instructed to turn back (if possible) after visiting the fourth camp on their trail*
- *And so on, with the length of an emissary's route, in terms of the number of camps to be visited before turning back, increasing by a factor of two*
- *A warlord will stay in contention and progress to the next round only if both emissaries dispatched in the current round return to camp*
- *A warlord learns that he is elected as the leader once he sees his emissaries arrive at camp from directions opposite to those of their departures*

In mathematical terms, round *k* will see an emissary visiting 2^{k-1} warlord camps in his assigned direction.

6.3.1 Updated election algorithm: mechanics

Let us try to follow the updated algorithm through the various rounds to figure out how it works. While doing so, we will also start to move ever so slightly away from the example scenario and towards a more formal mode of description involving mathematical quantities and such. This is keeping in mind that we will inevitably be working towards not just understanding the algorithm, but also arriving at a formal description of the *cost* of the algorithm in terms of the number of warlords (entities) involved.

To start with, let the following diagram represent the group of warlords camped out in ring formation, with each camp being assigned an integer number that represents the particular warlord's military prowess.

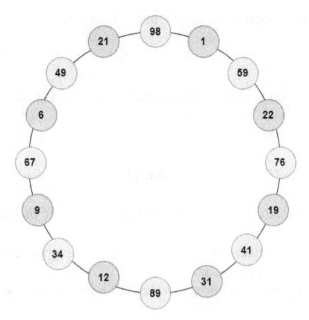

The election starts, and it is the first round. Each camp sends out an emissary in either direction, and the emissary will visit the first and nearest camp before turning back (if possible). Here's a pictorial representation of the proceedings in the first round:

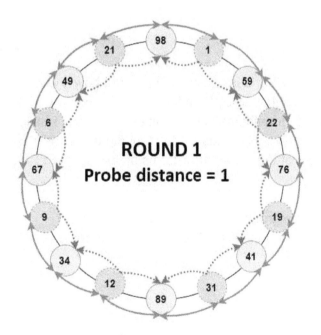

The blue camps (alternate ones, starting from 98) all represent those who survive the first round, because all of them have numbers higher than their immediate neighbours. Hence, the bidirectional arrows represent an emissary leaving in a particular direction, visiting the first camp, and coming back safely. On the other hand, the red camps (alternate ones, starting from 1) all drop out of contention; the dotted unidirectional arrow lines indicate the path of an emissary on a one way trip to prison. As you can see, the number of candidates has dropped to about half after the first round. Next, we proceed to the second round:

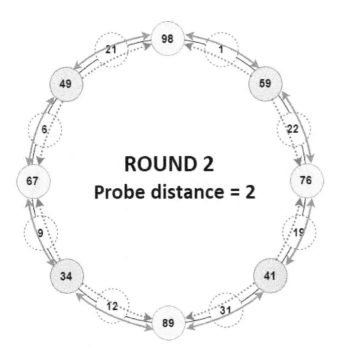

Starting with 16 candidates, we see that 8 candidates enter the second round. In the diagram, once again, a bidirectional arrow indicates the successful return of an emissary back to his warlord's camp while the unidirectional ones indicate the path of a losing warlord's emissary (to prison). At the end of round 2, only 4 candidates remain. Let us check out round 3, then:

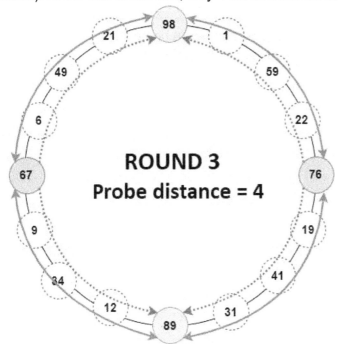

By the same reasoning, 67 and 76 drop out of contention, leading to a final shootout in round 4 between 98 and 89. The outcome is equally simple, as seen next:

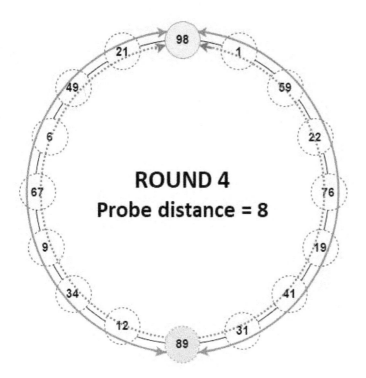

ROUND 4
Probe distance = 8

Both emissaries dispatched from camp 89 reach camp 98 and receive imprisonment (as indicated by the unidirectional arrows), while those sent from camp 98 turn back after visiting camp 89 and successfully return to their home camp (as indicated by the bidirectional blue arrows).

In the next (and last) round, the leader will see his emissaries return home from directions opposite to those of their departures, thus indicating his selection as leader:

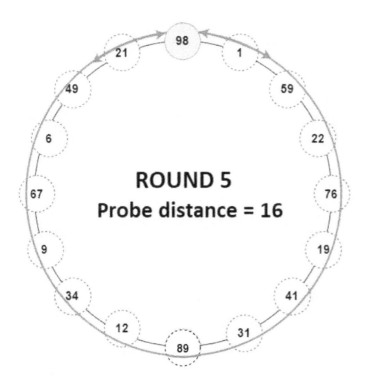

6.3.2 Updated election algorithm: performance

We will start off with a couple of propositions, which we will reason about afterwards with the intention of proving their validity.

- The scenario discussed in the previous section is the worst case one

We should pause here for a second to take note of how the best case scenario for contestants in any given round is a worst case scenario for the algorithm's performance; the more the number of survivors in a round, the longer the algorithm will potentially take to achieve completion.

- The performance of the updated algorithm has a *linearithmic*, i.e. *nlog(n)*, relationship to the number of warlords (*n*)

With that out of the way, let us approach the defense of the first statement in stages. We begin by demonstrating an alternate scenario that is considerably cheaper.

Consider the camps being arranged clockwise in sorted (ascending or descending) order of their military strengths. It is readily obvious that only the eventual leader will survive the first round; every other warlord will have an emissary ending up imprisoned at a neighbouring camp. The sole survivor did not have to work too hard at all; the rest of the pack took care of each other, to put it in simple terms. An illustration follows.

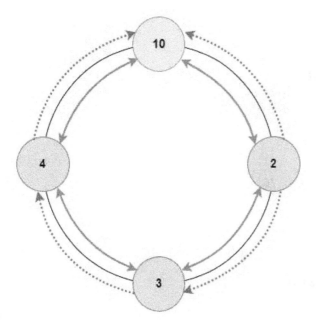

On the contrary, if you consider any round in the previous (worst case) scenario, both emissaries of each 'defeated' warlord were imprisoned at the first camp they came across (in other words, in no round did a losing warlord also cause the loss of one or more other warlords). The survivors of each round were directly responsible for the undoing of each of those who did not make it through that round.

We seem to have found the maximum limit of survivors for any round, then: a maximum of half the contestants. This is because each survivor of any given round survives by taking out at least one contestant, leading to at least half the contestants not surviving the round. This is exactly what happens in the first scenario that we analysed, and that is precisely why we label it as the worst case scenario for the performance of this algorithm.

Next, let us consider the mathematical perspective. The next diagram provides perspective on what follows afterwards.

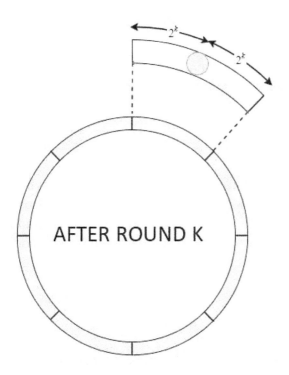

For each entity (warlord) that survives round k, it is a given that there are no survivors on either side for a distance that equals the probe distance for that particular round, i.e. 2^k. In other words, said entity is the only survivor in a stretch of distance 2^{k+1}. For example, consider the illustration from section *6.3.1* that depicts the second round: clockwise of node 98, there are no survivors for a distance of 4 miles. This implies a worst case scenario where $(n/2^{k+1})$ entities survive each round, which is just a different way of stating that the number of contestants drop by half with each passing round in the worst case. Armed with this information, we will start analysing the cost of the algorithm.

To begin with, let us understand that we need to take 3 steps to arrive at the cost of the algorithm:

- Figure out the number of rounds the algorithm will go through
- Calculate the cost per round, in terms of distance traveled by emissaries
- Multiply the two parameters to find out the total cost

Since the worst case scenario implies the number of contestants dropping to half with each passing round, it is clear that we will have a total of *log(n)* + *1* rounds. Let us now focus on the cost per round.

The cost in distance per round is calculated by multiplying the number of participating emissaries with the total distance traveled by an emissary. While the contestants (and hence, the number of emissaries) drop to half from one round to the next, this is canceled out by the probe distance going the other way (since the probe distance doubles from one round to the next). Thus, effectively, the cost in distance for any round remains a simple multiple of the total number of contestants, n.

Finally, putting both prior observations together implies that the cost of the algorithm is linearithmic, i.e. $nlog(n)$. Let us keep in mind that we are referring to the cost in terms of *distance traveled*, or in technical terms, the *communication cost*.

How about the cost in terms of *time*?

It helps to note that multiple messages (or emissaries) travel concurrently. This favours the simple reasoning that *time-cost* is determined by the message which gets relayed the most (the emissary who travels the most) - which is the eventual leader's message (the winning warlord's emissary) that gets transmitted n times (visits n - 1 camps and then finally gets back to home camp). In brief, the time cost is linear to the number of entities (warlords), or to use different words, the algorithm runs in $O(n)$ time.

6.4 Back to the real world

Let us move away from the world of warlords and emissaries and come back to a distributed environment consisting of message-passing entities existing in a ring formation. A warlord's camp becomes an entity, while an emissary is a message sent by one entity to a neighbouring one. Messages cannot be imprisoned, but they can be discarded. An emissary can decide to turn back and go to his home camp, but a message will have to be echoed back by the receiving entity. An emissary being allowed to continue his journey to the next camp is mirrored by an entity relaying on a received message to the next entity in the ring. Finally, a message cannot remember or count; but a message can carry an integer *hop count* that is set by the entity who generates the message. The hop count is decremented by each entity along the way. If the message reaches zero and the source entity is still in contention, the receiving entity (who decremented the message's hop count to zero) relays the message back towards the source. With said transformations in place, our findings remain equally valid and applicable to a real life distributed group of entities.

Finally, the basic algorithm presented in *6.2* is known as the *LCR algorithm* (after Le Lann, Chang, and Roberts). The optimised version introduced in *6.3* is the *HS algorithm* (Hirschberg–Sinclair).

6.5 Timing and synchronisation considerations

It is time to note that we never worried about messages (emissaries) getting delayed; we always assumed that when a message (emissary) does not return, the source entity (warlord's camp) knew when to stop waiting and start assuming the message to be discarded (imprisoned) by a 'higher' entity on the way (a more powerful warlord). In other words, we implicitly assumed a *synchronous distributed system*. How will these algorithms behave in an *asynchronous distributed system*?

A key observation is that the *rounds* in the HS algorithm are indeed asynchronous. In fact, at any given moment in the algorithm's execution, there is no guarantee (or requirement) that all entities are operating in the same round. For example, consider a message in the clockwise direction from A to B getting heavily delayed. Meanwhile, there is no such problem with the message that A sent out in the anti-clockwise direction; said message reaches a 'lesser' neighbour and gets echoed right back. Now A cannot proceed to the next phase until the 'other' message bounces back. While A keeps on waiting, the rest of the entities can well move ahead to higher rounds. Note that A continues to be a team player, relaying, echoing, and discarding messages as per the rules. Whenever the delayed message arrives, A moves on to the next round. This has no bearing on the eventual outcome (except that if A is the eventual leader, the final result is delayed).

We conclude by noting that a similar reasoning applies to the *LCR* algorithm.

6.6 Message failure considerations

In *6.2.1* we made the assumption that an emissary is never stopped or endangered during his travels; i.e. we assumed no *message loss*. Obviously, a message failure or loss can subvert the algorithm's behavior. We may still arrive at the final result in some cases, but not when one or more of the messages emitted by a potential leader gets dropped.

6.7 An interlude

Let us have a quick recess to take stock. We discussed two algorithms for leader election in rings, the second of which improved in performance over the first by implementing *bidirectional* communication along with a *probe-based* strategy involving multiple rounds. Now what if we assume the ring to be strictly unidirectional? So far, we are left with reverting to the first algorithm (LCR) and paying a price in terms of performance. Do we have a better option? In other words, can we retain a *nlog(n)* message cost while accepting the restriction of a unidirectional ring?

6.8 Improving performance for leader election in a unidirectional ring

The basic building block in leader election algorithms we discussed so far is:

- An entity communicates its 'value' to another entity,
- Who compares the incoming value with its own,
- And communicates back (explicitly or otherwise) the result to the first entity.

It is quite clear that step (3) is an impossibility when dealing with unidirectional rings.

Since two entities can only communicate one-way, how about seeking help from a *third party* to whom both entities will send their respective ids or values? The only possibility is another entity in the ring, situated clockwise (let us assume unidirectional clockwise communication) to both the entities. So, now it is up to this third entity to compare the ids of its two predecessors and take a suitable action based on the result. A basic plan seems to be emerging.

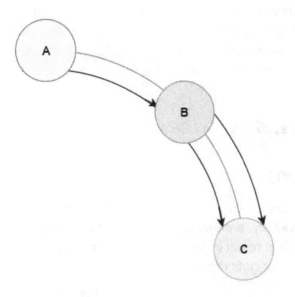

As the diagram illustrates, both A and B send their respective ids to C. What the diagram does not cover is that C does the same by sending its id (and relaying the id of B) in the clockwise direction. Similarly, A receives two messages from its two predecessors. Anyway, so how can C help?

It can be tempting to let C drop itself out of contention (and switch to a passive *relay mode*) if either A or B has an id that is larger. Conversely, If C is the largest, C stays in active mode and proceeds to the next round.

Let us apply this logic to a ring formation of ids in ascending order, clockwise. Each (active) entity sends its id to its immediate neighbour in the clockwise direction, while receiving two messages from its two immediate (active) predecessors in the anticlockwise direction, of which it will pick one (of the immediate (active) predecessor in the anticlockwise direction) and relay it along in the clockwise direction. It should be obvious that all contestants except the two least ids will survive the first round. This is not a good score, by any means. Why? The number of contestants that survive each round is fairly linear to *n* (rather than say, dropping by half), and hence, the number of rounds the algorithm will need is also linear to *n*. Putting together oth observations, we arrive at a message complexity of $O(n^2)$. This is not what we set out to accomplish.

What did we miss, essentially, in that ill-fated attempt? *For each surviving entity, we need to fail at least one other entity.* With that objective in mind, let us try a different strategy on how an entity deals with the ids of its two active predecessors.

The new approach is that, as any active entity in the ring network, it is no longer your headache to worry about your identity once you have passed your id to your successor (your immediate neighbour in the clockwise direction); you are solely concerned with how your predecessors (both of whom send you their ids) compare with each other as well as yourself. If your immediate predecessor is larger than the next predecessor *and* you, *you adopt the id of your immediate predecessor.*

That does not mean that your id is 'lost'; your successor will adopt your id if it finds your id to be larger than itself and your predecessor's. Now, if your predecessor does not compare well with you and the next predecessor, you immediately turn into a *relay entity*. In other words, 'you' are no longer in contention (technically, as far as the id is concerned, it is the immediate predecessor who has dropped out of contention). You, as an entity, no longer generate messages, but simply relay what you receive. You are no longer an *active entity*.

Let us consider this algorithm in stages using pictorial representations for each. While doing so, we will finally discover the condition for an entity to realise its own election as leader. To start with, here is a simple ring formation:

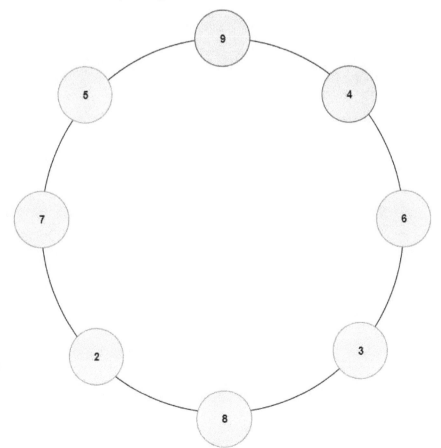

Let us see what happens during round 1. Consider entity 4 who receives two messages from 9 and 5. Obviously entity 4 finds its immediate predecessor (9) to be larger than itself and the next predecessor (5) and hence adopts the value of 9 - who in turns switches to relay mode upon receiving messages from 5 and 7 and finds its immediate predecessor 5 to be smaller than itself and 7. Similarly, entities 6, 8, and 7 also drop out of contention and switch to relay mode. Here's the situation, then, at the end of round 1.

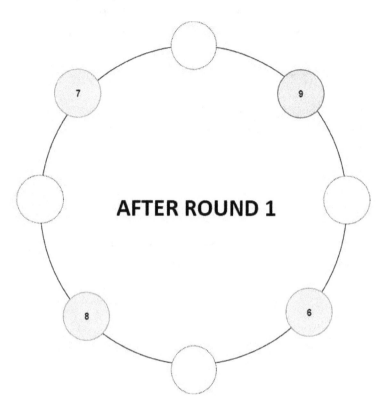

Predictably, we have two more drop-outs after round 2:

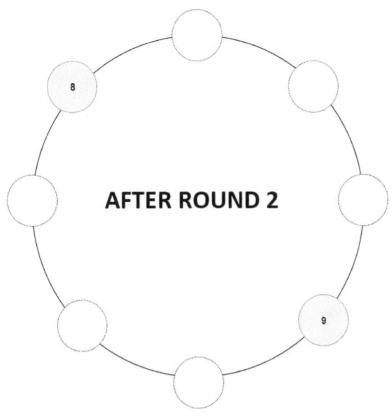

AFTER ROUND 2

How about round 3? The entity 8 would receive two messages - one from 9, appearing to be the immediate predecessor, and the other carrying a smaller id (8), which is nothing but its own message relayed on by 9. Conversely, it appears to 9 that its immediate predecessor (8) is smaller than the next predecessor (9) and promptly switches over to relay mode.Thus , round 3 ends with 8 adopting the value 9 while the original 9 is no longer active.

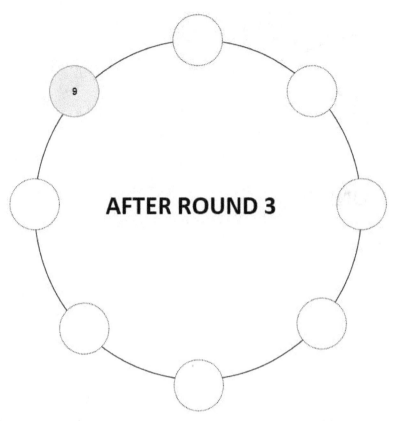

AFTER ROUND 3

In the next and final round round, 9 receives its own message - an equal value - and this specifically is the condition for an entity to realise that it has been elected as the leader.

As we saw with the *HS* algorithm, the number of contestants drop by half in each round - how, exactly? Consider 4 entities A1, A2, A3, A4 positioned clockwise. If A4 survives a round (obviously, in which case, it would switch to the id of A3), it implies (*A3 > A4 and A3 > A2*). This implies that A3 will not survive said round because the condition (*A2 > A3 and A2 > A1*) is false (because *A3 > A2*). In other words, each surviving entity in a round will have left a predecessor switching to relay mode.

This process implies a maximum of *log(n) + 1* rounds for the algorithm, each involving a number of messages linear to *n*, and finally a performance relation of *nlog(n)* to the total number of entities. This algorithm is known as the Peterson / Dolev-Klawe-Rodeh algorithm for leader election in unidirectional rings.

We round up by noting that timing and synchronisation considerations apply to the Peterson / Dolev-Klawe-Rodeh algorithm in a manner similar to the *LCR* and *HS* algorithms that we discussed earlier.

6.9 Conclusion

We made up a scenario stuffed with warlords and emissaries and discussed two algorithms for leader election in ring formations. We translated out findings to real life scenarios and worked out the math for deducing the cost for both algorithms. Next, we noted that either algorithm works fine for both synchronous and asynchronous distributed systems. Finally, we imposed a communication restriction in our rings and analysed a third algorithm that provides linearithmic performance even in the context of said restriction.

6.10 What's next?

We are not done with leader election algorithms just yet. Having looked at ring formations, let us now consider the case of general networks in the next chapter.

Chapter 7. Leader election in arbitrary networks

In the previous chapter, we considered multiple algorithms for ring networks. Moving on from rings, we shall now consider an algorithm for leader election in general networks.

7.1 Introduction

When we say *general networks*, in this context we will stick with arbitrary *directed graphs* (digraphs) that are strongly connected. In other words, we are interested in network topologies where:

- The component entities are connected by channels with a sense of direction
- If you consider any pair of entities in the network, there exists a *path* between them

Before proceeding further, let us recall from section *4.6* what the *diameter* of a network is: *the shortest distance between the two most distant nodes in the network.*

7.2 Leader election in a strongly connected digraph

To keep things simple, consider the following network topology:

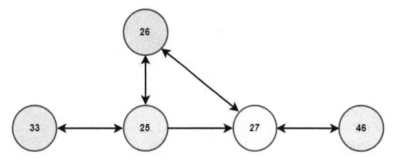

It should be easy to ascertain that we are presented here with a connected directed graph. The objective of this exercise is to come up with an algorithm, at the end of the execution of which, all nodes or entities will be aware of the leader. In this context, the leader is the one node or entity with the highest associated integer. Let us also note that the diameter of this network or graph is 4 (the distance in hop count along the route 46 - 27 - 26 - 25 - 33).

To begin with, each entity is only aware of its own assigned number. Obviously, we need a broadcasting strategy, so each entity will first broadcast its own value:

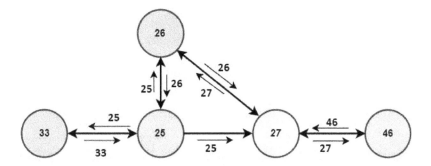

Now, consider node 27. After round 1, it is aware of 3 values: 27, 46, and 26. Naturally, node 27 goes ahead and modifies its knowledge of *highest value* from 27 to 46. Similarly, 26 is now aware of 27 as the highest value, meanwhile 25 has 33 noted down as the highest number it has seen so far. Moving on to round 2:

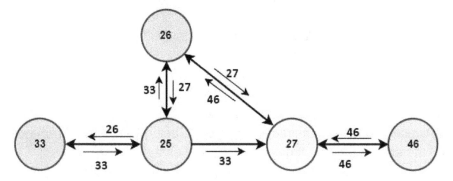

We can see the beginning of how 46 begins to propagate as the highest value in the network. At this point 26 has joined 27 in this awareness. Let us move on to round 3.

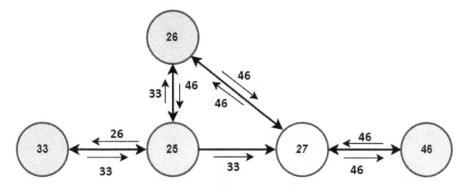

We are now left with 33 as the sole entity without an accurate awareness of the highest value in the network. This is corrected by the next round, as seen in the following diagram:

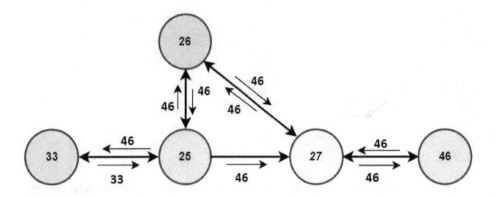

Finally, after round 4, we have all entities on the same page as to who the leader node is in the network. Let us also note that we needed exactly 4 rounds - 4 is also the diameter of this network, which is no coincidence. Thus, our algorithm reveals itself:

In successive rounds, each node propagates along each of its outgoing links the highest value it has seen so far. A node elects itself as the leader upon seeing its value being propagated as the highest value after d rounds, where d is the network diameter.

The following diagram represents the final configuration, with each node aware of 46 as the leader in the network. In particular, seeing the message value of 46 being transmitted from node 27 in round 5 gives node 46 the affirmation that it has been elected as the leader.

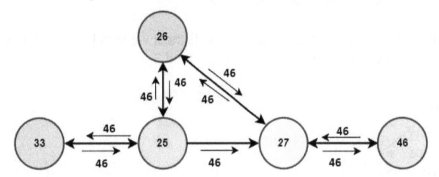

7.2.1 Performance

The message complexity can be calculated trivially: a message or two is sent along each edge or link during a round, and there are *d* rounds (where *d* is the network diameter) needed to achieve leader election. So, the message cost is $O(m \times d)$ where *m* is the number of links or edges in the network and *d* is the network diameter.

7.2.2 Optimisations

While it works, the algorithm in its current shape is message-heavy. We can consider at least two optimisations to address this issue:

- An entity can remain silent in a given round if its perception of the highest value remains unchanged from the previous round
- An entity need not send a message to another entity in a given round, if the latter produced a higher value in the previous round which the former entity used to correct its knowledge of the highest value

While the former would be quite obvious, the latter might deserve a bit of explanation. If A received a higher value from B in any given round, the next round will see A propagating that very value; B has no need to be a recipient of the same because, in said round, B will either resend the same value or send a higher value.

7.3 Synchronisation and timing considerations

So far in this chapter, we have assumed a synchronous distributed system. All the entities have to be in lock-step and communication delays are assumed to be bounded, failing which the end of a particular round cannot be determined by an entity. Switching to an asynchronous environment will have at least two impacts:

- Since messages may arrive out-of-sync and with unbounded delays, a message would need to carry not just a value but also the number or index of the round which the message belongs to. This helps an entity to identify the termination of a particular round (i.e. once it has seen a message specific to that round from all its neighbours)

- The optimisations which we listed earlier are compromised; since the entities do not go through each round in lock-step, each entity depends on the arrival of a message from each of its neighbours in order to identify the termination of a round

7.4 The Bully Algorithm

In 1982, Hector Garcia-Molina published what came to be known as the *Bully Algorithm* for leader election in synchronous distributed systems where the component entities are known to fail (and possibly recover). This is the last algorithm we will be looking at in the context of leader elections and let us once again use a simple hypothetical scenario to try and understand the bully algorithm clearly. Rather than warlords, we will be dealing with a bunch of politicians this time.

We begin by introducing a politically unstable republic that will remain unnamed; a small affair hardly larger than a medium-sized town. The government over here consists of a bunch of politicians, of which one stays elected as the leader or head of government at any given point in time. Major decisions in the republic are made under the scrutiny and approval of said leader.

To proceed further, a better description of the politicians of this republic is in order. Specifically, we need to know three things:

- First and foremost, each politician in this republic is a consummate workaholic. They work round the clock, with no sleep, day in day out. While this is beneficial for the prosperity of the republic as a whole, there are consequences. The stress and lack of sleep is an accumulating and telling factor; every now and then a politician drops down to a deep slumber than can extend for long durations. Even the leader is not immune to such involuntary 'disruptions'.

- Each politician has yet another curious character: whenever one rises from a deep sleep, it is with heavy brain fog - leading the confused person in sleep-induced stupor to exist oblivious of the prevailing political leadership, causing him or her to promptly and vehemently call for an election. Further, when the ruling politician drifts off to sleep, the resulting slow movement of matters of the state will cause one or more observant politicians to produce a call for election.

- The third and final aspect we need to know about these politicians is that there is a pecking order amongst them, in terms of skill, influence and money. In other words, we assume that each politician has a unique *strength* represented by the sum total of his or her intellectual, political, and financial capabilities. So, when a politician calls for an election, he or she may well be overruled by a *stronger* politician.

Let us see how this works. Consider the scenario where the leader falls into a deep sleep, slowing down official matters to such an extent that another politician notices the lethargy and decides to hold an election to pick a new leader. When a politician decides to hold an election, the procedure is quite simple: he or she rushes to the republic's radio station and broadcasts the following simple message:

- *It is time to elect a new leader*

This message is assumed to be received by every citizen, and in particular, by each awake politician. While each politician in the republic who is *weaker* (than the politician who made the election announcement) will take no action and stay put, the *stronger* ones will not sit back and watch.

Meanwhile, what does the election-announcing politician - let us call him or her X - do? X follows the constitution which clearly mandates a specific waiting period after making the election announcement and withdraws to the radio station's waiting room to...simply wait.

Next, let us assume that Y is a stronger politician who listened to the election announcement. Y will immediately deliver a personal message to X by dialling up the radio station's waiting room, and the resulting conversation is more or less one-way with Y saying:

- *Thanks buddy, but I will take it from here*

Upon receipt of such a message, X meekly withdraws from the scene. Now it is the turn of Y to arrive at the radio station, deliver a new election announcement, and move to the waiting room. Just like earlier, there is a possibility that another stronger politician Z will do to Y what Y did to X just a while back.

Obviously all this can go on for a bit but how does it end, if at all?

This is exactly where the constitution-mandated waiting period, which we briefly referred to earlier, comes in. If X does not receive a call from a stronger politician (asking X to step away) before the waiting period elapses, X leaves the waiting room and makes a beeline right back to the radio station's broadcast room to make the following announcement:

- *I am the newly elected leader*

That sums up the bully algorithm, in terms of the example. In more formal terms, let us list the three types of messages which we came across:

1. *Election announcement*
2. *Election announcement invalidation*
3. *Leader announcement*

Before moving on to a more technical form of analysis, let us quickly go through the whole sequence using a series of diagrams.

7.4.1 Diagrammatic representation

1. The beginning if it all, when the leader (the circle, with a 'strength' indicated by the integer 18) sleeps off - something which does not go unnoticed by the politician represented by 9.

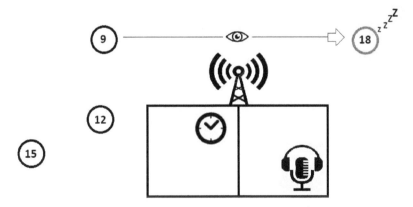

2. Without wasting any time, 9 heads over to the radio station and makes an election announcement.

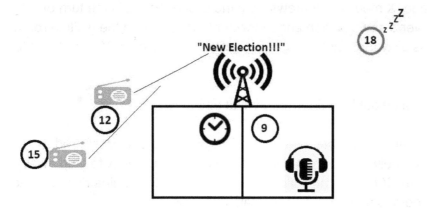

3. Both 15 and 12 receive the election announcement from 9. Without delay, 12 contacts 9 in the radio station's waiting room and orders 9 to back off.

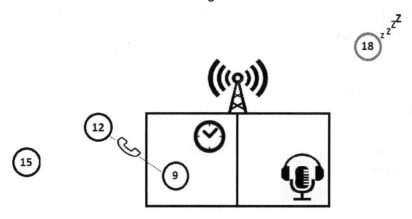

4. No surprise that 9 obeys 12, and now 12 makes his or her way to the radio station and announces an election. Note how 9 plays no further part in this scenario.

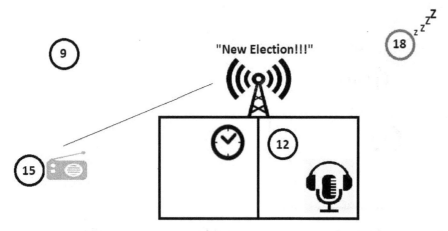

5. Next, 12 retreats to the waiting room - only to be contacted and dismissed by the more powerful politician represented by 15.

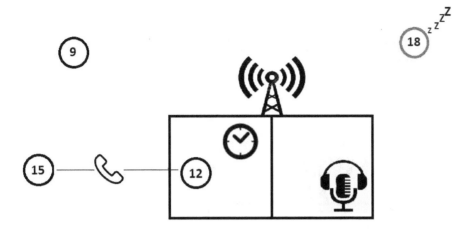

6. Now it is the turn of 15 to make an election announcement. Note how 9 and 12 play no further part in this scenario.

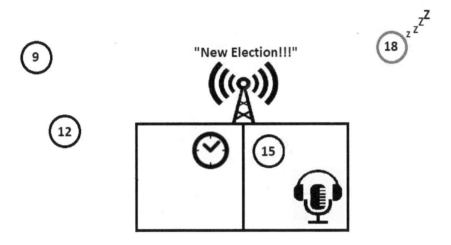

7. Like anyone else, 15 is now required to see out the mandatory waiting period.

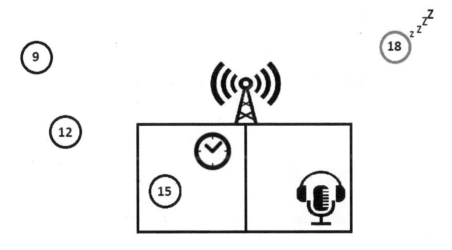

8. Unsurprisingly, 15 survives the waiting period unscathed, moves to the broadcast room, and announces his election as leader.

9. The final outcome, where 15 is represented as the leader while the old leader, 18, has been displaced (and continues to snore away).

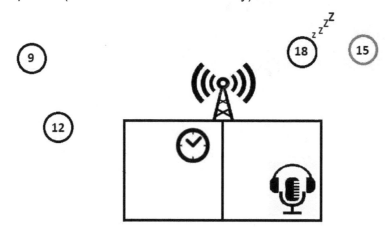

10. Perhaps 18 might wake up at some later point, raise a new election announcement, and possibly take back the top spot from 15.

7.4.2 Technical aspects

Moving away from the power play of sleep-starved politicians, let us review the bully algorithm more formally in the context of multiple entities working together as a distributed system. The use of the *waiting period* concept in the example should point out that we assume a *synchronous distributed system*. A politician deferring to another indicates an awareness of entities about each other and their respective 'values'. Finally, a politician 'dropping off to sleep' in an unpredictable manner represents *entity failures* of a similar nature in the system.

Before rounding up, let us consider the message complexity of this algorithm. In the worst case, the least powerful politician notices the leader in a failed state and raises an election announcement. If there are $n + 2$ entities in total, this can lead to n 'back off' messages directed at the weakest entity. If the 'next' entity (in ascending order of strength) takes over at this stage and generates an election announcement, it can lead to $n - 1$ 'back off' messages, and so on, leading to a total of $O(n)$ rounds and a final message complexity given by $O(n^2)$.

7.5 Conclusion

Moving on from the last chapter where we focused exclusively on leader algorithms for ring formations, we handled the case of generic networks in this one. The first algorithm that we discussed assumed strongly connected digraphs and synchronous distributed systems, while being allowed to be modified to work for asynchronous distributed systems as well (provided certain optimisations were dropped). The last one was specifically for synchronous environments, which we illustrated using a hypothetical scenario.

7.6 What's next?

This brings us to the end of our second and last chapter dedicated to election algorithms. Next, we move on to focus on a distributed algorithm with a related but broader sense of purpose: *consensus*.

Chapter 8. Synchronous Consensus (part 1)

By now, we ought to be pretty familiar with the concept and mechanics of leader election in distributed systems. If you think about it, leader election is nothing but the process of arriving at a *consensus* among all concerned entities on who the leader is. In this chapter, we will look at the broader aspects involved in the problem of reaching consensus in a synchronous distributed network. We will be starting with (a variation of) the fairly popular *two-generals problem*, but first we will attempt to nail down a formal structure and definition for the concept of consensus itself.

8.1 Introduction: consensus

Consensus is a fundamental problem in distributed computing, which addresses the challenge of *getting multiple participants in a system to agree on a value or opinion*. While simple enough at first glance, that illusion rapidly disappears once we start considering how communication links as well as participant nodes or entities can fail in a system. We shall be handling those two cases separately: the possibility of link failures first, followed by situations where entities can fail (crash or stop). The latter topic further divides into two subcases, but we will get there. For now, let us formally accept the following requirements for a consensus protocol that is to be executed by multiple nodes or entities in a distributed environment, with each one starting off with a proposed value for the final decision or consensus:

- *Termination*: every correct (non-faulty) node or entity in the system arrives at a decision (liveness)
- *Validity*: if all correct nodes propose a value *V*, then all correct nodes eventually arrive at a decision of *V*
- *Integrity*: every correct node decides on at most one value, and if it decides some value *V*, then *V* must have been proposed by some node
- *Agreement*: Every correct node arrives at the same decision (safety)

8.2 The Two-Generals Problem

Let us tweak the classic problem just a bit so that a pictorial representation becomes easier. The scenario begins to unfold in a form pretty much unchanged from the original one: two generals leading a two-pronged attack, from opposite directions, on a fortified enemy camp situated on elevated ground. Both generals and their divisions have to attack simultaneously, else their defeat and retreat, and possibly annihilation, is guaranteed. The generals and their divisions are several miles apart, on either side of the enemy camp. It is vital that the two generals communicate between each other and arrive at a consensus on the time of attack.

Before we start getting any further into their communication conundrum, let us name the two gentlemen: *General A* and *General B*.

Next, let us assume that the terrain is too hostile for a messenger or runner to reliably travel between the two divisions camped out on either side of the fortified enemy camp. Further, the enemy has jammed all electronic communication in the area for a radius of several miles. However, the Generals' signal engineers have located a 'bug' or loophole in the enemy's signal jamming mechanism, which enables them to identify intermittent 'windows' during which a very small amount of information can be sent with varying degrees of success. The engineers thus build a virtual communication channel on top of said mechanism, albeit one of incredibly low bandwidth and highly dubious reliability.

To sum up the communication aspects, each general has at his disposal a tiny computer using which he can send and receive messages to and from his counterpart. Thanks to the limitations of the underlying communication channel, a conversation consisting of a message in the form of a simple sentence and a similar-sized reply can take about an hour or more, with virtually no guarantee of safe delivery in either direction. Something is better than nothing - the Generals see it that way.

Let us come back to the plan of the impending attack. General A racks his brain over various military strategies and arrives at a conclusion: the best time of attack is *tomorrow 6AM*.

Having made up his mind, General A opens a chat window and sends the following message to General B:

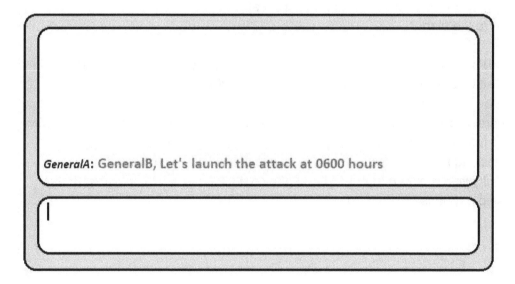

General B receives this message after about 30 minutes and replies in a positive fashion, which General A observes in his display after a further 30 minutes.

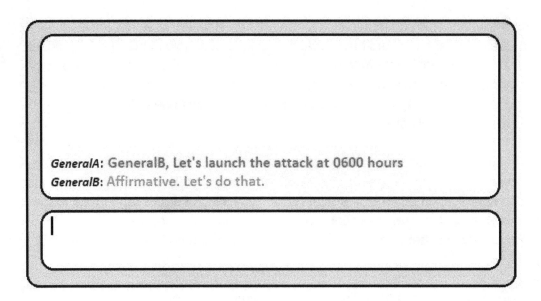

GeneralA: GeneralB, Let's launch the attack at 0600 hours
GeneralB: Affirmative. Let's do that.

What exactly is the situation at this point, which is about an hour after General A sent his first message? Let us consider the perspective of General A, first. General A knows without room for doubt that :

1. He successfully conveyed his attack plan to General B
2. B has agreed to the plan

What about General B's perspective? General B now knows what General A plans to do and has conveyed his positive acknowledgement and readiness for the same.

However, what General B *does not* know at this point is whether General A received his positive acknowledgement or not. Note that General A will not attack unless he knows for sure that General B will be attacking simultaneously. In short, at this point, *General B does not know whether General A will join the attack or not*. At first glance, this looks set to be easily sorted once the following step happens:

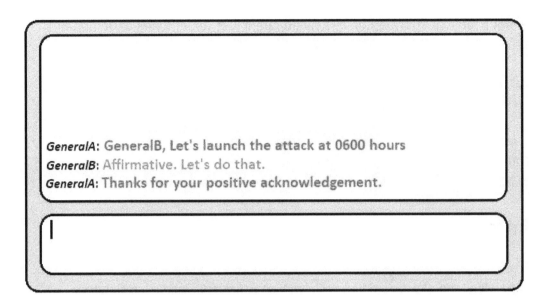

General A sends his acknowledgement of General B's positive acknowledgement, which General B receives and sees after half an hour.

They're not really out of the woods though. At this point, General A does not know if General B received his last message, i.e. whether his own acknowledgment of General B's positive acknowledgement has been received by General B. That brings a new requirement: General B has to acknowledge General A's acknowledgement of General B's positive acknowledgement of General A's plan.

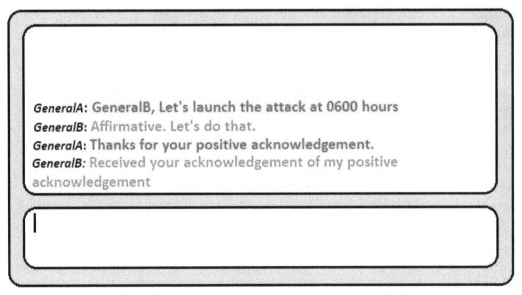

But now, General B would not know if General A received *that* acknowledgement unless General A sends a new level of acknowledgement. It is probably safe to say that we see where this is headed: nowhere.

The basic problem is simple but may not be readily apparent just yet, still we will go ahead and state it in a blunt fashion after which we will analyse the limitation more thoroughly:

If communication reliability is any less than absolutely 100%, a consensus between two or more entities in a distributed network is impossible.

It is important to note that *actual* communication failures need not happen; the *finite probability* of a communication failure is the deciding factor in this scenario. Let us now move away from the example and take a closer look at this impossibility in theoretical terms.

8.3 Consensus in synchronous systems with possibility of link failures

Since the two Generals in the example had a requirement to operate in lock-step (attack simultaneously), not to mention the nature of their communication strategies, it should be obvious that we were modelling a synchronous system. The unreliable communication channel implies that we assume the possibility of link failures.

Let us consider two entities, A and B, with a synchronous bidirectional communication link or channel between them. Without loss of generality, let us make three assumptions about A and B:

1. Each entity has an associated *state*
2. One entity sends a message to the other entity to communicate a *change in state* at the sender's side
3. When an entity receives a message, it will cause a change in state at the recipient's side

Going back (briefly) to the example: General A deciding to attack (at *0600* hours) is a change in A's state (from '*attack or not*' to '*will attack at 0600 hours*'), which induces a message from General A to General B. Similarly, the receipt of said message by General B changes B's state (from '*attack or not*' to '*join the attack at 0600 hours*').

Let us also note the following corollaries:

(1) If assumption 2 is contradicted by a message transmission, i.e. if a message is sent without a corresponding change of state, the message can be safely treated as a *dummy message* (which can be discarded without any consequences)
(2) If assumption 3 is contradicted by a message recipient, i.e. if a received message does not produce a corresponding change of state, the message can be treated as a dummy message (and safely discarded)

Let us assume that the consensus problem between A and B is to decide, together, between two values 0 and 1. As per section *8.2*, a consensus is impossible if the connecting link is assumed to be failure-prone. Let us defy this impossibility and claim that *A and B reached a consensus after say, 32 rounds of messaging* (note: each round consists of two messages, one in each direction). We will now demolish this claim and prove the original impossibility.

Let the last message, i.e. the 32nd one, be from B to A. Note that there is no 33rd message. If there was no 33rd message, the 32nd message did not cause a change of state at A (else, as per assumption 1, A would have generated a 33rd message to communicate the change of state). This gives us enough reason to consider the 32nd message to be a dummy message (as per corollary 2) and erase it from the scenario (which now transforms to '*A and B reached consensus after 31 messages*').

It should be readily obvious that we can extend the same treatment to the last message (31st message) in the new scenario: this message is from A to B, which obviously was sent without a change of state at A (else the 32nd message would not have been a dummy one, but instead, it would have been one generated due to a state change caused by the 31st message, which in turn was generated due to a state change at A), and hence, as per corollary 1, can be safely discarded as a dummy message. Now we have a new scenario where '*A and B reached consensus after 30 messages*'.

Continuing in this direction, backwards, we end up removing every single message and reach an impossible scenario where *A and B reached consensus after sending 0 messages*. This proves that our initial claim is wrong, and that the original impossibility holds intact.

Next, we will very briefly allow us the luxury of zero link failures before going back to reality and the lingering question of how best we can achieve consensus in the presence of communication breakdowns.

8.3.1 Alternate view

If the link between A and B is assumed to be *failure-free*, then a single message is all that is needed for consensus: a state change in A generates a solitary message from A to B, which is guaranteed to be delivered, and the resulting state change in B, and A's awareness of the same, is also guaranteed as a direct consequence of the failure-proof nature of the communication link. Note how this scenario does not violate, in any manner, any of the assumptions or their corollaries from the previous section.

This opens up an alternate view of consensus impossibility for synchronous systems in general:

Consensus is possible between two entities in a synchronous distributed system with a single message, or not at all with any number of messages.

If this statement appears brittle at first glance, think about this: consider a second message being needed, which obviously has to be an acknowledgement of the first one. This implies an element of unreliability in the communication link, which is equally applicable to the second message as well, leading to the need of a third message to act as acknowledgment of the second message, and so on in a never-ending sequence.

8.3.2 The Varghese-Lynch method

In this section, we come back to the possibility of link failures and consider the option of a 'compromise'. Having proved the impossibility of consensus in the presence of link failures, it is now a question of how to live with the situation in a practical sense. In other words, we will consider ourselves to be happy as long as we have a procedure that provides an acceptable *probability for consensus*. Let us expand and alter the two-generals scenario that we discussed earlier, which will in turn help us analyse the *Varghese-Lynch randomised coordinated attack protocol*.

In this modified scenario, we now have *n* Generals who need to achieve consensus among themselves. Let us also rid them of all means of electronic communication facilities and switch them right back to the old fashioned way of sending runners to deliver messages. Some things do not change, though: all Generals must attack together, or not attack at all. In mathematical terms, the consensus has to be from the set [0, 1], where 0 represents the *do-not-attack* option while 1 stands for *let-us-attack*. To begin with, let us list some conditions, all or most of which should be obvious:

- The process consists of multiple *rounds*
- Each round involves each General sending a message to everyone else
- Each General starts off with an *initial decision* of 0 or 1
- A message carries the sender's decision (0 or 1) among other information which we will identify shortly, one by one
- Even if one General decides on 0, the whole attack must be called off
- If all Generals decide on 1, *and there are no communication failures*, a consensus for 1 must result
- The consensus must arrive within a finite number of *rounds, r*
- We accept a certain probability that consensus does not happen after *r* rounds
- Each General assigns a unique runner to each other General; in other words, the communication network resembles a *complete graph*

Now, let us get familiar with the specific parameters and requirements of the protocol.

8.3.2.1 Knowledge Level

To proceed any further, we need a good handle on the concept of *knowledge level*. To understand this more, let us begin by accepting outright that each General starts off with a knowledge level of 0. This is another way of stating that a General is aware of only his own decision (0 or 1) at this point in time. Once a General hears for the first time from every other General, his knowledge level moves to 1: now the General knows the decision of every other General (because, as listed earlier, a message carries the sender's decision). Once the General knows that every other General knows every other General's decision, his knowledge level jumps to 2, and so on it goes. It should be becoming obvious, then, that the sender's knowledge level is specified in each message.

8.3.2.2 Key

All we need to know at this point about the concept of *key* in the context of the Varghese-Lynch protocol is listed below:

- The key is an integer value k such that $1 \leq k \leq r$ (where r is the number of rounds in which we target consensus)
- The key is selected by a single General right at the start and is advertised to everyone else by being specified in each message that is sent (by said General)
- Note that the key is selected randomly using a uniform distribution (i.e. each value in the set *[1, r]* have an equal chance of being selected)
- The key, along with the knowledge level, form a critical pair of information that each General use at the end of r rounds to make a decision

8.3.2.3 Initial Decision

We briefly touched upon how each General starts off with an initial decision of 0 or 1. Let us add to that information here by noting that the initial decision of each sender is yet another component of every message. By now, we have independently mentioned each component of a message; the next section will formally list all of them.

8.3.2.4 The Message

The following are the components of each message carried by a runner:

- Key (has a value in the range *[1, r]* if the sender is the General who chose the key, or -1 otherwise)
- Value of initial decision of sender (0 or 1)
- Knowledge level attained by sender (0, 1, 2, ...)

8.3.2.5 How it works (and how it may not)

We have all the necessary information in place, so it is time to look at how the protocol actually works. As mentioned earlier, the process consists of *r rounds*, during each of which, every General sends a runner to every other General. Each runner carries a message; but they make their way through extremely hostile territory, so there is no guarantee of safe delivery.

Every General starts off with a knowledge level of 0, which upgrades to 1 once a runner is first received from every other General. A General upgrades his knowledge level to 2 upon receiving a runner conveying a knowledge level of 1 from every other General, and so on. At every point, each General has a perceived notion of the knowledge level of every other General; his own knowledge level is set one higher than the lowest among the knowledge levels of every other General (as known to him).

This clearly means that knowledge levels among Generals can vary, but no more than by 1. Why? Because, for the knowledge level of say, General A, to reach L, every other General must first reach $L - 1$ (i.e. General A would have switched to L only upon seeing $n - 1$ runners, each conveying a knowledge level of $L - 1$). Every General also notes down the key once they first receive a runner from the General who chose the key.

As mentioned earlier, the process is simple if the initial decision of at least one General is 0; the consensus also will be the same. A bit more complexity ensues if all Generals have decided on 1, so let us look at that next.

At the end of r rounds, each General uses a comparison between the key and his knowledge level to take a decision. A General will assume communication failure(s) if his knowledge level is less than the key value, and switch to a decision of not to attack (i.e. 0). Otherwise, the decision remains the same (i.e. 1). Clearly, consensus will happen without a hitch if all Generals are at the same knowledge level at the end of r rounds.

However, communication failures can end up 'dividing' the Generals into two sets: one with a knowledge level of $L1$, and the other with a knowledge level of $L2$ (where $L2 = L1 + 1$). Here also, we find no problems with consensus if $L1 \geq K$ (*implying* $L2 > K$) or $L2 < K$ (*implying* $L1 < K$). The former assures a consensus of 1 (*attack*) while the latter leads to a consensus of 0 (*do not attack*).

All this brings us to the sole possibility where consensus may not happen: $L2 = K$. In such a scenario, all Generals with a knowledge level of $L2$ will (continue to) decide to attack (1) while those with a knowledge level of $L1$ will switch their decision from 1 to 0. The probability of this event can be easily calculated: since K is chosen randomly (with a uniform distribution) from $[1, r]$, we arrive at a probability $1/r$ of missing consensus for a given communication pattern (which decides L1 and L2).

8.3.3 Can we do better?

Having seen the Varghese-Lynch protocol that assures consensus with a failure probability of $1/r$, the question naturally arises as to whether an algorithm can be devised with an improved chance of consensus. As it turns out, there is not a lot of scope for improvement and that is what we will look at next. Without resorting to mathematical notations (much), we will try to understand the limitation as intuitively as possible.

Consider the same group of n Generals, who now run an arbitrary unnamed algorithm in an effort to achieve consensus after r rounds. Let them all decide initially on 1 (attack). Assume that General A ends up with an information level of 0 after r rounds. This implies that we have at least one participant - let him be General B - from whom General A never heard from; not one single message was received from General B. In other words, the situation from the perspective of General A remains utterly unaffected by the initial decision, communications, or final knowledge level of General B; let us exploit this fact and safely imagine that General B has an initial decision of 0, implying that General B will eventually decide for 0 (do not attack). Now let E be the utmost probability for consensus failure in this algorithm - which is exactly what will happen if General A opts for 1, implying that E represents the maximum possibility that General A opts for 1 upon finishing round r with an information level of 0.

Next, let us assume a second scenario where General A reached a knowledge level of 1 at the end of r rounds. Similar to the first scenario, there has to be a General B from whom General A has heard only once, when General B had an information level of 0; hence, from A's perspective, it makes no difference to assume that B arrives at the end of round r with an information level of 0. Let $E1$ be the probability that General A opts for 1. Now, General B is in the same spot as General A in the prior scenario, so the probability that General B will opt for 1 is E. We also know that E represents the probability of consensus failure, so the probability that A and B differ in consensus, i.e. $E1 - E,$ equates to a result of E, implying in turn that $E1 = 2E$. In other words, $2E$ is the maximum probability that General A will opt for 1 upon finishing round r with an information level of 1.

Proceeding in this direction, level by level, we arrive at the utmost probability $E(r + 1)$ that A will opt for 1 upon finishing round r with an information level of r. However, we know that A will opt for 1 with absolute certainty upon facing no communication failures (hence the final knowledge level of r) and everyone else having an initial decision of 1. Hence, we equate $E(r + 1)$ to at least 1, implying that E is at least $1/(r + 1)$. As we anticipated earlier, this is not much of an improvement over what the Varghese-Lynch protocol achieves.

So far, we have considered consensus in synchronous systems where link failures are a possibility while the participating nodes stay alive continuously. Next, let us assume reliable links while allowing the nodes or entities in the network to fail, i.e. to simply stop working.

8.4 Consensus in synchronous systems with possibility of entity failures

Let the following diagram serve as an introduction:

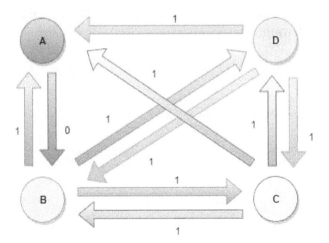

Obviously, we are considering a scenario involving 4 nodes or entities, each of which seem to communicate with each other (note: a *complete graph*). The presence of 0s and 1s as messages would imply that the consensus should be on one of those two values. It is interesting to see that node A sends out only a single message: implication being, node A *failed* before it could send the remaining two messages of its *message set*. We should also note that A seems to be the dissenter of the group, voting 0 while everyone else voted for 1, but only B has received or noted this aspect. Assuming, of course, that this is round 1 of this particular consensus mechanism that proceeds in rounds, how will this scenario unfold? We will assume that any entity will switch from a decision or vote of 1 to 0 upon seeing a vote or decision of 0 from anyone else.

So, the next round should be somewhat easy to imagine: B has heard of the negative vote from A, so B would be issuing a vote of 0 in the next round. C and D would continue to stick with their original decisions of 1. Let us, in fact, make things a bit trickier. Take a look at the next diagram:

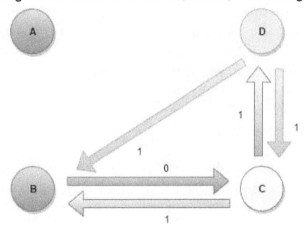

It seems that B has crashed in similar fashion; in fact, similar to the extent that B crashed after sending a single message to C. At this point, only C is aware of a negative vote, D does not know yet.

So, 2 rounds have passed, and what if there were no further rounds? We would not have a consensus, because C has switched to 0 while D is still at 1. It is obvious that 2 rounds would have been enough to cope with the single failure of A, but a second failure (of B) has broken the consensus. Well then, what if there was one more round?

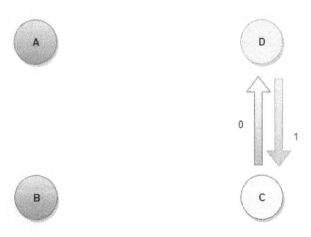

Now *that* works. The 3rd rounds allows C to pass on the negative vote to D, who will promptly switch to a decision of 0, ensuring consensus. What we have effectively seen so far is a simple version of a worst case scenario where *an entity fails in every round except one.* We shall call this the *simple-broadcast* algorithm for consensus in a synchronous distributed network with the following properties:

- The network resembles a complete graph
- Nodes or entities in the network can fail
- Nodes fail after sending a *subset* of their message set
- Every pair of nodes are connected by reliable bidirectional links

It should be evident that the simple-broadcast algorithm provides consensus in the event of up to a maximum of *f* node or entity failures where $f \leq r - 1$. In other words, *it is critical to have at least one round where no entity fails.*

8.4.1 Message cost of simple-broadcast consensus algorithm

We can easily see the element of n^2 figuring in the message cost since each round involves everyone communicating with everyone. Since there are f + 1 rounds, we have a final message complexity given by *n(n - 1)(f + 1)*, which implies $O(n^2(f + 1))$.

8.4.2 Optimising the message cost of simple-broadcast consensus

If we take a closer look at the earlier diagrams, we can easily convince ourselves on a definite room for improvement in message cost. For instance, consider D who sends one or more messages carrying the value 1 in each round. D could just send a single message to each other node for 1 and leave it at that (since the decision for D never changes until the last round). A diagram follows.

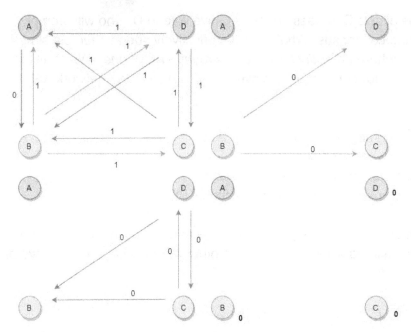

Top left indicates round 1 where all nodes send out messages, but node A fails after sending a single message (to B). Top right shows the next round, where only B is active - in order to propagate the 0 it received in the previous round. Round 3 (bottom left) finds D and C advertising the 0 it last received from B, while round 4 (bottom right) is a silent affair, in turn leading to a consensus (of 0).

This implies that each node needs to send a maximum of 2 messages to each other node - the second one being needed only if there is a decision change involved. We seem to have improved the original message cost to $2n(n - 1)$ but can we do better?

8.4.3 Another optimisation for simple-broadcast consensus

Why not let 1 be the default decision? This implies the following: an entity needs to resort to messaging only upon seeing (or initially having) a decision of 0. In other words, 1 is implied as default while a 0 is signalled exactly once. This tweak further improves the message complexity to $n(n - 1)$.

8.4.4 Single-consensus V. Multi-consensus

So far, we required the state of consensus to be one where all (surviving) entities selected the same, single, value out of a larger set of candidate values. What if we loosen the restrictions a bit? Perhaps we are a T-shirt company willing to issue free samples to a certain segment of the population, and we would like the target segment to arrive at a consensus that decides upon a final result of 3 distinct T-shirt sizes (say, Small, Medium, Large). In short, we are now prepared to accept multiple consensus values, to a certain limit - for example, we do not want a set of 100 people ending up choosing 100 distinct values, with each person deciding on a different selection. We will label this the *m-consensus problem*, where we would like n entities to agree on a maximum of m different values. We will continue to assume stopping failures, up to a maximum of f.

As usual, the algorithm will proceed in rounds; during each round, each entity broadcasts its choice to everyone else. An entity may fail after sending out only a subset of its intended message set. During any round, an entity will switch its preference to the smallest value it has seen from everyone else in that round. After the last round, we do not want more than m distinct values among the surviving nodes or entities. To better understand this algorithm, let us consider a simplified scenario and focus on the first round.

We will assume 6 nodes - A, B, C, D, E, F - starting off with initial values 1, 2, 3, 4, 5, and 6 respectively. If this first round is a complete success, i.e. if there are no failures, obviously everyone will agree on a consensus of 1. Let us not make things so easy, and instead, assume that A and B fail during the first round. In fact, A fails immediately after sending its value (1) to C, and B crashes right after sending its value (2) to D. Upon receiving the value of 1 from A, naturally C switches its choice to 1. Similarly, D switches own choice to 2 after receiving that value from B. Now, the message exchanges between C, D, E, and F go smoothly, with everyone receiving everyone else's values. The lowest value among this group is 3; hence, E and F settle for a choice of 3. In short, at the end of the first round, we have 3 distinct values in the system. Of course, this would have been lesser if A and B could reach out to more nodes before they crashed. The purpose of this example was to show that *the number of distinct values remaining after a round could be as much as one more than the number of failures during that round*. Also, let us carefully note one striking aspect of our current approach: we are no longer are held hostage to the condition that at least one failure-free round must happen. Any round with one or more failures will result in multiple distinct values prevailing in the system, and it just so happens that we no longer have a problem with such an outcome!

Let us next get a grip on the worst case scenario. Assume an arbitrary number of nodes in the system. To start with, what if all or most of the failures happened during the first round? Note that we design our algorithm around an assumption that failures do not exceed a particular count. The next round would be relatively failure-free, and hence, would immediately yield a low number of distinct values. For example, consider that $f = 4$ and $m = 2$. The first round sees 4 failures (and hence, 5 distinct values in the system, in the worst case failure behaviour). The second round sees no failures, and thus, a single consensus value. This is definitely not a worst case situation.

How about the other extreme, then, in terms of how failures appear? Let the first round be quite failure-free. In this case, we have a low number of distinct values after the first round, and we can only improve from here. Let us note that the number of distinct values in the system can only *decrease* as the rounds pass. For example, if there are no failures during the first round, we immediately have a single consensus value in the system - and we are done right there, and quite happy.

So, it looks like the worst case scenario is when failures accumulate at a constant rate across rounds, without any sharp spikes. In other words, the worst case scenario happens when failures are distributed as uniformly as possible across the various rounds. To analyse this further, let us assume that f is *not* a multiple of m. This means that we distribute f failures across r rounds in the following manner: the first $(r - 1)$ rounds see m failures in each, and the last round sees $(f \% m)$ failures (i.e. the 'remaining' failures). Hence, in the worst case, the last round sees $(m - 1)$ failures, since $(m - 1)$ is the maximum possible value of $(f \% m)$. This means: even in the worst case, we end up with m distinct values after the last $(r$-th) round. The final step is to arrive at an expression for the number of rounds needed by the algorithm, in the worst case:

$(r - 1)m + (m - 1) = f$

$rm = f + 1$

$r = f/m + 1/m$

It follows that we are looking at a minimum number of rounds given by $f/m + 1$ to ensure that no more than m distinct values remain by the final round. Next, let us try to defeat this relation that we just obtained. Our attempt will fail.

Assume that the algorithm ran for $f/m + 1$ rounds, but we were left with $m + 1$ distinct values. We will now try do defeat this assumption. The assumption implies that the last round saw m failures, which in turn implies that *every* previous round saw at least m failures. In other words, the total number of failures is given by the following expression:

$m(f/m + 1)$

However, this is a value which is greater than f. This hands us a contradiction, which in turn defeats our assumption that we were left with $m + 1$ distinct values after $f/m + 1$ rounds.

8.5 Conclusion

In this chapter, the first of several ones dedicated to consensus algorithms, we started off with the two-generals problem before switching to a theoretical view of how and why consensus is impossible for synchronous networks in the presence of possible link failures. Having understood the impossibility, we considered a realistic possibility of consensus using the Varghese-Lynch protocol. Next, we turned our attention to consensus in synchronous systems where communication links and reliable while the participating entities are not. We concluded by looking at a simple broadcast algorithm designed to provide consensus in the presence of entity failures.

8.6 What's next?

In the next chapter, we will continue to look at consensus for distributed systems. Initially picking up from where we left in this chapter, we will subsequently look at situations that allow participating entities to behave in a more 'interesting' fashion than what we have seen till now.

We will see that endowing network entities with such 'enhanced' character will take a significant toll on the number of entity failures that an algorithm with a given number of rounds can tolerate.

Chapter 9. Synchronous Consensus (part 2)

9.1 Introduction

We concluded the last chapter with a quick look at consensus in synchronous systems where communication links are reliable while participating entities may *stop* or *fail*. We will follow the same thread, while also taking a seemingly backward step by first discussing an algorithm that is much costlier in terms of message size, local storage, and possibly, computation. Let us start with a closer look at the concept of *knowledge level* as introduced and used in the previous chapter.

9.2 Knowledge Level : a closer look

What does an entity mean when it advertises its knowledge level to be, say, 3? The answer should be obvious to us; an entity saying *"my knowledge level is 3"* means something like:

- *At first, I knew only my own decision*
- *Then, I came to know about everyone else's decision*
- *Then, I came to know that everyone knows about everyone else's decision*
- *Most recently, I came to know that everyone knows that everyone knows about everyone else's decision*

In brief, a knowledge level of 3 is an efficient contraction of the following:

Everyone knows that everyone knows about everyone else's decision

However, while this mechanism is indeed efficient, there is no mention anywhere of the actual decision values as heard by anyone from anyone else at any given time or round. What any entity knows about another entity's decision is based entirely on what the former entity heard directly from the latter. This, then, is the price we pay for the efficiency we enjoy with this particular approach.

So, what if we decide to lose this efficiency and permit each entity to communicate in a (much) more verbose manner? In particular, we ponder an ulterior motive: will not this give us an opportunity to inspect what any given entity communicated (as decision value) to each other entity? With aforementioned data, can we make judgements on the trustworthiness of any given entity?

It may be obvious where this is headed: we will soon be dealing with network entities that are unreliable not just in terms of *availability* but also *behavior*. Before getting there, let us look at an algorithm which tries to accomplish the result of the *simple-broadcast* consensus algorithm from section *8.4* albeit with much reduced efficiency.

9.3 Consensus in synchronous systems with entity failures: a verbose alternative

We will consider a simple arrangement involving 4 entities talking to each other, in synchronous rounds, over reliable links that form a complete graph (just as in section *8.4*). Consider the following communication pattern during round 1 for the algorithm:

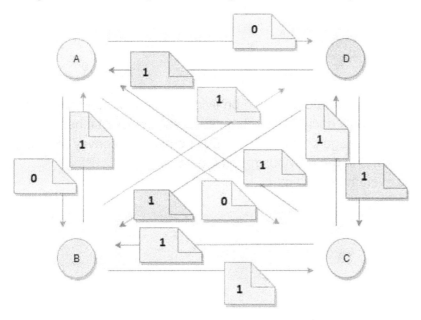

Clearly, not much has changed: each entity simply advertises its own decision to everyone else. How about round 2, then:

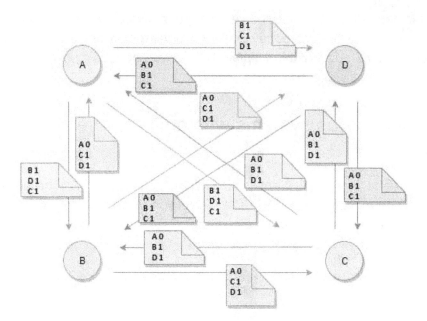

Now, clearly, things have changed. The strategy should be evident: in each round after the first (when each entity simply advertises own decision), each entity advertises what it heard in the previous round. For example, the message content *(A0 B1 D1)* from C to B convey the values *(0 1 1)* which C received from A, B, C in the previous round (i.e. round 1).
Unsurprisingly, then, round 3 is even more hectic:

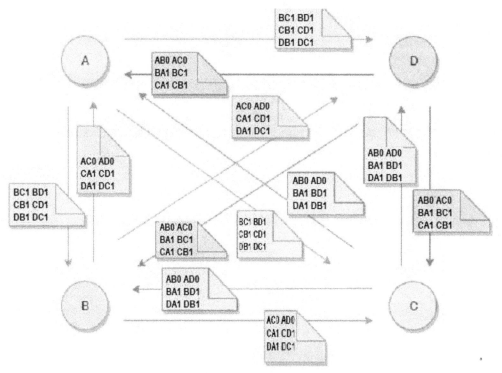

Note that each node includes only information about *other nodes* that it received in the previous round. For instance, A's message in round 3 does not contain *AB0* (meaning *A passed 0 to B in the previous round*) or *AC0* or *AD0*.

It is easy to see this algorithm working exactly like the simple-broadcast consensus algorithm as far as the end result is concerned. If A crashes after sending a single message (carrying a decision of 0) to B, C and D will come to know of A's decision during the next round. In other words, as earlier, f failures can be tolerated if the algorithm ticks for $f + 1$ rounds. What has changed specifically is the cost in terms of message size and local storage (memory at each entity). In fact, there is something more: now any given entity can *cross-check* the consistency of any other entity's decision by referring the message content of other entities. For example, B can verify that A sent a decision of 0 to not just B, but to C and D as well. We do not have occasion to exploit this new-found capability yet, but that will change soon.

9.3.1 Local storage and computation

As we noted earlier, this 'verbose' algorithm sacrifices efficiency not just in terms of message size, but for local storage and computation as well. Clearly, each entity has to store the non-trivial information received from every other entity in a manner that is friendly for lookups as well as updates. The first step on the course to deciding a data structure for the task is to look at how information accumulates as each round pass. Let us consider the general case of having n entities. The first round is the simplest; each entity sends out a single piece of information, $n - 1$ times. In other words, each entity receives $n - 1$ pieces of information, one piece per message. This naturally leads to a second round where each entity sends out $n - 1$ pieces of information, $n - 1$ times - which implies that each entity receives $(n - 1)(n - 1)$ pieces of information, $n - 1$ pieces per message. We see the implication: information accumulates exponentially. This leads to an intuitive option of having a *multi-level tree* as the data structure of choice for the job at hand. A formal definition and a diagrammatic representation are next.

9.3.2 EIG Tree

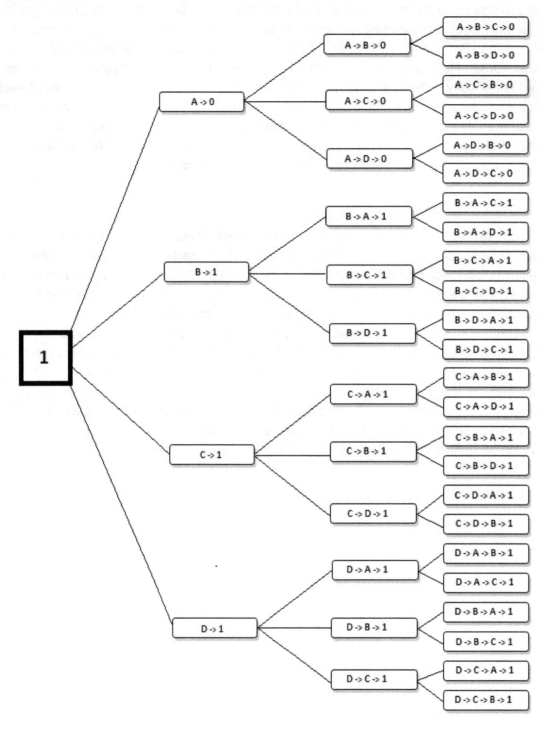

For the sake of readability, the tree is tilted horizontally. Since the strategy employed by the algorithm to accumulate information is formally known as *Exponential Information Gathering*, what we have at hand is an *EIG Tree*.

9.3.2.1 Structure of an EIG Tree

The EIG tree for an algorithm that uses r rounds has a height of $r + 1$, including level 0 which contains the root node. Each non-zero level is updated during the corresponding round of the algorithm. Since the algorithm is required to have $f + 1$ rounds, where f is the number of entity failures that can be tolerated, the height of the EIG tree is also equal to $f + 2$. Looking at the first level, we see n nodes where each node has $n - 1$ children, each of which has $n - 2$ children and so on, till the last level (level $f + 1$). In other words, (obviously) exempting the leaf nodes, each other node in the tree has $n - l$ children where l is the level the node is at.

Before moving on to the specifics of how an EIG tree is maintained, let us quickly note the two distinct factors which determine the layout or shape of an EIG tree:

- The number of participating nodes in the network (which really has got nothing to do with the algorithm), which determine the horizontal layout of the tree
- The number of entity failures that the algorithm is designed to tolerate (which decides the number of rounds involved), which determines the vertical height of the tree

9.3.2.2 Maintaining an EIG Tree

Needless to say, a copy of the EIG tree is maintained by each entity in the network. The root node of the EIG tree contains the decision value of the host or local node. This implies that the previous diagram could represent the EIG tree maintained by B, C, or D. What about the rest of the nodes?

Each node (other than the root) has two associated attributes: one being a label, and the other being the value. If you consider the right-most (top-most in the diagram) leaf node marked as "A -> B -> C -> 0", the label is "ABC" while the value is 0. This particular node is updated with the value 0 upon receiving a message from C which describes what C received (in the previous round) from B about what B heard (in the round previous to that) from A. Note that at the start of round 1, all nodes have an associated value of *null*. In other words, an EIG tree is initialised with all node values set to *null*. The implication follows that messages require a specific format in order to be compatible with the choice of EIG tree as the data structure for local storage at each node or entity. Let us look into that part right after we mull over something rather interesting about EIG trees.

Fundamentally, each node in an EIG tree represents a piece of information from the maintainer's point of view - for example, the node "$D \rightarrow 1$" represents the information "D's decision is 1" as heard directly from D - and each child node represents a confirmation or refutation of this information as obtained through another (relevant) party. For example, "$D \rightarrow C \rightarrow 1$" represents the information received from C that "D's decision is 1". This leads to an interesting implication that "$D \rightarrow 1$" having a child node "$D \rightarrow C \rightarrow 0$" would mean food for thought, at the very minimum.

9.3.2.3 Message formats as implied by the EIG tree

It should be evident by now that a message should contain two types of parameters: one or more labels, and an associated value for each - to mirror the corresponding target nodes (i.e. the nodes whose values will be set upon message receipt) in the EIG tree. To provide an example, consider the first round: every message sent out by A would specify the label as "A" and carry a value of 0. Similarly, B will send out messages with a label of "B" and value of 1, and so on for C and D. In the same fashion, the next round will see A send out messages with the labels "BA", "CA", "DA", each with an associated value of 1, to represent the data it received in the prior round. Refer the following diagram:

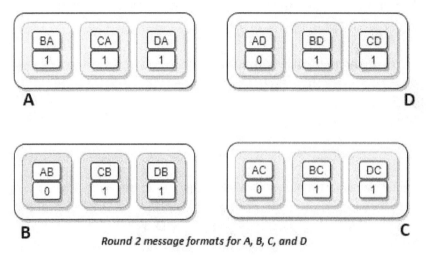

Round 2 message formats for A, B, C, and D

This process applies for each entity and accelerates through each round, with the number of label/value pairs increasing exponentially as the rounds progress.

9.3.2.4 Entity failure

Note that an entity failure during a round will cause the corresponding nodes in the EIG trees of each other entity to be left with a value of *null*.

9.3.3 Consensus using the EIG tree as input

As with the simple-broadcast consensus algorithm from section *8.4*, the verbose and inefficient version runs its course for *f + 1* rounds where *f* is the maximum amount of entity failures that can be tolerated for consensus to happen. By that point, the EIG tree is fully updated at each node, matching the diagram from section *9.3.2*. Now, to put it in simple terms, each node *plucks* its EIG tree. In a technical sense, the values from *all* non-root nodes are noted, and the unique ones among those are combined to form a set which will be the basis for the consensus process. Very simply, if only a single value results - i.e. the formed set is a *singleton* one - then we have a consensus, obviously. Otherwise, there is a conflict (or maybe even a null set) and a pre-agreed default value (for example, 0) will be the decision by consensus. In the particular example we have been handling, the set will clearly be *(0, 1)*, leading to a consensus of *0*.

Let us also note the implication that we can expand the decision set of this algorithm beyond the current limited one of *(0, 1)*. In other words, each entity can opt for a decision value in some set $(v_0, v_1 ... v_m)$ and the algorithm will work in an equivalent manner.

9.3.4 Message complexity

Following up from section *9.3.1*, the message complexity is clearly $O((f + 1)n^2)$. This is another way of saying that, in each of *f + 1* rounds, every entity messages every other entity. The information complexity, as we noted earlier, is exponential and is given by $O(n^{f + 1})$.

Let us conclude here by noting that the simple-broadcast optimisations described in sections *8.4.2* and *8.4.3* are applicable in this case, too.

9.4 Interlude to take stock, and a slight detour

Together with the previous chapter and so far in the current chapter, we looked at consensus algorithms for synchronous networks where either links or entities can fail. We have mentioned it in each case but let us note here that we consistently dealt with networks that are *complete graphs* - which, of course, means the existence of a *direct* link from every node in the network to every other one. In comparison, a *connected graph* implies only a *path* between every pair of nodes in the network. Before turning our attention back to entity failures, let us take a moment to understand how a consensus algorithm is affected by a switch from complete graphs to connected graphs. This means that we are essentially interested in how the broadcast capability of a connected graph or network is affected by the failure of one or more entities or links.

Let us first focus on a complete graph, actually. Assuming a *n* node graph where *n > 1*, the broadcast or consensus capability is not affected by removing or failing a particular link or node - because each available node has a dedicated link to every other one. You would need to remove all *n* nodes to declare broadcast capability to be disabled. In other words, a complete graph can be thought of as a *n-node-connected* network, as in, removal of *n* nodes will disable broadcast capability in the network. Equivalently, we can define an n-node-connected network as one which retains broadcast capability despite removal of up to *n - 1* nodes. In much the same manner, we can define *n-edge-connected* networks as those which allow broadcast despite failure of up to *n - 1* links.

Since consensus depends directly on broadcast capabilities, we arrive at the following two conclusions:

- Consensus in a synchronous network is possible despite *f* entity failures only if said network is *(f + 1)-node-connected*
- Consensus in a synchronous network is possible despite *f* link failures only if said network is *(f + 1)-edge-connected*

Let us also note, well in advance actually, that asynchronous networks are a completely different proposition altogether. We will get there in the next chapter.

9.5 Byzantine behaviour

The Byzantine empire or *Byzantium* was an ancient city under Greek occupation which went through several transformations over the centuries to become what we now know as Istanbul. History aside, our interest in the term *Byzantine* arises due to its appearance in the 1982 paper by Lamport, Shostak, and Pease; *"The Byzantine Generals' Problem"*. The paper initially used the term Byzantine only to provide a common allegiance to those Generals, but the term caught on to be used widely for the purpose of describing a particular type of behavior or failure. So, what exactly does it represent?

Let us first recollect that we are still on the subject of entity failures in synchronous distributed networks. By introducing *Byzantine Failures*, we allow failing entities to not just stop working, but also behave in an *arbitrary* manner. Depending on an observer, byzantine behavior might appear random, calculated, incompetent, or even devious to a fault. As an example, consider the possibility that a subset of the *n* Generals in the problem discussed in section *8.3.2* is on the payroll of the enemy; any one of them can send conflicting votes in multiple directions, with the malicious intention of subverting the forthcoming attack. Or maybe some of them are plain incompetent; or amnesiacs; maybe drunks; the point of interest is the havoc wreaked by such behavior and the algorithms we can devise to salvage a consensus out of such chaos. While we relied so far on knowledge levels, initial decisions, pre-agreed defaults, and so on to handle consensus in cases of link or entity failures, now for the first time we will be employing the concept of a *majority*. Let us consider a simple example and see how an EIG tree might help, as we have been hinting at more than once earlier.

9.5.1 Consensus with Byzantine failures using EIG trees

Consider the following situation in a 4 node complete graph:

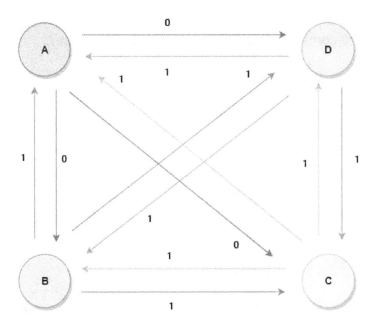

We assume three entities to be in unflawed shape, while one behaves in a byzantine fashion. A single entity failure implies 2 rounds for the algorithm, the first of which unfolds as the diagram represents.

We do not notice anything out of place, yet; everyone except A decide on 1, and everyone is truthful in their messages to everyone else in this round. The second round is different, though:

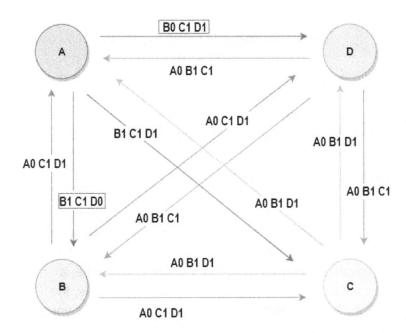

Here, the byzantine failure reveals itself as A sending not one, but two wrong pieces of information. One is A informing B that A received 0 from D, and the second is A informing D that A received 0 from B. Now, B did see a 1 from D in the first round, so do B assume that D was lying during round one? Or do B assume that A is being dishonest? A similar situation applies for D, in terms of B's truthfulness versus that of A. The solution should be evident already for such a simple scenario, but observing the corresponding EIG tree makes it even clearer:

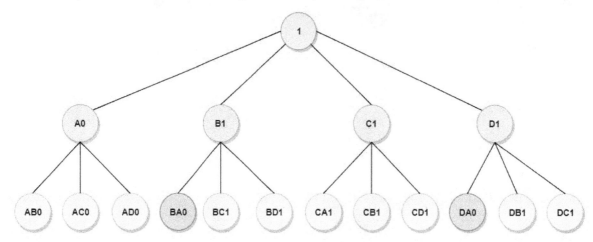

Picking up from where we left in section *9.3.2.2*, what B and D need to do is to check the validity of values at nodes *D1* and *B1*, respectively. It should be clear that we can rely on a *majority* in this situation. Considering B1 first, the anomaly *BA0* is invalidated by the two other nodes *BC1* and *BD1* - both of which confirm a 1 from B. Similarly, in the case of D1, *DA0* is invalidated by the presence of the majority composed of *DB1* and *DC1*. Interestingly, this would not have worked if we had at least one more byzantine entity - or if we had one less non-faulty entity. Let us note casually that, at least in this specific situation, we needed the total number of entities to be greater than thrice the number of entity failures. Next, we will see if we can prove this limitation.

9.5.1.1 Defining the requirement for a majority

We know from section *9.3.2.1* that the number of children under a tree node at level *l* is given by $n - l$. For a majority in this crowd over *f* byzantine members, we need $n - l$ to be greater than *2f*. We also know that the maximum value of *l* is *f + 1* (the lowest level), which implies that $n - l$ is greater than $n - f$, allowing us to switch to the equivalent condition that $n - f$ must be greater than *2f*. In other words, *the number of entities n must be greater than 3f for the EIG tree algorithm to achieve consensus despite a maximum of f failures.* We have thus formally confirmed the limitation that we casually introduced in the prior section.

For a more intuitive understanding of the aforementioned requirement (*n > 3f*), consider the following line of thinking: an algorithm designed to produce consensus from *n* entities of which *f* are byzantine, must be prepared to work with a minimum of $n - f$ votes. Why? Because, a byzantine quantity may not even put in a vote. That said, while working with $n - f$ votes, the algorithm also need to accept the fact that all *f* byzantine quantities could have put in a vote. This leads to the conclusion that one is working with $n - 2f$ reliable votes, a quantity which must be greater than *f* to avoid the byzantine entities forming a majority. It follows that *n* must be greater than *3f*, i.e. *f < n/3*.

9.5.1.2 Using the EIG tree for consensus

We described (and proved) how the EIG tree helps us resolve conflicts caused by byzantine entities, but we have yet not laid out a formal process for the same. Quite simply, each entity *fixes* its EIG tree first. In order to fix the EIG tree, an entity starts from the lowest level of non-leaf nodes (i.e. level *f*), going all the way up to the root node, and validates, modifying if needed, the value at each node using a majority from the child nodes of the same. If a majority (of child nodes) points to a different value, the node value is replaced by the value held by the majority (of child nodes). If no majority is possible, the node value is invalidated and replaced by a pre-agreed default. Also note that the default will replace any *null* values (see section *9.3.2.4*) found at any nodes. Once the EIG tree is fixed, we will see that all non-faulty nodes will converge on the same value at the root node of each EIG tree.

As an example, consider a revised version of the scenario described in section *9.5.1*. Let node A continue to be the sole byzantine entity. B has an initial decision of 0, while C and D opt for 1. In the first round, A sends 0 to B and 1 to C and D. A remains truthful in the second round. Here is what B sees while attempting to fix its EIG tree:

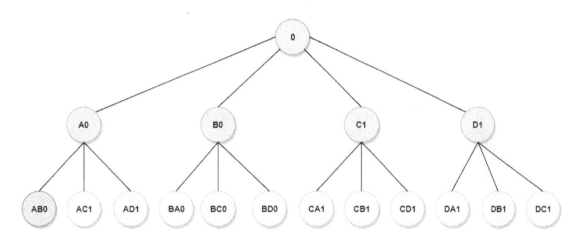

Clearly, the value of 0 at node *A0* is refuted by the majority formed by *AC1* and *AD1* (i.e. nodes C and D both claiming that A issued a decision of 1 in the first round).
On the aforementioned basis, B fixes level 1 of its EIG tree with the following result:

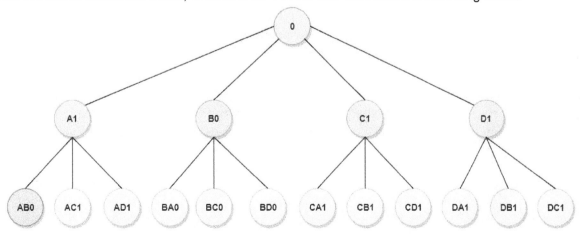

As the next and last step, the root node's value is adjusted to match the values held by the majority of its children (i.e. level 1 nodes):

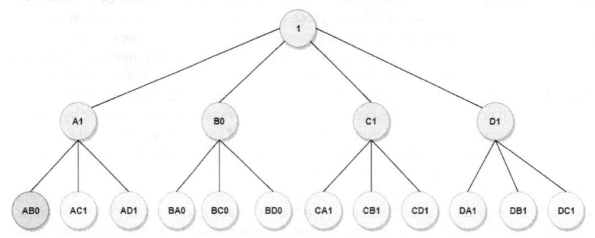

Each other non-faulty node goes through a similar process - i.e. C and D follow the same routine - ensuring that all three non-faulty nodes reach a consensus of 1. Note how and why we remain flatly unconcerned about A's treatment of its own EIG tree: *we are only interested in the final decisions of non-faulty entities.*

9.5.1.3 Message complexity

Clearly, the message complexity remains the same as described in section *9.3.4* for the non-byzantine use of EIG trees: $O((f + 1)n^2)$. Information complexity remains unchanged too, given by $O(n^{f + 1})$.

9.5.2 Byzantine consensus and network connectivity

So far, we have assumed complete graphs in our analysis of byzantine failures. Let us remember that a complete graph of *n* nodes enjoys the luxury of *n - 1* paths between any pair of nodes. To rephrase, the *connectivity* of a complete graph is *n - 1*, implying that connectivity refers to the minimum number of nodes to be removed for a network to be either disconnected or be reduced to a single node. Let us now try to understand the relation between connectivity and the tolerable number of byzantine failures in a network.

Consider any two nodes A and B in a given network having a given connectivity. Let the network contain *f* byzantine entities. Assuming *f* paths between A and B such that each pass through a unique byzantine entity, we need at least another *f + 1* paths between A and B that do *not* involve a byzantine node in order for A and B to take majority votes on the validity of the information they receive from each other. In other words, A and B must be connected in at least *2f + 1* ways for majority decisions on either side to be feasible. Let us prove this further for the simple case of *f =1* and *connectivity = 2* using a set of diagrams.

9.5.2.1 Single byzantine failure in a 2-node-connected network

Consider a simple 2-node-connected network which will serve as our base or reference network:

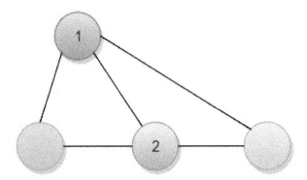

Clearly, removal of node 1 and node 2 would separate the network into 2 disconnected nodes. The other two (unnamed) nodes can talk to each other only through 1 and 2. If either of the pair (1 and 2) is byzantine, the two unnamed nodes will find it impossible to majority-check any information which they receive from each other - simply because there are only two routes between the pair of them.

Next, we will prove this impossibility in more formal terms. We will assume that the algorithm being executed in the network produces correct consensus, and then derive a contradiction which will defeat that assumption.

Consider the configuration in the next diagram that is built by fitting together two *copies* of our reference network, i.e. the one illustrated in the previous diagram. One copy has all nodes using 0 as their initial decision, while 1 is the choice for all nodes in the other copy. Note that 'copy' is the key word here - even though one copy is named A, B, C, D, and the other is named E, F, G, H in the illustration, corresponding nodes act just like each other, like a pair of nodes with the same identity. For example, A and H will send out messages containing the same identity information, so does E and D, C and F, B, and G.

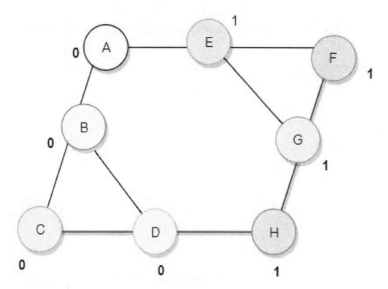

Our specific interest is in how we can primarily view a subset of them as a single byzantine node - which the remaining nodes will attempt to deal with in the context of a consensus. First, we imagine replaced EDFGH to be replaced with a byzantine entity:

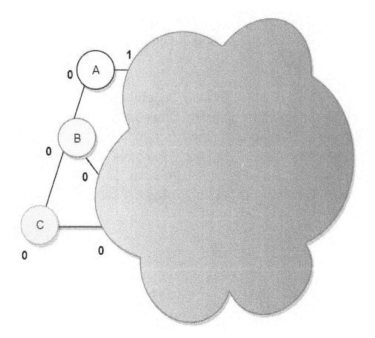

Since D and E act exactly similarly (identity-wise; their initial values of choice are different, though), it would appear that the trio A, B, and C receive conflicting value information from the same node. In other words, it is the same as if A, B, and C are connected to a byzantine entity.

Since all correct nodes (A, B, and C) in this configuration have the same initial values, the correctness conditions from section *8.1* dictate that they must agree on 0 as the decision. That done, let us consider a different subset to be viewed as a byzantine quantity.

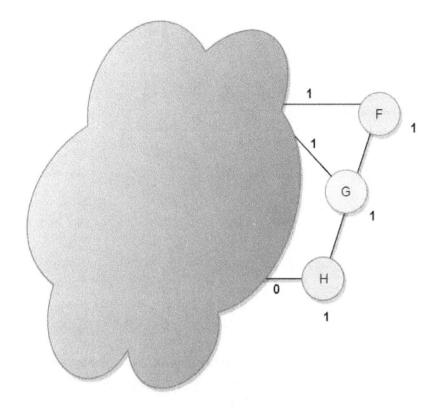

Now, it is the group *AEBCD* that is replaced by a single byzantine entity. This case is similar to the previous one - the non-faulty nodes (F, G, and H) must reach a consensus on 1 if the algorithm being executed is a correct one. Once again, E and D provide the illusion of a byzantine node sending out conflicting values - this time, to the trio of F, G, and H. Lastly, we have the group *BAEGF* forming the byzantine node, as represented in the next diagram. Here, it is the turn of B and G to simulate a byzantine node that sends conflicting values to the trio of C, D, and H.

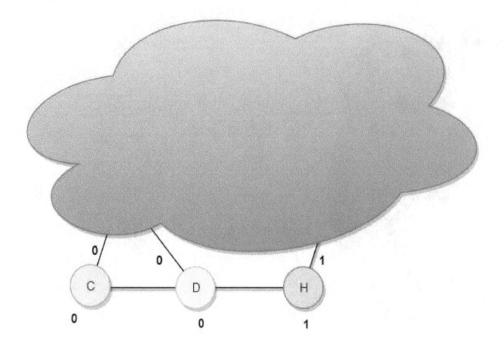

Going by the correctness conditions which guided the previous two scenarios, the third scenario should result in a consensus, too. However, we notice that consensus in the third scenario is infeasible because we have already established using the first two scenarios that C and H decide on differing values. This firmly precludes any scenario where C and H can agree. This is a contradiction which proves that the algorithm implemented in this case is not a correct one.

9.5.3 The Berman-Garay-Perry algorithm for byzantine consensus

To conclude this chapter, let us consider one more algorithm for consensus in the presence of byzantine failures. Starting with a simple-but-flawed voting procedure as implemented in a fictitious scenario, we will finally arrive at a consensus algorithm originally proposed by P. Berman, J.A. Garay and K.J. Perry. We go right back to our battlefield scenario, where a given number of Generals need to reach a consensus on the battle plan (*whether to attack or not - 1 or 0 respectively*). That said, some changes are in order.

9.5.3.1 A revised consensus procedure for the battlefield

The King, to whom all Generals swear allegiance to, has ordered some modifications to the consensus strategy:

- A single round of message exchanges (binary *vote - 0 or 1*) should produce a consensus
- The decision must be based on a strong majority - at least *3/4th* should be the majority of a winning vote
- In absence of a majority, a single General (selected by the King) will break the tie using his vote

This sounds easy enough, as far as all Generals are concerned. A single round where everyone messages everybody else, resulting in $n(n - 1)$ messages; followed by each person inspecting the received votes - including the specially appointed General, whom we will name as General A - and deciding on the *3/4th* majority if there is one. Either way, General A ends the process by broadcasting a single additional message (carrying his own preference, which will be the same as the *3/4th* majority if there was one) which will form the final consensus. Further, all communication links are assumed to be reliable.

Everything looks good; after the briefing, the group of Generals leave the King's palace with a satisfied frame of mind. Each lead their divisions to the battlefield and set up camp at their assigned locations, study the enemy fortifications from their vantage points, and reach their individual decisions regarding the *attack-or-not* question. Finally, the vote happens, producing a consensus of 1 (*attack*) and the battle takes place. However, the Generals take a heavy pasting at the hands of the enemy. The reason is simple: several Generals (and naturally, the divisions they lead) never joined the battle, leaving the enemy vastly superior in numbers. Obviously, the voting process was flawed to say the least. What went wrong?

Needless to say, an intense round of recriminations and post mortem ensue. Soon, an unequivocal conclusion is arrived at: one or more Generals are of a treacherous nature and did their best to 'game' or subvert the voting process.

Now, the king is not one to give up. He orders a second round of attack, predicated of course on the outcome of a preceding consensus, but is not stupid enough to persist with the same voting procedures.

9.5.3.2 Further revisions to, and relaunch of, the consensus algorithm

This time around, the following additional changes are mandated:

- Multiple rounds of voting
- Multiple special appointees to break ties

So, how does this work? Let us begin by assuming a simple case involving a total of 5 Generals. The King has learnt somehow that exactly one of them is not to be trusted, though his true identity remains unknown. This forces the King to select not one but *two* Generals with tie-breaking privileges(if there was only one, he could very well be the one on the enemy's payroll - any tie-breaking decision by said individual might lead to an eventuality best suiting the enemy's interests).

As far as the voting rounds are concerned, the King has been advised to have $f + 1$ rounds where f is the (suspected) number of treacherous Generals. Each round is assigned to one of the Generals who is a special appointee, implying that there are $f + 1$ special appointees (one more than the number of suspected traitors, which is by intention). The key idea is to ensure at least one 'clean' or 'safe' round.

Moving on to the mechanics of the algorithm, each round consists of a *first part* where every participant broadcasts his vote, and then counts the received votes to identify a majority. In the *second part*, the special appointee (in charge of the round) broadcasts his vote (which will be the same as the *3/4th* majority if there was one). Each receiver of this vote will change his decision to this vote if the majority he identified during the first part did not meet the *3/4th* criteria (or if there was no majority at all). Note that the special appointee could have faced the same conundrum of not being presented with a suitable majority, in which case his vote would be based on his initial decision which in turn relied upon his own study of the enemy fortifications from his vantage point.

9.5.3.2.1 How does it work?

In fact, let us consider how it may *not* work - i.e. what can go wrong. We have 5 generals, of which one cannot be trusted (even to make a vote, let alone an honest one). So, that leaves us with 4 individuals who behave in an honest manner and a required majority of *3/4th* (which implies 4 out of 5 voters). We have 2 rounds (*f + 1*, where *f* is 1), and let us assume 2 honest Generals voting *for* the attack and the other two, voting *against*. In other words, there is no majority - let alone a *3/4th* one. To make matters worse, let the dishonest General be in charge of one of the two rounds - say, the first one. We will let some diagrams do (most of) the talking.

Consider the following diagram to view the first round of voting, specifically part one of the first round:

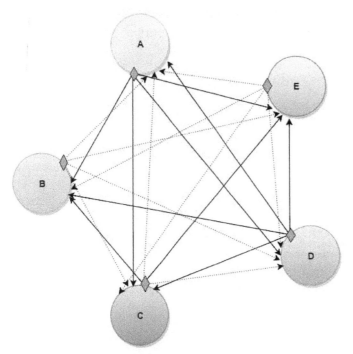

Each directed line represents a message from one entity to another, with dotted lines representing 0s and 1s being represented by the solid lines. Clearly, C is up to no good - two of C's votes are against an attack (0) while the other two signal a readiness to attack (1). As far as the others are concerned, A and D are for the attack while B and E prefer not to attack. Obviously, there is no majority. Let us see what happens in the second part of round one, next.

The second part of each round, as mentioned earlier, involves the special appointee (in charge of the round) broadcasting his vote. So, the next diagram represents exactly that:

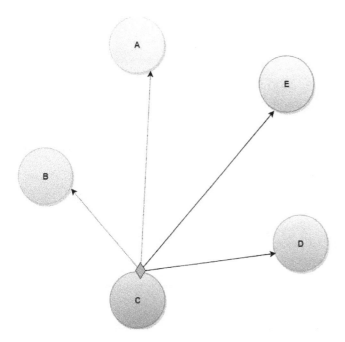

Note how the dishonest special appointee broadcasts votes that are inconsistent not just with each other, but with his votes in the first part of round one, too. Having not seen a majority, A, B, D, and E switch to the decision of C, as seen by each: i.e. 0, 0, 1, and 1 respectively. Clearly, round one was neatly sabotaged by the lone traitor, C. Can a consensus be salvaged in round 2? Here, then, is what happens in round 2:

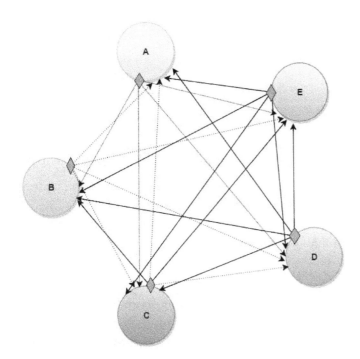

Now, A and B vote for 0, while E and D vote for 1. C, as usual, sticks to a mix of both votes to confuse the proceedings.

Once again, there is no majority; however, the second part of the second round is pending. As mentioned earlier, we have two special appointees. We know C is one and handled the first round, so let this round be in the control of E.

Now, the first round forced E to switch from a decision of 0 to 1. Having seen no majority in the first part of the second round, E continues with the decision of 1 and broadcasts the same in the second part of the second round.

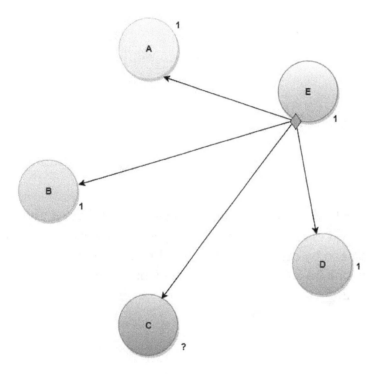

As a result, each (non-faulty) entity switches to a decision of 1. The second round being the final one, the consensus is 1.

Note how the algorithm would still provide consensus even if C got to 'manage' the second round instead of the first one. In such a situation, the first round (under the control of a non-faulty entity, i.e. a honest General) would generate a majority (either an actual majority identified in the first part of the first round, or one enforced by the in-charge General during the second part of the first round) which will in turn persist in the second round, effectively leaving C's broadcast ineffective in the second part of the second round.

9.5.3.2.2 Relationship between *n* and *f*

We know that byzantine entities behave arbitrarily, including refraining from voting. So, each entity may have to pick a majority from a total as low as *n - f* votes in (the first part of) any given round. Let us recollect the king's criteria for a majority (*3/4th*) and consider the situation where all $n - f$ votes received by any given entity are unanimous; which means that $n - f$ must be greater than $3N/4$, which in turn leads to $n > 4f$ being the requirement for this algorithm to be effective.

9.5.3.2.3 Message complexity

There being $f + 1$ rounds each of which involving everyone messaging everyone else, we easily arrive at a message complexity given by $O(n^2)$.

9.5.4 Source verification

While considering the problem of consensus in the presence of byzantine elements, we need to take note of a crucial loophole: a byzantine participant can behave in all sorts of weird manners, but if we allow one to get away with impersonating another participant, i.e. forge messages from other entities, then consensus clearly becomes impossible. This implies the following: *we assume that an entity is capable of verifying the source of a message*. For example: If A receives a message from C (a byzantine entity) crafted to appear as if B is the sender, then A is assumed to be capable of identifying the forgery (leading to the message being discarded).

9.6 Conclusion

We started off this chapter by coming back to fundamentals and scrutinising the concept of knowledge levels, and subsequently moving on to a 'costlier' version of consensus algorithms for synchronous systems where entity failures can happen. We did this with an ulterior motive, that of introducing the concept of EIG trees. Having briefly covered the relationship between consensus and network connectivity in terms of both edges as well as links, we finally took the challenge of dealing with byzantine failures. We analysed how algorithms can use EIG trees to determine consensus using majorities in the event of byzantine failures, came up with the corresponding message complexity and possible optimisations, while also noting how an algorithm for byzantine consensus is affected by the relationship between the total number of entities and the number of byzantine ones. Next, we established the requirements for byzantine consensus in terms of network connectivity, before finally analysing one last algorithm for byzantine consensus in synchronous systems.

9.7 What's next?

In the second part of this book, we have so far dealt exclusively with synchronous distributed systems. Let us now move on to the topic of consensus in asynchronous distributed systems. This is where things get really interesting, and we will soon be coming across a very important impossibility proof - in fact, one of the most important ones in distributed systems theory.

Chapter 10. Asynchronous Consensus

Leaving behind the relatively well-choreographed and streamlined efforts of finding consensus in synchronous distributed systems, we finally arrive at a much murkier world where unbounded communication delays are the norm and network entities exist and operate without the notion of a common clock. Some even call it the real world. While it is very obvious that we will be dealing with a considerably different environment, our focus will continue to be on consensus problems in the presence of network entity failures. We shall follow the pattern used in the last chapter, where we considered stopping failures before moving to the topic of byzantine ones. To start with, let us do a quick recap on how synchronous distributed systems compare with their asynchronous counterparts.

10.1 Synchronous v. Asynchronous distributed systems

We have already seen that synchronous distributed systems have the following properties:

- Bounded communication delays
- Entities operate in lock-step
- Entities have access to a common clock, or local clocks that are synchronised with each other

In contrast, asynchronous systems have these characteristics:

- Unbounded communication delays
- Entities operate independently, i.e. not in lock-step
- No common clock or synchronised local clocks

As discussed in section *1.2.2*, person A sending a letter by post to person B can be viewed as an asynchronous form of communication. The sender is free to shift his or her focus elsewhere the moment the letter is dispatched and remains oblivious of the communication status until a reply arrives. More importantly, in the context of this chapter, the sender can make no assumptions on the availability of the receiver (to the letter headed in his or her direction) or the possibility of a subsequent reply. In contract, consider a phone call. Person A can try ringing up person B on B's cell phone and decide with much more exactitude on B's availability. If B picks up, of course B is available. If B does not answer the call despite, say, 3 phone calls, and further, does not call back in the next shall-we-say one hour, A can consider B to be unavailable. Note that certain assumptions or pieces of 'inside information' are always helpful to make definite conclusions; for example, A knows that B always carries his or her cellphone, or if the call is to B's office phone, A knows that B is at his or her desk every weekday by 10AM, and so on.

Let us also note, then, that an inherently asynchronous environment can be the foundation for synchronous transactions as long as a set of reasonably accurate assumptions are set in place. For example, assume that one does a survey or research on the nature of postal communication in a given area and comes up with worst case delivery speeds and delivery failure probabilities. Also, we let A and B have clear and specific information regarding the availability of each other at their respective delivery addresses: for example, A is available on all weekdays, B is available on all days except wednesday and thursday, etc. With such information in place, one can arrive at a *timeout* period - if no reply is seen until when, the recipient can be considered unavailable. For instance, a letter is sent by A to B on monday. A assumes a worst case delivery time of 2 days, hence the letter should be in B's postbox by wednesday. However, A also knows that B is not available on wednesdays and thursdays, so B will pick up the letter only on friday. So, A would expect a reply by the next monday, failing which, A would consider B to be not available for communication.

To warm up in the general direction of where we are headed, we shall consider an example using the plight of a GPS receiver trying to calculate its location using intermittently insufficient data. Granted, there is no consensus involved in this scenario; but there is, as you will see, a never-ending loop of indecision which we just might find interesting.

10.2 Warm up: a (buggy) GPS receiver

Consider a GPS receiver installed in a moving car. As we all know, a GPS receiver works with messages received from multiple satellites to calculate its own location. Since the equations tackled have 4 unknowns, availability of at least 4 satellites are mandatory for the location to be accurately determined. However, a GPS receiver can work with 3 satellites to calculate its location - indeed, with reduced accuracy. While we have no interest in delving into the details of how GPS works, let us assume loosely that our receiver is programmed with multiple algorithms, each to be selected for specific scenarios differentiated based on satellite availability.

Let the example scenario start off with the receiver being able to hook on to 3 satellites. The device recognises the situation and adapts accordingly to select an algorithm designed specifically to calculate location using 3 satellites. Remember that the car is moving, so the situation is dynamic in terms of satellite coverage. For the sake of easy reference, let this algorithm be named *A3S*.

As the calculation is in progress, a 4th satellite makes itself available. Our device detects the 4th signal and responds accordingly to abort its current calculation and switch to a different algorithm *A4S* - of course, one designed to work with 4 satellites. So, the *A4S* algorithm is launched, and starts to execute. However, the 4th satellite seems to be available no longer; the receiver drops its attempts after a while and reverts to the only solution: switch to *A3S*. Now we see how this loop can go on and on, with no real work being done, and no result (location) being ever arrived at. Of course, the advance of technology would certainly have addressed and resolved such scenarios a long time back, but our interest is primarily in establishing an example; an ever-looping scenario to build further on.

10.2.1 A formal analysis

Before leaving our obviously outdated and flawed GPS receiver to its endless and fruitless iterations, let us attempt to capture the gist of what we just saw:

A system programmed with plan A to get some specific work done using n entities, while also having a backup plan B that will make do with n - 1 entities, vacillating endlessly between the two plans due to the intermittent availability of one particular entity.

Next, let us sit back for a moment and wonder if any of this is related to the topic of consensus in asynchronous environments where entity failures are a possibility. In the example, the endless loop was generated primarily due to the intermittent availability of a single satellite. The satellite did not fail; its availability was simply not consistent or reliable. How can we translate or transform this to the behavior of entities in an asynchronous environment?

In fact, we used a particularly loaded phrase in section *10.1* while referring to the behavior of asynchronous systems: *unbounded communication delays.* If you ask somebody a question, any question, while granting the person an unbounded amount of time to answer the same, at what point will you decide that, *okay, this person does not know the answer*? In fact, can you ever reach that decision, at all? Since the person can take all the time he or she wants, a lack of reply need not mean the person is stumped. It should be obvious what is being hinted at, here: *in an asynchronous environment, you cannot distinguish between an entity that has failed and one that is simply taking an inordinate amount of time to communicate.* This, then, is the key factor (limitation, actually) when it comes to reaching consensus in asynchronous systems while tolerating one or more entity failures. With all this in mind, let us list the following harsh realities that a consensus algorithm will have to factor in while attempting to produce a correct execution:

- Entities can fail (by stopping or crashing)
- An entity failure cannot be reliably detected
- Silence from an entity need not imply the same in future
- An entity can take forever to generate a message, but the algorithm cannot wait forever on an entity and must carry on along alternate paths
- Any alternate path following the silence of an entity can be interrupted in future by a message from said entity

Does this look like an impossible task? Let us consider another example, and this one involves consensus among a bunch of gentlemen who are up to no particular good in the middle of the night.

10.3 A tale of 5 robbers

So, this story is acted out by 5 bank robbers who have made their way into a bank some time way after midnight. Two of them are break-in specialists, who work together to disable the bank's alarm system and penetrate the bank's side entrance to gain entry to the main hall. Another two are armed lookouts, their job being to take station at different spots outside the building and watch out for any activity outside - a job at which the break-in specialists join them once their particular task is done. This produces a situation where you have four lookouts on four corners of the building while the fifth individual does what he does best - he goes inside, and starts working on the bank's vault, because he is an expert safe-cracker.

The cracker sets about his job with intense focus, while the four lookouts anxiously wait and monitor the environment for any suspicious onlookers or approaching law enforcement personnel. They have agreed on a plan in case of emergencies; a consensus have to be quickly formed - abort and escape (0) or stay put and wait for the cracker to finish with the vault door and see the job through (1). The communication is by hand-held walkie-talkies, with each of the robbers carrying one.

Now to the kicker, before this situation begins to look like a comfortable one for all concerned parties: due to the intense concentration demanded by his particular task, it had to be accepted by all that the cracker may not be able to respond synchronously to any communication from others. In fact, the lookouts may also not be particularly free to communicate at will; their precarious situation will demand complete silence and invisibility in certain situations, such as having a late-night pedestrian walk by, or a roving patrol car. Further, silence from any of the lookouts may mean anything - that he is currently unable to respond or perhaps even that the gentleman has been spotted and arrested by an alert cop. In other words, these lawless gentlemen are equipped with enough hardware capability to facilitate synchronous communication, but the limitations of their working environment reduce their communication capabilities to one of an asynchronous nature.

Now, the time of the night and the risk of the situation starts playing with one's mind. One of the lookouts (say, A) is suddenly unsure whether what he heard, or thought he heard, for a split second was the vague sound of police sirens in the distance. He loses his nerve, and immediately uses his walkie-talkie to transmit an abort (0) into their communication channel. The following situation results:

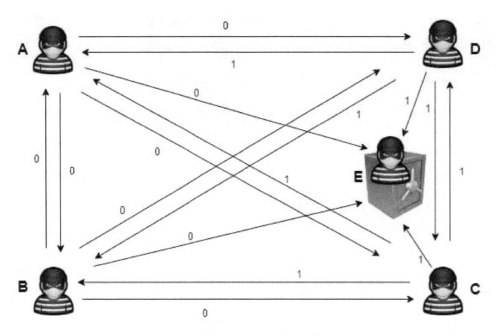

As seen above, A votes for an abort and so does B - perhaps unsurprisingly, as B is closest to A and fancies himself to have also heard something that can remotely pass for a police siren. Meanwhile, D and C have no particular visions of law enforcement vehicles hurtling towards them, and vote for sitting tight and going ahead with their robbery. Nothing is heard from E, who is obviously busy and brain-locked with his work on the vault's combination. Is a consensus possible at this point?

In fact, anticipating such scenarios, a pre-agreed tie-breaker decision is in place: *in the event of a tie, the safe decision must prevail*. In other words, abort and run. So, D and C must reverse their decisions and agree to ditch the ongoing operation. At this point, none of them can make any assumptions about E's availability or preference. Let us see what happens next:

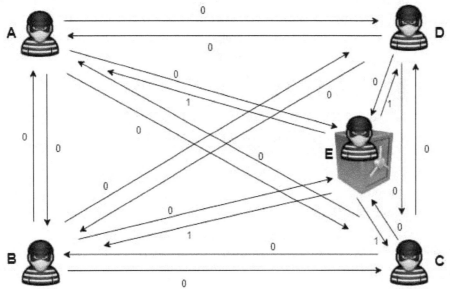

While A, B, C, and D have converged on to a decision of 0, E seems to have come alive, albeit a little late, and voted for 1. How will this affect the proceedings?

On one hand, they have a majority; on the other hand, D and C could very well reverse their decisions after seeing that E favours their original decision. After all, the element of greed may outweigh the risk factor - abort and run, and there is no loot; risk everything and stay, and the potential haul can be very rewarding. Further, it is not hard for C or D to justify their aversion to a profitless abort: since E voted to continue, perhaps he is extremely close to cracking the safe? Hence, the next stage unfolds thus:

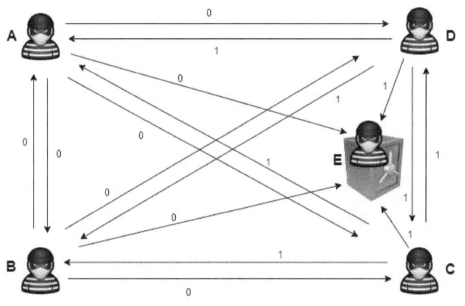

We have a curveball, at this point. D and C have switched their decisions, *but* - no more is heard from E. In other words, no progress has been made as far as a consensus is concerned - back to a tie-breaker.

Now, we can easily extend this situation infinitely if we assume E to interfere with each tie-breaker decision, only to remain silent elsewhere. A decision is never reached. Note how a timely vote by E would have resulted in a *3-2* majority, and subsequent consensus, in favor of continuing the operation. The delayed response from E led to an 'intermediary' stage - which, in fact, would have resulted in a sure decision (of 0)...had E remained silent.

To sum up, at this point we have analysed two hypothetical scenarios where the common factors were the following:

- The lack of a definite result in finite time
- The inconsistent availability of a participating entity

We have perhaps warmed up enough to take a close look at the *FLP impossibility result*, so we will first state the impossibility outright before proceeding, in stages, to understanding and finally proving the same.

10.4 The FLP Impossibility result

Known after Michael J. Fischer, Nancy Lynch, and Mike Paterson, the authors of the landmark 1983 paper ("*Impossibility of Distributed Consensus with One Faulty Process*"), this impossibility result is considered to be one of the most important findings in the formal study of distributed systems. At first blush, it says something quite simple:

It is impossible to devise a completely correct consensus protocol for an asynchronous distributed system where even one entity failure is possible.

It is important to note that the *FLP* impossibility result does *not* claim that consensus is impossible; just that there is no algorithm or protocol which will *always* work correctly, i.e. always arrive at consensus, in an asynchronous system where at least one entity is likely to fail by stopping. In other words, one can always devise an infinite *execution* or *run* for any given algorithm in which no result, ever, happens. Unsurprisingly, the cornerstone of this result is a key observation that we made in *section 10.2.1*: *in an asynchronous environment, you cannot distinguish between an entity that has crashed and one that is simply taking an inordinate amount of time to communicate.* Any alternate plan as incorporated by the 'system' to go past the apparent unavailability of an entity can, in theory, be scuttled by the future availability of said entity.

To decipher the *FLP* impossibility result in a better, step by step manner, we shall switch to yet another example which, unsurprisingly, has certain elements of similarity with the earlier two scenarios which we went through. In addition to being more complete, this example will also help us establish certain key definitions which we will eventually be employing on our way to understanding and proving the *FLP* impossibility. First, let us quickly contrast and compare the earlier two examples to better understand what further advantage we gain to hope by introducing a third one.

Our first example - the buggy GPS receiver - contained two critical elements: a perpetual vacillation between two different states, and the concept of a final result or decision. The second example (bank robbery) had these two, and some more; there was an element of actual consensus involved. However, the example did lack something - the relevance of the initial decision of each participating entity. In fact, the initial decision of each entity was implicitly 1, else said entity would not be present in the scenario at all. Our third example, as mentioned earlier, will aim to be more complete.

10.4.1 A tale of 5 Generals

We are back to the familiar scenario of a group of generals, five of them in fact, camped out around an enemy stronghold. The need of the day, as usual, is a consensus on whether to attack or not. We will assume asynchronous communication (of course) in the form of dispatched runners who are allowed unbounded time durations to reach their destinations. Note that eventually all runners do reach their destinations.

10.4.1.1 Univalent configurations

Consider a scenario of unanimous agreement for the *attack* option as depicted by the next diagram. We have our 5 generals surrounding the enemy's castle, and the initial decisions of all are without conflict.

As indicated by the thumbs-up gestures, each General is in favor of going ahead with the attack. Which is to say, the initial decision set in this case is *{11111}*. What we know unequivocally at this stage is that a consensus of 1 (*attack*) is guaranteed - i.e. this initial configuration of *{11111}* has but a single outcome (that of 1). We shall call this a *univalent configuration*.

How about we start turning some of those bits off, i.e. let some of those thumbs point downwards? In fact, let us switch right to the other extreme where not even one General wants to attack.

We now have an initial decision set of *{00000}*, which is again guaranteed to provide a consensus (of 0). The following diagram represents this situation which is diametrically opposite to what we considered a minute back.

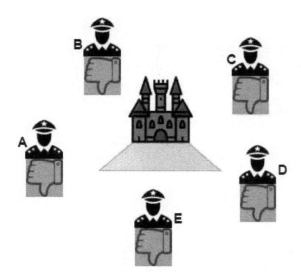

We have identified another univalent configuration, then. While the first one was *1-valent*, this one is *0-valent*. However, we have only been operating at the extremes. What lies in between?

10.4.1.2 Bivalent configurations

Compare the following two initial configurations:

As the circles indicate, these two configurations differ only by a single vote - that of General E. The left configuration results in a consensus of 1 by majority, while the right one produces a consensus of 0, again by majority. It seems exceedingly obvious that both are univalent configurations, the left being 1-valent and the right, 0-valent. However, there is one aspect which we have not considered yet: the possible unavailability of an entity. How will this pair of seemingly secure and straightforward situations be affected by the unavailability of E?

Let us assume that all runners dispatched by E are delayed heavily. There is no more a majority in either configuration, and more importantly, it is impossible to distinguish between the two scenarios anymore, now that E is no longer in the picture. This implies that both produce the exact same consensus (0 or 1), which in turn implies that one of these two scenarios are capable of both results, depending on the 'availability' of E. We state that one of these two scenarios form a *bivalent configuration*.

For example, let the pre-agreed tie-breaking decision be that of 0 (*do not attack*). This implies that the configuration on the right will always produce a consensus of 0, either due to a majority or due to the tie-breaking decision (induced by a perceived silence from E). Hence, the configuration on the left turns out to be bivalent - leading to a consensus of 0 if it comes to a tie (when E is unavailable), or a decision of 1 by majority (when E is available). Note that we succeeded in establishing the presence of a bivalent initial configuration only because we brought in the possibility of an entity failure; this brings us to the first of two key observations that are required to build a proof for the *FLP* impossibility:

Any consensus algorithm designed to work in the presence of entity failures has at least one bivalent initial configuration.

It may be somewhat obvious at this point as to how we will go about proving the FLP impossibility. To prove that any consensus algorithm can find itself in a scenario where it never arrives at a result, we started off by establishing the presence of a bivalent configuration in the set of all initial configurations. So, this could be our argument: any given consensus algorithm can be trapped in an unending sequence where it moves from one bivalent configuration to another, a result-deciding univalent state perpetually remaining out of reach, thanks to a very specific order of events in the execution of the algorithm.

To accomplish this, we need another key observation: we need to establish that *a bivalent configuration can always move to another bivalent configuration*. Intuitively, this is not hard to accept; a bivalent configuration implies that it holds the potential to head in the direction of either univalency. In both cases, there has to be a defining *step* or *event* which triggers the definitive transition from a bivalent state to a univalent one. If we sufficiently withhold this specific event, we can imagine the system proceeding towards the opposite univalence and switching back to a bivalent state once said event is finally applied (in a delayed fashion). With a basic understanding in place, we shall strive to achieve a more formal clarification.

Starting with a bivalent configuration, assume that 0-valency is made possible by an event E0 happening on entity A, and that 1-valency is achieved by an event E1 happening on entity B. In other words, we assume two distinct scenarios: one where E0 applies on A, leading to a decision of 0, and another where E1 happens on B, leading to a decision of 1. Now, if we allow that A and B are independent entities, just as E0 and E1 are independent events, we can also allow the following: let the first scenario be extended such that E1 happens to B after E0 happens to A, and the second scenario be similarly updated such that E0 happens to A after E1 happens to B. Clearly, the two scenarios have gone through the exact same transformations at this point, and hence, must produce the same result. This implies that one of these two scenarios must be bivalent - either the first scenario resulting in 0 if E0 on A was not followed by E1 on B, or 1 otherwise, or the second scenario resulting in 1 if E1 on B was not followed by E0 on A, or 0 otherwise. The next diagram represents the aforementioned transitions:

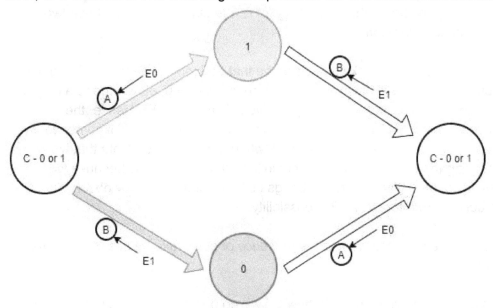

Clearly, this is equivalent to delaying an event (which, otherwise, would have produced a univalent configuration), only to introduce it in a later configuration (which, otherwise, would have yielded a univalent configuration) to produce another bivalent configuration.

Naturally, this brings up the question: what about an alternate scenario where both univalent configurations (0-valent and 1-valent) are made possible by different events happening on the same entity? For example, E0 on A paves way for a decision of 0, and E1 on A leads to a decision of 1. Since A is obviously the key entity here, we consider the scenario where A fails; if the algorithm has any claim to fault-tolerance, it still needs to produce a result. Let us assume that result to be 0, without loss of generality. Now, what if we 'pause' A and let the rest of the system proceed in the direction of 0-valency, after which we 'unpause' A to allow the receipt of E1? We can go the other way, too: we assume the system to be capable of 1-valency in the absence of A, let the proceedings move in said direction, and allow A to come 'alive' with the receipt of event A0.

What we need to take away is: *any event applicable to a bivalent configuration, even one that can change the configuration right away to a univalent one, can be delayed just enough such that, once said event is actually applied, the result is not a univalent configuration but a bivalent one.*

This is hardly a surprising observation, since the state of bivalency exists *only* because of the possibility of future events happening in different orders. We will consider a related problem and employ a similar line of reasoning in section *20.3*.

10.4.2 Putting together the proof

We have at our disposal the two key observations needed to build a proof for the FLP impossibility:

- *Any consensus algorithm designed to work in the presence of entity failures has at least one bivalent initial configuration*
- *A bivalent configuration can always move to another bivalent configuration*

Putting these two together, we place any given asynchronous consensus algorithm in an initial bivalent state and initiate a never-ending sequence where the algorithm perpetually moves from one bivalent state to another. We always ensure the delayed arrival of that one event which *could have* directed the sequence to a univalent configuration (had it arrived in time), ensuring that the sequence never terminates in a decision. This is more or less what we enacted in our second example (the bank robbery), and is equally applicable to our third example, i.e. the battlefield scenario. Note that we really do not need to get an entity to actually fail; the fault-tolerance built into an asynchronous consensus algorithm is exactly what that leads to the *FLP* impossibility manifesting itself.

10.4.3 Accepting the FLP impossibility result

All this seems to imply a very unpleasant form of reality where you cannot devise a fault tolerant, totally correct, consensus protocol for asynchronous systems. How about a compromise, just as we did in section *8.3.2*? We shall begin by observing the *deterministic* nature of the algorithms we considered so far; every decision was made as per a set of rules, based on prior events. There was no element of chance or randomness, which in turn allowed the possibility of an infinitely recurring pattern of execution. What if we allow participant entities the freedom of a coin flip when it comes to making certain decisions? To illustrate this point, consider an example of two gentlemen attempting to cross a narrow bridge from opposite directions.

The bridge is barely wide enough for one person to walk along. We will assume both parties to be perfect gentlemen, always severely eager to defer to the other person. Let them step on to the bridge simultaneously from opposite directions. They spy each other at the same moment, and without surprise, each decide to step back off the bridge to offer the opportunity to the other. Now, both are off the bridge - a fact which each perceive simultaneously, resulting in each calling out a 'thank you' and stepping back on the bridge - again, simultaneously. This can go on endlessly, so how do we disrupt this sequence?

We begin by confirming the root cause of the infinite sequence that we just considered: there was no concept of chance or free will, so to speak. Both participants had a limited and deterministic set of options as far as their actions were concerned. While we cannot give the gentlemen unlimited options, we can certainly take away the deterministic nature which they are bound to. Instead of taking a decision that is completely determined by a prior decision by the other entity, we allow each to take a *random* decision based on the result of a coin flip. Now, we have a finite possibility that (at some point) the results of their coin flips will conflict so that one decides to step off the bridge while the other decides to step on and cross the bridge.

However, we also have a possibility that their coin flip results will match and keep both off the bridge (of course, by a probability that moves to zero as the number of flips keeps increasing). Here, then, is an example of a *Las Vegas algorithm*: one that terminates with some probability but has surety of a correct result upon termination. Conversely, a probabilistic algorithm that is sure to terminate but only probable to produce a correct result is known as a *Monte Carlo* algorithm. A memory aid: Monte Carlo hosts the Monaco F1 Grand Prix race, and a Formula 1 race is one is a process that always ends after a fixed number of laps or rounds. The result of the race may not always be, say, what a Ferrari fan prefers, or what a Renault supporter would like to see, but a result is guaranteed all the same. Contrast this with someone of infinite wealth gambling away at Las Vegas with a solemn determination that he or she will not stop until making a profit of X. Since he or she can afford to play endlessly, a termination is not guaranteed, but - upon termination, the final result (profit of X) is guaranteed.

10.4.3.1 Las Vegas v. Monte Carlo: Safety v. Liveness

This might be an opportune moment to contrast between the concepts of *safety* and *liveness*. Consider a Las Vegas algorithm: the accuracy of the final result is paramount while the time delay involved in reaching there, not so much. Imagine a mad scientist working away to solve a difficult problem; he or she is determined not to come out of the research facility till a 100% confirmed solution is found. It is not hard to imagine such a person effectively dropping 'off the grid' and people beginning to wonder if 'that crazy person still alive or not'. Here, liveness is sacrificed in pursuit of safety (i.e. a safe and guaranteed solution).

In contrast, a less 'extreme' person might place more emphasis on life as a whole, work/life balance and so on, and decide that it is time to end the research once a near-enough solution has been arrived at. Note that said solution has a certain probability of being off the mark. However, the priority of this person is to make sure that the research is not of a never-ending nature; he or she wants to get back to life. In this particular case, safety is sacrificed in the interest of liveness.

We should note the element of a gamble (i.e. probability) involved in either scenario. The former researcher gambles for a termination (which may not happen) while refusing to compromise on safety (accuracy); the latter rolls the dice for a safe solution (which may not be the case) while insisting on a finite duration of research. The former might use up a whole life searching for an elusive perfect solution, while the latter might end up with a solution that is eventually proven to be suboptimal.

To round up, we give up certainty once we introduce an element of randomness. Having gained a clearer understanding of this approach, we shall consider a few algorithms that use randomisation to generate consensus in the event of entity failures.

10.5 randomising the consensus strategy: stopping failures

Let us start with the case of stopping failures before moving on to the topic of byzantine behavior. Assuming that our current approach of randomisation allows us to keep the FLP impossibility result from manifesting itself, our first question is as follows: *how much of entity failures (of the stopping kind) can we live with?*

Consider a consensus requirement from the decision set *{0, 1}* among *n* entities of which *f* can possibly fail, assuming an asynchronous system. We will use a Las Vegas algorithm with multiple rounds of voting, where each entity will not expect to see more than *n - f* votes, including its own. How much can we allow *f* to grow? To answer this question, we shall consider an example where a maximum of half the entities are allowed to fail. In other words, the algorithm specifies that each participant entity must work (in each round) with *n/2* votes. Consider the following complete network of 8 entities:

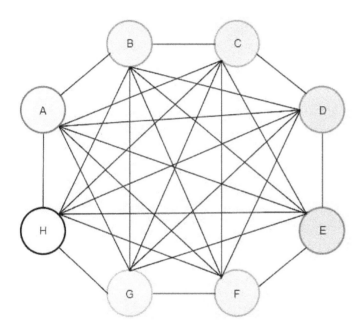

Let the algorithm commence its execution, and we will select and examine a specific sequence where the order of of received messages (in every round) essentially divides the network into two disjoint halves. To explain further, let us remember that each entity will attempt to work with only 4 votes (including own vote). Let *A* receive its first 3 messages (other than own) from *B, H,* and *G*, with a similar behavior from each of them - *B* receives its first 3 messages from *A, H,* and *G, G* receives its first 3 messages from *A, B,* and *H,* and lastly, *H* receives its first 3 messages from *A, B,* and *G*. We have a similar situation on the other half of the network as well.

Looking at this another way, we seem to have allowed the algorithm to pick a limit (*f <= n/2*) that allows the system to be described as, or operate as, two disjoint sets. The following diagram illustrates this condition:

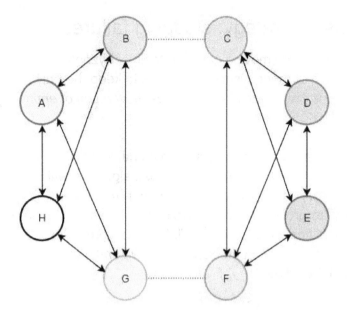

The 'missing' messages - for example, the message from F to A or from H to D - can be considered (effectively) delayed. Since the algorithm requires any entity to work with only 4 votes (including own) in any given round, any message reaching an entity which has already received 3 messages in said round will end up being ignored.

It follows that A, C, H, and G will function and decide as a separate network while C, D, E and F will do the same. There is no reason or guarantee that both will reach the same decision because there is no contact between the two halves. To avoid such a scenario, we are forced to tolerate a maximum of $f < n/2$ failures.

Further: since a majority for n entities is $n/2 + 1$, it follows that $n - f$ must be at least that; i.e. $n - f > n/2$, or $f < n/2$. In other words, our algorithm will be prepared to let less than half the entities to fail, but no more. Let us now attempt to predict a few rules that a randomised algorithm for asynchronous consensus can be expected to follow.

10.5.1 Rules for a randomised algorithm

- As mentioned earlier, each entity, in each round, is prepared to work with only $n - f$ votes
- Each entity will aim to look for a majority, which, as we have seen in the previous section, is $n/2 + 1$
- The last statement implies that each entity will look for a condition where all $n - f$ received votes agree - because, f can be as much as $n/2 - 1$, implying that $n - f$ is a majority
- Since entities may not receive messages in the same order, each entity may not receive $(n - f)$ votes from the same set of entities. For example, if $n - f$ is 3, entity A might receive votes from B, C, and D, while C might end up working with votes from B, D, and E
- The last statement implies that, even if there is a majority, all entities may not see the majority simultaneously. Reusing the previous example, A might see $\{1,1,1\}$ while C would receive $\{1,1,0\}$

- Hence, any entity seeing a majority should also advertise the fact for the benefit of others (who have not seen the majority yet) - for example, with a message '*I saw a majority for 1*'
- Which in turn greenlights one possible approach: each round will consist of two parts: part one where everybody broadcasts their votes and everybody tries to identify a majority, and a second part where everyone broadcasts whether they saw a majority (and if so, for which value) or not
- In the second part of any round, all entities receiving an intimation of majority from anyone else will switch their preference to said majority (and advertise said majority in the second part of the next round)
- A decision is finalised by an entity once it sees a majority intimation from $n - f$ entities
- At this point, naturally the question arises: where exactly is the randomisation part?
- To address that last question, let us consider the possibility that an entity did not receive even a single intimation of majority in the second part of a round. In such a situation (during part 2 of a round), every such entity does a *coin flip* and sets its preference based on the result

Critically: if there is a majority, only one entity needs to see that majority; said entity will advertise the same in the second part of that round, swinging everyone else's decision to the majority which it saw, causing all to see a majority in the first part of the next round, and thus to advertise the majority and lead to a decision in the second part.

Critically: assume that an entity reaches a decision after seeing an intimation of majority from $n - f$ entities in (the second part of) a particular round. Every other entity may not see the exact same $n - f$ votes; however, since $n - f$ is a majority in n (because $n/2 > f$), every other entity will see *at least one* intimation of majority; which is enough to swing its preference in that round, and thus lead to a decision in the next round.

In brief, we have k rounds, each having two parts - which is exactly what the *Ben-Or algorithm* specifies, so we shall go through the formal specifications of the same. We assume that entities can stop or die but will not display any kind of malevolent nature.

10.5.2 The Ben-Or Algorithm for non-byzantine entities

In a landmark paper that appeared in 1983, Ben-Or presented the first ever randomised algorithm for asynchronous consensus in the presence of crash failures. The significance of this finding should not be underestimated, because Ben-Or published his paper shortly after the paradigm shift which was the *FLP* impossibility result. Each round of the algorithm has two parts. Let us briefly describe the two corresponding sets of activities performed by each entity in any given round:

- Every entity broadcasts its vote, receives $n - f$ votes, and looks for a majority - i.e. whether those $n/2 + 1$ votes (including own vote) agree, in which case its preference is set to said majority. Note: since $f < n/2$, we know that $n - f$ is at least $n/2 + 1$

- In the second part of a round, every entity broadcasts an intimation on whether it saw a majority (in which case, the majority decision is also included) or not, and then receives $n - f$ intimations (including own). If more than f intimations are on a majority seen, the entity decides accordingly (on the majority decision). If there is at least one such intimation, the entity sets its preference (not decision) accordingly. If all received intimations are for *no majority seen*, then a coin flip is done to set the entity's preference. Note: since $f < n/2$, we know that $n - f$ is greater than f

A pictorial representation of the aforementioned process follows:

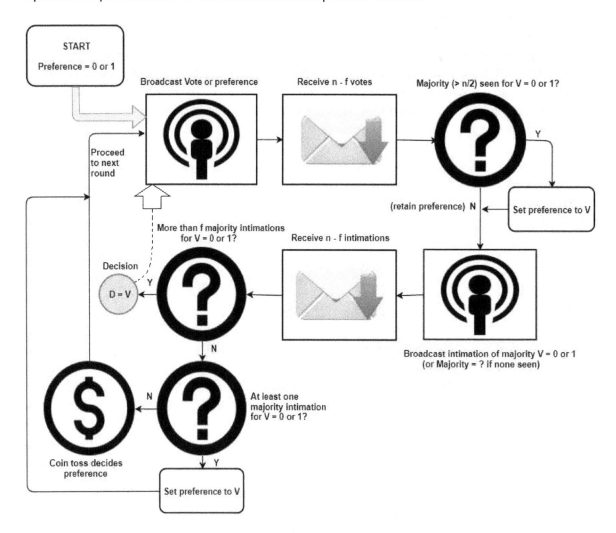

As seen above, a decision of V (as indicated by the circle labelled "D = V") is reached once at least f intimations of majority are seen (for 0 or 1) in the second part of a round. Note that an entity continues to contribute its votes/intimations for at least one more round after a decision is made - so that yet-to-decide participants can reach a decision in the next round.

10.5.2.1 Message formats

The following diagram represents the message format for part 1 of any given round:

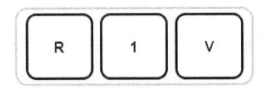

Clearly, R indicates the round number - and indeed is essential in an asynchronous algorithm. The next parameter, 1, stands for part 1 of the specified round. Finally, V is the sender's vote, being 0 or 1. The next diagram shows the layout of messages issued in the second part of any given round:

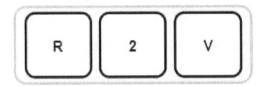

R represents the round, as usual, while 2 indicates a message sent during the second part of the specified round. In addition to the possible values of 0 or 1, V could also be a suitable character like ? to represent 'no majority seen'.

10.5.2.2 Analysis

To begin with, what are the odds of this algorithm never terminating? Consider the following pattern: the initial decisions are such that there is no majority. In other words, half the entities begin execution with a decision of 0, while the other half has opted for 1. This will result in no entity discovering a majority in part 1 of round 1, leading to each entity opting for a coin flip in part 2 of round 1. Assume that half the entities end up with a result of 0 while the other half end up with 1, leading to part 1 of round 2, where nobody yet again observes a majority. This proceeds to part 2 of round 2 where everyone goes for a coin flip (again). What if this pattern repeats? It should be obvious that an indefinite repetition of such a sequence has a probability that drops to zero. So, the natural question, next, is: what is the probability, then, that the algorithm terminates in a result?

We will consider a scenario where one or more entities observe a majority during part 1 of a certain round. Such entities will produce intimations of majority in part 2 of the same round, leading to recipients of the same switching their preference (or even decision) to said majority. The key observation here is: a preference of an entity may be non-random (forced, based on firsthand or secondhand knowledge) or otherwise (coin flip). Broadly speaking, all preferences set in a non-random manner are based on a majority and will agree (on 0 or 1) - because there is only one majority. What we are arriving at is the following point: in any round, we can divide the entities into two groups; one whose preferences are set in a non-random or forced manner (all of which have the same preference), and two, who set their preferences based on a coin flip. How can this line of thinking help us?

We know that the latter group arrives at their (forced by majority) preferences first, after which the coin flips (by the second group who has not seen or heard of a majority, yet) happen. Hence, we can think of a probability where the results of all coin flips (i.e. preferences of the second group) match the already-established preference of the first group - i.e. the probability where all entities agree in a particular round. The probability of n coin flips resulting in a matching result is $1/2^n$, so the required probability (of a *subset* of n entities having their coin flips providing a matching result) is at least the same. Going in the opposite direction, we have a maximum probability of at least one mismatch as given by $(1 - 1/2^n)$. If this disturbance has to persist across k rounds, the probability is at best $(1 - 1/2^n)^k$. The minimum probability of avoiding said (unwanted) event is given by $(1- (1 - 1/2^n)^k)$. With that established, we shall consider a corner case next.

10.5.2.2.1 A corner case

We know that $n - f$ is a majority (of $n/2 + 1$) even in the worst case (where $n/2 - 1$ entities fail) but consider the following majority: $n/2 + f + 1$. What exactly is special about this (large) chunk of agreement?

If $n/2 + f + 1$ entities have the same vote or preference, we have a guarantee that every non-faulty entity, even one entity ignoring f of those votes (we know that each entity will work with only $n - f$ votes, and thus ignore f votes), will see a majority of at least $n/2 + 1$, and switch preference accordingly. This results in all non-faulty entities deciding in the second part of that round, due to seeing at least f intimations of a majority. What are the odds of this happening within the first k rounds?

We know the odds of $n/2 + f + 1$ parties agreeing (on 0 or 1) - obviously, $1/2^{n/2 + f + 1}$. What are the chances of at least one disagreeing among $n/2 + f + 1$ entities? Again, obviously, $(1 - 1/2^{n/2 + f + 1})$. How about this happening k times in a row? We end up with $(1 - 1/2^{n/2 + f + 1})^k$. The opposite of the same is given by $(1 - (1 - 1/2^{n/2 + f + 1})^k)$, which represents the probability where you *do not* have k straight rounds where at least one entity among $n/2 + f + 1$ ones disagree - which is exactly the probability for success.

Let us next consider an algorithm which deviates from the dual-step nature of each round as specified by the Ben-Or algorithm: the *Bracha-Toueg consensus protocol* as described in the 1985 paper by Gabriel Bracha and Sam Toueg. Once again, we will consider the case of consensus among non-byzantine entities.

10.5.3 The Bracha-Toueg algorithm for non-byzantine entities

This *weight-based* or *cardinality-based* algorithm uses a message format which mandates (along with a round or phase number, obviously) a vote (of 0 or 1) and a *weight* or *cardinality* for the same and uses the concept of a *witness* which describes a message carrying a weight of more than $n/2$. The algorithm proceeds in asynchronous rounds. Here are the salient features, along with a diagrammatic representation:

1. Each entity starts off with a vote (random choice of 0 or 1) and an associated weight of 1. This makes complete sense, since each entity is aware of only its own vote at this point
2. Each round involves every entity broadcasting a message of format as described earlier, followed by receiving *n - f* messages (including own)
3. Any entity seeing a majority against its vote will switch its vote accordingly (obviously, an entity seeing a majority *for* its vote will retain the same)
4. Any entity *not* seeing a majority will switch (if needed) own vote to 0

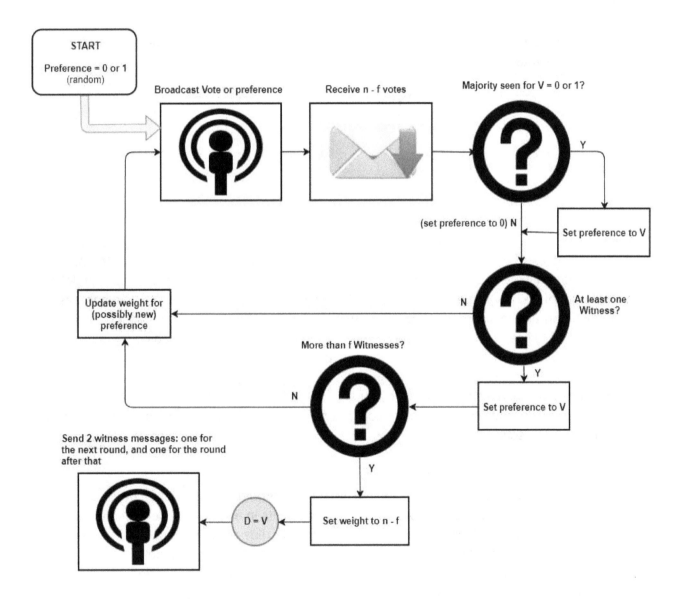

5. Any entity will update the weight of its (possibly updated) vote according to the number of votes that support the same

6. Any entity receiving a witness (i.e. a message with *weight > n/2*) for a particular vote will change (if needed) its own vote to match the same (and update the weight accordingly)
7. Further, any entity receiving more than *f* witnesses to a particular vote sets its decision to said vote
8. Once a decision is made (in a round, say *r*), each entity sends out two witnesses (for the next two rounds), specifying the decision and associated weight (of *n - f*). Why two? The first message (in the next round, *r + 1*) swings the votes of all correct entities which receive the same (see *6*), and the second message is for the following round (*r + 2*) in which all correct entities inevitably decide (after noting more than *f* witnesses - see *7*)

10.5.3.1 Message format

As mentioned earlier, the message format requires the round or phase number, weight (of the vote), and the vote (0 or 1) to be specified:

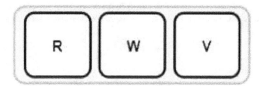

10.5.3.2 Analysis

Note that we never came across an instance where a coin flip is involved. What does this mean? As an example, assume 10 entities starting an execution of this algorithm with half of them having an initial preference of 1 while the other half opt for 0. Since *n* is 10, we can let *f* be a maximum of 4 - implying that each entity will work with 6 votes in each round. We can easily imagine a non-terminating sequence where each among the first group (that had initially opted for a value of 1) keep receiving the set of votes *{111110}* in each round (leading them to perpetually retain a preference of 1) while each in the second group (that had initially opted for value of 0) keep receiving the set of votes *{000001}* which in turn keeps them glued to a preference of 0. Such a sequence will never produce a consensus. In fact, the Bracha-Toueg algorithm explicitly specifies the assumption of a *fair scheduler* to preclude a similar eventuality. So, what *is* a fair scheduler?

10.5.3.2.1 Fair scheduler

Before getting to a fair scheduler, how do we define a *scheduler*? In fact, let us begin by formally defining a *schedule*: a sequence of steps or events in a specific order. A scheduler can be thought of as an *agent,* an abstraction of a set of properties of the system, which determines each step or event in a schedule. In a given system, there are several schedules or patterns of events possible, in various orders. In fact, we assumed a very specific scenario just a minute back - when we considered two groups of 5 entities each, receiving a specific set of messages in any given round, perpetually, while all other possibilities are ruled out.This situation can be thought to be enforced by a scheduler having a very specific or vested nature, which obviously, is by no means fair. Perhaps the system being considered is skewed in some manner, which assigns or provides a disproportionate level of opportunity for a particular schedule to take place. With this background in place, let us assign a formal definition for a fair scheduler in our current context.

A fair scheduler is one such that, in any round, there is a constant probability p that all processes receive messages from the same set of processes. Applying such a behavior to the system in our earlier example, we can imagine a pattern where all 10 entities receive messages from the same set of senders for 3 consecutive rounds - obviously with a probability given by p^3. Once this pattern kicks off - let the first of the three rounds be r where the set of votes seen by all is {111110} - each entity switches preference to 1 in round r, thanks to the 5:1 majority seen for a vote of 1. The associated weight in each case would be 5 (since each entity sees 5 votes for 1 in round r). In the next round ($r + 1$), each entity sends a vote for 1, with an associated weight of 5, and next receives $n - f$ similar votes (including own) of the same content. This causes the weight to increase from 5 to $n - f$ (6) for each entity. Naturally, round $r + 2$ would see each entity issue a witness message for 1 and then receive $n - f$ similar witness messages, causing each to arrive at a decision of 1.

Another way of representing a scheduler is by using the concept of an *adversary*. As a rough example, let us consider a new consensus algorithm designed by professor A, which he or she presents for peer review. Let professor B, who is a nemesis and competitor of professor A, be part of the review committee. We can easily imagine professor B going through all possible execution schedules of professor A's algorithm - with the express aim of identifying and choosing a specific pattern which will prevent the algorithm from terminating correctly. The adversary in this case is professor B, a *strong adversary*, i.e. one who has knowledge of not only the algorithm, but also the state of each participant entity and its messages at any given point in a particular execution of the algorithm, enabling him or her to determine the order of events which is best suited to disrupt the effectiveness of the algorithm. Applying such an adversary, working doggedly *against* the algorithm's success, to a real life execution environment might sound far fetched, but it need not be so in all cases. Ultimately, the point is that an adversary model is a primary design specification when it comes to developing algorithms.

10.6 Randomising the consensus strategy: byzantine failures

Following the practice we adopted in chapter 9, we will now move on from stopping failures to failures of the byzantine kind. Conveniently, each of the earlier two algorithms have variants for dealing with byzantine failures. Respecting the earlier order, we will start with the Ben-Or algorithm for asynchronous consensus in the presence of byzantine entities.

10.6.1. Rules for a randomised algorithm

Most of the rules from section *10.5.1* will carry over unchanged, except for a few that are specifically meant to decide a majority in the presence of byzantine behavior. We already know from section *9.5.1.1* that a consensus algorithm among n entities *cannot* tolerate $n/3$ or more byzantine entities. We follow the usual practices while dealing with byzantine entities:

- While collecting votes, assuming the worst case scenario where none of the byzantine entities decide to vote - i.e. never attempt to collect more than $n - f$ votes
- While examining a set of collected votes, assume a worst case scenario where all the byzantine entities *did* put in a vote - i.e. while working with $n - f$ votes, assume than (only) $n - 2f$ are from non-faulty entities

Note what the last point implies: if $n - 2f$ must be a majority (among non-faulty entities; of which there are $n - f$), then $n - 2f$ must be greater than $(n - f)/2$, implying that $n > 5f$. We will see an application of this limit right away.

10.6.2 The Ben-Or algorithm for byzantine entities

In his 1983 paper (mentioned in section *10.5.2*), Ben-Or also describes a modification of the algorithm which enables the handling of byzantine failures.; the algorithm is designed to work with less than $n/5$ byzantine entities. As earlier, each round consists of two steps. Here is how it works:

- In part one of any round, every entity broadcasts own preference and receives $n - f$ messages or votes. If more than $(n + f)/2$ votes agree, a majority is sensed and the preference set accordingly
- In the second part of a round, an intimation is sent - for a majority (if seen in part one), or for a *no-majority*. Next, $n - f$ intimations are received. If more than f intimations of majority for a particular vote (0 or 1) are seen, the preference is set accordingly. Further, if the number of said intimations is at least $(n + f)/2$, the *decision* is set accordingly. If neither is the case, then a coin toss decides the preference

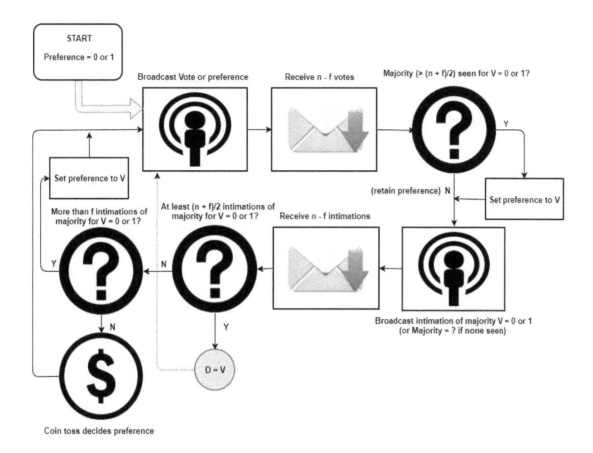

START
Preference = 0 or 1

Broadcast Vote or preference

Receive n - f votes

Majority (> (n + f)/2) seen for V = 0 or 1?

Y

Set preference to V

More than f intimations of majority for V = 0 or 1?

At least (n + f)/2 intimations of majority for V = 0 or 1?

Receive n - f intimations

(retain preference) N

Set preference to V

Y

N

Y

N

D = V

Broadcast intimation of majority V = 0 or 1 (or Majority = ? if none seen)

Coin toss decides preference

10.6.2.1 Analysis

Let us consider the part one of any given round. First of all, note that an entity A cannot receive more than $(n + f)/2$ votes for say, 1, while another entity B receives more than $(n + f)/2$ votes for 0. Why?

Let us assume that A received $(n + f)/2 + 1$ votes (for 1). Let f of these be from byzantine entities. Which means, the number of non-faulty votes that A received is $(n + f)/2 + 1 - f = (n - f)/2 + 1$. That leaves $((n - f) - ((n - f)/2 + 1)) = (n - f)/2 - 1$ non-faulty entities for B to receive votes of 0 from. Also, let all byzantine entities send a vote of 0 to B. So, the total 0-votes received by B is $(n - f)/2 - 1 + f = (n + 1)/2 - 1$, which is less than the number of 1-votes received by A.

From a more generic perspective, a quantity *greater than* $(n + f)/2$ can be thought of as the sum of $(n - f)/2$, f, and at least 1. The first and last of these, together, amount to a majority among the number of non faulty entities, so even if f votes among $(n + f)/2$ votes are from byzantine sources, an assurance of a majority in the non-faulty faction is still in place.

As for the second part of a round, the proceedings are equally straightforward. More than f intimations of a majority would imply that at least one non-faulty entity noticed a majority (and issued an intimation of the same). Similarly, more than $(n + f)/2$ majority intimations indicate a majority being observed by a trustworthy majority.

10.6.3 The Bracha-Toueg algorithm for byzantine entities

The Bracha-Toueg algorithm deals with byzantine entities by the use of an additional 'vouch' message broadcast in any given round by each entity for each vote said entity has seen. If we visualise a module that accomplishes the specific task of accepting $n - f$ messages as specified by this algorithm, it can be represented thus:

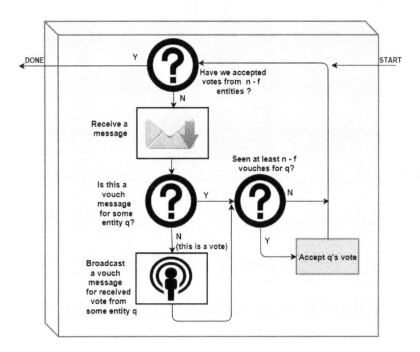

As represented in the diagram, an entity A will not trust or *accept* a particular vote V (0 or 1) from B solely based on the receipt of the same; A will accept the vote only upon seeing at least $n - f$ vouch messages from other entities. This implies two types of messages broadcast by every entity in each round:

- A regular message carrying own vote
- A special *vouch* message - one for each vote received by the entity - using which each other entity can validate received votes

The preference carried by each vote message is vetted or validated using the vouch messages (corresponding to said vote) received from other entities. We have seen various versions of the same approach before, and the underlying tactic is the same: before one believes what an entity (a byzantine one, possibly) has to say, one checks with everyone else what said entity told *them*. The following diagram represents the complete process, using the '*message-receive module*' described earlier:

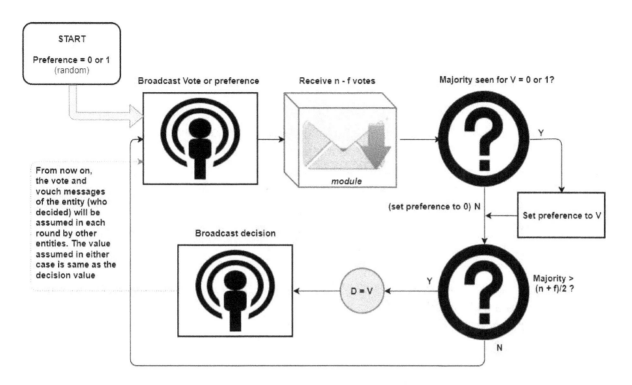

As seen above, the preference of an entity is set to a majority if one is seen, or to 0 if not. Note that the complexities involved in vote validation and acceptance have been hidden away inside the message-receive module. As far as a decision is concerned, one is made upon seeing more than *(n + f)/2* votes in agreement - at which point, an entity broadcasts a 'decision intimation' (which specifies the decision value). An entity, once having reached a decision, need not participate in the consensus process any longer; from that point onwards, in each round, the rest of the entities *assume* vote and vouch messages (for the value specified in the decision intimation) from said entity.

10.6.3.1 Analysis

Can a node A receive *(n + f)/2* vouch messages for (a vote of) *1-from-C* while B receive *(n + f)/2* vouch messages for (a vote of) *0-from-C*? The answer is *no*, and the reasoning is the same as in section *10.6.2.1*. Let us assume that A received *(n + f)/2 + 1* vouch messages (of *1-from-C*). Let *f* of these be from byzantine entities. Which means, the number of non-faulty vouch messages that A received is *(n + f)/2 + 1 - f = (n - f)/2 + 1*. The total number of non-faulty entities is *n - f,* which leaves *((n - f) - ((n - f)/2 + 1)) = (n - f)/2 - 1* non-faulty entities for B to receive vouch messages of *0-from-C* from. Also, let all byzantine entities send vouch messages of *0-from-C* to B. So, the total *0-from-C* vouch messages received by B is *(n - f)/2 - 1 + f = (n + f)/2 - 1*, which is less than the number of *1-from-C* vouch messages received by A.

Also, note that the requirement specified in section *10.5.3.2.1* - for a fair scheduler - is equally applicable here; the algorithm requires a probability *p* that a set of *n - f* nodes will find themselves in a round where all messages are received from within the set. This leads to a probability p^2 of two such consecutive rounds, which in turn will lead to consensus.

10.7 Failure detectors

We have seen how the *FLP* impossibility is no longer applicable once we choose probabilistic algorithms over deterministic ones. What about alternate techniques to achieve a similar result? While discussing the *FLP* impossibility in section *10.4*, as well as in the earlier section *10.2.1*, we noted the crucial role played by a participant's inability to *differentiate between a failed node and one that is operating excessively slowly*. So, it stands to reason that we should be able to build correct (and deterministic) algorithms if we have a mechanism in place that helps to detect failed nodes. This section is dedicated to such an approach.

Failure detectors or fault detectors can be thought of as additions or 'extras bolted on' to each participant node in a distributed system. In a realistic sense, we can imagine anything from fault-detecting code being added to the algorithm executed by each node, to a specialised (hardware) module being wired in. Think of a synchronous system as one where each entity comes with a built-in fault detector, because of the unique guarantees provided by such an environment (all nodes operate in lock-step, with bounded message delays) which in turn makes it fairly straightforward to detect a faulty entity. While an asynchronous system is vastly different, we can adopt similar techniques that help point out crashed or failed entities. For example, an algorithm designer can carefully observe the target network and come up with a reliable number for network latency, which then becomes the timeout enforced on communication. This is obviously not a perfect system, but it does lead us in the direction of applying different *standards* for failure detectors. To understand this better, let us take a closer look at what exactly a failure detector has to do.

In a simple sentence, a failure detector must pick out failed entities. Thanks to a failure detector, each participant node in a network can be thought of as having access to a *list* of failed nodes; a list that is updated dynamically as time goes by. At this point, we have enough information to consider or raise four questions:

- Will the list include all failed entities or (only) some?
- What if the list includes non-faulty entities?
- Since the list is dynamic, will the quality of its content change over time?
- Since each entity maintains a list, will the contents be same across all?

Thankfully, we have standard definitions which address these questions. A failure detector is said to be *strongly complete* if *all* faulty entities are detected by *all* entities. A weaker version is one such that, eventually all failed entities are detected by - not all - but *some* of the participants. With the concept of completeness in place, we shall introduce the concept of accuracy: a failure detector is *accurate* if no non-faulty entity is ever detected (as failed) by anyone. In fact, that is *strong accuracy* right there. We can weaken such a condition to let some non-failed entities, instead of all, to be never detected as failed by anyone. We round up with the concept of time or eventuality: using the idea of each entity holding a dynamic list, we have *eventual strong accuracy* and *eventual weak accuracy* if the corresponding condition is eventually reached by the contents of the individual lists. For example, let us go back to the example of the algorithm designer selecting a particular value for network latency - say, *s* seconds. Next, he or she comes up with an algorithm that requires each node to broadcast a *hello-I-am-alive* message every *K* seconds. If *K* + s seconds elapse without node A receiving such a message from node B, node A immediately marks B as failed. Now, assume that B's message does reach A afterwards. In such cases, A corrects its list (by erasing B's entry) and also increases its concept of network latency by a suitable amount. Such a 'learning' process ensures that all false suspects in a list are weeded out - eventually. This would also be a good opportunity to note a critical requirement that any fault detector should fulfill: while (it is acceptable that) a non-faulty node may be wrongly listed as a faulty one, any activity or step in the algorithm made by said node, such as a message delivery, must not be blocked out or ignored by the rest of the system. This not only gives a chance for the algorithm to make progress towards its goal, but also, as seen earlier, provides room for the fault detection process to improve its accuracy.

Having listed out the quality criteria for failure detectors, what expectations should we carry along while setting out to design and implement (or use) failure detectors for real life systems? As it turns out, a weak failure detector with the following completeness and accuracy properties is hard enough to achieve:

- Eventually some nodes become aware of all faulty ones
- Eventually some non-faulty nodes are not marked as faulty by any node

While this might come across as a hard bargain, the key is for some measure of completeness and accuracy to apply across sufficient windows of time which enables the algorithm to achieve its primary objective; for example, for a consensus algorithm to reach a decision. In other words, we do not need these conditions to start applying right away (i.e. right from the first step of the algorithm's execution), and we do not need them to persist 'forever' once they apply. To understand how all this will actually work, we shall proceed in stages. As a first step, we consider an example scenario to understand how a failure detector works, and is utilised, in a distributed environment that is executing a particular algorithm. We will not be concerned with specifics of the algorithm as such; our only interest will be in how the failure detector is made use of by the algorithm. With such understanding in place, we will then go ahead and analyse a couple of consensus algorithms that employ two different failure detector models.

10.7.1 An example implementation

If we look back at the asynchronous consensus algorithms we discussed so far, the failure model determined the number of messages each node or entity worked with in each round. For example, if the algorithm is prepared to accept a maximum of *f* failed entities (among a total of *n*), each round would see each entity working with *n* - *f* votes or messages. The introduction of a fault detector changes all that. If an entity, let us call it node A, can query a module which replies that, for example, *currently all nodes are up and running*, then A can go ahead and attempt to receive all *n* messages. This looks good, but there is a snag. What if a node fails right after the module gives an all-clear (that all nodes are up and running) to A? This can cause A to deadlock trying to receive a message from the (newly) failed entity. Hence, we also equip a failure detector with the capability to *interrupt* a node, one that is possibly waiting for a message, with news about recently-failed nodes. We shall see how we can incorporate these findings into a simple example scenario.

Consider a distributed environment of *n* nodes, where each node is a piece of hardware running a very simple operating system (*OS*). The algorithm is executed as a *user-level process* running on top of said *OS*. The *OS* provides the process with basic services - for example, a routine *receive(addr, buffer)* that accepts a node's address, receives a message from the specified address, and stores the same in the provided buffer. Let us also assume a *get_address_list(array)* routine which the process invokes upon startup; this routine (somehow) collects the addresses of all other nodes in the system - i.e. *n - 1* addresses - and stores them in the specified array. Once this is done, the process has the capability to receive messages from any other entity in the system. Next, we shift our focus to the failure detector.

The failure detector (*FD*) is implemented as a kernel module. Broadly, the *FD* has two distinct jobs:

- Every *K* seconds, the *FD* sends a *hello-I-am-alive* message to every other node
- Listen for a similar message from other nodes, and mark or list any nodes which seem to go silent

The first job is simple enough, while the second one involves a bit more activity. To accomplish the latter, each *FD* maintains *n - 1* timers, one for each other node. Each timer is set to go off at *K + s* seconds, where *s* is the network latency. The following two cases are possible:

- Once a *hello-I-am-alive* message is received from a node, the corresponding timer is reset
- If a timer expires, i.e. if *S + k* seconds elapse without a *hello-I-am-alive* message seen from a node, that node is marked as faulty

Clearly, the *FD* maintains a list of faulty nodes, which may or may not be empty. Now, this list holds information that is of great value to a process; so, it follows that the *FD* provides a routine, say *get_failed_list(array)*, which the user-level process invokes to obtain the list of failed nodes. The following diagram represents the mentioned arrangement:

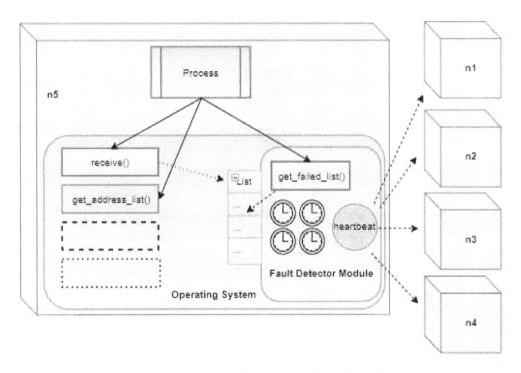

At this point, we have all the required components to imagine how the algorithm goes about its business. The algorithm starts off by obtaining the addresses of all other participants by invoking the *get_address_list()* routine. Next, the asynchronous rounds kick off. In each round, the algorithm uses the *get_failed_list()* routine to obtain a list of failed nodes, and then invokes the *receive()* routine for each node that is *not* present in the list of failed nodes.

Lastly, we consider the scenario where a node can fail immediately after the routine *get_failed_list()* is invoked. Being a kernel or *OS* module, the *FD* has the capability to inspect the state of the user-level process; if the timer corresponding to a node expires, the *FD* (after marking the node as failed) checks whether the process is blocked (i.e. waiting) in a *receive()* routine. If so, the *FD* compares the address passed to the receive routine with that of the newly-failed node, and if there is a match, the *receive()* routine is interrupted so that it stops blocking and returns immediately with a corresponding error (for example, *E-NODE-FAILED*). The user-level process wakes up to see the receive() routine returning with an error, which it inspects, and understands that the node (from which it was trying to receive a message from) has failed, abandons that receive attempt, and moves on to the next node. Note that the *OS* implementation of the *receive()* routine can also be optimised so that the *FD* is consulted before getting into the (potentially blocking) receive operation - in case the specified address belongs to a node listed as faulty. If that is indeed the case, the routine will return an error right away.

Let us now consider two consensus algorithms proposed by Chandra and Toueg. The first one requires the services of a failure detector that has strong completeness and weak accuracy but will tolerate up to *n - 1* entity failures (of the crashing or stopping kind). The second one will only accept a maximum of *n/2 - 1* failures (again, of the crashing or stopping kind), but requires its failure detector to provide (only) eventual weak accuracy (and strong completeness).

10.7.2 Chandra-Toueg consensus algorithm (using failure detectors with weak accuracy)

This algorithm assumes the following: each entity has access to a failure module (which can be queried for a list of failed nodes), that, right from the get-go, will be accurate enough that some non-faulty nodes will never be listed. The process consists of three phases. Let us go through each of them. As usual, each entity or node starts the algorithm by first adopting a proposed value or initial decision.

10.7.2.1 Phase 1

The first phase consists of $n - 1$ asynchronous rounds where the participants *broadcast and relay* their proposed values. In the first round, each node broadcasts only its own proposed value. From the next round onwards, a node will no longer broadcast its proposed value; only one or more proposed values received in the previous round from other nodes (hence the usage of the term *relay*). Note that no node will broadcast another node's proposed value more than once - for example, once node A sees node B's proposed value for the first time in a given round (round 1 if received directly from B, or relayed by another node in a later round), node A includes the same in the *next* round's message (but never again in any of the rounds after that). To summarise:

- Each node broadcasts own proposed value in round 1
- In subsequent rounds, each node broadcasts values newly seen in the previous round

Each participant can be thought of as broadcasting a message that contains (along with own identity and round number) a list or array - which may have multiple null entries. For example, the list in first round messages will have $n - 1$ empty or null entries, because said list will contain only the proposed value of the sender (which is all the sender is aware of, at that stage). Also note that, in any given round, a node may attempt to receive messages from only a subset of the participants - i.e. only those not present in the list of faulty nodes as maintained by the 'local' fault detector module. Since we assume the failure detectors to have (perpetual) weak accuracy, there will always be entities that never appear in the list.

As the rounds progress, each participant builds up a local list of proposed values as received from other participant nodes. Under perfect conditions, of course, each node will finish phase one with a complete list of n entries which would contain the proposed values of all participants. Since we assume perpetual weak accuracy for our failure detectors, every functioning node will receive the proposed value of at least one other node, and hence, will finish phase 1 with a list that contains at least two values (own value, and that of at least one node that was never marked as faulty).

10.7.2.2 Phase 2

Phase 2 is simple: every (functioning) participant broadcasts the list which it built in phase 1. This means that each node will receive up to $n - 1$ such lists, depending on the output of the local failure detector. Each node compares its local list with each received one; if any entry is null in the received list, the corresponding entry is made null in the local list as well. This ensures that all the lists effectively 'converge' to the same content. Next, we go to phase 3.

10.7.2.3 Phase 3

If phase 2 was simple, phase 3 is even simpler. The decision is made by each participant node by picking the first non-null entry in the local list. This ensures consensus, since we know that all entities end up with matching lists by the end of phase 2.

10.7.2.4 Analysis

Since we have perpetual weak accuracy for fault detection, there is a group of *c* nodes that are never marked as faulty by anyone. This means that all functioning nodes will end phase 1 with lists that include proposed values of all these *c* nodes. The remaining contents on everyone's list may or may not vary, but that does not matter because of the correction process employed in phase 2 (as described in section *10.7.2.2*).

10.7.3 Chandra-Toueg consensus algorithm (using failure detectors with eventually weak accuracy)

This algorithm, which will tolerate up to *(n - 1)/2* entity crash failures, is prepared to weather out or see through an initial period of turbulence, because it assumes the failure detectors available to each entity to *not* provide weak accuracy right from the start, but only in time, i.e. eventually. Such a period is followed by a stage where a value is locked on (but not yet decided), and finally a third period where a decision (matching the locked value) happens. Of course, these three intervals span across multiple asynchronous rounds. The key feature of this algorithm is that each round is assigned a coordinator node, and this happens in a round-robin fashion. For example, *n1* coordinates round 1, *n2* is in charge of round 2, and so on. If there are a total of 10 entities, the control rotates back to *n1* in round 11, and the process continues. So, what does a coordinator do? What exactly happens during a round? As with the previous algorithm, each round has multiple phases; in fact, four of them. Let us go through each.

10.7.3.1 Phase 1

In the first phase, each participant sends its proposed value to the node who is the coordinator of the round (it is assumed that all nodes have enough awareness of who coordinates which round). The message format is mostly predictable: since the rounds are asynchronous, the round number is mentioned; so is the sender's identity; and of course, the proposed value. Interestingly, there is a fourth element which is a round number - not the current round number, but the round where the sender last updated its proposed value. Clearly, this field will be set to 0 in all round 1 messages, because they carry the initial proposed value of the sender - which is set before the algorithm kicks off. Let us label this element as *last-updated-round*. Every node holds a local copy of its *last-updated-round* value which it updates whenever it makes a change to its proposed value. More on this in phase 3, but meanwhile that is all there is to phase 1.

10.7.3.2 Phase 2

The second phase is slightly more involved. The coordinator collects or receives $(n + 1)/2$ messages, inspects them to identify a subset of one or more messages that carry the largest value of *last-updated-round*, and selects a proposed value from among this subset of messages. Then the coordinator broadcasts this selected value to all.

10.7.3.2 Phase 3

The third phase starts with all nodes waiting for a selected value to be broadcast by the coordinator. Once received, each node updates its proposed value to the one broadcast by the coordinator, and also updates its local copy of *last-updated-round* to the number of the current round. Once that is done, the node sends a positive acknowledgement to the coordinator. Now, a node may not receive this broadcast (from the coordinator) if the node's fault detector module finds the coordinator to be faulty. In such cases, the node sends a negative acknowledgement to the coordinator.

10.7.3.4 Phase 4

In the fourth phase, the coordinator waits for $(n + 1)/2$ messages from other nodes. If all are positive acknowledgements, the coordinator broadcasts a *decision* message which carries the decision value. Every receiving entity (of the decision message) takes the same decision.

10.7.3.5 Analysis

The algorithm appears quite simple overall, but in reality, has to deal with more complexity than it would give away at first glance. The essence of the mechanism is how a particular proposed value is locked on, and once that happens, no other proposed value can ever be a contender. Let us try to understand why this is the case.

When things work just fine and smooth, it is easy to see how the algorithm will reach a decision; a coordinator receives proposed values from $(n + 1)/2$ members, picks one specific value (that arrived in a message that has the largest value for last-updated-round) and informs everyone, who in turn reply with positive acknowledgements, $(n + 1)/2$ of which will cause the coordinator to announce a decision. Let us see what can go wrong in multiple steps of this seemingly simple and innocuous process

1. A coordinator may not receive $(n + 1)/2$ messages in phase 4, thanks to several nodes perceiving the coordinator to be in a failed state, resulting in an insufficient number of positive acknowledgements
2. The coordinator can actually crash before it is able to announce a decision

Since we assume fault detectors to achieve weak accuracy eventually, sooner or later we will have one or more coordinators that appear non-faulty and stable from everyone else's perspective. This takes care of the first issue, but what about the second one - what will happen if a value is locked on by a coordinator who then fails to see the job through?

If a coordinator has decided on a value (let us call it *v0*) in a given round r, that implies the receipt of *(n + 1)/2* positive acknowledgements; which in turn implies that

- we have *(n + 1)/2* entities at that point who have set their proposed values to *v0*
- each of them has set their last-updated-round value to *r*

At this point, the only nodes in the system with *last-updated-round* values of *r* are those that have adopted a proposed value of *v0*. Everyone else will have a lesser value for *last-updated-round*. Now, assume that the coordinator crashes before announcing a decision. Sooner or later, all functioning entities recognise this event (and stops waiting for a decision announcement in round *r*) and moves on to the next round.

Let the next round *(r + 1)* commence, with a different coordinator. As usual, the new coordinator receives *(n + 1)/2* messages in phase 1; at least one of them will be from an entity that belongs to the set of *(n + 1)/2* nodes which sent a positive acknowledgement in the prior round (this is easy to see, since *(n + 1)/2* is a majority in *n*). This means said entity will not only have sent a proposed value of *v0* in round *r + 1* but will also have specified the largest value for *last-updated-round* (*r*). ensuring that the coordinator can arrive at no other decision other than *v0*. This condition applies to any subsequent round until a decision is made, and *v0* is the only decision possible.

Finally, let us inspect if the algorithm can block or hang at any stage. Phase 1 involves everyone messaging the coordinator, but what about phase 2 when a coordinator waits to receive *(n + 1)/2* messages? All *(n + 1)/2* messages must eventually arrive, since we assume a maximum of only *(n - 1)/2* failures. Moving on to phase 3, we have all functioning entities sending acknowledgements to the coordinator, which leads to the coordinator waiting for *(n + 1)/2* acknowledgement messages in phase 4. Again, *(n + 1)/2* message must arrive in phase 4, because again we assume at least *(n + 1)/2* functioning nodes, and even if we split those into two sets, *set 1* who finds the coordinator to be non-faulty, and *set 2* who finds the coordinator to be faulty, the former will send positive acknowledgements while the latter will issue negative ones.

10.7.4 Reality check

After having seen two algorithms that solve asynchronous consensus in the presence of multiple crash failures if a suitable failure detector is present, we can either consider the *FLP* impossibility to be beaten fair and square *or* accept that such reliable failure detectors cannot be implemented in practice. Indeed, the latter is the case - which should be fairly evident from the fact that we assumed our failure detectors to work with reliable assumptions on communication delays - which holds only for networks that are at least *partially synchronous*. In other words, even the weakest failure detector we considered so far is impossible to implement in a completely asynchronous system! This really should not come as any surprise, because, fault detection is nothing more than a modular abstraction of a key activity that any participant node should engage in. Separating it out and giving it exclusive attention is never going to help us beat a fundamental impossibility result, but it will help us think more effectively when it comes to algorithm design within the limitations of our problem context. Lastly, real-life systems are closer to partial synchrony than either of the two extremes (synchrony and asynchrony); which makes the application of fault detectors very much relevant to distributed systems on a practical basis.

10.8 Conclusion

We started off this chapter on asynchronous consensus with a few warm up scenarios that eventually led to us coming face to face with the famous *FLP* impossibility result. Having built a proof for the same, we switched our attention to practical workarounds: we considered a series of algorithms which used the technique of randomisation, some of which addressed crash failures, while some were designed to work with byzantine faults. We also looked at other mechanisms that could possibly help us evade the *FLP* impossibility. In the end, however, we do not ignore the stark reality that such mechanisms cannot be reliably implemented in a completely asynchronous environment.

10.9 What's next

We have gone through a lot of theory on the problem of consensus in distributed systems, and now it is time to look at some practical applications. In particular, we will consider a popular and widely used consensus protocol. To set the stage for analysing an industrial-strength consensus protocol, we will first consider a fundamental problem to be tackled while handling transactions in distributed systems - the problem of *distributed commits*.

Chapter 11. Distributed commits, Paxos and Raft

In this chapter, we start off by taking a close look at the problem posed by *distributed commits* and a couple of solutions for the same before moving on to the *Paxos* consensus protocol first and the *Raft* protocol next. We will see that the commit problem in a distributed setting is essentially one of consensus; and hence the idea of analysing such a subject before attempting to understand a practical and popular consensus protocol like paxos. Also, focusing on the more complex paxos before the sleeker and easier-to-understand raft gives us a clear perspective on not only the functional aspects of consensus protocols, but also on the various critical tradeoffs involved in protocol design. As been the practice followed in earlier chapters, the initial sections in this chapter assume synchronous distributed systems and we move on to the asynchronous variants later on.

11.1 Distributed commits

We start off with an example. Imagine an unmanned lunar module (*LM*) attempting to land on the moon's surface. The plan is for the *LM* to land, conduct various experiments, collect data and samples, and return to a control module (*CM*) that is currently in lunar orbit. The *LM* is at an altitude of a couple of thousand feet and is descending at a rate of, say, 100 feet per second towards the lunar surface. The critical decision of whether to go ahead with the landing, or abort the landing (and return for docking with the control module), is to be taken by a consensus (*GO/NOGO*) among four important modules on the *LM*:

- Module 1 monitors the data produced by the *descent radar* on the LM, watching out to avoid the *LM* landing on a dangerously uneven surface leading to a crash and/or subsequent inability to take off (a *NOGO* must be raised in the event of a safe landing zone being unavailable)
- Module 2 is the monitoring component of the *main computer* aboard the *LM*, and watches out for critical error codes thrown by any part of the system (a *NOGO* must be raised in the event of critical faults)
- Module 3 monitors and manages the *fuel level/usage* of the *LM* (If the fuel usage rises sharply, potentially leading to a situation where not enough fuel is available for a take-off later, a *NOGO* must be called)
- Module 4 is in charge of the *battery cells* that power the spacecraft, and must watch out for deteriorating power levels or failures

If everything goes according to plan, a consensus of *GO* will be arrived at a point when the *LM* is at an altitude of 200 feet above the lunar surface. In such an event, each module listed above will *commit* to the landing by sending an approval to the main computer on the *LM*. As long as conflicting messages are not received, the main computer will issue the appropriate instructions to let the landing program take over control of the *LM*, and the landing process will be initiated. If even one module decides for a *NOGO*, it is imperative that all modules decide accordingly so that a smooth return back to the *CM* can be accomplished. For example, consider module 3 which is in charge of fuel management. In the event of a *NOGO*, it is critical that module 3 works the thrusters correctly to let the LM break away from the lunar gravity field and towards the orbiting *CM*, rather than throttling off with the intention of landing on the lunar surface. In brief, we have 4 nodes among which a consensus (to commit or not) is required. Let us look at a simple process to fulfill this requirement: *the 2-phase commit* or *2PC*.

11.2 The 2-Phase Commit

A diagram speaks best, so we will present one right away:

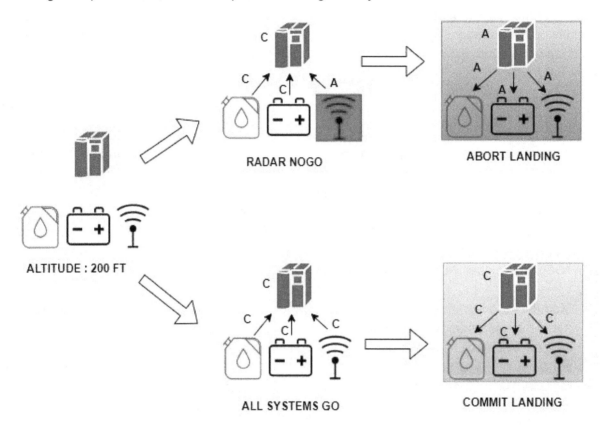

The consensus process kicks off once the *LM* reaches an altitude of 200 feet. Two possible scenarios are depicted in the diagram above: in one, all systems are *GO* and every module sends a *C* (for Commit), resulting in a landing. In the other, the radar subsystem sends an *A* (for Abort) since it has failed to locate a safe landing zone. All other systems report a *C*.

In either case, it should be obvious that 2 rounds are involved in the process:

11.2.1 Round 1

The first round involves all nodes messaging a *distinguished node* with their proposals. In our scenario, the distinguished node (*DN*) is module 2, in charge of the main computer aboard the *LM*. The *DN* decides to commit if all nodes agree on the same. Otherwise, even if one node prefers to abort, the *DN* also decides to abort.

11.2.2 Round 2

In round 2, the *DN* sends its decision to all other nodes, which each node respects and obeys by switching own decision accordingly. As seen in the abort case depicted by the diagram, the abort decision of module 1 has the desired effect of reversing the decisions of first the *DN* (module 2), and next, the rest of the modules (3 and 4).

11.2.3 Analysis

The *2PC* algorithm is remarkably simple, and herein lies its weakness: what we have is a *blocking algorithm*, which will hang without reaching a decision if the *DN* crashes or goes silent for whatever reason in round 2, causing all other nodes to wait or block till a decision announcement is seen from the *DN*. In other words, this algorithm has the *weak termination* property: all participants eventually reach a decision (only) in the event of no failures.

As far as message complexity goes, it is easy to see that $n - 1$ messages are issued in round 1, followed by another $n - 1$ in round 2. This adds up to a total of $2n - 2$ messages being required. We can actually show that one cannot do better; i.e. one cannot reduce this message count without introducing the possibility of breaking consensus.

11.2.3.1 A lower bound on message complexity

To start with, let us accept that any pair of nodes in a system of n nodes (where a distributed commit must happen) are 'connected' in the sense that the proposal or vote of one influence that of the other. To prove this, assume the opposite: in the system, there is a pair of nodes A and B such that their votes do not influence each other. Then A could vote for 0 (abort), and everyone else could vote for 1 (commit) - a situation where the final decision should be 0 because at least one node (A) voted for 0 - and B could arrive at a decision of 1 (since B is not concerned with the opinion of A), while everyone else decides for 0, thus breaking consensus.

So, now we know that every node can affect the decision of every other node. Once again, consider a system of n nodes, and let us look at any one node, say *n1*, among those. For *n1* to influence every other node, *n1* would need to send $n - 1$ messages (to the other nodes, and there are $n - 1$ of them). Next, consider a different node, say *n2*, from the remaining $n - 1$ nodes. For *n2* to influence every other node, *n2* must send a minimum of...a single message! To see this, we just need to imagine *n2* sending its vote to *n1*; that is, *n2* only needs to influence *n1*, who in turn can influence every other node in the system. We can apply the same argument to each of the $n - 1$ nodes (i.e. all nodes other than *n1*) and attribute a message cost of 1 to each of them. Finally, we have a minimum total message cost of $n - 1$ (for *n1*) + $n - 1$ (for the remaining nodes, at 1 message each) = $2n - 2$.

11.2.3.2 Coping with failure of the distinguished node

Consider the beginning of round 2. We know that all nodes are blocked on a message from the *DN* at this point. If the *DN* fails, why not let the other nodes adopt a termination protocol so that the algorithm switches to a non-blocking nature? The termination protocol can be as simple as *'everyone will abort if the DN has failed'*.

11.2.3.3 Coping with failures of both the distinguished node and an ordinary node

Well, what if both *DN* and another node fails in round 2? Fall back to a termination protocol just like the previous case (where only *DN* fails)? We have a serious problem here, once we accept the following sequence of events to be entirely within the realm of the possible:

1. The *DN* is in a *Decided-C* (decision is to commit) state at the start of round 2
2. The *DN* issues the first of the series of 'Decided-C' messages
3. Said message goes to node A
4. Node A receives the message, moves to a commit state, and *commits*
5. The *DN* fails before it could send another message
6. Node A fails right after its commit operation

At this point, all that the other nodes know is about the failure of *DN* and node A. No further details are available, i.e. nobody is in a position to confirm or refute whether node A has done a commit.

Now, can we improve on the *2PC* algorithm and arrive at a non-blocking version that does not suffer from the above-mentioned weakness? We will consider the *3-phase commit* or *3PC* next, which is a *non-blocking algorithm* and has the property of *strong termination*: all non-faulty participants eventually decide.

11.3 The 3-Phase Commit

As should be obvious from the name, *3PC* consists of 3 rounds. Before we get to round 1, let us take note that *3PC* requires any node to be in one of four different states. The following are the allowed states:

- *Undecided*
- *Ready*
- *Decided-C* (decided to commit)
- *Decided-A* (decided to abort)

While the first, third, and fourth states have rather self-explanatory names, the second one might sound a bit mysterious. *Ready*? Ready for what? Ready to commit in fact, but we should not get ahead of ourselves at this point. We start with round 1. At this point, all nodes are in an *Undecided* state.

11.3.1 Round 1

Round 1 is very similar to the *2PC* variant. We have a distinguished node (*DN*), to whom everyone else sends their votes or preferences (*C* or *A*). If the *DN* receives even a single abort (or sees even a message receive failure; remember that we assume a synchronous system), it decides to abort and moves to a state of *Decided-A*. If not, i.e. if all *n - 1* received votes are for the commit option, then the *DN* moves to the *Ready* state.

11.3.2 Round 2

At this point, there are two possibilities:

1. If the *DN* has decided at this point (which will happen only if *DN* decided to abort in the first round, after seeing at least one vote for the abort option), a 'Decided-A' message is sent to every node. Each receiving node moves to a state of *Decided-A*.
2. If the *DN* is in the *Ready* state, a 'Ready' message is sent to every node, and once that is done, the *DN* moves to a state of *Decided-C*. Every node moves to a *Ready* state upon receiving the 'Ready' message. We can also imagine the *DN* finishing round 2 in a *Ready* state, moving to a *Decided-C* state only in the beginning of round 3.

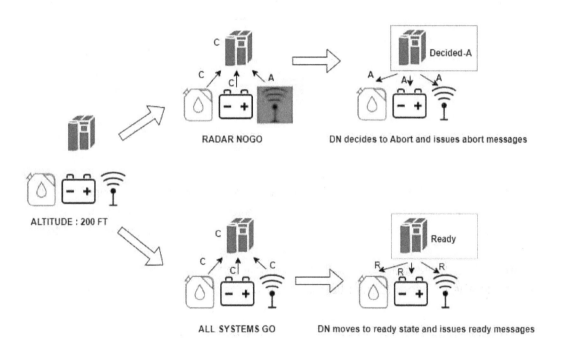

The above diagram represents the two possibilities by the end of the second round. Let us now see what happens in the next round.

11.3.3 Round 3

If the *DN* is in a state of *Decided-C*, a 'Decided-C' message is sent by the *DN* to every node. Each node moves to a state of *Decided-C* after receiving the same. As depicted in the next diagram, the *DN* starts round 3 in either a *Decided-C* state or in a *Decided-A* state. In the latter case, the rest of the members would already have transitioned to a matching (abort) state; there is nothing more to be done. As for the former, the *DN* has something left to do: issue a 'Decided-C' message to each node, leading all to transition to a *Decided-C* state.

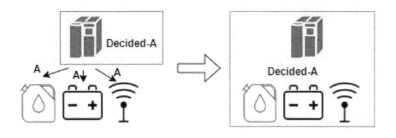

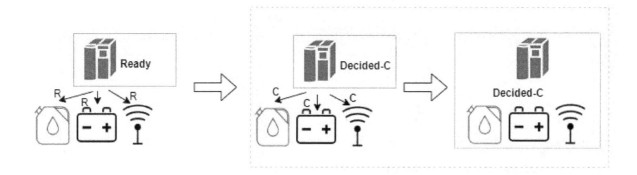

11.3.4 Analysis

Just how is *3PC* a better proposition than *2PC*? The *Ready* state is the key. At the end of round 2, a *DN* in *Ready/Decided-C* state have issued 'Ready' messages to everyone (note that we assume a synchronous system; thus, message deliveries in bounded time are guaranteed for all non-faulty recipients), and thus is in a position to confirm that every (non-faulty) entity is ready to commit. Even if the *DN* and another node fails in the beginning of round 3, other nodes can detect the same and go ahead with a termination procedure that can possibly greenflag a decision to commit.

Next, let the *DN* fail at any arbitrary point during the whole process. Perhaps the *DN* fails right at the start, without sending out a single message; this would see everyone finishing round 3 in an *Undecided* state, timing out through the receive attempts in each round. Or maybe the *DN* failed in round 2, after sending out a few - not all - messages of the 'Decided-A' kind. This would leave some nodes in an *Undecided* state, while some would be in the *Decided-A* state. What if the *DN* failed in round 2 after sending out a few 'Ready' messages? Then we would end up with some *Ready* nodes and a bunch of *Undecided* ones. The point is this: the *3PC* algorithm can always be extended to continue beyond 3 rounds, stopping only when all nodes have decided (a simple broadcast procedure can help achieve this).

So, if there is a fourth round, a decision has not been arrived at - thanks to the *DN* having failed. The obvious strategy is for the fourth round to have a new *DN*, who will then solicit *status* messages from everyone. First of all, we can easily see that certain combinations (of statuses) cannot exist:

- If we have a node in state *Decided-A*, there cannot be another one in *Decided-C* and vice versa
- If anyone has decided, then nobody else can be in an *Undecided* state (at minimum a *Ready* state is expected)

Consider the first claim. If a node, let us say node X, had decided to abort, then it has received such a decision message from the *DN*. If the *DN* has sent such a message, then the *DN* has seen at least one vote or preference to abort from one of the nodes - in which case, the *DN* will never have sent a commit-decision message to any node, precluding any node from being in a state of *Decided-C*.

The second claim is even more obvious. If any node has decided, then the *DN* did broadcast a 'Ready' message - which all functioning nodes would have received (and moved to a corresponding state, so the minimum expected state is that of *Ready*).

So, getting back to where the new *DN* inspects the status of everyone as the 4th round kicks off:

- If anyone is found to be in a *Decided-A* or *Decided-C* state, the new *DN* will subsequently lead everyone else to the same decision
- If all are *Undecided*, the *DN* will force a *Decided-A* state
- If even one node is *Ready*, the *DN* will move to a *Ready* state, and subsequently force a *Decided-C* state

The above activities will consume rounds 4-6. Now, if the new *DN* proves no better than the original one and does not last long enough to get the job done (by the 6th round), the algorithm continues into a 7th round - with a different *DN*. The process repeats till a decision is done (and detected), at which point the algorithm terminates.

11.3.4.1 Verdict?

Is everything alright with *3PC*, then? We have seen how *3PC* can never block, once we arrange a little 'help' in the form of an efficient termination protocol. However, we never considered a specific type of failure: that of a network partition. Consider the end of round 2, when the *DN* has issued its set of 'Ready' messages. Assume a network partition to take place around this time, such that all nodes which received the 'Ready' message are partitioned from the ones that did not. The nodes in one partition can possibly end up with a commit decision (possibly after running a termination protocol amongst themselves), while those in the other partition would very well opt for the opposite course of action. This is hardly surprising, because *3PC* is designed to be non-blocking at the cost of being safe - quite the opposite of *2PC*!

11.4 Moving on to a practical consensus protocol

So far, we have gone through formal descriptions of two distributed commit protocols, both of which consider the chance of entity failures but assume the safety and comfort of a synchronous network. Let us now take a 'long jump' to real life situations and try to understand how a distributed consensus algorithm is used to solve the problem of distributed commits - while assuming node failures, but in an asynchronous distributed environment.

11.5 The Paxos consensus protocol

Leslie Lamport came up with the Paxos consensus algorithm in the 1980s and published the same in 1989 as the paper *"The Part-Time Parliament"*. Here is what Lamport had to say about a fundamental choice which he made at the time of writing the paper:

Inspired by my success at popularising the consensus problem by describing it with Byzantine generals, I decided to cast the algorithm in terms of a parliament on an ancient Greek island.

At first blush, this is a master stroke that cannot go wrong. After all, the original approach was so successful to the point that even folks who have absolutely nothing to do with distributed systems are aware of the sinister connotation possessed by the word *byzantine*. Lamport further elaborates on his enthusiasm at that time:

To carry the image further, I gave a few lectures in the persona of an Indiana-Jones-style archaeologist, replete with Stetson hat and hip flask.

So, how was the paper received? More from Lamport, on that very subject:

My attempt at inserting some humor into the subject was a dismal failure. People who attended my lecture remembered Indiana Jones, but not the algorithm. People reading the paper apparently got so distracted by the Greek parable that they did not understand the algorithm.

While all this might sound borderline gloomy, most of us should be well aware of the subsequent 'happy' ending as paxos turned out to be immensely popular and widely adopted across the industry in various shapes and forms. The fact remains, though, that a significant chunk of readers still finds the paxos protocol to be rather hard to digest. But we will ponder on this curious aspect a bit later on.

Right now, let us move *away* from the specific topic of the paxos protocol - without even having discussed any of the why/what/how of it - because we will first focus on building a proper foundation of the problem context, and the best way to do so would be to consider a few examples. We will make progress in stages; starting with a generic template for the problem before moving on to progressively concrete variations with increasing validity in real life. Once the problem is clearly defined, and one or more high level solutions considered, we should find ourselves with a clear understanding of where and how the paxos protocol 'fits into' the overall scheme of things - at which point we will finally look at what exactly paxos is, and how it does what it does.

11.5.1 A generic template: distributed event ordering

The description *distributed event ordering* may not sound very meaningful, but the situation should improve once we assume that each *event* has an associated piece of *information*. These are the salient features which will broadly define the class of problems which we will be looking at, going forward:

- An asynchronous distributed system
- Certain events happen in this distributed system (example: users entering inputs)
- There are a set of responsible entities or nodes in this distributed system (example: compute nodes or workstations or servers, etc)
- These entities *observe* and *record* events (example: receive, process, and store data)
- All events may not be visible to each entity (i.e. distributed processing of events, load balancing, etc)
- Each entity or node must maintain a record or list of events - of *all* events in the system
- To rephrase the previous item, each record or list contains an entry for each event that has happened in the system - i.e. not just the ones visible to the maintainer node
- And last but not the least, the content of each list must match that of every other list in the system

A pictorial representation follows:

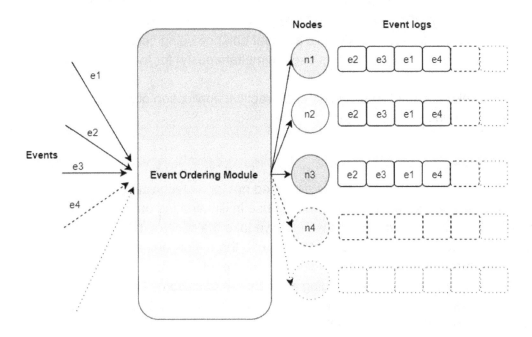

For example, we can imagine each entity or participant in the system carrying a notebook. Whenever the entity hears of an event (directly, or indirectly through another entity or participant, or by any other means), the entity will make a note of the same in a page in the entity's noteback. The pages in each notebook are numbered, and each page is used to record (only) one event. At the end of the day, each entity submits its notebook to a common supervisor who verifies that each notebook contains a matching set of events in the exact same order.

What is the fundamental service rendered by such a distributed system or arrangement? We have essentially described a system that:

- Collects events
- Assigns a sensible order to collected events
- Processes/applies/stores collected events in the established order
- Ensures that the result of the prior step is *replicated* at multiple nodes

Each step provides a valuable service, but the last one in particular stand out as a key element of defence against node failures in the distributed system. The replicated information could very well be the set of transactions on a bank account, for instance - we would expect an online service providing access to a bank account to be implemented as a fault-tolerant distributed system. A bank account has an associated balance, which is the result of a set of prior transactions on the same. While certain transactions can happen in any order, that is obviously not true for all cases. If the bank decides to debit a certain amount of money as interest (which in turn is calculated based on the current bank balance) to the account, it makes a difference as to whether said action is done before or after another credit or debit is made to the account. This implies that any distributed system providing an online access to such a bank account must respect the order of events (transactions) that might happen concurrently at different nodes in the system, and accurately replicate the transaction log of the account across multiple storage nodes in the system. After all, a user checking his account balance using server A must receive a matching result compared to when server B is used (simultaneously) for the same purpose.

While on the topic of bank accounts, let us consider a practical application of distributed consensus and commits in the same context.

11.5.2 A concrete example: distributed password creation

We shall consider a hypothetical scenario that is designed not for its technical efficiency, accuracy, or relevance to real life, but for its immediate use in illuminating our current context of interest. We need a distributed system to start with, so we take the case of three computer terminals, each being operated by an individual. Now, these three individuals - we shall call them A, B, and C - are family members trying to set up a joint bank account. In particular, they are at the step which is all and only about deciding on a shared password. The bank insists that the password must be exactly 9 characters long. Each person insists that 3 characters must be of his or her choosing. We shall also assume that each person is located in a different city in the world, and at the moment, are in front of that computer terminal which allows them to make their contribution to the password: remember, the contribution of each person is exactly 3 characters.

The following diagram is a representation of the described system, leaving out any details like the actual software executed by each terminal, etc:

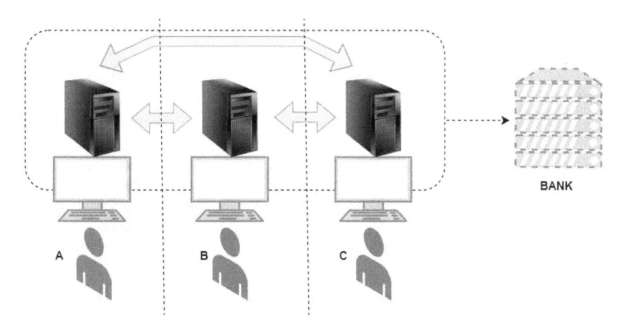

All terminals have computational power (i.e. they are not dumb terminals), and expectedly, all three are linked together so that messages can be broadcast, thus enabling the three units to work together as a 'system' that is capable of arriving at a consensus (somehow) on matters of common interest. Finally, the system is also linked to the bank's server so that the password, once finalised (we will shortly see how, in a broad sense), can be sent over to be linked with the joined account. The vertical dotted lines imply the geographical separation between the terminals/users.

At this stage, it is important to distinguish between *network entities* and *users*. These 3 computer terminals form 3 entities that are part of the network; each of them executes a distributed algorithm which we are interested in. The users are *drivers*, that 'push' each entity to generate an event in the system.

As the password-generation process kicks off, here is the screen that each person is provided by his or her terminal:

Needless to say, quite simple: 9 slots are presented. Each empty slot is supposed to hold a character that is part of the password. As seen, the cursor is present in the first slot. Once the cursor starts blinking, each person must hit a key (a character) of his own choosing. Each key press generates an event in the system. Only one among these three events will be selected to be entered into the first slot. Let us suppose that A hits the key 'P', B hits 'Q', and C goes for 'R'. We shall assume that the system 'somehow' decides to choose the input provided by A from among the three inputs. So, the screen subsequently presented to A will look as follows:

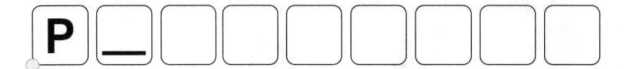

As seen above, the character 'P' has been entered in the first slot. The small circle (towards the bottom left of the slot) is an indication to A that his or her choice made it into the first slot. This follows that both B and C would simultaneously see the following version (where the mentioned circular hint is absent):

At this point, three events have been generated in the system:

- A choosing the character 'P'
- B choosing the character 'Q'
- C choosing the character 'R'

Of these, the first event has been selected for slot 1. Before allowing any more events to be generated - i.e. before allowing any more key presses - the remaining two events need to be 'consumed'. The solution is obvious: whatever technique or algorithm was used to select A's input (as the selection for slot 1) from three inputs can be used to choose the next one (as the selection for slot 2) from the remaining two inputs (i.e. the those provided by B and C). Let us say that the input provided by B was selected (again, magically, as far as we are concerned at this point). So, within no time, B ends up seeing the following:

What does C have on his or her screen at this instant?

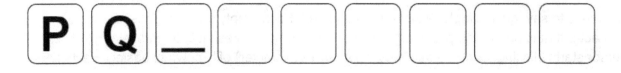

Naturally, the 'Q' has no green marker in the view presented to C because C opted for 'R' and not 'Q'. Note that all these steps flash by in quick succession, leading to the last step of this 'round' - which is to consume the remaining event, i.e. the remaining input of 'R'. Dealing with that sole remaining event requires no more than assigning the same to the third slot, leading the display of C to be refreshed to:

Note that the displays of A and B would be refreshed by now to the same content, except for the position of the green circle. At this point, the cursor has moved to the fourth slot and started blinking - this indicates the next round (of keyboard inputs) starting, leading to each individual entering another character, each of which will be selected and distributed across the next 3 slots, after which the process repeats for one final round which takes care of the remaining 3 slots - at which point the password of 9 characters is complete. Each participant would see the same password in front of him or her, 9 characters each, of which 3 would be marked with green circles to indicate his or her contribution to the password.

Once the completed password appears on each of the three terminals, satisfying each user of his or her own (equal) contribution to the process, the following two things happen:

- Each user notes down (or commits to memory) the password displayed on his or her screen
- Each terminal updates the bank's database with the password

Note that the last action would mean the password being set three times at the bank's database, the last two of which will overwrite a previous entry; however, that does not matter as long as the distributed algorithm is 'correct' - in which case, each terminal would have arrived at the same password.

To sum up, what exactly just happened? To understand that, let us first ask this question: what exactly was the final result? The result, of course, was the creation of a password string *agreed upon by all participants (entities) involved*. In a general sense, the result was a set of *units of information* (characters) in a specific order. All participants proposed multiple units of information (3 characters each) and together arrived at a consensus on the order in which said units of information must be arranged. In fact, *the 9-character password was the result of 9 executions of a consensus protocol*. Each execution (i.e. each *instance* of the consensus algorithm or protocol) had a slot number associated with it and was concerned with arriving at a consensus (on the character to be assigned to the specified slot) between three participants.

Armed with all this information, we can think of each entity (i.e. computer terminal) as having access to a *consensus module*. An entity makes a *proposal* to the consensus module and receives a reply. In this case, a proposal contains two pieces of information: a slot number (for example, 1), and a character value (for example, 'P').The module will provide a reply that can be positive or negative. In the former case, the module says sometimes along the lines of:

Congrats, your proposal to insert 'P' at slot 1 is accepted

In the latter scenario, the message would look like, for example:

Sorry, your proposal is rejected. The chosen value for slot 2 is 'Q'

The consensus module can also send an unsolicited (i.e. with no corresponding proposal) informational message to a terminal:

FYI: The chosen value for slot 3 is 'R'

In such a scenario, the role of the terminal or entity is not that of a *proposer*, but that of a *learner*. During round 1, the terminal of user A updates the values of slots 2 and 3 based on such messages from its consensus module. The following diagram represents the communication pattern between terminal A and its consensus module during round 1 in the earlier example, using a hypothetical communication protocol:

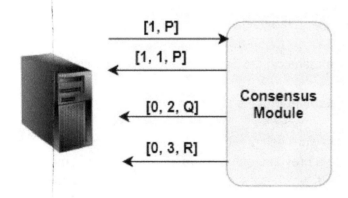

The communication starts off with a proposal and a corresponding reply: the proposal consists of a pair of information *[1, P]* that indicates the value of 'P' being proposed for a slot number of 1, while the corresponding reply is a triplet *[1, 1, P]* that consists of a flag, a slot number, and a value (in that order). The flag is 1, indicating the proposal being successful (whereas a 0 would have meant a rejection), followed by a slot number (of 1), and then a value selected ('P') for that slot number.

The next two messages are unsolicited informational messages (corresponding to the selections for slots 2 and 3) where terminal A plays the role of a learner. The first one is *[0, 2, Q]*, where the flag 0 indicates the nature of the message (either informational with no corresponding proposal, or a reply to a proposal that was not accepted), 2 indicating the second slot, for which 'Q' (proposed by terminal B) is the selected value. The second of *[0, 3, R]* represents the selection of the proposal from C to be used as the value for the 3rd slot.

The previous diagram can be misleading in the sense that the consensus module available to terminal A is represented as a standalone entity; obviously, the consensus modules of all three entities are linked together (else consensus will not be possible), so the following diagram is a more realistic and complete representation of all transactions happening during round 1:

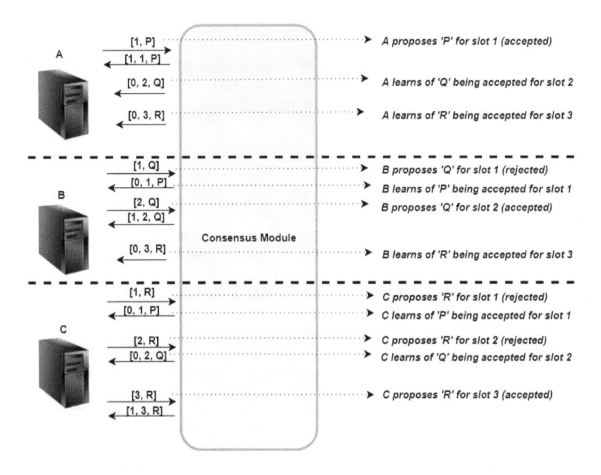

11.5.2.1 Roles

Now, before we slowly move away from this example, let us take a second to focus on the concept of an entity playing different roles during the described process. We did touch upon how terminal A acts as a *learner*, when it receives information on the characters assigned to slots 2 and 3. Right from the start, we also saw how each terminal can operate as a *proposer* who suggests a character for a particular slot. Can we think of more roles? Note that we assumed the consensus process to happen inside a black box of some kind, one which we called a *consensus module*. While this is a fair assumption as far as an abstraction goes, it should be fairly obvious that our consensus process would be simply an algorithm that requires participation from all terminals involved, and *not* a separate mechanism or service which each terminal can depend on (without participation). This more or less paves way for yet another role being played by each node or terminal in the system: that of a *voter*, because it is fair to assume that a consensus mechanism involves some system of voting by all interested parties. To summarise, we identified three roles (note: just *roles* played by each participant or entity or node; we are not talking about separate components dedicated to each role), so let us list them before moving to a different example:

- *Proposers*
- *Voters*
- *Learners*

Think about candidates participating in an election, the opinionated ones who vote for them, and a set of indifferent non-participants reading about the election result in newspapers! Needless to say, these categories indeed overlap; a proposer (or candidate, as per the last analogy) does vote, and any voter would subsequently learn the result of the election.

11.5.3 Another concrete example: replicated log

The last example we considered, as mentioned earlier, is admittedly a 'toy' one. We assumed a synchronous environment in terms of communication as well as user actions. We noted how there is not much of a consensus required for every third character, since we resume user inputs only after a set of 3 characters are decided in their order. That said, we can easily extend this toy example to a more complex and practical arrangement with the following characteristics:

- A set of nodes or entities (computing nodes, possibly spatially/geographically separated) connected together to form an asynchronous network
- The input to the network is a (possibly unending) 'stream' of events
- Each event arrives at one node or entity in the network
- Each event carries an associated value or input (which may be more complicated than a single character)
- Each node or entity manages a (possibly infinite) sequence of slots, starting from slot 0
- Each node or entity keeps track of number of the first empty slot available in its sequence of slots (initially all slots are empty) at its disposal
- When an event arrives, the recipient node makes a proposal to the system to place the event's value in the first slot available (i.e. the first empty slot, as per its knowledge)
- The proposal may succeed (in which case, the recipient node, i.e. the node who made the proposal, as well as every other node, assign the event's value to the slot as specified in the proposal)
- The proposal may fail (perhaps due to another node's proposal, for the same slot, having succeeded - in which case, every node updates the specified slot with the value mentioned in the proposal that succeeded)
- When a proposal fails, the proposer tries again - possibly with a different slot as target
- This process goes on, as a series of consensus instances manage to distribute incoming events across available slots

A readily apparent industrial-strength example is that of a *replicated log*. Imagine multiple servers, geographically separated, each maintaining a copy of a log file - this could be the access log of a web server, for example - and all the copies must be faithful replicas of each other. Clients contact any of the servers and submit a log entry, which must then be replicated correctly to all copies of the log file. At the beginning, each server starts off with an empty log file; in other words, the first available slot is 0 - representing a file offset of 0. Let us assume 3 clients contacting this system simultaneously from different locations, and submitting a log entry each to 3 different servers:

- *server1* receives *entry1* of length *l1* from *client1*
- *server2* receives *entry2* of length *l2* from *client2*
- *server3* receives entry3 of length *l3* from *client3*

At this point, the system has three events - each of which has associated information (i.e. a log entry of some length). Each of server1, server2, and server3 make a proposal:

- *server1* proposes that *entry1* be appended to offset 0 of the log file
- *server2* proposes that *entry2* be appended to offset 0 of the log file
- *server3* proposes that *entry3* be appended to offset 0 of the log file

A consensus algorithm is kicked off and assume the proposal of *server2* to be accepted. Each server in the system appends *entry2* to the beginning (since the offset is 0) of its copy of the log file and updates the offset or slot to the value *l2*.

Now, *server1* and *server3* retry their proposals; assume that the proposal of *server1* is accepted. Subsequently, each server in the system appends *entry1* to offset (or slot) *l2* of its copy of the log file and updates its offset or slot to *l2 + l1*. Next, it is up to *server3* to try proposing *entry3* again, this time targeting a slot of value *l2 + l1*, resulting in each log file replica to be updated/appended with *entry3* (to offset *l2 + l1*) and each server updating its offset or slot to the value *l2 + l1 + l3*. Of course, this is a highly simplified scenario; the system could continue to receive events from clients while all this is happening, and there could be many more proposers concurrently attempting to push values to the first available slot or log file offset. Further, servers could go down and come back up - which is what we will consider next.

11.5.3.1 Failure and recovery

So far, the mechanism of maintaining a replicated log appears fairly straightforward. Each slot (file offset) is filled up using a consensus procedure, and the file grows in equal increments of matching contents across all nodes. However, what if a node, say node X, fails or stalls? Obviously, the local *state* of node X will become increasingly out-of-date. For example, if node X had failed before it got a chance to do anything at all, the first free slot as known to X will remain at 0. What if X recovers at some point? Assume a load balancer who becomes aware of the fact that X is no longer in a crashed or unavailable state but is now up and running; as a result, X is forwarded a client request (carrying a new log entry). Expectedly, X will propose the addition of the newly arrived log entry to slot or offset 0 in the file.

Now, that is *not* going to work - because other nodes have 'moved on'. Imagine node Y receiving such a proposal: node Y is up-to-date with the rest of the system and has processed and stored, say, 10 log entries - i.e. filled up the first 10 slots and is ready to guide the next log entry to the 11th offset in the file. And here comes X suggesting a proposal for slot 0. Though the specific details may vary, we can imagine X receiving multiple replies of the form:

Sorry, slot 0 is occupied by the following log entry: ...

This gives a chance to X to do two things:

- Update first-free-slot to 1
- Update slot 0 with the specified log entry (as received in the response(s) to its proposal)

This still leaves X with a new log entry that is yet to be assigned to a slot, so X initiates a new proposal - this time using slot 1. Again, a similar result is possible, causing X to update first-free-slot (to 2) as well as the contents of slot 1. This can go on till X effectively 'catches up' with the rest of the system, after which the newly arrived entry finally gets assigned to a slot. We can see how a rejoining node will have to go through a work-intensive phase before it can actually start contributing to the system in terms of handling incoming load.

11.5.3.2 Implication of a fault-tolerant replicated log

Think about it: once we can replicate a log (a series of entries, in effect) in a fault tolerant manner, what we end up with is a powerful foundation layer on which we can build useful services. The entries in such a log can be viewed as a sequence of instructions consumed by a higher application layer and can be anything from bank transactions to generic database commands. The state of the higher layer (which sits on top of the foundation layer) is a function of the underlying command sequence, and thus inherits the consistency and fault-tolerance guaranteed by the latter. An analogy follows.

11.5.3.2.1 An analogy: a hotel chain

Consider a chain of restaurants. Each unit in the chain consists of a three-storied building; the ground floor is a communication or public relations office, the first floor is the kitchen, and the top floor is the actual restaurant where customers sit down to dine. The ground floor facilities enable all units to be linked together by 'some' communication protocol. We assume that customers give regular and honest feedback, based on which the recipes used by the whole chain are constantly updated or adjusted. Note that the kitchen owns the recipes; the chef 'consumes' the feedback log to 'fix' his or her recipes before preparing food in a manner consistent with the latest feedbacks, across all units belonging to the chain.

Needless to say, the feedback log is the replicated information of interest in this analogy. In each restaurant, the quality (or state) of the dining experience in the top floor is a direct function of the replicated information (i.e. feedback log) utilised by the underlying kitchen.

Now, a customer would only contact the specific restaurant (where he or she had dined) for providing feedback; perhaps the feedback is provided along with payment of the cheque:

Fix the seasoning in the french onion soup please, with a bit more of salt and pepper

No matter, the efficient communication protocol used by the restaurant chain ensures that the feedback is propagated in a consistent manner across all units. Note that there could be conflicting feedback from customers:

The french onion soup will probably be better off with a little less pepper

This may even be expected, if we imagine that a prior suggestion would have caused the chef to go overboard with pepper! The idea is that feedback helps, if applied in a consistent and sensible order. One way or the other, a consensus algorithm would have to be part of the communication protocol. As far as the kitchen is concerned, none of this is their problem: they receive and consume feedback from the lower floor, apply the updated recipes, ensuring that food is always prepared in a reliable and consistent manner. A customer having provided valid feedback to one unit may visit another unit the next day and would find his or her feedback to be correctly honoured.

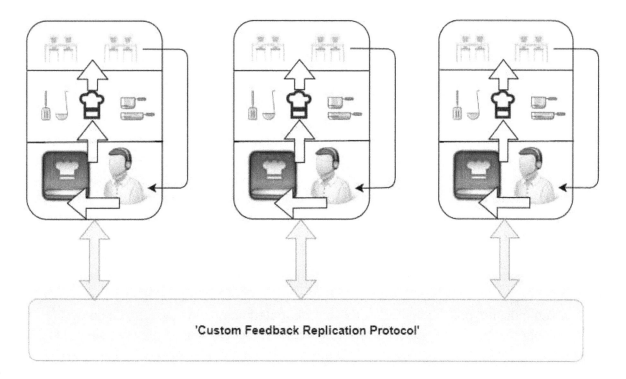

'Custom Feedback Replication Protocol'

11.5.4 State machine replication

This might be a good opportunity to take a broader view of what we are attempting to accomplish: in this specific case, we were interested in a consistent dining experience replicated across multiple locations. In other words, we desired a consistent *state* of affairs across all nodes in the system. The states change (hopefully for the better, as far as dining experiences are concerned), but we want those changes to be consistent everywhere, and not specific to a particular node or two. This brings us to the concept of a *state machine.* Each node in our system of interest can be thought of as a state machine: i.e. a *device* of some description, with an associated state. We accept (maybe even desire) that the state keeps changing, and we want the evolving state to be replicated consistently across all entities or nodes that operate in our system. In other words, the fundamental problem that interests is *SMR* or *State Machine Replication*. To achieve *SMR*, we first arranged a solution to log replication; which in turn depended on a faultless consensus algorithm. The following diagram represents the relation between these three problems: state machine replication, log replication, and consensus.

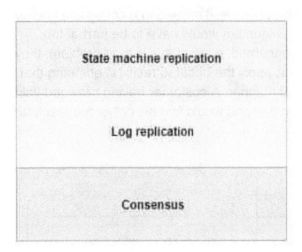

It is not hard to see how we found ourselves in a situation where *SMR* is the key priority. First and foremost, *state matters*. When we use the word 'state', it could stand for anything from the information in our email account, or the state of a bank account, the result of a business transaction, a purchase order, to a dining experience. In fact, state mattered so much that we chose to replicate it for the sake of availability. Once we did that, consistency became a problem that must be addressed.

To gain more perspective, we imagine a bunch of nodes or *replicas* - across which state must be replicated - driven by multiple clients. A client contacts a particular node with a *state change request*, which must not only be fulfilled but also propagated across the system. Once we imagine multiple clients operating concurrently, it is easy to accept that a consensus protocol plays a key role in accomplishing *SMR*. This is exactly where paxos comes in. In fact, paxos can be thought of as a consensus protocol as well as a solution for *SMR*. Over time, paxos has come to be widely described in both terms.

11.5.5 The road to Paxos

In previous examples, we worked with consensus modules - opaque boxes which we assumed to solve the consensus problem by running 'some' algorithm. Paxos is one such algorithm, probably the best known and most widely used one. The original paxos paper ("*The Part-Time Parliament*") as well as the follow-up ("*Paxos Made Simple*") dealt with three related problems:

- Developing a consensus algorithm to get multiple participants to agree on a single value

- How to use multiple instances of said algorithm to generate agreement on a *series* of values
- How the whole mechanism can be used to implement state machine replication in real life, with tentative suggestions and guidelines for implementers

The papers focused on the core consensus problems to be addressed and left a fair bit of details to be determined by the implementers of the system - explicitly in some cases, implicitly in others. Our approach to understanding paxos has been the opposite, because so far, we have considered multiple implementations that used consensus, and we are yet to delve into the paxos protocol as such.

In general, we will assume the following, which is a condensed version of the listing in section *11.5.3*, during our discussions on paxos:

- A bunch of nodes or replicas forming an asynchronous network
- Each replica holds a (possibly infinite) sequence of slots
- Each slot can hold a value
- One or more clients who issue requests to these replicas
- Each client request specifies a value
- A value could be anything, depending on the actual application: maybe a log entry, maybe a database command to be executed

Next, the concept of roles: we discussed and listed various roles in section *11.5.2.1*, and those are exactly applicable to paxos, which assumes a distributed system where entities or replicas play the following roles in an overlapping fashion:

- *Proposer*
- *Voter*
- *Learner*

Referring to the concept of *SMR* as introduced in the previous section, the proposer can be thought of as one among the set of replicas to whom a client issues a request for state change. More accurately: upon receiving such a request, the replica adopts the role of a proposer. So far things sound very uncomplicated: we have a proposer, who wants to propose a value. To keep things even simpler, let us step away from the concept of multiple slots (per node) for a while, and assume a single slot (per node). So, we have a strictly one-time phenomenon at hand; a single value has to be selected (and replicated at each node).

In fact, this is somewhat like an election where a single candidate (out of possibly many) has to be elected as the leader. Normally, elections are coordinated or synchronous affairs in the sense that there is a single planned and scheduled election, a single process, in which all candidates and voters participate to produce a result. This assumes the governance of an overseeing agency that arranges and schedules the election, issues notifications, conducts the election, determines and announces the result, etc. What if there was no such coordinating unit? After all, we are dealing with decentralised distributed systems. To get a firmer grip on the problem at hand, let us consider a fictitious island republic in the next example (and the last one, before we finally meet paxos) and see how a president is elected by rather unconventional means.

11.5.5.1 Presidential election in an unnamed island republic

In this island country which will remain unnamed, the process of presidential election is a bit different from most places. The citizens of this extremely small country are assumed to be well-meaning responsible individuals, with no greed towards power or wealth; the well being of the republic comes first. When there is a vacuum of power at the top, any citizen is free to propose himself or herself as the president. Also, as voters, the people of the land do not have individual preferences and are concerned only about completing the necessary task of electing a leader rather than lobbying for, or rallying around, any specific person for the job. To aid the proceedings, the constitution of the country lays down some simple rules as to how the election mechanism must be implemented:

- *An individual can be elected as leader upon receiving votes from a majority of the population*
- *It is an individual's responsibility to trigger an election (and propose himself or herself as the leader)*
- *Multiple individuals can hold elections simultaneously (!)*
- *Only one leader must be elected eventually*

So far, it sounds quite simple - maybe except for that part about multiple concurrent elections of which each is triggered by a different candidate. However, that bit of complication is to be expected, given that there is no central agency for handling elections. The constitution tries to be helpful by going on to describe more details; in particular, more guidance on the election process:

- *As the first step, the candidate will assemble a quorum (i.e. a majority) by interacting with (all or a majority of) the population of the republic. Candidates are encouraged to reach out to the mayor's office to avail any (contact) information required for this purpose*

- *If one or more members in the newly-assembled quorum has already voted (in another election, started by a different candidate) for other candidates, the candidate will consider himself to be no longer in the running, but is free to continue the process (i.e. the election which he or she started) with one of the other candidates (to whom one or more members in his or her quorum has already voted) as the proposed leader*

- *On the contrary, if a candidate chances upon a quorum of non-voters, he or she is then free to propose himself or herself as potential leader to the quorum*

- *A candidate is free to back out of the election process at any stage*

- *Any citizen is free to abstain from, or back out at any step of, an election if he or she so desires*

- *To capture the attention of the voter population, candidates are permitted to distribute gifts along with election messages, provided that said gift values are always approved by, and registered with, the ethics committee housed by the mayor's office*

The constitution deliberately kept certain aspects a bit vague, but over time the people of the republic worked out enough details, ironed out the flaws, and developed an effective leader-election method which broadly had the following steps to be followed by a candidate:

1. Assemble a quorum
2. Propose a candidate to the quorum
3. Accepts votes from the quorum
4. If a majority of votes are received, send success messages to the quorum

So, one fine day the head of state decides to retire, leaving a sudden vacuum at the seat of power. Let us see what follows.

11.5.5.1.1 John

John wakes up early that morning and comes to know of the situation. Fancying himself to be a good leader who can contribute much to his country, he decides to have a go for the top man's job. Having procured a copy of the constitution and acquainted himself clearly with the process involved, he first contacts the mayor's office and obtains the list, including mailing addresses, of all voters (we assume a small and manageable list of voters, because this is a very small island republic). John then follows the established method of forming a quorum: he sends an election gift of price 1$ to each voter (or a majority) in the country. John is also required, by the mayor's office, to report the price of the gift (1$) to the in-house ethics committee. Along with each gift is a message, an *election-intimation*:

- *Hi, please accept this election gift of 1$*

At this stage, we assume that John is the sole candidate. As we will see later, that explains why John had the 'freedom' to choose an arbitrary gift value of 1$. The reliability and speed of postal services in the tiny island are good in general; an hour or so of delivery time usually, but there may be the occasional delay or message loss which in turn might see to it that all voters may not receive John's message (in time). However, the process works as long as a majority of the voters receive (and respond to) his message. So, let us consider that John receives affirmative responses from a majority which then forms his quorum:

- *Thanks for the 1$ gift! Please provide your candidate details*

Per process, John next sends the following *vote-request* message to his quorum:

- *I am John, and I am the candidate. Please vote for me*

In response, he receives affirmative responses from his quorum:

- *I vote for John*

Finally, John sends out success or victory messages to his quorum and considers himself elected:

- *Thank you! John is the newly elected president!*

Now, time to bring Smith into this scene.

11.5.5.1.2 Smith

Assume that Smith wakes up that fine day a bit late: perhaps by 11AM. He comes to know of the resignation of the head of state, but not about what happened later on. He is not particularly aware of John's activities - maybe he did not receive john's election-intimation message due to a delivery delay or failure. Smith wastes no time and follows the same initial procedure as John. However, when he contacts the mayor's office (to obtain postal addresses of all voters), the ethics committee duly informs him about John's election process having kicked off, including the gift price used by John to generate election-intimation messages.

Now, to get the attention of voters, Smith has to use a larger gift price; he decides on a gift cost of 2$ and keeps the ethics committee informed accordingly. Long story short, Smith sends out a 2$ gift to all voters, with an accompanying message, i.e. an election-intimation similar to the one issued by John:

- *Hi, please accept this election gift of 2$*

As in the case of John, Smith receives responses from a majority, which will form his quorum. However, this is where Smith's situation deviates from that of John's. Smith sees two types of responses:

1. *Hi, thanks for the 2$ election gift! I'm required by law to inform you that I have voted for John after receiving a 1$ election gift*

2. *Thanks for the 2$ election gift! Please provide your candidate details*

The second type of messages are obviously from voters who have not received John's message (yet). However, the presence of the first type of messages sees to it that Smith has no choice but to send the following message (i.e. vote-request) to his quorum as the next step:

- *Please vote for John*

This is because of what the constitution mandates for this specific situation, as specified earlier:

- *If one or more members in the quorum has already voted for other candidates, the candidate will consider himself to be no longer in the running, but is free to continue the process with one of the other candidates (to whom one or more members in his or her quorum has already voted) as the proposed leader*

The next steps are same as what John went through; Smith receives responses from his quorum of the type:

- *I vote for John*

Following which, Smith sends out success or victory intimations to his quorum. The set of voters present in both John's and Smith's quorums will indeed receive a second or duplicate victory intimation, but no harm is caused by such an event.

Note one advantage of Smith switching sides (from own side to that of John): Smith's quorum may have contained one or more voters who never received John's election intimations. Such parties effectively join the election mechanism thanks to the efforts of Smith, and the result of the election is thus propagated wider across the population. Note also how the prompt backing-out of Smith (as candidate) results in a simple conflict resolution mechanism that leads to smooth operation and a final result.

11.5.5.1.3 John and Smith

What if John and Smith triggered their elections concurrently? This is where we must note that any citizen will ignore messages (election-intimation or vote-request) part of an election carrying a 1$ gift once an election-notification carrying a more valuable 2$ gift is seen! This implies a very real possibility that John may not see enough responses to his election-intimation message. Meanwhile Smith does hear from a majority and sends out vote-requests to that quorum. Coming back to John, he is free to start a new election if he prefers so - he can check with the ethics committee, discover the last entry (i.e. Smith) into the election game with a 2$ election gift, and very well decide to up the game by using a 3$ gift for his second election-intimation message.

Remember that John, like all citizens in this land, is not driven by personal ambition but a strong sense of civic duty. Think about how John triggering a second election can be useful: imagine that Smith did not see through his election process due to whatever reasons; maybe he was rather overwhelmed by the sense of responsibility and backed out right at the last round, without dispatching his success messages (he does not have much choice, as we will shortly see). His quorum is still waiting for the final confirmation/victory message which may never come now. As such, the election is in a blocked stage. But now, John triggers his second election by sending out election-intimation messages carrying a 3$ gift (which will get the attention of a majority of the voters). Since both John and Smith work with quorums or majorities, John has to receive at least one response to his latest election-intimation that says:

- *Hi, thanks for the 3$ election gift! I'm required by law to inform you that I have voted for Smith after receiving a 2$ election gift*

Expectedly, John now generates the following vote-request to his quorum:

- *Please vote for Smith*

Upon seeing votes from a majority, John goes ahead and closes out the election by issuing the required victory messages for Smith:

- *Thank you! Smith is the newly elected president*

What if John falls sick right before he could generate vote-request messages to his quorum? No matter - assuming an abundance of duty-bound citizens, we can imagine someone else stepping in to create a new election, discovering in the process one or more voters who have already voted for Smith, and carrying the process along to the end just like John would have done. Thanks to the records maintained and shared by the ethics committee, each new election starts off with an election-intimation message that brings a gift costlier than any seen till that point. This ensures that the most recent election messages hold the attention of the public over messages from any prior ones.

11.5.5.1.4 John, Smith, Paul

Let us now consider a slightly more complicated situation. John sends out his 1$ election-intimation messages and successfully assembles a quorum. At around the same time, Smith does the same using his 2$ election-intimation messages. A certain number of people that are also part of John's quorum end up receiving Smith's election intimation *right after* John's election-intimation is received (and replied to). Now, these good folks will no longer pay any attention to the soon-to-arrive vote-request from John, since John's election carried a lesser gift as compared to what Smith provided. As a result, John fails to see a majority response to his vote-request, and rather uncharacteristically, gives up his election effort.

At this point, some voters have voted for John, but some were distracted away by Smith's election-intimation. Let us assume that Smith goes ahead with his vote-request, gains a majority response from his quorum, but 'fails' to go ahead any further (i.e. he does not generate the success messages that are required to close out his election process).

By now, we have two sets of voters in the system - those who have voted for John, and those who have voted for Smith. Currently the election is stalled. Enter Paul, who decides to create a new election (the 3rd one - carries a 3$ gift) and get things moving.

Paul receives a majority response to his election-intimation, and the results are interesting because there are three kinds of messages:

1. *Hi, thanks for the 3$ election gift! I'm required by law to inform you that I have voted for John after receiving a 1$ election gift*

2. *Hi, thanks for the 3$ election gift! I'm required by law to inform you that I have voted for Smith after receiving a 2$ election gift*

3. *Thanks for the gift of 3$! Please provide your candidate details*

Now, obviously Paul is no longer in the running - thanks to the existence of quorum members who have already voted. However, Paul sees a quorum containing voters for John as well as voters for Smith. Which candidate will Paul favour in his soon-to-be-issued vote-request messages? The answer is simple, as per existing practices of the land: *Smith*, because his election was the latest entry (as indicated by the higher valued gift). Hence, Paul carries along the election process and gets Smith elected.

Refer the following diagram for a pictorial representation of the mentioned procedure. John sends out his election intimations first (*El-J*) for which the quorum [A, B, C, D] is formed by responding with *El-J-OK* messages. Right behind is Smith, who generates his own election intimations (*El-S*) to the quorum [B, C, D, E]. This disrupts John's quorum, thanks to B, C, and D switching preferences. Unaware of the winds of change, John issues his vote-request messages (*V-J*), to which he receives only a single response (from A). Meanwhile, Smith does the same with much better results - his quorum stays intact, and he receives votes from B, C, D, and E. However, for whatever reason, Smith makes no further move - he does not generate a success/victory message - leaving the process blocked for the moment. Paul enters the scene and generates his *El-P* election-intimation messages to [A, E, F, G] which then forms his quorum. Seeing existing votes in the quorum (A and E admit to having already voted for John and Smith, respectively), with the latest vote being for Smith, Paul next issues *V-S* messages (vote-requests for Smith), which succeeds in drawing votes from the full quorum, leading to Paul declaring Smith as the elected leader.

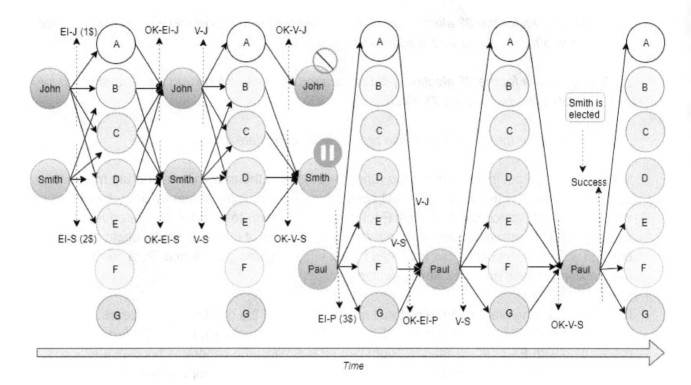

11.5.5.1.5 Learners?

Consider the state of D in the previous example, who seem to be out of the picture once Paul arrives. Indeed, D is not part of Paul's quorum - the quorum that finally pulls off a result. The point is that a mechanism is needed to convey the results to folks who never played an active role in the final result, or perhaps no role at all during any stage. To address this, the island rules request voters to inform the nearest press office as soon as they receive a success/victory message. This ensures that the election result gets published in the next morning (or evening) editions of one or more newspapers. Also, note the availability of alternate mechanisms by which a citizen can learn the result:

- D can very well grow impatient and trigger an election mechanism, allowing the result to be learnt (and possibly propagated to wider audience)
- Someone else could do the same and D might end up being part of the subsequent quorum, leading to the same result
- That 'someone' could even be John (coming back with a new election) or Smith (restarting his paused election process)

11.5.5.1.6 A thought on quorums

While we've been using the word 'quorum' extensively, it is easy to underestimate the role played by the concept of a quorum in the overall procedure. As we defined very early on, a quorum is defined as a majority; if the island has a voter population of 200, then 101 is the (minimum) quorum. For example, John obtains 200 postal addresses from the mayor's office, sends out 200 election-intimation messages, and moves to the next stage (of issuing vote-request messages) once he receives the 101st response. We can think of three types of quorums:

1. A *fresh* or new-born quorum
2. An *active* quorum
3. A *deciding* quorum

A fresh quorum is considered to be in existence once a proposer or candidate receives a majority of responses to his or her election intimation messages; in the example earlier, this is the case once John receives his 101st response. Note how even this preliminary step can fail, in which case the proposer would need to try again to create a fresh quorum. The quorum in this newly-formed stage can be considered to be rather fragile. A new election intimation from someone else can very well break this up right away (as we have seen earlier). In other words, a fresh quorum is not a guarantee of anything at all. One needs to convert a fresh quorum into an active quorum, i.e. a fresh quorum needs to be *activated*, and once that is done (for the first time: see next paragraph), the result is *locked*.

So, what is an active quorum? An active quorum is one from which the proposer has received responses (note: from *everyone* in the quorum) to his or her vote-request messages. From this point onwards, any newly-formed or fresh quorum will contain at least one member who is part of the active quorum, and the proposer (who created said fresh quorum) will be forced to issue vote-requests for the candidate selected by the active quorum. The first active quorum formed in the system, hence, can be thought of as the deciding quorum. All subsequent active quorums will inevitably agree with the deciding quorum as far as the result is considered. Refer the following diagram for the various transitions just described:

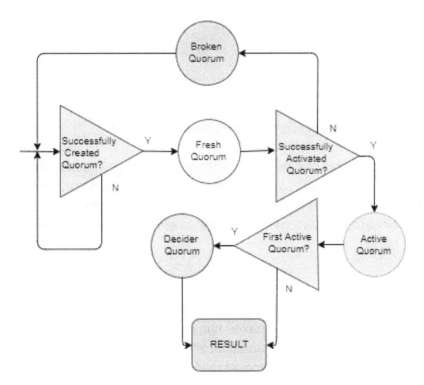

Finally, from this current perspective of ours, the broad steps involved are:

1. Attempt to create a quorum
2. If step 1 fails, try again
3. Attempt to activate the forum
4. If step 3 fails, try again
5. If the newly activated quorum is a decider quorum (i.e. the first active quorum), the result is now locked
6. Announce the result

11.5.5.1.7 Switching back to multiple slots

Remember that we had decided to switch temporarily to a simplified scenario of a single slot (presidential seat, in the ongoing example) to which a value (candidate) must be selected. As an introduction to moving back to the real-life world where multiple values must be selected, one for each slot in a sequence of multiple slots, how about expanding the current example such that a president is aided by a vice-president, and a certain number of advisors? Now, consider the case of Paul in the example where he is first introduced. Maybe Paul comes in with the intention of running for president, but he dutifully does the last-leg donkey work for Smith and gets Smith elected. Once that job is done, Paul does not have to sit back. He can start a new election, this time proposing himself for vice-president. Who knows, he may very well get elected as vice-president. Then again, he might find a similar situation and end up closing out the process to get someone else elected as vice-president. No matter, Paul can still create another election, this time for the post of 1st advisor, and so on. Note a subtle change to the message formats as a direct result: till now, all messages in this example were implicitly associated with the presidential seat election, but now each message will have to explicitly specify the target seat (i.e. slot). Some examples follow:

- *Please vote for Paul as vice-president*
- *Please vote for Robert as presidential advisor (1)*
- *Hi, thanks for the 3$ election gift! I'm required by law to inform you that I have voted for Quinn as presidential advisor (6) after receiving a 1$ election gift*

The point is to see how a well-refined protocol can be used to obtain consensus in a quorum, effectively selecting a value (candidate) for a particular slot (seat) and how the same protocol can be executed as multiple instances to handle multiple slots. We start looking into the details of paxos next, and from this point onwards we assume the existence of multiple slots per each participating node or replica.

11.5.5.2 How Paxos does it

The procedure which we described at length in section *11.4.4.1* very closely resembles the paxos protocol. Just like election-intimation messages, paxos has *proposals*. The concept of a proposal is a key one in paxos, and each proposal has an associated integer number, a unique identifier for the proposal. This is exactly similar to election-intimation messages having an associated gift of some (unique) cost. It is up to the system implementor to ensure that duplicate proposal numbers do not happen, say by having a set of non-overlapping monotonously increasing streams of identifiers, one for each proposer in the system. To exemplify this arrangement, perhaps an implementation involving 10 replicas would let *node1* use proposal numbers from the sequence *1, 11, 21, 31…*, *node2* use numbers from the sequence *2, 12, 22, 32, ...*and so on. In the previous island election mechanism, we assumed proposers to be accurately informed about the gift value of the latest or last election, and also to be sensible enough to use gifts of continuously increasing values.

As an example, let the proposal from node or replica A be the following:

- *Proposal #22 : I propose the value V12 for slot 16*

Here, the proposal identifier or proposal number is 22. The value *V12* could be, for example, a command of the type "*add 10% to the current balance*". Whatever *V12* may look like, instruction, database command, or log entry, it has to be 'applied' across the system - which is the problem that node A must begin to address. It should be interesting, then, to note that the value has no role to play in the first step that node A takes. This is exactly like an election-intimation message not mentioning the candidate details, and is easier to accept if we consider the following: as a proposer, node A has a two-step job just like John, Smith, or Paul in the previous scenario:

- Assemble a *quorum* of nodes (a quorum of voters or *acceptors*)
- Get the quorum to accept the proposal

Obviously, the quorum must be large enough to form a majority in the system. The first step for node A, as it assumes the role of a proposer, is to advertise the fact that it is a proposer with some proposal.

11.5.5.2.1 The *prepare* stage

To achieve this, node A sends out a '*can-I-make-a-proposal*' message (to other nodes - the voters or acceptors) which contains two pieces of information:

- A proposal number (22, in the earlier example)
- A slot number (16, in the earlier example) for which a value is being proposed

Let us call formally call this 'can-I-make-a-proposal' message a *proposal-prepare* message, or more simply, a *prepare* message. Note the absence of the actual value in this message; only the proposal number and target slot are present. If all goes well, all recipients (or at least a majority - the quorum) respond with a *proposal-OK* reply which can be of two types:

1. *Alright, let us hear your proposal #22*
2. *Alright, let us hear your proposal #22. Do note that the last proposal that I voted for was proposal #19, for value V99*

If all replies are of the first type, then node A is free to use a proposed value of own choosing in the next stage. If one or more replies are of the second type, then node A will keep aside own proposed value (if there is one), and pick the value associated with the highest numbered proposal that was voted for by a member in this quorum. Once again, this is similar to the procedure which we described in section *11.5.5.1.4.*

11.5.5.2.2 The *accept* stage

Next, node A would send the actual proposal, a '*please-accept-this-proposal*' message, that specifies the following:

- The proposal number
- The proposed value
- The slot number for which a value is being proposed

Let us formally call this 'please-accept-this-proposal' message an *accept-proposal* message, or in a simpler fashion, an *accept* message. Again, if all goes well, a majority of acceptors would send an *accept-OK* reply. Upon hearing replies from a majority, node A commits the proposal (i.e. writes the proposed value to the associated slot) and issues *Success* messages to the quorum. Each recipient of the success message performs a commit. Refer the following diagram:

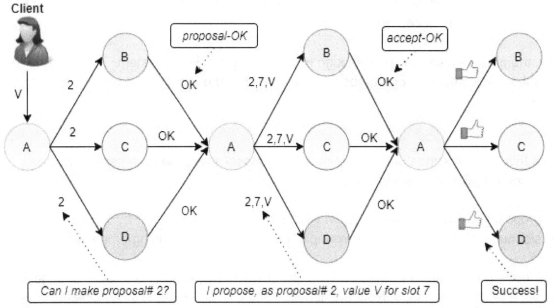

We noted in *11.4.4.1* how a voter will start ignoring messages associated with a particular election once he or she sees an intimation message for a new election that carries a gift of higher value. In paxos, this concept is formalised to the agreement that *an acceptor will stop honouring lower-numbered proposals once a higher-numbered one is seen.* For example, assume that node X receives a proposal numbered 33. This implies the following:

- X starts ignoring prepare messages associated with lower-numbered proposals
- X starts ignoring accept messages associated with lower-numbered proposals

Another way of looking at a proposal-OK response is as a promise from an acceptor that the above two behaviors have come into force.

Note that an implementer can choose to use negative-acknowledgements (*nacks*), at the risk of higher message complexity and traffic, instead of silently ignoring prepare and accept messages. Such nacks can have the advantage of resolving ambiguity (*Why am I not hearing from anyone in my quorum? Did the network fail, or did all those nodes fail, or did they all receive higher-numbered proposals?*), with the added benefit of conveying useful information as exemplified next:

- Sorry, I cannot accept your prepare message for proposal #44, because I just happened to see a prepare message for proposal #51
- Sorry, I cannot accept your accept message for proposal #37, because I just happened to see a prepare message for proposal #41

11.5.5.2.3 Distinguished proposer

In our discussion so far, we assumed any replica to turn proposer upon receiving a client request. There is indeed a 'race condition' if we allow multiple concurrent proposers. As we saw (equivalently) in section *11.5.5.1.6*, a fresh quorum can be demolished immediately by a new and higher-numbered proposal from an 'opponent'. The 'loser' may come back with a new proposal, which in turn disrupts his opponent's quorum just when it was about to be turned into an active quorum. This can go on and on. A solution would be to use a leader-election mechanism of some sort during 'system startup' to ensure a single *distinguished proposer*. Only a distinguished proposer makes proposals; a replica (who is not the distinguished proposer) receives a client request, prepares a proposal, and passes on the proposal to the distinguished proposer who in turn issues the proposal. Alternately, we can think of 'normal' replicas *forwarding* client requests to the distinguished proposer. Once we bring fault-tolerance into consideration, we could imagine one or more distinguished proposers who in turn are backed up by one or more nodes who are ready to step into the role in the event of failure.

11.5.5.2.4 Distinguished learners

We have already discussed one consequence of proposers working with majorities, which is to potentially leave a minority set of nodes unaware of the final result. Our island elections from *11.4.4.1* addressed this by having the result propagated via the news medium, whose press offices are fed the result by voters from an active quorum. The press offices can be thought to play the role of *distinguished learners*, who in turn propagate the result to the rest of the learners.

In a real-life set of replicas, distinguished learners handle the critical job of serving *read operations* from clients. A read request from a client which requests the latest state of affairs should not be provided a reply fetched from a 'regular' replica, after all. The reason is obvious: there is no guarantee that such a replica is up-to-date.

11.5.5.2.5 Rounding up 11.4.4.3.4 and 11.4.4.3.3: a high level view

Let us divide client requests (broadly) into read and write operations, combine the conclusions of the last two sections, and come up with the following high-level modus operandi:

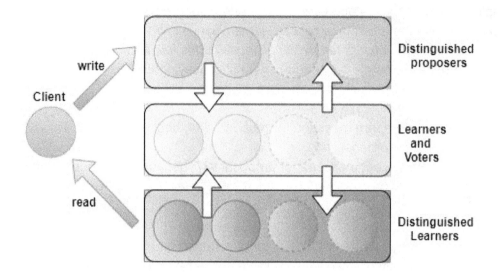

Lastly, let us always keep in mind that these are overlapping roles. The same node could serve as an acceptor in some proposer's quorum, do the job of a distinguished learner, or take over the role of a distinguished proposer, and so on.

11.5.5.2.6 Holes

Since we assume multiple concurrent clients 'driving' our system of replicas, we can certainly expect multiple concurrent paxos instances to be executing simultaneously for various slots. A given replica may be a member of quorums for some, and not a member of quorums for others. This could lead to a replica being part of a successful consensus instance (i.e. one that ran to completion and selected a result) for a particular slot while one or more lower slots are yet to be filled (maybe the corresponding consensus instances are in a stalled state) - leading to 'holes' in a replica's sequence of slots.

As an example, assume that node X participates in the paxos instance for slot 33, while slots 30, 31, and 32 remain empty as far as the local state of node X is concerned. Maybe node X was not a member of the quorums for those consensus instances. If those instances had successfully completed, the learning mechanism (section *11.4.4.3.4*) would have have (eventually) updated node X, thus filling up those slots at node X. Perhaps those paxos instances are currently in a stalled state - maybe the proposer failed. Let us indeed assume exactly such an eventuality, that the distinguished proposer failed. Let the failed distinguished proposer be node Y. At some earlier point, during healthier times, our node Y triggered paxos instances for slots 30, 31, 32, and 33. The first 3 instances dragged on slowly, perhaps victims to slow-responding members in their quorum, while 33 sprinted to a quick conclusion. This is when node Y failed.

We will assume that node X is the successor to node Y. Now, node X takes over as distinguished proposer and finds an immediate problem to worry about. Node X sees that slots 1 - 29 as well as slot 33 is filled, but slots 30-32 remain empty. To top it up, node X has just received a client request. Should it propose the command (associated with the new client request) for slot 34 or should it target slot 30?

The problem with the latter approach is simple: node X has no information on the history associated with these three empty slots; perhaps their paxos instances stalled after values (commands) were proposed for those slots; perhaps one or more members in their quorums have already accepted those commands; node X cannot assume one way or the other. Hence, to avoid inconsistency, node X first triggers paxos instances for each of these three 'suspect' slots, proposing a *null command* (a *no-op*, for no-operation) for each. The paxos protocol will ensure that either the no-op or a previously accepted command will be selected for these slots, depending upon the state of their individual paxos instances. As far as the command associated with the new client request is concerned, node X issues a proposal for slot 34.

11.5.5.2.7 Reconfiguration

We assumed implicitly all along that the exact number of replicas in the system, and the identity/address of each, is public knowledge shared by all parties involved. We can imagine this information being passed to each replica as the system comes up. What if this information needs to change at some later point in time? Perhaps we want to remove one or more replicas. Maybe we want to add a few more nodes to the system. One option obviously is to bring the system down, i.e. shut down all replicas, and restart them - only this time, we pass the updated information regarding system membership to each replica. This is not very efficient or clean, not least because such a reconfiguration mechanism interrupts availability of the cluster.

Let us look at what we essentially need: we want each replica to update its local knowledge regarding who else is participating in the system and how each one of those can be communicated with. Clearly, this can be achieved by running 'some' command at each node. The command could be something very simple, say, one that reads a file to obtain the updated cluster membership information. Now, as we have seen earlier, state machine replication is all about executing a sequence of commands at each replica, in the exact same order everywhere. Hence, we can always insert or 'slip in' the reconfiguration command along with the 'regular' ones (i.e. the client-supplied ones). Imagine the system administrator issuing a reconfiguration request, just like any other client, which is then handled by a proposer and gets voted upon by acceptors to be selected for a particular slot. The admin's request would contain two crucial pieces of information, one being a command identifier, and two, some 'parameter' for the command - like the path location of a file which contains the updated membership information. This sounds good, but as usual there is a hitch.

We have seen that a particular command is actually a 'result' chosen for a particular slot, thanks to a consensus protocol run among the participants in the system. Execution of a reconfiguration command is an action that modifies the participants in the system - which means that, executing a reconfiguration command at, say, slot 10 will provide a new *configuration*, one which the system's consensus protocol has to use from that point onwards when it comes to selecting commands for slot 11, 12, etc. This is perfectly fine if consensus instances for no other higher slots are being executed concurrently: we execute the reconfiguration command; which in turn updates the configuration (the participant list and contact info) at each replica; and whenever consensus instances are run for slots 11, 12, and higher, the updated participant list will be used to select commands for those slots. But then, thanks to concurrent activity from multiple clients, it is quite possible that consensus instances for multiple slots like (10, 11, 12,...) are concurrently in progress - which precludes a reconfiguration command running at a particular slot from modifying the configuration immediately. Well, the configuration can be modified immediately, in the sense of time, but there is no guarantee that a certain number of higher slots will be affected by the change. This is because, as we just saw, those slots could very well have their consensus instances already in progress.

What we need to do, then, is to first fix an upper limit C on the number of concurrent requests allowed by the system. Think of C as a configuration parameter specified during system startup. A reconfiguration command is committed (to a slot) just like any other command, but *not executed immediately* by any replica. As an example, let C be 32 and let the reconfiguration command be written down to slot 13 at each replica. At that moment, there could be consensus instances running for a slot as high as 45 - because C is set to 32. However, slot 46 is 'safe' because it lies outside the window set by C in this example. Therefore, every replica will execute the reconfiguration command just before initiating or processing a consensus instance for slot 46. This ensures that all commands from slot 46 onwards will be selected using the updated list of participants. Note how this adds a minor step at each replica: before slot n is handled, check if the command at slot $n - C$ is a reconfiguration command; if so, execute the reconfiguration command and get the configuration updated before proceeding any further.

11.5.6 The good, bad, and ugly

So, what went wrong with paxos? Nothing much, in fact: most went right. Paxos turned out to be very popular and widely used, to the point that 'paxos' is synonymous with the word 'consensus'. However: there remained the problem of lucid comprehension as far as a good chunk of the population is concerned. This is applicable not only to the original paper, but also to a follow-up one by Lamport ("*Paxos Made Simple*") and many other articles, blogs, and publications, all done with (and subsequently having failed at) the single definitive objective of uncomplicating the original topic.

Let us start with the original paper, the 1989 "*The Part-time Parliament*". The information is presented in an interesting context, using a fictitious scenario which describes the law-making process adopted by the parliament of a greek island called Paxos. While this particular choice of backdrop for a distributed consensus protocol certainly evokes curiosity and interest, it mainly succeeded in letting the paxos protocol gain a certain amount of notoriety as a hard-to-comprehend subject. In fact,such a choice for storytelling can be seen as the first step in the direction of building an unnecessary layer of complexity over a relatively simple protocol. Considering that the english phrase 'Greek and Latin' stands for 'something hard to understand', the choice of a greek parliament as the primary mechanism of illustration is at best a dubious one and does not exactly inspire confidence in readers!

Indeed, the popular opinion is that the original paper is unreadable. Now, that is not entirely true, because the paper is in fact simple and easy to read compared to many other ground-breaking papers in the subject of distributed systems. The problem is a particularly long-winded style of narration through the abstruse details and mechanisms of a greek parliament, all of which is beautifully written and most likely with the best of intentions, but one which finally produces one of two results on a reader based on the way the subject is approached by the same:

- For the curious kinds, the learners, those with a passing interest, those catching up with distributed systems, and so on - who form the majority, in fact - the readers are left wondering, probably after multiple passes through the entire paper, '*well, that is all nice and good but what exactly did I just learn, and how exactly can this be applied practically, if at all?*'

- If the reader is a seasoned professional, maybe a researcher in the field of distributed algorithms, a senior student of the subject, or one who have been actively working hands-on with commercial distributed system projects involving replication, consensus, and so on, then the result is entirely different: everything will be clear as day, coming together nicely to provide a new step or solution which he or she can build on existing knowledge and experience, even possibly leaving said reader to wonder, '*it is so obvious, why did none of us think along these lines earlier?*'

Indeed, the second effort by Lamport - *Paxos Made Simple* - is a huge improvement over the first, written with a lot of sensitivity and sense of purpose (of demystifying and uncomplicating). For most of the paper, Lamport uses simple and clean english to show how obvious - and almost inevitable - the protocol is. However, one cannot help but imagine that the damage is already done by the time this paper arrived. A casual reader never gets stuck at any point in this paper but is prone once again to be left 'in a vacuum' towards the end, with more questions than answers. This brings us to a fundamental drawback - if one can use such a term for an intentional choice - present in both papers: there is very little discussion or guidance on how a practical implementation of paxos should look like. Now, as we have seen before, a real-life implementation for state machine replication has at its heart a replication mechanism for a series of values; which in turn is built on top of a core protocol that provides consensus on a single value. Such a core consensus protocol should provide both safety and termination (liveness) properties. Reading either paper, one often gets the impression that Lamport has focused primarily only on 1. such a core protocol, and 2. its safety property. Starting with the termination property of the consensus protocol, then the replication mechanism, learning mechanisms, fault tolerance, leader election, and so on, the subsequent 'gap' or distance to a practical implementation is covered in an increasing relaxed or vague manner, with only a few high level guidelines or tentative suggestions for implementers. This will certainly work for many experienced professionals, but the beginners and uninformed will usually have a hard time with the subject.

11.5.7 Moving on - to a consensus algorithm which is easier to understand

Having dealt with paxos and its complexities, how would one react to a new consensus protocol whose genesis is introduced thus by its authors?

After struggling with Paxos ourselves, we set out to find a new consensus algorithm that could provide a better foundation for system building and education. Our approach was unusual in that our primary goal was understandability: could we define a consensus algorithm for practical systems and describe it in a way that is significantly easier to learn than Paxos?

With extreme interest, no doubt. Let us move on to the Raft consensus protocol, then. We will not yet let go of paxos completely though, because a certain amount of comparison is inevitable as we get started with raft.

11.6 The Raft consensus protocol

The paper which introduced raft - as a consensus algorithm for managing a replicated log - was named *"In Search of an Understandable Consensus Algorithm"*. True to its name, the paper is quite friendly to read through as compared to the paxos paper(s). The authors, Diego Ongaro and John Ousterhout, make their priority very clear before getting into the details of their protocol:

We had several goals in designing Raft....But our most important goal—and most difficult challenge—was understandability. It must be possible for a large audience to understand the algorithm comfortably....There were numerous points in the design of Raft where we had to choose among alternative approaches. In these situations, we evaluated the alternatives based on understandability....we used two techniques that are generally applicable. The first technique is the well-known approach of problem decomposition....Our second approach was to simplify the state space by reducing the number of states to consider...

This is indeed a refreshing and reassuring approach to introducing a new protocol or algorithm. This attitude faithfully reflects in the finished algorithm, which is quite clean, sleek, and modular. There is no denying that paxos has a very elegant core; however, in comparison to raft, paxos as a final product tends to appear a bit fuzzy and muddled except to the brightest minds and thoroughly seasoned professionals. We have seen how paxos adopts a very decentralised or asymmetric peer-to-approach to log replication: individual log entries may be proposed by different nodes, and the protocol only suggests a weak form of leadership (as covered in section *11.5.5.2..3*). While such an approach has undeniable mathematical beauty, all subsequent complexities in terms of comprehension and implementation - and there are several - are left as responsibilities to the respective parties, i.e. the readers and implementers.

11.6.1 Strong leadership

Right off the bat, raft takes a different approach when it comes to leadership:

- *There is a single leader, and the rest are followers.*

All client requests get redirected to the leader. It is the leader's responsibility, and the leader's responsibility alone, to see to it that each log entry is replicated at each follower. A leader never modifies or delete existing entries in its log; any inconsistencies are always resolved by forcing followers to duplicate the leader's log. All this is in stark contrast to paxos, where a node could play the role of proposer in one or more concurrent elections while simultaneously acting as acceptor in others. Indeed, such a paxos node may also operate as a learner at the same time, receiving updates from one or more distinguished learners. None of this complexity happens in raft, which places a clear emphasis on the problem of electing a leader. True to their stated aim of reducing complexity by problem decomposition, raft splits the consensus problem broadly into two independent subproblems:

- Leader election
- Log replication

In addition, addressing the safety property can be thought of as a third major subproblem. However, the solutions to the first two subproblems contain key elements which directly address the safety factor. For example, the leader election mechanism has safeguards to prevent an outdated node (i.e. a node whose state is not recent) from being considered for leadership. This is critical because information, in terms of log entries, always flows in only one direction - from the leader to followers, and this requires only qualified nodes (in terms of information state) to be considered for the post of leader. As another example, the process of log replication contains mechanisms to correct inconsistencies in the state of followers; a follower who is lagging behind, or holding on to incorrect log entries, will be 'pulled' back to an updated state by the leader. Let us also quickly note that raft uses RPCs (Remote Procedure Calls) for communication between nodes.

11.6.1.1 Leader failure and term

Just like any other node, it is possible that a leader does crash. The protocol is designed to ensure detection of such an event, and a subsequent election of a new leader. The possibility of changing leadership implies that a leader has an associated *term.* The concept of term is a key one in raft and stands of the duration of time during which a specific node served as leader. In raft, the passage of time can be thought of as a series of *terms* (1, 2, 3,...), each of which is the tenure of a particular node as leader. For example, term 2 refers to a period in the system when a new leader has been elected following the failure of the first or original leader. If this new leader fails at some point, another node is elected as leader and term 3 starts from that point onwards. This brings about an interesting implication as far as log entries are concerned: we have already seen how each log entry reaches a follower from the leader, and hence, each log entry is not only associated with a particular slot, but also its origin, i.e. a term number which in turn represents the leader during that period. In other words, to compare log entries for a particular slot between two nodes, it is sufficient to check if the term associated with the log entry in either case is the same. If so, the contents of the slot are guaranteed to be the same. Note that each node stores the current term number, which is updated (increased) each time a new leader is elected. Also, the term is a key information carried by most messages in raft. For example, a follower will not honour a log replication message from a leader that carries an older term. This naturally suggests that term is a piece of data that each node should keep on persistent storage. Next, let us take a closer look at the mechanism of leader election as proposed by raft.

11.6.2 Leader election

Raft mandates that a leader send regular heartbeat messages to all followers. If this stops happening, followers end up timing out. This is called an *election timeout*. The protocol ensures that all followers do not timeout simultaneously - by the simple measure of requiring the use of random election timeouts. For example, one node will allow a maximum interval of 200 milliseconds between heartbeat messages while another node will not be prepared to wait more than 150 milliseconds. Each timed out node immediately starts an election, and the use of such randomised election timeouts restrict the possibility of multiple elections being triggered concurrently. A follower who starts an election after losing patience waiting for a heartbeat from the leader is called a *candidate*. Naturally, the first thing a candidate does is to increment its term value. Next, it sends out vote request messages to other nodes. A follower (i.e. a node who has not timed out yet) sends a vote reply upon receiving a vote request, and also updates its term value to the current one as indicated in the vote request message. Note that a follower, during a particular term, will vote for only one candidate. This implies that a follower must note down the fact on persistent storage once it votes for a candidate, to prevent the following sequence from happening:

1. Node A receives vote request from candidate B and provides a vote
2. Node A crashes and immediately restarts
3. Node A receives vote request from candidate C and provides a vote, its second vote in the current term

A candidate receiving a majority of votes becomes the leader and informs others accordingly by initiating heartbeat messages. A candidate becomes a follower upon seeing a heartbeat message with a term that is at least as large as own value of term. If multiple candidates appear simultaneously, none might obtain a majority - the term ends with no leader, and each candidate backs off (again, for a random period of time) before trying again, starting the next term. Overall, the leader election mechanism benefits tremendously from the relatively simple technique of using randomised timeouts, which reduces the possibility of conflicts and complicated scenarios.

Having come across the concept of nodes acting as candidates, let us take a moment to list and contrast the three different roles played by nodes in a raft cluster:

- Leader

- Followers
- Candidates

Of these three, followers are completely passive; they never issue *RPC*s of any kind, and only respond to incoming *RPC*s. In contrast, a leader is always center-stage; playing an active role, issuing *RPC*s to effect log replication as well as to provide proof-of-life heartbeats. Candidates also issue *RPC*s, as we just saw, to solicit votes from followers.

11.6.2.1 Criteria for leadership

As we have noted before, a node must be qualified enough to be considered for leadership. This is critical because the information content of follower nodes is controlled solely by the leader; a raft cluster is dictatorial in the sense that a leader forces every follower's log to become a duplicate of the leader's log. Hence, a node who is 'lagging behind' in terms of state must not be allowed to become a leader. Raft requires that a vote request message contains the status of the candidate's log. A vote will be denied if a recipient finds own log to be more up-to-date than the candidate. Here is how the raft specification requires that two logs be compared:

Raft determines which of two logs is more up-to-date by comparing the index and term of the last entries in the logs. If the logs have last entries with different terms, then the log with the later term is more up-to-date. If the logs end with the same term, then whichever log is longer is more up-to-date.

Since votes from a majority are required for a candidate to win an election, and a recipient will not vote for a candidate with a log that is not as up-to-date as own log, the conclusion is simple: *a candidate can win an election only if its log contains all committed entries in the system.* This is a direct result of commits happening by the criteria of majority; implying that any majority in the system will have at least one member who has the latest commit, and that such a member will effectively 'block' a candidate whose log is not as up-to-date as own log, by denying a vote. Note the implication of such an election criterion: *if a leader commits an entry, it is guaranteed that said entry will be present in the logs of all future leaders.*

11.6.2.2 Function of a leader

All client requests reach the leader, as mentioned before. Think of a client request to be carrying a single command, which, when executed, produces a state change. The leader's responsibility is to distribute the command to followers, at a specific target slot. Once this step is successful for a majority of followers, the leader does a commit - i.e. executes the command, thus updating the state of its state machine - and instructs its followers to do so as well. In the coming sections, we will look into the details of how a leader goes about its job of ensuring log replication and resolving any inconsistencies or conflicts.

11.6.2.3 Criteria for a successful leader election

We have already seen one possibility where an election does not select a new leader: split votes, resulting in no majority. Of course, the chances of this happening can be highly reduced by a correct use of randomised timeouts. In particular, the election timeout should fall within a sensible *range* of values. Since elections effectively use a broadcast strategy, the broadcast messages must reach the intended recipients before their individual election timeouts expire. Since the broadcast time is part of the system specification, election timeouts should be chosen based on the same. Also, the participant servers should stay up long enough to give a chance to the election mechanism to make progress. With all this in mind, the raft specification mentions the following requirement:

Broadcast time << Election timeout << Mean time between server failures

It is interesting to compare the paxos approach with that of raft, in this context. The more complex paxos mechanism which allows multiple proposers, has a distinct edge when it comes to availability in the presence of node failures - at least theoretically. Raft has a design which invests a lot in strong leadership, hence the system implementer must take extreme care to make sure that leader elections work effectively - because a raft cluster remains unavailable during a leader election. A paxos cluster is more 'distributed' in a sense and is better suited, at least theoretically, to be implemented in a looser fashion over more heterogeneous hardware.

11.6.3 Log replication

In section *11.5.1*, we noted how raft requires a leader to never modify or delete any entries in its log, and instead, resolve conflicts by forcing followers' logs to be modified to match the leader's log. Let us consider an example to see how this is actually done. In the process, we will also get to see the details of the message formats used by raft. To begin with, we will consider a simple situation where the system is running fine and the elected leader is up and healthy.

11.6.3.1 An example - without leader failure

Consider a raft cluster consisting of 5 machines or nodes - A, B, C, D, E. Let node A be the leader. Node A is up and running and going about its duties in a fine manner. So far, the system has processed 10 client requests. This means that commands have been written to 10 slots in each node, and all 10 commands have been committed (i.e. applied to the state machine) at all nodes. Now, a 11th client request comes in and reaches the leader, i.e. node A.

Node A notes that the first unoccupied slot is 11. This might be a good time to compare quickly with paxos and note that raft does not provide a similar opportunity for holes to develop in logs. Coming back to the example, node A parses the client request and identifies the associated command. Let the command be *C11*. Now, node A first writes *C11* to slot 11 in its log, and then generates a message to each of the followers. The message content is (broadly) something like:

- *Please add C11 to slot 11 in your log*
- *Oh, by the way, the command in slot 10 in my log is C10*

The second part of the message is a conflict resolution mechanism, a sanity check of sorts. Each node compares this information with the status of its log - in this case, verifies that slot 10 in its log contains the command *C10* - and if there is a mismatch, refuses to process the leader's message. In either case, the corresponding reply is dispatched to the leader. We assume no mismatch scenarios in this case, as everything has been working just fine. Once the leader receives success responses from a majority, the leader commits *C11* and informs each node to do so as well. This action happens through a heartbeat message, and predictably, the heartbeat message contains a slot number which indicates the slot up to which the leader has committed its log entries. In other words, the leader issues the next heartbeat message with the following content:

- *I have committed commands up to and including slot 11*

This is a cue for each node to check own commit status and update the same. In this situation, each node has committed only up to slot 10 before receiving the heartbeat message described earlier. Upon receiving the heartbeat, each node commits C11 and updates local commit status (eg: *all commands up to slot 11 have been committed*) accordingly.

Note that a leader is free to include multiple new entries in a message. As ever, this is accompanied by information regarding the slot previous to the first new entry. For example:

- *Please commit command C7 to slot 7*
- *Please commit command C8 to slot 8*
- *Please commit command C9 to slot 9*
- *Please commit command C10 to slot 10*
- *Oh, by the way, the command in slot 6 in my log is C6*

Note: while providing information regarding the slot previous to the first new entry, the actual content of the slot need not be mentioned at all. As noted in section *11.6.1.1*, the term of a log entry is sufficient for this purpose. So, an equivalent and shorter version of the sanity-check would be:

- *Oh, by the way, the term of the command in slot 6 is 1*

To understand this, we only need to note that the same slot in two different nodes can hold different commands only if those commands were received from different leaders.

Let us next consider a different example, a more complicated one that contains leader failures.

11.6.3.2 Another example - with leader failure

Consider the same cluster, having recently started up from a fresh initial state. Node A was elected the leader. A client request came in, which node A processed and replicated successfully. As a result, the command *C1* has been written to slot 1 and committed at every node. A second client request comes in. Let *C2* be the associated command. Node A inserts *C2* to slot 2 in own log, and generates a message to node B, as a result of which node B writes *C2* to slot 2 in its log. Before getting a chance to generate any more messages, node A crashes. This results in silence as far as heartbeat messages are concerned. We have seen how (and why) raft mandates the use of randomised election timeouts; let node B timeout first and trigger an election. Note that all nodes are equal at this point as far as commit status is concerned. Node A and node B do have an extra log entry at slot 2 as compared to nodes C, D, and E. But this entry is not committed yet because node A crashed before it got a chance to issue messages to C, D, and E. Due to the equal commit status, any of the followers can turn into a candidate and have equal chances of getting elected. In this case, node B had an advantage thanks to its election timeout being shorter than others and was elected as a result. Here is what the cluster looks like, at this point:

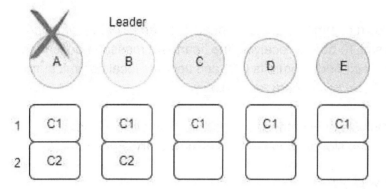

Let a third client request come in, carrying a command C3. As leader, node B receives and processes this request. As the first step, B adds C3 to slot 3 in its log. Next, it sends a message to C, D, and E with a similar content:

- Please add *C3* to slot 3 in your log
- Oh, by the way, the command in slot 2 in my log is *C2*

Now, as expected, each message receives a negative response. This is because C, D, and E have their second slot empty. What node B does next forms a key aspect of how conflicting follower logs are updated eventually by the leader. Upon receiving each negative reply, node B sends the following message:

- Please add *C2* to slot 2 of your log
- Please add *C3* to slot 3 of your log
- Oh, by the way, the command in slot 1 in my log is *C1*

Now, this generates a positive response in each case, as the sanity check is satisfied at C, D, and E. We can see what node B did here: upon seeing the initial conflict (for slot 2), it moved a step back (to slot 1), and issued a new message requesting for additions from that point onwards. This process is repeated till a common matching point is found, even though in this example only a single iteration was required. Once B notices that all nodes have updated commands for slot 2 and slot 3, and also that its current commit status is only up to slot 1, it executes *C2* and *C3* and updates its commit status accordingly. The next heartbeat message carries this updated commit status, resulting in each follower committing *C2* and *C3* as well. Next, let us consider a stormier set of events in the same cluster.

11.6.3.3 Yet another example - with multiple leader failures

We consider a different train of events now. Let the original leader, node A, crash at the exact same point as in the previous example. A leader election happens, and let node E get elected - rather than node B - as represented below:

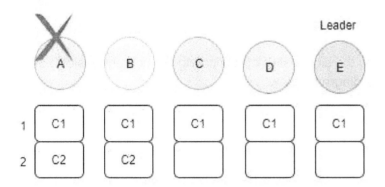

At this point, a third request arrives and reaches node E. Processing the third request, assume that node E makes progress till the point described by the following diagram, and promptly crashes:

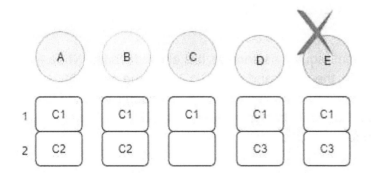

Note that node A is back up by now. The failure of node E triggers a new leader election and let node A get re-elected as the new leader. Node A quickly notices that the content of slot 2 has been replicated to only B; so, its first action is to generate messages to C, D, and E to remedy the situation. There are four distinct possibilities here:

1. Assuming node A stays up long enough, it would ensure that *C2* is replicated at slot 2 in nodes C, D, and E (assuming E is up by then), overwriting existing entries at D and E. Refer below:

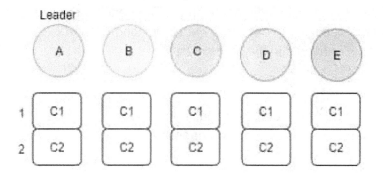

2. Assume that node A makes no progress, before crashing again

3. Assume that node A accomplishes the single step of replicating the content of slot 2 at C, before crashing again. See the diagram below:

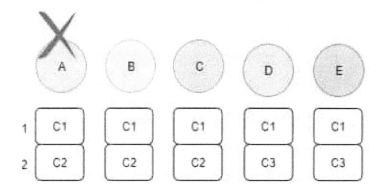

4. Consider that node A receives a client request as soon as it is elected leader. Node A stays up long enough to replicate *C4*, the command associated with the new request to, B and C, before crashing. This allows A to commit *C4* since it has been replicated to a majority. Note how the conflict resolution mechanism ensures that slot 2 of C also gets updated in the process. Refer the following diagram:

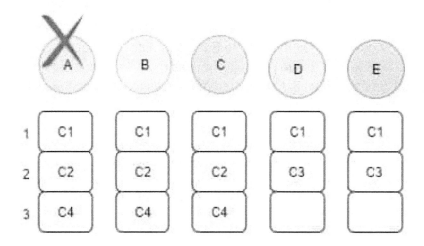

In scenario (1), node A notices that slot 2 has been replicated everywhere - and goes ahead with the commit. In scenario (2), obviously nothing happens because node A crashes right away without making any progress. Subsequently, for example, node D could get elected as leader next, and would replicate *C3* in slot 2 at all followers, thus overwriting the content of slot 2 at A and B. This eventuality is represented in the next diagram:

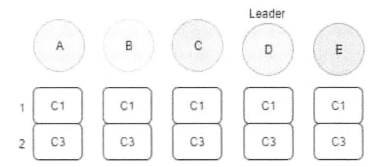

The 3rd scenario is interesting: node A does get slot 2 updated at a majority, so does it try and commit *C2* for slot 2? Raft says *no* to such an action, because the majority is spread across multiple terms - the updates in slot 2 for A and B happened during term 1, while that in slot 2 for C happened during term 3, when A was re-elected. The commit was allowed in scenario (1), despite the updates being done across different terms, because the update happened at all nodes. Since *C2* is not committed to slot 2 by node A, and node A crashes, we can imagine a similar result as the first scenario: perhaps node E gets elected next and updates all followers to have *C3* written at slot 2. The following diagram shows this outcome:

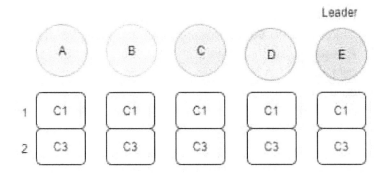

The 4th scenario is perhaps even more interesting: node A handles a new request, managing to replicate it at a majority of nodes (A, B, and C) before crashing again. However, unlike the previous situation, A is allowed to commit the new entry to slot 3 - because slot 3 at A, B, and C were updated in the same (current) term - and manages to do so before crashing. This also firmly places D and E in a not-up-to-date state, preventing either of them being elected again right away. Either B or C would be elected next, and ensure that both D and E are updated to match the log contents held at A, B, and C. This would mean that the content of slot 2 at D and E would be overwritten with *C2*. Note how the commit of an entry (*C4*) allows the commit of all preceding entries (*C2*) as well. The next diagram shows the result just discussed, with B acting as leader following the crash of A:

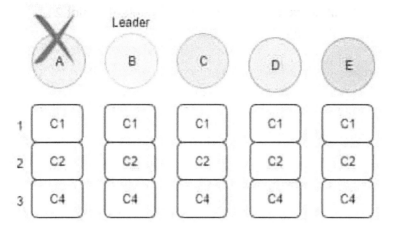

These examples also outline the broad algorithm followed by a leader:

- Service client requests if there are any
- Send regular heartbeat messages
- Work on catching up any followers who seem to be lagging behind in terms of last-written log entry

The last item requires that a leader keep track of the status of each follower, in terms of the last/latest slot that was written to. Just like every node keeps track of the first empty slot in its own log, the leader keeps track of this info for *every* node. Upon assuming leadership for the first time, a node assumes that each follower has the same first empty slot as itself and generates update messages based on such info. This might produce negative responses initially, but the conflict resolution mechanism described earlier ensures that each follower log is soon updated to match that of the leader. A leader crashing while in the midst of replicating a log entry, as happened to node A earlier, will find itself in an uneven state upon reacquiring leadership later - an entry has been updated at some nodes, but not at others. As seen earlier, such a node, upon assuming leadership again, immediately starts working on fixing this asymmetric situation.

11.6.4 Reconfiguration

In this section, we discuss how raft facilitates modifications to the cluster membership. Raft approaches this functionality in a rather restricted manner, albeit with good reason. Only a single node can be added to, or removed from, a raft cluster at a time. Consider such an operation a *step*; more complex operations can then be built using a series of such steps, thus making major modifications to the cluster membership. The idea is to prevent the formation of independent majorities (leading to multiple simultaneous leaders) in the cluster during the process of reconfiguration. If only a single server is added, such situations are impossible: any two majorities will overlap.

11.6.4.1 The mechanism

As we saw with paxos in section *11.4.4.3.7*, a reconfiguration command is processed (written to log and committed) just like any other command. There is a subtle difference, though: as soon as a reconfiguration command is written to the log, the new configuration takes effect. Note that this is a direct consequence of the centralised nature of raft. Commit happens next, once a majority of nodes from the new configuration has written down the reconfiguration command in their logs.

11.6.4.2 Adding a server

Now that we have described how the actual reconfiguration step works, it is time to note that the addition of a node requires something else to be done *before* executing the actual reconfiguration step. In other words, replicating and applying the configuration change is only the second step. The first step, then, is to introduce the new node to the leader, and to catch up the new node in terms of log content. It is the leader's responsibility to replicate its log content at the new node and then trigger the reconfiguration step. Naturally, a newly added node does not get to vote while it is executing the first step. Indeed, the new node is not part of the cluster configuration during this phase due to the simple reason that the reconfiguration step is yet to execute.

11.6.4.3 Removing a server

Removing a server follows a similar yet simpler mechanism, since only the reconfiguration step needs to be executed - which is executed by all nodes except the one being removed. This also leaves the removed node somewhat 'in the dark', a situation not helped by the sudden silence in terms of heartbeats. A removed node, unless shutdown immediately by the leader as part of an established post-reconfiguration process, can start a new election, thus interfering with the smooth functioning of the cluster. To prevent such scenarios, raft allows nodes to prevent voting when the node knows that the leader is intact and functioning (i.e. the node has heard recently from the leader).

11.6.4.4 Changing the leader

Raft provides a simple mechanism for effecting a change in leadership. Assume that node A is the leader, and the admin now wants node B to be the leader (for whatever reason(s)). From what we have learnt about raft so far, it should be easy to deduce that two things need to be achieved for this to happen:

1. Node B must be as up-to-date as the leader, i.e. node A
2. Node B must trigger an election

As is the convention in raft, these two responsibilities land squarely with the leader - node A. The first thing node A does is to catch up node B, if required, by sending additional log entries to node B. Once this is accomplished, node A sends a message to node B, asking it to trigger an election. Upon receiving such a message, node B acts as if its election timeout just expired and takes the appropriate step - i.e. triggers an election.

11.6.5 Rounding up: messages in Raft

To conclude our journey on raft, let us look at the formal messages as specified by the protocol. Raft specifies that nodes communicate using remote procedure calls or *RPC*s. Let us look at the various *RPC*s and their formats, next.

11.6.5.1 AppendEntries

The *AppendEntries RPC* is issued by the leader for two distinct purposes:

1. To replicate one or more log entries
2. As the heartbeat

The message contains the following fields:

- The term of the leader (eg: 3)
- The address of the leader (a hostname or IP address)
- A set of new entries
- The log index of the entry preceding the new entries
- The term of the entry preceding the new entries
- The log index up to which the leader has committed

Note that *AppendEntries* does not contain any new entries while being used as a heartbeat.

11.6.5.2 RequestVote

The *RequestVote* RPC is issued by a candidate during an election process and is a '*vote for me*' request as implied by its label. The various fields are the following:

- The candidate's term
- The candidate's address
- The index up to which the candidate's log is filled
- The term of the last entry in the candidate's log

As discussed elsewhere, the last two fields help a potential voter make a decision on the candidate's qualification for being a leader; if the candidate is holding on to a log that is not as up-to-date as the voter's log, a vote is declined.

11.6.5.3 AddServer

The *AddServer RPC* is issued to the leader, by the system administrator, to introduce a new node to the cluster. Predictably, this message contains a single piece of information: the new node's address.

11.6.5.4 RemoveServer

The *RemoveServer RPC* is issued to the leader, by the system administrator, to remove a new node from the cluster. Again, as expected, this message contains a single field: the address of the node to be removed.

11.6.5.5 TimeoutNow

The *TimeoutNow RPC* is issued by the leader, to the next leader, to trigger a change in leadership. This is an empty message; a simple trigger that has the sole purpose of making the recipient start an election.

11.7 Conclusion

We come to the end of a rather intense chapter, where we started off with the 2-phase commit, followed by the 3-phase commit, examined multiple example scenarios introducing log replication and state machine replication, before finally discussing two practical consensus and replication strategies in the form of paxos and raft. We analysed and compared both protocols in detail, observing how paxos can be hard to comprehend and how raft takes explicit steps to avoid a similar outcome. In a sense, paxos has undeniable beauty while carrying an extreme *handle-with-care* label; raft is more methodical and less adventurous, placing heavy emphasis on simplicity and understandability. They are not unlike two different maps to a particular destination: one map containing only a basic direction backed up highly cryptic clues and tentative suggestions to reach the destination, while the other one contains highly specific instructions right down to the last mile. The first one is for seasoned explorers, and each one might end up at the destination using very different routes. The second one is for a wider audience, including beginners and hobbyists, and most of them are likely to deduce the same route from the map.

11.8 What's next

Consider a class of algorithms that fall within the following range of functions:

- Monitoring
- Search
- Snapshots
- Measurements

Let us label such as 'investigate' algorithms. They typically execute in a distributed environment to produce a certain result, which is then exploited by a 'consumer' distributed algorithm. The essential idea always is to scan or analyse the network in a deep and systematic manner, in order to come up with data which will then aid future calculations. We move on to such algorithms from the next chapter onwards.

Chapter 12. Graph Algorithms

12.1 Graphs: an introduction

We have already referred to, and used, the concept of graphs during several occasions in earlier chapters: starting with section *4.2* where we analysed a network which resembled a *connected grap*h, we dealt with *directed graphs* of the *strongly connected* kind in chapter 7, came across *complete graphs* in section *8.4*, and even contrasted connected graphs with complete ones in section *9.4*. For the sake of formality, then, let us introduce a graph as a collection of *edges* and *vertices*, where the edges connect some or all of the vertices to each other. Applying this description to our current field of interest, it should be obvious that vertices become compute nodes or entities, while edges represent the communication links between them. Note that we also consider scenarios where edges have weights associated with them, and the weights are always assumed to be non-negative quantities.The graph view makes it highly convenient to represent several properties of interest in a networked distributed system, and to formulate algorithms which measure or calculate such properties. We will begin with the challenge posed by network traversals.

12.2 Traversals

Consider an arbitrary network; a set of nodes or entities with connecting links among them. Perhaps these are a bunch of houses in a given neighbourhood. We will assume each house to be connected to one or more houses in its immediate neighbourhood by a dedicated pathway. The challenge involves circulating a piece of information to each house, or conversely, collecting a piece of information from each house. Either way, each house needs to be visited; in other words, the network needs to be *traversed*, starting at a given origin. In this example scenario, consider that one of the residents, Mary, is assigned a responsibility by the town council. She has to circulate a memorandum in her neighbourhood and get each resident to sign the same. Finally, the fully signed memorandum has to be submitted back to the town council. How does Mary go about this task?

12.2.1 A Depth-first approach

For simplicity, consider that Mary has only one immediate neighbour, Paul. In turn, Paul has two immediate neighbours - John and Smith - and that is it. That is the whole small neighbourhood right there, to keep things simple. Mary walks over to Paul, updates him on the task at hand, hands over the memorandum, and walks back to her house. What does Paul do? Paul has a pathway to John, and another to Smith. John and Smith are not connected by a pathway. Paul walks to John, provides an update, and hands over the memorandum. All John has to do is to sign the memorandum, and hand it back - because John is not in a position to propagate it any further. Having collected John's signature, Paul walks to meet Smith, where a similar situation unfolds. Having collected two signatures, Paul walks back to his own residence, signs the memorandum, and delivers it back to Mary. What does Mary do? Mary signs the document and delivers it to the town official. Job done.

The following diagram shows the configuration assumed by the example.

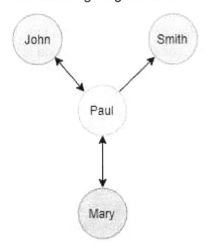

One immediate takeaway from this very simple example is how the memo travels to the edge of the network before the first signature is collected. Indeed, it is John who signs the memo first, followed by Smith, and then John, and finally it is Mary who signs the memo last. This is known as a *depth-first traversal* (*DFT*), due to the probing nature of the mechanism involved.

Now, what if John and Smith were connected? Paul could hand over the memo to John and walk back home. John would then approach Paul and collect Paul's signature. We will assume that Smith is new to the neighbourhood and is not aware that he has a pathway to Paul's house. This is represented by the unidirectional link between Paul and Smith in the earlier diagram as well as the next one.

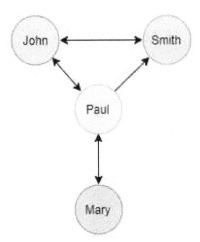

So, Smith is not connected to anyone else, as far as he is concerned; he immediately signs the memo and returns it to the waiting John, who then delivers it back to Paul. Now, as in the earlier scenario, Paul makes his way to Smith's house with the memo - Smith informs that he has already signed the document, so Paul walks back to his home, signs the memo and returns it to

Mary - same process as earlier. Can this be optimised a bit further so that Paul saves a quite unnecessary stroll to Smith's house? Of course, Paul can check the memo and quickly realise that Smith has already signed it and avoid a trip to Smith's house. Also note how this new neighbourhood model - where one can reach Smith's house from Paul's house in either a direct manner, or via John's place - is different from the original one in the sense that the new one is no longer a *tree*. A tree, then, is a graph variant such that loops are absent; there is exactly one path between any given pair of nodes.

Coming back to the optimisation that we just considered: this works well for signatures, specifically assuming that John could identify Smith's scrawl. What about an entirely different scenario where, say, the memo was an informational one of scant interest that required no signatures? In such a case, Paul's walk to Smith's place will indeed happen and indeed go wasted. Unless of course, each recipient of the memo takes a specific informational action - like hanging a sign-board outside his or her place - which can be viewed by any immediate neighbour - that says '*Okay, I received the memo already*'.

Now, a further twist: what if Mary has another neighbour, Linda, who in turn has one or more immediate neighbours of her own? As soon as Paul returns with the document, Mary would make her way to Linda's place, and the same algorithm repeats. In other words, Mary processes 'the tree' starting with Paul first, then addresses the one beginning with Linda. The next diagram shows this scenario where Mary is effectively connected to two networks, with Linda being her 'contact point' to the second network. There are possibly one or more other residents in Linda's network, which the diagram does not explicitly show.

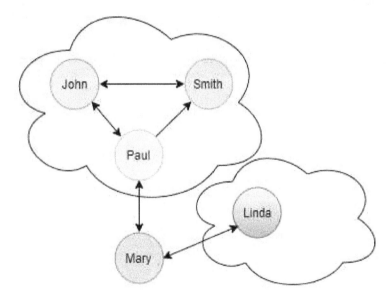

Let us try to formally present the algorithm which we just used in multiple configurations. Here is a flowchart representation of the procedure that we implemented:

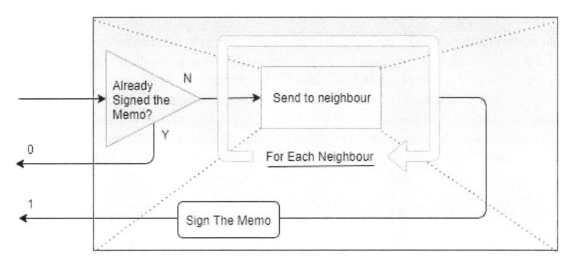

The inner rectangle contains the same mechanism as the outer one, a recursion as represented by the dotted lines. The 'output' of *0* represents the reply *'Oh I've already seen and signed the memo'*, while *1* represents the 'normal' scenario where a memo is returned by a person after having signed (and propagated) the same. Irrespective of the specific configuration, the strategy is the same: from each point, explore all options to go forward; when out of options at any point, execute the action of interest at the local node (in this case, collect a signature), retreat to the prior point, and repeat the procedure.

12.2.1.1 Effort - message delivery

We will first focus on the original neighbourhood that we assumed, where there is no pathway between the residences of John and Smith. When we use the word 'message', we imagine, say, Mary walking to Paul's house with a memo that needs to be signed, or Paul walking back to Mary's place with a signed document. Let us think of the message cost this way: each participant receives a message (the memo) and generates a return message (the signed memo). In fact, the previous statement is not totally correct - because it is not applicable to the source, who is Mary in the example. Of course, Mary does receive the memo from someone (a town official) and does submit it back in a fully signed form, but we consider those actions to be 'outside' of the algorithm. So, the total message cost is 2 messages per person, excluding the individual who triggered the signature collection drive - for a final message cost given by *2(n - 1)* where n specifies the number of houses in the neighbourhood. In other words, the message cost is linear to the number of participants, i.e. *O(n)*.

Needless to say, we are missing something here. This relatively simple calculation is applicable only if the original neighbourhood configuration which formed a tree in graph-speak - i.e. where a participant receives the memo only once. In other words, we were considering a situation where the number of links is *n - 1* among a set of *n* participants. Once we insert more links that in turn create loops, as we did when we decided to add a pathway between John and Smith, we have to consider two more messages for each such link that is added. Imagine this for a *complete graph* where each node has a link connecting it to every other node - there are *n(n - 1)/2* links, and obviously the message cost becomes $O(n^2)$. There should be a way to optimise this further, and we will get to that soon.

12.2.1.2 Applicability to a network of compute nodes

How do we apply this to a network of compute nodes? The memo in our example can be imagined as a network packet of some sort. The system administrator sends a trigger to some node, which then plays the role of the source node S from where the algorithm kicks off. Node S creates a message packet and gets things moving. Each recipient, and finally node S, appends certain local information to the packet. The information could be, for example, performance numbers of interest - like *CPU* utilisation, or requests processed per second, memory usage, and so on. In the end, node S finishes the process by adding own information to the packet and returning the same to the system administrator, who now has valuable information regarding the health of the whole system.

Just as we considered earlier, a message packet could possibly be analysed by any node to obtain the list of recipients that the message has already passed through. But then again, the message content may be of a type which does not lend itself to such comprehension. In the latter case, message cost can possibly suffer; unless of course, we implement the message equivalent of the 'hanging sign-board' technique from earlier - a node informs all neighbours upon receiving the message packet, by sending a brief notice that says, *'hey I received the message packet'*. This would keep everyone informed about who (among one's neighbours) has received the message packet already and who has not.

Coming back to the example with this information at hand, we note that John realises, one way or the other, that Smith does not need to be approached in a future situation where, say, a second memo needs to be signed by everyone. This is a powerful concept as far as a network is concerned: the network has effectively transformed itself into a new version where information dispersal or retrieval is easier or more efficient as compared to the original one. In particular, a loop has been eliminated. The next diagram depicts this achievement:

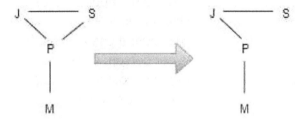

If we compare the two versions, we note that no participants have been removed; in graph parlance, all vertices remain intact while some edges are not longer present. The newly constructed variant is called a *spanning tree* of the first or original graph. Note that the spanning tree must retain all vertices, as well as the minimum number of edges such that connectivity is not reduced. All nodes reachable from the source or root node in the original graph must remain reachable in the spanning tree, too.

This technique can be extremely useful in more complicated network configurations, as in the case of complete graphs which we considered in the prior section. Indeed, we can modify the previous diagram to see how a complete graph network would be simplified by an initial depth-first traversal step:

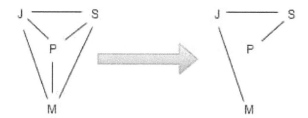

To summarise, once a spanning tree algorithm is executed, the network enriches itself with enough information that will increase the efficiency of future traversals. In particular:

- Each node, except the root node, identifies a single node as its 'parent' in the spanning tree
- Each node identifies a possibly reduced subset of its neighbours as its 'children'

There is room for improvement, though; a closer look at these transformations do indicate that communication costs could have been optimised further. In the previous diagram, the transformed network has P (Paul) three hops away from Mary (M), while Smith (S) is two hops away. In the original configuration, both Paul and Smith were a single hop away. Can we optimise the spanning tree any further? We *do* seem to have a target: assuming a root node, we do not want any node in the transformed network to end up being further away from the root node. This seems to suggest an entirely different form of traversal, altogether. It is time to look at *breadth-first* traversal (*BFT*), then.

12.2.2 A Breadth-first approach

We will use the following approach towards understanding breadth-first traversals: we will introduce *BFT* in the context of our original example (memo circulation), followed by an analysis of how *BFT* could be implemented in a distributed network of compute nodes. The first step is primarily intended as an illustration mechanism to broadly contrast *BFT* with its *DFT* counterpart; it involves steps that are vastly different, as we will subsequently see, to how *BFT* is used in an actual network of nodes to produce a spanning tree.

12.2.2.1 A second memo

Let us now consider a different neighbourhood in town and see how they circulate a similar memo. This is a slightly more populated neighbourhood, which will help illustrate the *BFT* technique clearly. As earlier, our story starts with a town official approaching a resident in the neighbourhood to hand over the responsibility of circulating a memo. The following diagram depicts the layout which the memo must traverse:

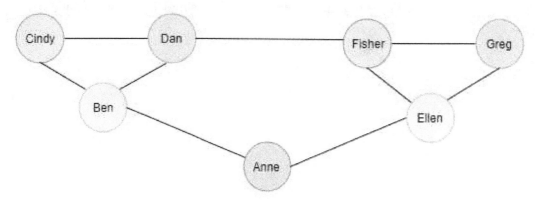

Here, Anne is the source node to whom the memo is first handed over for circulation. Before starting off, let us consider for a second the spanning tree which a *DFT* approach would have generated for this layout:

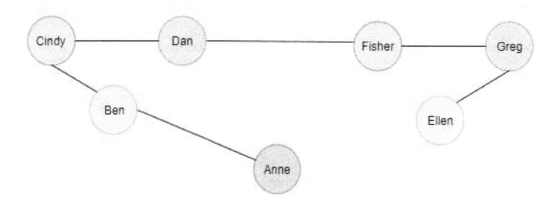

Not so great - considering that, for example, how far Ellen has ended up from Anne in the resulting transformed network. Let us next see how the residents actually go about their way of collecting signatures, so that we get to see and contrast the result produced by a *BFT*.

Anne notes that the content of the memo is on a single page, leaving the whole other empty side for collecting signatures. She first draws a vertical line down the middle of the empty side of the page, dividing the page into two sections: one side is for a list of names, the other side contains the corresponding signatures. Broadly, the following is the simple process which each resident follows upon receiving the memo, and it consists of two parts:

Part *one*: steps applicable when a resident receives the memo for the first time:

1. Note the sender as his or her 'parent'
2. Locate own name in the left column, and sign alongside on the right column
3. Add the names of all immediate neighbours to the left column, but do not add a name in case it is already present. To each name added on the left column, append own name as a hint, in brackets along side - for example: Ellen (Anne)
4. Return memo to sender (i.e. parent)

Part *two*: steps applicable when a resident receives the memo from the second time onwards:

1. If the sender is the parent, locate the first unsigned entry in the left column - i.e. the first name in the left column which does not have a signature alongside on the right - and relay on the memo in the direction of that person
2. If the sender is not the parent, relay on the memo to the parent

Seems a bit messy but let us see how it works out. Anne obviously starts off with an empty list, so she executes step (2) of the first set of instructions herself - she adds her own name as the first entry of the list in the left column, then signs alongside in the right column. Then she adds the names Ben and Ellen to the list, so that the left column appears as follows:

Anne (signed)
Ben (Anne)
Ellen (Anne)

At this point, the entry "Anne" carries her signature alongside, so step (3) in the first set of instructions mandates that she should send the memo to Ben.

What does Ben do? Ben notes Anne as his parent, and next, finds his name present in the left column list and signs alongside. Next, Ben adds the names of Cindy and Dan to the list of names in the left column, which now looks like the following:

Anne (signed)
Ben (Anne) (signed)
Ellen (Anne)
Cindy (Ben)
Dan (Ben)

That done, the memo in the current form is sent back to Anne - as per step (4). Anne examines the received memo and notices the first entry which does not carry a sign alongside: that of Ellen. So, Anne dispatches the document to Ellen. Ellen follows a procedure exactly similar to that of Ben, remembering Anne as her parent, adding the names of Fisher and Greg, and finally returning the memo to Anne. The list reads as follows at this point:

Anne (signed)
Ben (Anne) (signed)
Ellen (Anne) (signed)
Cindy (Ben)
Dan (Ben)
Fisher (Ellen)
Greg (Ellen)

Anne receives the memo back, and now Cindy is the first unsigned entry. Anne does a bit of 'path resolution' by noting that Cindy's name was added by Ben, so dispatches the memo to Ben. Now, Ben is not receiving the memo for the first time, so starts following the second set of instructions: by passing on the document to Cindy. Of course, Cindy signs against her name, refrains from adding Dan's name since it is already present, and returns the memo to Ben, who notices that the sender is not his parent (Anne), and hence forwards on the memo to his parent - as per rule 2. Anne notices the updated document to read as follows:

Anne (signed)
Ben (Anne) (signed)
Ellen (Anne) (signed)
Cindy (Ben) (signed)
Den (Ben)
Fisher (Ellen)
Greg (Ellen)

"Den" appears as the first unsigned entry, so the memo is now off to Den, via Ben, in a process exactly similar to how Cindy came to receive the document. Once the document comes back with Den's signature, Anne focuses on Fisher: the memo is sent to Fisher, via Ellen. As the last step, the memo reaches Greg via Ellen, and returns to Anne - who sees no more unsigned entries and returns the fully signed document to the town authorities. The diagram below shows the exact order in which signatures were collected, even though the actual communication pattern was far more complex and messier:

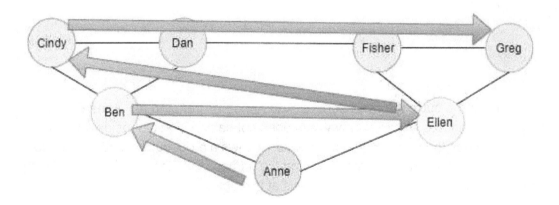

The 'overlay' constructed by the thicker arrows indicate a more disciplined or methodical manner in which signatures are collected, which actually belies the underlying complexity - a veritable maelstrom of path resolutions and messages, with Anne acting as the overall orchestrator who makes her way through the list, collecting signatures one by one. With *DFT*, each node benefited from a fair amount of delegation. For comparison, here is the order in which nodes are 'visited' when *DFT* is used:

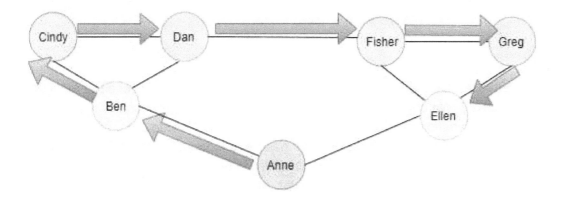

Also, note that Cindy and Dan added Ben as parent, Fisher and Greg added Ellen as parent, and Ben and Ellen added Anne as parent. This results in a simpler and more efficient spanning tree as shown in the next diagram:

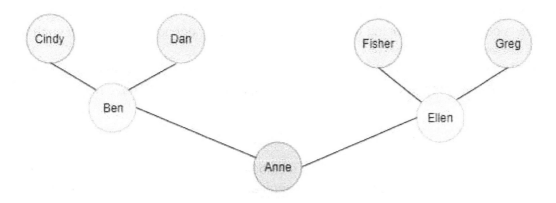

All the loop-producing links have been cleaned out, and there are exactly 6 links connecting a set of *6 + 1 = 7* nodes.

12.2.2.2 Applicability to a network of compute nodes

The previous example only served to highlight and contrast the order in which participant nodes are visited during a *BFT*, as well as to broadly illustrate the overall mechanism involved. The example used a communication mechanism that was costly, sequential, and rather centralised. Let us now look at how we can produce an efficient spanning tree by implementing *BFT* in a network of nodes, in an efficient, concurrent, and distributed manner.

12.2.2.2.1 A BFT algorithm

We start by remembering that we need each node to identify a single neighbour as its parent. A subsequent acknowledgement mechanism also achieves the opposite - parents identifying children among their neighbours. As ever, our algorithm is triggered at the root or source node, which sends a specific message to all its children. All recipients mark the sender as its parent, and pass the message on to each neighbour, who in turn identify its parent, and so on. This looks fairly simple. However, there is a question and a potential problem. We will look at the question first.

12.2.2.2.2 Termination

How will the described process end? At what point does the root node 'know' that the spanning tree has been constructed, i.e. the network has acquired the full knowledge needed to make future traversals efficient? We can solve this by assigning an additional responsibility to each recipient: generate a *termination message*. This process starts in a reverse order as compared to the 'main' mechanism; once a node realises that it has no neighbours to send the message to (or if it turns out that none of its neighbours are its children) - such a node ends up being a *leaf node* - it generates a termination message to its parent. A parent node waits till it receives termination messages from all its children before sending a termination message to its parent. Finally, once the root node receives termination messages from all its children, it knows that the job is complete. In fact, the termination mechanism directly exploited the newly-constructed spanning tree! If we try to imagine this whole operation, we see how the termination information flows from the extremities of the network and converges to a single point, i.e. the root or source node. This particular technique, hence, is known as *convergecast*. What we have just seen is an example of how a constructed spanning tree lends itself for implementing functionalities such as broadcast and convergecast.

We mentioned a potential problem in the previous section, so now we shall move right on to that.

12.2.2.2.3 A closer look

Assume that we are operating in an asynchronous distributed environment. Message delivery speeds are unpredictable; if A, B, and C form three vertices of a triangle, where A is the root node, there is a possibility that B receives the message from C - which is issued by C after it receives the message from A - and identifies C as its parent before it sees the direct message from A. In other words, we do not necessarily end up with a 'proper' spanning tree as *BFT* should ideally provide. What is evident here is that we allow a node no opportunities to correct its information regarding who its parent is. In the triangle example, B will receive the message from A, eventually. Once we allow A to modify its knowledge of parent from B to A, we have a solution. There is one slight hitch, however; in such situations, the node must not only correct own information, it should propagate the new knowledge to its neighbours. Refer the following pictorial representation of the mentioned sequence of events, starting with the original network configuration, followed by the first (flawed) version of a spanning tree, a partially corrected one next, and finally, the one that is fully corrected.

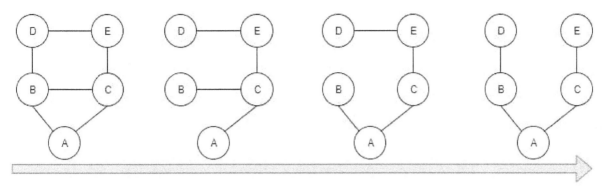

The second stage illustrates the result of B receiving C's message before the one from A. Once B corrects itself, it 'somehow' updates D as well. This results in D modifying its local state to replace E with B as parent. Our challenge, then, is to produce an algorithm which allows such corrective measures.

12.2.2.2.4 Another BFT algorithm

Returning momentarily to the previous example, it is obvious that B's corrective update to D must contain some (comparable) piece of information which D can use to override its current knowledge (that E is its parent). An integer value lends itself very well to such a requirement, so how about each message carrying the distance (in hops) of the sender from the root node? Obviously, the root node would use the value 0, then. Each recipient increments the received value before relaying it on to its neighbours. When node X sends, say, 5, to node Y, what node X is saying is 'I'm 5 hops away from the root node'. This leads node Y to conclude that 'In that case, I must be 6 hopes away from the root node' - based on the information it has so far, at least. Refer the next diagram to see how this would work for the prior example:

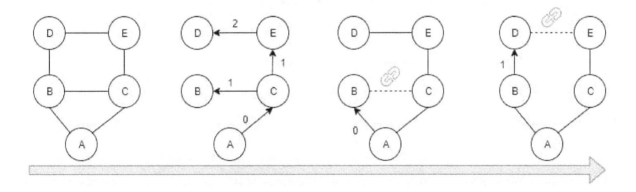

The above illustration shows how the link from B to C is 'broken' by the arrival of a 0-message from A, and how the same happens to the link between D and E thanks to a 1-message from B. The final result is a correct *BFT* spanning tree: no node is further away from the root as compared to the original configuration of the network. Note that termination works exactly as before, using convergecast. However, also note that a node could generate multiple 'correctional' messages, each of which would be acknowledged. This would imply that acknowledgements need to be tracked separately without any mix-ups.

12.2.2.2.5 Message complexity

It is easy to see that message cost is a product of the number of edges and number of nodes; a given node can receive multiple distance notifications, and each such message has to be acknowledged back as well as propagated in other directions (to neighbours). As a result, we state that the message cost is given by $O(mn)$ where m is the number of links and n is the number of nodes.

12.2.2.2.6 An optimisation

Let us go back to the network configuration depicted in the diagram from section *12.2.2.2.4*. Here, one can travel from any node to any other node with a maximum of two hops. This is another way of saying that the network diameter is 2. We will assume that the algorithm 'knows' what the network diameter is. With this perspective, let us rethink the action of E sending a 2-message to D. Since the network diameter is 2, E can cannot be more than 2 hops away from the root node; hence there is absolutely no point in E receiving D's 2-message and setting its concept of distance (from root node) to 3, because sooner or later that is going to be corrected to 2 (or less). We have our optimisation, then: suppress all messages that would carry a distance equal to, or more than, the network diameter. This approach reduces the message complexity to $O(dm)$, where d is the network diameter.

12.2.2.2.7 Introducing link costs and the Bellman-Ford algorithm

In this section, we introduce a new paradigm: each link in the system has an associated cost of usage. We shall assume that a recipient is billed a certain amount upon message delivery. When a recipient passes on the message to a neighbour, the total cost incurred so far by the message is also included in the message. This would mean that a root or source node will issue messages that carry the value '0'. A recipient takes delivery of the message after paying a bill of say, x units, and updates the '0' in the message to 'x' before forwarding the message to a neighbour - who in turn, might end up paying y units upon receipt, modify the message's content from 'x' to 'x + y' before forwarding to its neighbours, and so on. Needless to say, different links may have different costs associated with them. This is a crucial aspect of our new system, because this means that a direct link between two nodes will not make it to the spanning tree if there is a cheaper indirect route. In graph terminology, we say that the network now forms a *weighted graph*, where each edge (link) has an associated weight (cost).

The method of creating a spanning tree remains broadly unchanged, with the source initiating the process by broadcasting 0-messages to all neighbours, each of whom might update the message with a different cost - depending on the cost of the link along which the message arrived - before relaying the message to neighbouring nodes. This process repeats, propagating the message across the network, with each node selecting a parent whose message delivery yielded the lowest cost. This algorithm is known as the *Bellman-Ford* algorithm and it produces a spanning tree such that each node is located at the shortest distance (in terms of cost) possible from the source node. It is important to contrast such a *shortest-path spanning tree* with a *minimum spanning tree* - one which is not concerned with nodes being as close as possible to the root node, but only requiring that the *total* cost of the links present in the spanning tree be a minimum. The next diagram exemplifies the difference between the two concepts:

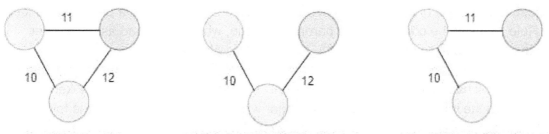

| The base network | The shortest-path spanning tree | The minimum spanning tree |

It is not hard to see how message complexity is affected once we start assigning costs to communication links: while paths were identified only by the number of hops earlier (before we considered link costs), now routes involving the same number of hops could have distinct weights or costs associated with them. This increases the message complexity exponentially, because of the sheer increase in the number of distinct routes in the system. If we imagine a link connecting node X to a set of n nodes, we note that the number of distinct distance notifications that can reach X along said link is $O(n^n)$ simply because that represents the possible number of different routes among a set of n nodes. This implies a message complexity given by $O(n^n m)$ for n nodes and m links.

12.2.2.2.8 Single-source V. Multi-source spanning tree construction

In the algorithms discussed so far, we assumed a single root or source node initiating the process of constructing a spanning tree. This is an ideal situation, one that is not necessarily available in real-life networks where there could be multiple simultaneous initiators. For example, in a cluster that is being 'booted up' all nodes could simultaneously attempt to create a spanning tree of the network. If we do assume that nodes have unique identifiers (which can be compared), we can allow each node to participate in multiple spanning tree constructions of which the one initiated by the node with minimum id will prevail in the end. Naturally, this requires more housekeeping at each node - since there are multiple 'instances' of spanning trees being built at any given moment. A node participating in the construction of a spanning tree initiated by node X will end such participation as soon as it sees (a message from) a node Y of lower id initiating its spanning tree. This would also imply that all messages carry the id of the initiating root node.

12.2.3 Tarry's algorithm

Let us conclude the current section on graph traversals by a quick look at one of the oldest graph traversal algorithms - one from the late 19th century, in fact. Gaston Tarry, a french mathematician, published a simple graph traversal algorithm for undirected graphs in 1895. The algorithm assumes an initiator node, i.e. a source node, who kicks off the proceedings by sending out a token which gets forwarded along by its recipients. There are only two simple rules:

1. A recipient of the token can forward the token along an edge only once
2. A recipient can forward the token back to the parent only when it is out of other options

Rule (1) is just another way of stating that a node will receive the token from a particular sender only once. Rule (2) uses the concept of the *parent* of a node, which is defined as the sender from whom the node received the token for the the first time. We can easily see that the algorithm terminates with the token arriving back at the source: each node sends the token back to the sender when it has no more options left to explore, so it is inevitable that the token will find its way back to the initiator - because each sender will sooner or later receive the token back. The following diagram illustrates an example execution of Tarry's algorithm in a 7-node and 7-edge network:

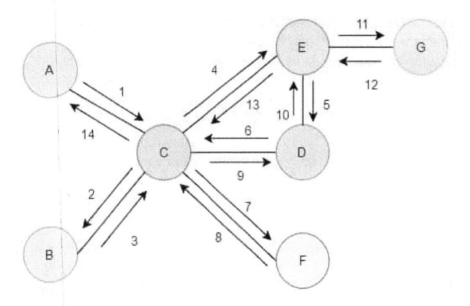

It is readily seen that the message complexity is given by *2m* for a graph consisting of m edges or paths. This is obviously because a token may be sent only once along an edge in a particular direction, leading to the token using each edge twice.

Interestingly, Tarry's algorithm can be trivially converted to provide *DFT* behaviour by the addition of a simple third rule:

    3. A node is allowed to immediately send the token back to its sender if rules (1) and (2)
    and are not violated by doing so

For example, the example in the previous diagram does not follow the *DFT* order. Node G is processed dead last, even after node F is processed. When node C receives the token from D, it sends the token to node F next. It could very well have sent it right back to node D, because D is not the parent of C (node A is the parent of C). Making this subtle tweak provides a *DFT* pattern, as seen below:

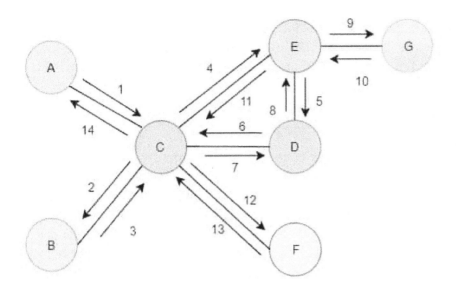

Next, let us shift focus to a concept that we briefly referred to elsewhere in this chapter (section 12.2.2.2.7).

12.3 Minimum Spanning Tree (MST)

We briefly introduced the concept of a minimum spanning tree in section *12.2.2.2.7*. In fact, the concept of an *MST* is important and useful enough to warrant a dedicated section of its own. Building an *MST* is a critical component of several real life applications: broadcasting, layout planning, circuit design, monitoring systems, and so on. We will look at an asynchronous distributed algorithm which a network can execute to construct its *MST*, as described in the 1983 paper *"A Distributed Algorithm for Spanning Trees"* by R.G. Gallager, P.A. Humblet, and P.M. Spira. Before diving into the algorithm, let us first try to gain an intuitive understanding of how we can build an *MST* - by considering how we can break down a fully built *MST*.

12.3.1 A bit of reverse engineering

Let us assume that we have an *MST* at hand. Our *MST* has a certain number of nodes and a certain number of edges or links. We assume edges to have distinct and finite weights. In other words, no edges have identical weights. We now consider a methodical process to break down this *MST* into individual nodes. We start off by identifying the edge with the *highest* weight, and then promptly remove it. What do we end up with? Starting with a single tree, we now have a forest consisting of exactly 2 subtrees. We apply the same process to each subtree, recursively, generating 'lower level' subtrees and processing them in turn, till we can continue no more - i.e. we are left with a forest of single-node subtrees, i.e. a group of independent, unconnected, nodes. If we imagine this process in the reverse fashion, starting with a collection of unconnected nodes, and then adding edges in order of increasing weight to connect two separate subtrees, we have an intuitive solution to building an *MST* out of its component nodes. This procedure, in fact, is known as *Kruskal's algorithm* for building an *MST*.

While our current discussion yielded a useful tool for understanding the theory of *MST* construction, the actual problem of building an *MST* in a distributed fashion presents its own challenges. Next, let us look at how the algorithm proposed by Gallager, Humblet, and Spira approaches this problem.

12.3.2 The Gallager-Humblet-Spira algorithm

We begin by defining the concept of a *fragment*: quite simply, a fragment is a subtree of the *MST*. A fragment could even be a single node. In fact, this algorithm begins at 'level 0' which consists of the single-node forest, the set of all single-node fragments. The basic step in the algorithm is the following: each fragment will 'reach out' along its shortest outgoing path (*SOP*) - i.e. outgoing edge of minimum weight - to another fragment and join with it, thus forming a larger fragment. A continuous and concurrent execution of multiple such steps finally yields a single fragment, the final *MST*. For ease of illustration as well as terminology, let us associate the weight of an edge with its length. As a result, we refer to paths instead of edges, and lengths instead of weights. We can intuitively come up with the following requirements:

- Each fragment must have a 'control center' that issues certain key messages which are then propagated through the fragment
- For a single node fragment, the sole member *is* the control center
- Each fragment must be able to identify 1. its outgoing paths, and 2. the shortest one among them (*SOP*)
- The former requirement implies that a node must be able to identify whether a neighbour lying at the other end of an incident path is part of the same fragment or not - because an outgoing path is, by definition, one that leads from a fragment member to a member of another fragment
- The former requirement would imply that each fragment have a unique identity
- The identity of a fragment is the identity of its control center
- The control center emits a special message that informs all fragment members of the fragment's identity as well as level
- When two fragments join to form a single, larger, fragment, the control center can possibly 'shift' to another location
- Information in the form of messages must pass between the control center and other fragment members, in both directions
- Interior nodes (i.e. non-leaf nodes) receive *SOP* information from leaf nodes, and propagate the least among incoming *SOP* values towards the control center
- The previous requirement implies that each node must know the direction, i.e. path, which leads to the control center, a problem that is solved easily enough by 'remembering' the path through which informational or special messages arrive (i.e. the messages which advertise information such as fragment identity)
- Each interior node 'remembers' the path from which it received the least *SOP* value, so that a route or trail is effectively marked out from the control center to the node which discovered the *SOP*
- A single-node fragment is at level 0, with higher fragment levels being 1, 2, 3, etc

- The final *MST* will also have a node as its control center, naturally, and hence the *MST*-generation process also serves as a leader election mechanism

Next, some key rules of the algorithm which may not be as obvious or intuitive:

- For a multi-node fragment, the control center is the *pair* of nodes on either side of the *SOP* through which it last joined with another fragment of the same level
- The identity of a multi-node fragment is the length of its *SOP*, which works because distinct path lengths are assumed in the system
- A fragment can *merge* with another fragment of the same level, to form a new, bigger fragment of the next level (i.e. $L + L = L + 1$) which will then have a new control center, which being the pair of nodes on either side of the *SOP* across which the merger happened
- A fragment can be *absorbed or acquired* into a higher level fragment, with the level and control center of the larger fragment remaining unchanged

It is readily seen that, broadly, two types of events happen during *MST* construction:

1. Mergers
2. Absorptions or Acquisitions

As a result of the first type of event, two fragments which existed at the same level effectively 'disappear', to be replaced by a new, bigger, fragment that exists at the next higher level, with a new identity and control center. In comparison, the second event type does not produce a new fragment; an existing fragment effectively disappears, while another fragment grows larger while retaining its original control center and level. In either case, a key step is for a fragment to identify its *SOP* - shortest one among all outgoing paths in the fragment, i.e. among all paths that start from a fragment member and lead to a member of another fragment. This requires that each node classify the paths incident on it as one of three types:

1. *Branch* - the path is a branch or link in the *MST* being built
2. *Not-a-branch* - the path does not belong in the *MST* being built
3. *Unknown* - this path is yet to be determined as *Branch* or *Not-a-branch*

As an informal example, imagine that a node sends a *what-is-your-fragment-id* message along one of its paths, and a reply comes, carrying an id which is the same as its own. Such a path has to be of type (2) because adding the path to the *MST* will create a cycle. The dotted path between nodes C and B in the following diagram illustrates this case:

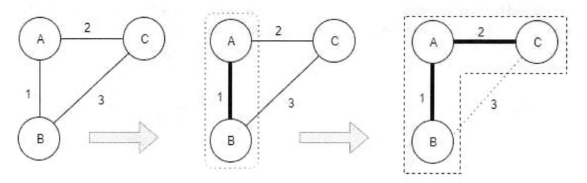

The first multi-node fragment formed in this example is the 2-node fragment consisting of A and B. Each node starts off with all its paths marked as *Unknown*, and proceeds to 'process' the shortest path incident on it. The results in A and B processing the path with distance 1, resulting in their 2-node fragment being formed. Once this is done, the fragment considers its outgoing paths - 2 and 3 - and processes the path of length 2 first, resulting in the 3-node fragment being formed. There is one more path, the one of length 3, to be processed; this path gets rejected as *Not-a-branch* once C and B communicate and come to the realisation that they are on the same fragment. The *MST* is now complete, as there are no more paths left to be processed.

Note that these are just the broad strokes in the context of a trivial example; we will look at the various details and complexities of the actual process, soon. We will imagine a network where each node has an embedded *MST-construction module*; our goal is to understand the various mechanisms inside such a module. The module constructs the *MST*, hands over the finished *MST* to a 'parent' module, and switches to a *Sleeping* state. The 'parent' module is in charge of 'some' algorithm which acts as a consumer of the generated *MST*. The parent module monitors all incoming messages and passes on *MST*-specific ones to the *MST* module; possibly waking it up from a *Sleeping* state. Sometime the parent algorithm detects a change in the network layout; maybe it notices that new nodes have joined the cluster. In such cases, we imagine the parent module sending a 'wakeup' message to the *MST* module, thus initiating a new instance of *MST* generation. Having woken up, the *MST* module starts executing our algorithm of interest, and in the process, generating messages which in turn wake up corresponding modules in its neighbouring nodes, and so on. Let us first see what steps are executed by the *wakeup* routine of the *MST* algorithm - the routine which our MST module invokes when it wakes up from a *Sleeping* state.

12.3.2.1 The wakeup routine

The first step is to make a list of the node's incident paths, and sort them in increasing order of path lengths. Each path is initially assigned a state of *Unknown*. The shortest path is then selected, and a *CONNECT* message is issued along it.

12.3.2.2 The CONNECT message

This message carries a single piece of information: the level of the sender's fragment, which is obviously 0 at this point. Having done this much, the state of the shortest path (along which the *CONNECT* is issued) is set to *Branch*. This makes sense, because the shortest path incident on each node must be part of the final *MST*. From this point onwards, the module executes the following loop in a broad sense:

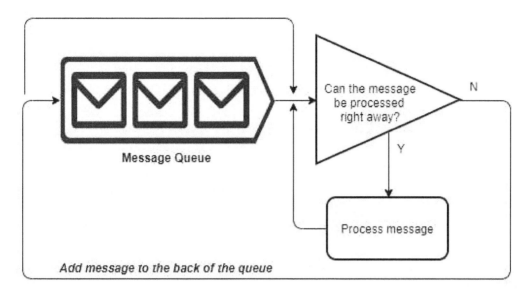

Messages to the *MST* module of a node are pushed to a message queue by a parent module. The *MST* algorithm executed by the module keeps fetching messages from the queue; each message is handled immediately if possible. Depending upon the state of the algorithm, certain messages cannot be handled right away. Such messages are pushed to the back of the queue, and will have to wait for their next turn, possibly making their way through the queue multiple times before the algorithm is ready to handle them. An example would be the case of node C from our prior 3-node example. Node C wakes up, and sends a *CONNECT* message along the path of length 2 to node A. However, node A does not service this message immediately, because it is in the process of forming a fragment with node B.

A single-node fragment does not have too many 'responsibilities' to fulfill - all it needs to do is to wake up, and issue a *CONNECT* message, as just described. However, once it evolves into a larger fragment, the nodes of the fragment get far busier. Let us assume that a single-node fragment, node A, woke up and sent a *CONNECT* message to another single-node fragment, node B, waking up B as a result. Node B executes the *wakeup* routine, which identifies the smallest path incident on B and issues a *CONNECT* along it. Let us assume this path to be the one that leads to node A, along which node A issued a *CONNECT* message a few moments back - which B will be processing shortly. Long story short, each node sees a *CONNECT* message in reply to the one it sent. This is a green flag for the formation of a new fragment of the next level (1), and the single-node fragments inform each other of this fact by sending *INITIATE* messages to each other. Note that an *INITIATE* reply subsequent to a *CONNECT* message causes the recipient to mark the corresponding path as a *Branch*.

12.3.2.3 The INITIATE message

The complexities of multi-node fragments begin with the topic of an *INITIATE* message. An *INITIATE* message informs each recipient that it is now part of a larger fragment, and carries the fragment level and the fragment identity, among other pieces of information. Obviously, recipients must pass on an *INITIATE* message so that all members of the fragment receive it. In the current example, node A and node B send *INITIATE* messages to each other which specify the fragment level as 1 and length of the path between them as the fragment identity. With the receipt of the *INITIATE* message (from each other), nodes A and B start executing the tasks of a multi-node fragment. The first step is to remember the direction, i.e. path, from which the *INITIATE* message arrived - this path is labelled to be remembered as the *control-direction*, for future routing of information from leaf nodes towards the control center. For a 2-node fragment, each node marks the path to each other as the *control-direction*, and the pair of nodes form the *control center* of the 2-node fragment. The second step is to propagate the *INITIATE* message through the fragment; i.e. to relay the *INITIATE* message along each incident path which is marked as *Branch*. The third step for both nodes is to start probing the neighbourhood. This is accomplished by each node issuing a *TEST* message along the next shortest path. Remember, the shortest path incident on each node is the one connecting them to form the 2-node fragment, and this path is now marked as *Branch* by both nodes (which was done as soon as each node issued a *CONNECT*). Hence, the process of a node issuing a *TEST* message first involves looking at all paths incident on the node that are marked as *Unknown* and selecting the shortest one among them.

12.3.2.4 The TEST message

In brief, multi-node fragments use the *TEST* message to determine outgoing paths. The *TEST* message carries two pieces of information: one being the fragment level, and the other, the identity of the fragment. In our current example of a 2-node fragment, the *TEST* messages issued by A and B carry 1 as the fragment level and the length of the *SOP* between them as the fragment identity. A *TEST* message can be either accepted or rejected by an appropriate reply. If the recipient of a *TEST* messages belongs to the same fragment (as determined by the fragment identity in the *TEST* message), the reply would a negative one. This results in the path being marked as *Not-a-branch* by both the sender as well as the recipient of the *TEST* message. This path will not be part of the *MST*, and no further messages of any kind will traverse this path. A positive reply, an *ACCEPT* message, will happen only if both of these conditions are satisfied:

1. The recipient is part of a different fragment
2. The recipient's fragment is at least at the same level as the sender's fragment

If the first condition is not satisfied, a *REJECT* message is immediately generated as reply to the *TEST* message. If the first condition is satisfied but the second condition is not, the *TEST* message is sent to the back of the recipient's message queue, for being processed later - once the recipient's fragment rises to at least the same level as the sender's fragment. This may happen in time if the recipient's fragment has other outgoing paths which are being processed at the moment. We can imagine each fragment, single-node or multi-node, as an entity that is processing its outgoing paths, one by one, in order of increasing length - a process that keeps increasing the fragment's level. Now, even if we assume otherwise, that the recipient's fragment does not reach the same level as the sender's fragment - maybe this fragment does a few acquisitions but no or not enough mergers - sooner or later the recipient's fragment will process the same path (along which the *TEST* message arrived) and issue a *TEST* message itself, to the sender of the original *TEST* message. This message will be accepted because condition (2) is now satisfied. Once a *TEST* message is accepted, the recipient of the *ACCEPT* message has discovered a neighbouring fragment which is closest to it. Its job now is to report this fact, to the control center. To be more specific, the length of the path to the discovered fragment is sent to the control center.

12.3.2.5 The REPORT message

As we noted earlier, each node knows its *control-direction*. A *REPORT* message is issued along this path, and it carries the length of the path between the source node of the message and the fragment which it discovered. Note that a *REPORT* message may not reach the control center, if relaying nodes along the way have seen other *REPORT* messages carrying smaller path lengths. Also, each relaying node remembers or marks the path along which it received a *REPORT* message carrying the shortest path length - i.e. the value carried by the *REPORT* message that it chose to relay along its *control-direction* path. This path is labelled as the *sop-direction* by each node that relays the *REPORT* message. For leaf nodes generating *REPORT* messages, the *sop-direction* is the very path connecting it to the discovered fragment. The final 'competition' is between the two *REPORT* message values reaching the pair of nodes forming the control center, which they sent to each other. Of the pair, one node receives a larger value than the one it sent to the other; now the control center knows the shortest outgoing path or *SOP* for the fragment as a whole. The following diagram provides an example:

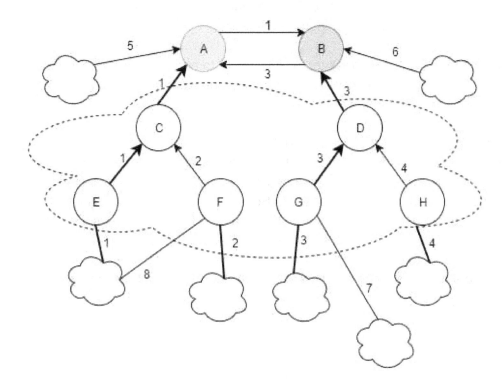

The control center (nodes A and B in the diagram) knows something more, actually: that either a merger or acquisition is about to happen, and it will cease to be a control center in either case.

In the case of a merger, the control center of the new fragment is the pair on either end of the *SOP* between the two fragments. In the case of an acquisition, the lower-level fragment (whose *TEST* message was accepted, which in turn initiated this whole process) becomes part of a higher-level existing fragment (which provided the *ACCEPT* reply to the lower-level fragment's *TEST* message) whose control center will remain unchanged. Either way, the next step is for the control center - specifically, the one among the pair of nodes who sent the *SOP* to the other - to generate a *TRANSFER-CONTROL* message, which is then passed along the path that the *SOP* arrived, following the *sop-direction* as remembered by each node on the way, till it finally reaches the leaf node which discovered the *SOP*.

12.3.2.6 The TRANSFER-CONTROL message

Upon receiving a *TRANSFER-CONTROL* message, the *SOP*-discovering leaf node sends a *CONNECT* message to the fragment that it discovered. If the discovered fragment is of the same level and has the same path as its *SOP*, a *CONNECT* message will arrive as a reply - due to the exact same process happening in both fragments. This is similar to the 2-node fragment formation which we covered earlier, except for the timing of events. For single-node fragments, their wakeup routine involves sending a *CONNECT* message before anything else, including the processing of any incoming messages. As a result, each of a pair of single-node fragments that wake up and process the same path, will end up seeing a *CONNECT* reply to the *CONNECT* message which it sent. For multi-node fragments, only If both fragments happened to be processing the same outgoing path simultaneously, and generated *CONNECT* messages simultaneously to each other, will each node see a *CONNECT* reply to its *CONNECT* message. Otherwise, one of the fragments will see a *CONNECT* message before it actually got around to sending one. Let us look into this timing aspect in more detail first.

Consider that the node *n1* from fragment *F1* issued a *CONNECT* to node *n2* located in fragment *F2*. We will assume that *F1* is at the same level as *F2*. Now, *F2* could be processing a different outgoing path at that point in time. In other words, while *n1* has marked the path to *n2* as *Branch*, *n2* still has the path in an *Unknown* state - precisely because there is a shorter path to a different fragment from *F2*, which some node in *F2* (could very well be *n2*) is probing at the moment. So, what *n2* sees is a *CONNECT* message, from a sender of equal level, along a path that is currently marked as *Unknown*. When this happens, the *CONNECT* message is sent to the back of the message queue for deferred processing. Sooner or later, and let us assume that the level of *F2* has remain unchanged till then, *F2* identifies the path from *n2* to *n1* as the next shortest outgoing path to be processed, as a result of which *n2* sends a *CONNECT* message along this path and marks the path as a *Branch*. When the deferred *CONNECT* message from *n1* makes it way to the front of its message queue next, *n2* will see that the corresponding path is marked as *Branch* - and processes the *CONNECT* right away. Similarly, *F1* sees a *CONNECT* message coming along a path marked as *Branch*, and services the *CONNECT* message without delay.

An *INITIATE* message is generated towards each other by the nodes on either side of the *SOP* joining the two fragments, once each realises that *CONNECT* messages have been exchanged. Once the other's *INITIATE* message is received by each, it is forwarded along to the rest of the fragment members on either side so that everyone becomes aware of the change in fragment identity and rise in fragment level. What happened just now is a merger.

On the other hand, if the discovered fragment is at a higher level, it absorbs or acquires the fragment which reached out in the first place using a *TEST* message. Going back to the example, this is the case where *F2* is at a higher level when it processes the *CONNECT* message from *F1*. When this happens, the *CONNECT* message is replied to *immediately* with an *INITIATE* message, which the recipient leaf node (*n1*) of the absorbed fragment (*F1*) propagates to the rest of the members (in *F1*). Note how the processing of a *CONNECT* message is *not* deferred only when the sender is found to be at a lower level than the recipient. The next diagram shows the flow of the various events and messages just described, at each node in the network:

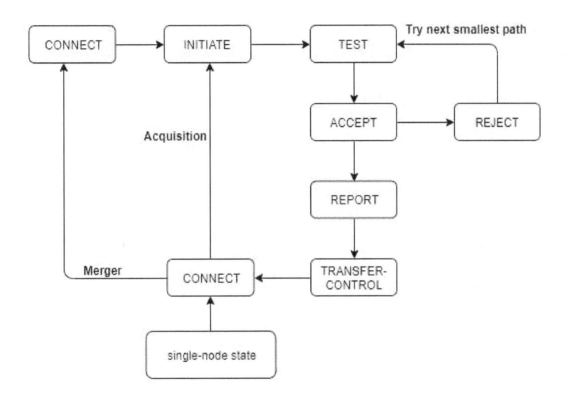

12.3.2.7 The INITIATE message: a closer look

We made the following statement in section *12.3.2.2*: this message carries the fragment level and the fragment identity, among other pieces of information. What other pieces of information? We know that *INITIATE* messages not only inform recipient nodes about the fragment level and identity, but also ask them to start probing the neighbourhood in order to find the shortest outgoing path of the fragment. In other words, an *INITIATE* message brings information and a task. However, there is a corner case where the task is absent.

Consider a fragment *F1* being acquired by a fragment *F2*. In detail, a node *n1* in *F1* identified an *SOP* to a node *n2* in *F2*, sent a *TEST* message, received an *ACCEPT*, subsequently sent a

CONNECT, and received an *INITIATE* as reply from *n2*. Consider the case that when *n2* received a *CONNECT* from *n1*, *n2* had already sent its *REPORT* message towards the control center of *F2* as tasked by the last *INITIATE* message it received from the control center. This would mean that *n2* did identify an outgoing path which is smaller than the one connecting *n1* and *n2*, and naturally, also smaller than any outgoing link in *F1*. This means that *F1* does not need to start probing its neighbourhood in response to the *INITIATE* message received by *n1*, and the *INITIATE* message will make that aspect clear by a suitable flag. The role of such an *INITIATE* message is purely informational and it triggers no *TEST* actions from its recipient nodes in the acquired fragment.

12.3.2.8 Termination

At what point does the algorithm realise that *MST* construction is complete? This is answered by the following simple mechanism: upon receiving an *INITIATE* message, a node that has no more paths left in the *Unknown* state generates a *REPORT* message carrying a value of ∞ (infinity) or a suitably large value. Sooner or later, the pair of nodes forming the control center of the sole and final fragment notice themselves reporting such a value to each other. This is the termination point, which can be followed by a last act of broadcasting the halt status across the fragment.

12.3.2.9 A complete example

Let us consider the following network as an example:

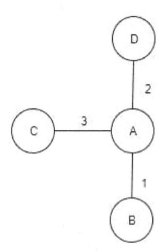

We will imagine that all nodes are initially in a sleeping state (i.e. the *MST* modules of all nodes are in a sleeping state). Node A comes alive at some point, and initiates *MST* construction. At this point, we have 4 single-node fragments, of which only one (node A) is awake. Node A executes the *wakeup* routine - which identifies the *SOP* as the path of length 1 to node B and sends a *CONNECT* message. This wakes up node B, which does the same - identifies the path of length 1 to node A as its *SOP*, and sends a *CONNECT* message along it to node A.

This leads to both node A and node B seeing *CONNECT* responses to their *CONNECT* messages, and immediately forms a 2-node fragment by sending *INITIATE* messages (carrying a fragment level of 1 and fragment identity of 1) to each other. As we discussed in section *12.3.2.6*, the default *INITIATE* message carries information as well as a task. Hence, node A and node B set upon the task after receiving each other's INITIATE message; the task is, of course, to find the shortest outgoing path to another fragment of the same or higher level. Now, node B has no *Unknown* paths left to process; the sole incident path (of length 1) is now marked as *Branch*. As a result, node B sends a *REPORT* to node A, which carries a value of infinity (∞).

What about node A? Node A sends a *TEST* message to node D, thus waking it up. As always, the first action of node D upon waking up is to execute the *wakeup* routine. Node D next considers the *TEST* message from node A and defers processing it after noticing the sender's level to be higher than own (1 > 0). Meanwhile, the execution of the *wakeup* routine by node D has resulted in node A receiving a *CONNECT* message. Node A sees the sender's level to be less than its own (0 < 1), and immediately replies with an *INITIATE* message (and marks the path to node D as *Branch*) which carries a fragment level of 1 and fragment identity of 1. This *INITIATE* message has the task flag set, because node A has not yet issued a *REPORT* message along its *control-direction*. Node D has no more paths left to process, so it sends a *REPORT* message to node A that carries a value of infinity (∞). This particular *REPORT* message is not yet processed by node A, because it is yet to generate a *REPORT* message of its own; in fact, node A is still waiting for a reply to the *TEST* message which it sent to D. The reply comes soon - a *REJECT* message - as node D could finally process the *TEST* message because its level has risen to 1 (as informed by the *INITIATE* message from node A). And why was the *TEST* message rejected by node D? Because, node D is now in the same fragment as node A (again, as informed by the *INITIATE* message from node A). So far so good, but how does node A react to the *REJECT* reply to its *TEST*? Normally, node A would mark the path (along which a *REJECT* message was seen) as *Not-a-branch*; but not in this case, since the path is already marked as *Branch*, which happened upon processing the *CONNECT* message from node D.

At this point, node A has not generated a *REPORT* message of its own. Its attempt to process the path to node D was interrupted and extinguished by the acquisition process of node D along the same path. Hence, node A turns its focus to the only remaining incident path, which is the one to node C, of length 3. Node C is asleep at this point. Node A generates a *TEST* message to node C, waking it up, and subsequently producing a similar sequence as in the case of the interaction between node A and node D. It ends with a similar *REPORT* (carrying ∞) from node C. This leaves node A with no more paths to handle, and two *REPORT* messages - one from node C and one from node D - carrying an equal value. So, the *REPORT* message which node A sends to node B is the same one, carrying a value of infinity. At this point, both node A and node B realise that they exchanged *REPORT* values of ∞ with each other and executes the halt step.

12.3.2.10 One more example

Before concluding the section on this most beautiful of network algorithms with an analysis of its message complexity, let us quickly consider one more example. Specifically, the idea is to understand the non-default variant of the *INITIATE* message; i.e. the one that does not require recipient nodes to start probing their neighbourhood. We will use the following network in this example:

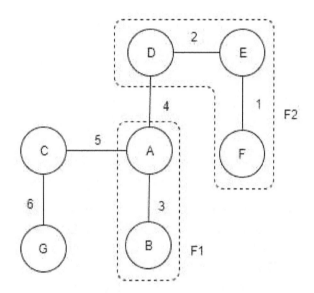

As seen in the diagram, nodes D, E, and F has formed a fragment *F2*, while nodes A and B form *F1*. Looking at the fragment *F1*, node B has no more outgoing paths to process, while A has two - of which the path of length 4 is selected first and a *TEST* message issued. Since *F2* is at the same level as *F1* (1), this *TEST* message is serviced immediately with an *ACCEPT* response. This results in A issuing a *REPORT* message along its control-path, which is the path to B, carrying a value of 4.

Let us assume that C wakes up at this point and sends a *CONNECT* message to node A. Since the recipient node's fragment is at a higher level (1), an *INITIATE* message is immediately sent back to C, signalling its acquisition into the larger fragment (*F1*). As section *12.3.2.7* explained, this *INITIATE* message makes it clear using an unset flag that the recipient need not explore its neighbourhood right now - because node A has already issued its *REPORT* message corresponding to the last *INITIATE* message that it received (the one from node B). Now, node C has an outgoing path, to G, which it is yet to process. We will assume that G is fast asleep. When and how will the path to G be added to the *MST*? We will next see when C finally gets around to exploring this path.

As mentioned earlier, node A has sent a *REPORT* message to node B. Node B, having no further paths to process, has already sent a *REPORT* message carrying ∞ to node A. Having

sent the shorter of the two values, normally node A will issue a *TRANSFER-CONTROL* to the leaf node who reported the *SOP*. Now, Node A *is* the leaf node of *F1* which discovered the SOP; since there is no point in issuing a *TRANSFER-CONTROL* to itself, node A immediately executes the next step, the one expected from an *SOP*-finding leaf node upon receipt of a *TRANSFER-CONTROL* message. In short, node A sends a *CONNECT* message along the SOP to node D. Since D belongs to *F2* which in turn is at the same level as *F1*, sooner or later a *CONNECT* arrives in response. This causes *INITIATE* messages to pass in either direction along the path between A and D, and the *INITIATE* message received by A is passed along not only to B, but also to C as well. Now, *this* particular *INITIATE* message is of the default kind, and leads to C exploring its path to G, waking G up, and soon acquiring it into *F1*. Before we look at message complexity, let us tweak the current example a bit to explore the non-termination and deadlock possibilities of this algorithm.

12.3.2.10.1 Possibilities for non-termination and deadlock

What if *F2* had another, shorter, outgoing path from node D, to another fragment *F3*, which it had identified as its *SOP*, and was currently processing, while the *CONNECT* message from node A arrived at D? This implies that D had already dispatched its *REPORT* message; and that the *INITIATE* message sent to node A would be the non-default kind. In other words, the second *INITIATE* message received by node C does not prompt it to explore the path to node G, either. The question is: can this go on? What if *F3* was processing an outgoing path shorter than the one from *F2*, when the TEST message from F2 arrived, and so on? Can node G 'somehow' end up being never woken up, and the the path between G and C remain undetected?

Obviously, this chain (*F1* → *F2* → *F3* ...) cannot go on endlessly; otherwise we would be dealing

with an infinite number of fragments and nodes. What about a cycle, then? For example, can *F3* be working on an *SOP* to *F1*, incident on node B in *F1*, when the *CONNECT* message from *F2* comes in? This also does not make sense for the described sequence of events, because, in that case A would get a chance to probe its path to *F2* only *after* B processes its path to *F3*. This follows, because we assumed that *F2* has a path to *F3* which is shorter than the path from *F2* to A, and that *F3* has a path to node B in *F1* which is even shorter. The following diagram represents this configuration:

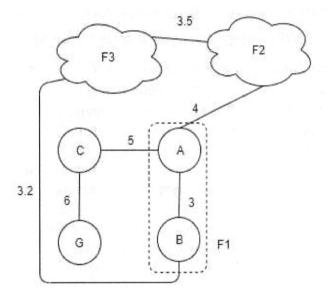

Let us assume that *F3* is at a higher level than *F2*, and that *F2* is at least at level 2. Once A and B form fragment *F1*, the path from B to *F3* is processed next, leading to *F1* being absorbed into *F3*. Next, *F2* gets absorbed into *F3*. Note that the path between A and *F2* does not make it into the *MST*. Finally, F3 (node A, actually - but node A is part of F3 by now) gets around to processing the path to C, leading to first C and then G being absorbed into *F3*.

We shall now move on to the question of message cost of this algorithm, which, incidentally, will also round up the topic on minimum spanning trees. Afterwards, we will shift our focus to the concept of *Maximal Independent Sets*. We will analyse an algorithm that is exquisitely simple, yet one whose (strictly) mathematical proof is anything but trivial. As usual, we will try to understand the proof by the best possible intuitive means available.

12.3.2.11 Message complexity

Let us first look at message complexity from the perspective of the number of paths or edges, denoted by *m*. Each path in the network must be selected or rejected as a part of the *MST*; either case involves a *TEST* message and a corresponding response (*ACCEPT* or *REJECT*). This implies that we have a message cost of *2m* messages for the specific communication mechanism by which paths in the network are selected into the *MST*.

Next, let us consider the rest of the message activity from the perspective of the number of nodes. We have seen a fixed set of messages which the algorithm uses, and none of these messages have to be received or transmitted by a node more than once for any given level of the fragment. Since we know that fragment level increases only when fragments of equal sizes merge together, we know the maximum possible level - which is *log(n)*, for a total of *n* nodes. This implies a message cost of *clog(n)* where *c* is some constant representing the number of messages handled per node per level.

Putting together the results from both observations above, we arrive at a final message cost of *2m + clog(n)* for the *MST* algorithm being executed in a network consisting of *n* nodes and *m* links or paths.

12.4 Maximal Independent Sets

A famous E-commerce company is evaluating drone delivery possibilities by conducting a trial project in a town very close to their headquarters. People order items using their website, and delivery happens in a day or two - using drones. The trial project members quickly establish, after analysing the specifications and capabilities of the drones at their disposal, that a special delivery platform (a physical structure which allows the drone to hover above, and deposit its payload at, in a safe manner) needs to be built at each delivery point, i.e. at each delivery address. There are hundreds of houses in their trial town, and the project being a trial or tentative one, their budgets do not allow the construction of so many delivery platforms. A quick sociological survey indicated very good relationships between the population of the neighbourhood, so an optimisation is quickly arrived at:

- Delivery platforms will be built only at select residences in the neighbourhood
- If a resident does not get a delivery platform at his or her residence, he or she will find one at his or her neighbour's residence

In short, as a resident, you either get your purchases delivered to your doorstep, or to your neighbour's house (a short walk and you pick up your purchase from your friendly neighbour). The project members decide to come up with a list of residential addresses where delivery platforms need to be built. What is special about such a list? Obviously, the list should not contain two neighbouring addresses - which is inefficient. If A and B are neighbours, delivery platforms are not needed at both their houses. Resident A can use the one at B's place, or vice versa. Also, the list must be complete - i.e. the addition of even one more address would violate the previous condition; i.e. the newly added address will be the neighbour of one already in the list. Such a set is called a *Maximal Independent Set* or *MIS*. From a graph perspective, an *MIS* is a of subset of the graph's vertices such that no pair in the subset is connected to each other directly. In other words, it is a *no-neighbour subset* of the set of vertices of a graph which cannot be expanded any further without destroying the no-neighbour property.

12.4.1 A sequential algorithm for computing MIS

Computing *MIS* for a graph in a sequential manner is anything but hard. Assume that we are presented with a graph for which *MIS* need to be computed. The result will be stored in a set, which is initially empty. Start going through the nodes of the graph, one at a time, starting at an arbitrary node. For each node considered: If adding the node to the set does not violate the no-neighbour property, do so. If not, reject the node and move on to another node. Stop once all nodes have been considered. That was not complicated by any means, but what about a distributed or parallel variation of such an algorithm?

In 1986, Michael Luby published a simple yet beautiful synchronous distributed algorithm for *MIS* calculation in undirected graphs. In particular, Luby described a randomised version of his *MIS* algorithm, and that is our next topic of interest.

12.4.2 Luby's MIS algorithm

For a start, let us consider an arbitrary vertex in the graph. Next, we define the concept of the *neighbourhood* of the vertex as the set including the vertex and all its neighbours. Going back to the example, we consider an arbitrary house and all its neighbouring houses. Now, this house should have a delivery platform or one of its neighbours should. Long story short, there must be a single delivery platform in a neighbourhood. This is equivalent to a leader election which selects a single house in the neighbourhood. This is exactly what Luby's algorithm does; the whole graph can be viewed as a collection of (overlapping) neighbourhoods, and a leader is elected in each. The algorithm may have multiple rounds, and each phase involves a set of concurrent leader elections - one for each neighbourhood that participates in the phase. Any neighbourhood that succeeds in finding a leader, stops participating in further rounds. When a neighbourhood succeeds in electing a leader, the leader is removed from the original graph and added to a *result set*. Note that the result set starts off as empty. Also, all the leader's neighbours are removed from the graph (but *not* added to the result set). If the graph is still non-empty, the algorithm moves to the next round to repeat the aforementioned steps. Let us look at a more formal description of this process.

1. At the start, have an empty set called *result*
2. Each node uses a random number generator to select a random number between 0 and 1 (example: 0.67)
3. Each node sends its random number to all its neighbours
4. A node knows that it is the leader if its random number is smaller than all the random numbers it received from its neighbours
5. The leader sends a victory message to all its neighbours, removes itself (and all its edges) from the graph, adds itself to the result set, and ends its participation in the algorithm
6. Each recipient of a victory message removes itself (and all its edges) from the graph, and ends its participation in the algorithm
7. If the graph is non-empty, go to step (2) and start the next round

How can a node participate in multiple rounds? If a node has one or more neighbours whose random values are smaller than its own (thus preventing its election as leader), and yet it does not receive a victory message from any of its neighbours (because all of them had neighbours whose random numbers were even smaller, in turn preventing any of them being elected). Such nodes move on to the next round. This is a simple consequence of the fact that neighbourhoods overlap.

Note that a round can see isolated nodes existing in the graph - a node who, in the previous round, did not have a low enough random number to get itself elected, but whose neighbours were all deleted from the graph because each of them received a victory message from its neighbour. Such isolated nodes, naturally, will elect themselves as a leader in that round and move to the result set. Also, let us not forget the possibility of 'collisions' where a unique leader is not elected in a neighbourhood thanks to multiple nodes choosing the exact same random number. In fact, the termination property of the algorithm is predicated on the effectiveness of the randomisation being used. For example, assume that each node which executes the algorithm uses the same pseudo-random number generator algorithm. A pseudo-random number generator needs to be seeded as an initialisation, so think about what will happen if the same 'seed' value is hardcoded in the algorithm code which is executed at each node. In every round, each node will arrive at the exact same random number, and no leader will ever be elected, and the algorithm will never make progress. The result set starts off as empty and stays empty after each round in an infinite sequence of rounds. Discounting such possibilities, let us try to (roughly) estimate the rate of progress of this algorithm.

12.4.2.1 Performance

We have seen how the graph progressively 'shrinks' across rounds as nodes and their edges are removed due to successful leader elections. To get an intuitive idea on the rate of progress at which the graph shrinks, let us look at the process from the context of the number of edges in the graph and try to approximate the rate at which edges disappear from the graph as rounds progress.

As a start, consider an arbitrary edge from vertex u to vertex v. From graph parlance, the *degree* of a node is the number of edges incident on it, i.e. the number of neighbours. Let us use the notation $d(u)$ or $d(v)$ to represent the degree or u or v, respectively. Let us consider one possibility how the edge from u to v can be removed from the graph: the random number generated by u is the least among the set of nodes including itself and its neighbours. This is just one possibility, one of several. Any of the neighbours of v can emerge as a leader, causing v to be dropped from the graph, taking the edge along with it. However, what if we focus on only that single possibility which we considered earlier? We assume that none of the neighbours of v play a role in the removal of the edge between u and v. To facilitate this, we consider the situation where the random number generated by u is not only the smallest in its neighbourhood, but smaller than the random numbers generated by the neighbours of v as well. What is the probability for this event happening? We are talking about a set of size $d(u) + d(v)$, so the answer is: $1 / (d(u) + d(v))$. If v gets removed, we know that $d(v)$ edges get removed; so, we are talking about an expectation of $d(v) \times 1 / (d(u) + d(v))$ edges being removed. Now, the reverse could happen - the edge could be taken out by the vertex v. The number of edges removed in this scenario is, symmetrically, given by $d(u) / ((d(u) + d(v))$. Since we have two mutually exclusive possibilities by which each edge can be removed, we can average it out (across the two possibilities) and sum it up (across all the edges) in the following fashion:

$$1/2 \sum_{u,v} \frac{d(u)}{d(u) + d(v)} + \frac{d(v)}{d(u) + d(v)}$$

Since this is a loop of *m* iterations, we arrive at a result of *m/2*. We therefore state the rate of progress as logarithmic in terms of the number of edges, i.e. *O(log(m))*.

How can we state this in terms of the number of nodes rather than the number of edges? We know that there could be as much as *n(n - 1)/2* edges among *n* nodes. Let us assume that *log(n)* rounds go by. How many edges will remain? Each round will reduce the number of edges by a factor of ½, so, approximately:

$$(n^2/2) \times (1/2)^{logn} = (n^2/2) / 2^{logn} = (n^2/2) / n = n/2$$

We are left with half the edges by the end of *log(n)* rounds. This is not much of a progress, so let us try jumping ahead to see what happens after *4log(n)* rounds:

$$(n^2/2) / 2^{4logn} = (n^2/2) / n^4 = 1/(2n^2)$$

Now we have a very small value, in fact less than $1/n^2$.

Note that we are considering a random variable here, and we arrived at an expected value of (at least) $1/n^2$ after *4log(n)* rounds. Let us use *Markov's inequality* here to help us out further: *the probability that the value of a non-negative random variable be k times its expected value is given by 1/k*. The expected value after *4log(n)* rounds is $1/n^2$, so the probability of the expected value being 1, i.e. of at least one edge remaining, which is n^2 times the expected value, is given by $1/n^2$. Considering the opposite possibility of *no* edges remaining, we have a result of *(1 - $1/n^2$)*. Hence, we state that the algorithm will terminate in *4log(n)* rounds with a probability given by *(1 - $1/n^2$)*.

12.5 Conclusion

In this chapter dedicated to graph algorithms, we visited various concepts such as traversals, shortest paths, spanning trees, and independent sets. Starting off with traversals, we analysed and contrasted depth-first and breadth-first approaches for the same, including algorithms for each. The topic on breadth-first traversals led us to shortest-path spanning trees, and then to a broader and more complex section on minimum spanning trees. The Gallager-Humblet-Spira algorithm dominated our *MST* section, with multiple examples being presented to cover various corner cases. Finally, we switched to the topic of Maximal Independent Sets, where we presented and analysed Luby's algorithm.

12.6 What's next

After discussing shortest paths and minimum spanning trees, perhaps it is only natural that we move on to a closely related topic - of routing, the mechanism by which a path is selected for moving data in a network. While doing so, we will have the opportunity to see how some of the concepts and utilities discussed in this chapter play the role of building blocks that facilitate a 'higher' purpose.

Chapter 13. Routing algorithms

13.1 An introduction

The topic we handle in this chapter is closely related to the ones broadly covered in the last chapter, and unsurprisingly then, we will continue to rely heavily on graph terminology. The essential idea of *routing* is about moving data from one point to another; thus, it involves the concept of a source and a destination. In particular, we are interested in *efficient* routing. If we are lucky enough to have a complete graph, routing is a no-brainer because every node is directly linked to every other one. In a more realistic sense, we assume connected graphs as the model for our networks. We also assume every node to be 'aware' of the identity or address of every other node in the network. For example, node A would know that node B is part of the network. However, node B need not be a neighbour of node A, in which case node A will not be aware of how to direct traffic to node B, let alone the most efficient way to accomplish the task. In general, we assume a routing algorithm to execute in the network - i.e. with the participation of all nodes - in two distinct situations: network initialisation and network reconfiguration. The latter might involve the addition or removal of nodes, or simply a change in network layout. We will remain unconcerned about the exact details of how or when a routing algorithm is executed and will remain solely focused on the algorithms and their internals. The output of a routing algorithm is a correctly filled data structure which we will call the routing table. Before diving into the details of various algorithms, let us look more closely at the concept of routing tables.

13.2 Routing tables

During steady state functioning of the network, we assume each node to have access to a fully constructed and accurate routing table. Such a data structure allows each node to transmit data to any destination in the network. A routing table can be a set of complete routes, one for each pair of nodes in the network. However, this is clearly overkill; a source node only needs to know the *next hop* for a particular destination. Simply put, for a given destination, the source node is only interested in knowing the answer to this question: *which neighbouring node must the data be sent to*? Needless to say, we are always interested in shortest paths. Otherwise, there could be multiple answers to the aforementioned question. We should assume routing tables to be periodically updated, without any particular prior warning. Also, we do not want any update to the routing table to render it less efficient; the information in a routing table should get only better. All this implies that an efficient routing table will consist of the following pair of information for each route in the table:

1. The shortest path length currently available
2. The first hop

As in the previous chapter, we assume undirected graphs with non-negative edge weights. The shortest path, hence, is the one with the least cumulative weight of all the edges traversed by the path. However, do we really need to store the shortest path length? Can we not store just the first hop, knowing that it is the first hop on the shortest path? We can, but this approach does not lend itself well to dynamic updates of the routing table; any new incoming route information should be compared to the existing one at hand and applied only if found to be more efficient. The presence of the shortest path length in a routing table entry directly allows such a facility.

Finally, we assume a whole routing table to be an array or vector of pair values - each entry in the array containing route information [*shortest path length, first hop address*] for one node in the network. Naturally, such an array has *n* entries where n is the number of nodes in the network. The question arises, next: how is such a routing table calculated? Let us look at a rather naive solution before moving on to more efficient ones.

13.3 Generating a routing table: a naive implementation

Let us define the *initial* stage of a network as one where all nodes are up, but there is no routing table at any node. Next, let us correct that statement thus: each node *does* have a routing table at hand, but one that is mostly empty. This means that each node during the initial phase knows something about its network. Let us define that bare minimum information:

1. The identity and address of each node in the network
2. The identity and address of its direct neighbours

In fact, the second piece of information facilitates a third one: the edge weight or path length to each of its neighbours. For example, we can assume that each node has a subroutine which, given a direct neighbour's address, will probe the corresponding path to provide the message transmission delay or latency along the same. In short, each node during the initial phase knows the address of all nodes in the network, who its neighbours are, and the edge weights to each of its neighbours. This is another way of saying that the routing table of each node will have entries of the kind [∞, -] for each non-neighbouring node. On the other hand, for a node who is a neighbour, the corresponding routing table entry would contain valid and useful information: for example, node A would store [*10, B*] as the routing table entry corresponding to its neighbour node B, where 10 is the path length or edge weight between A and B, and (naturally) B is marked as the next or first (and only) hop on the shortest path between A and B. So, starting with bare-minimum routing tables, how do we fill up the rest of the information?

An obvious solution is for each node to broadcast its initial routing table. As a result, everyone ends up with everyone else's initial information. The broadcast can be made possible by a prior step of creating a spanning tree for the network. We have already visited an algorithm in section *12.3.2* which accomplishes this with a message cost of *2m + clog(n)*. The broadcast round is followed by each node using the assimilated information to locally calculate shortest paths to every other node in the network. What we are talking about here, then, is a two step process: executing a distributed algorithm to facilitate efficient broadcast, followed by a centralised routing algorithm that runs at each node in the network. Let us accept this method for now and focus on the second step. The broadcast round ensures that each node knows the neighbourhood details of every other node; how will that help to create a routing table? Let us consider the following example:

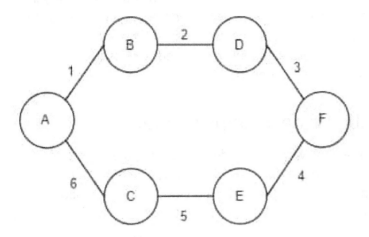

Once node D receives the routing table from A, can it make a step forward as far as its own routing table is concerned? Definitely yes; node D can inspect A's information and immediately realise that A is 1 unit away from B, and hence, there is a path from D to A, via B, which is of length 1 + 2 = 3 units. Node D can immediately update its routing table to modify the entry for A from [∞, -] to [3, B]. Similarly, once D receives routing information broadcast by node F, it can update its entry for E from [∞, -] to [7, F]. If routing information from node E comes in next, node D will update the entry for C from [∞, -] to [12, F]. This is because the incoming routing information from E specifies that C is 5 units away from E, which in turn is already noted by D as being 7 units away. Now, what happens if node D receives routing data from A, next? This message would inform D that A is 1 unit away from B (which D knows to be 2 units away) and that C is 6 units away from A. This immediately allows D to update its routing table so that the entry for A is changed from [∞, -] to [3, B]. Using this information, it can also deduce the more efficient route of length 9 units to C, ensuring that the existing entry of [12, F] for C would be replaced by [9, B]. Similarly, each node updates its routing table to full size, using local information supplied by every other node. This centralised algorithm is known as the *Floyd-Warshall routing algorithm*. The next section goes through the various steps in this algorithm in a more formal manner.

13.4 The Floyd-Warshall algorithm

As in the example used by the previous section, the floyd-warshall algorithm assumes that all required information is locally available; i.e. the identity of each node in the network, as well as its neighbours and their respective distances. In our current context, we assume the algorithm to execute immediately after the broadcast round as described in the previous section. Therefore, each node receives *n - 1* messages right before the algorithm commences its execution, where each message contains membership and proximity information of the immediate neighbourhood of exactly one (other) node in the network. Here are the formal steps involved, as executed on every node in the network:

1. Have a set *S* which is initially empty
2. Have a queue *Q* which consists of (the ids of) all other nodes in the network in any order
3. Remove a node u from the head of *Q*
4. If u *is* present in *S*, put u back to the tail of *Q* and go back to step 3 to select another node
5. Is the distance to u marked as ∞ in the local node's routing table entry? If so, put u back to the tail of *Q* and go back to step 3 to select another node
6. For each other node X in *Q*, check if the distance to X as marked in the local routing table is greater than the distance to X *via u* (i.e. the distance from the local node to u, as per the local routing table + the distance from u to X, as conveyed by u during the broadcast round). If so, replace the local entry for X with one that specifies the shorter value as the distance to X and the first hop as u
7. The algorithm is finished processing node u; add u to *S* so that it will not be considered again (see the restriction enforced in step 4)
8. If all the members of *Q* are present in *S* at this point, all nodes have been processed; go to step 10 to conclude the algorithm
9. There are more nodes to be processed; go to step 3 to select the next node
10. Halt after performing pre-termination broadcasts and/or other actions (if any)

Note the following properties of the initial state of every local routing table:

1. The distance to self is marked as 0
2. The first hop on the path to self is marked as self
3. The distance to an immediate neighbour is marked as the weight of the path to said neighbour
4. The first hop on the path to an immediate neighbour is marked as the immediate neighbour
5. For every node who is not a neighbour, the distance is marked as ∞ (infinity) and the first hop is marked as '-' (*NIL*)

The algorithm's 'philosophy' should be straightforward; the local node goes through an outer loop, in which each other node is considered as a *transit* or thoroughfare node; for each transit node, an inner loop considers every other node (i.e. every node other than the local node and the transit node) to see if there is a shorter path to that node from the local node, via the transit node, than what is recorded in the local routing table; if so, the local routing table is modified to reflect the shorter path via the transit node. Note that the next or first hop specified in the updated entry would be the same as that of the entry associated with the transit node. The following sequence illustrates the various steps involved in the algorithm as executed on node F from the earlier diagram:

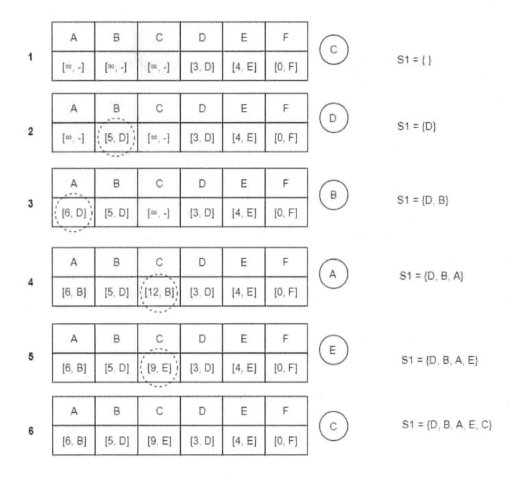

Step (1) involves node C being removed from Q. At this point, node F has no route to node C at all. In other words, node F can learn nothing from C. Hence, node C is sent back to the tail of Q for later reconsideration. Things move smoothly from then onwards, starting with node D being picked from the head of Q. This helps node F to mark the route to node B. Incidentally, node B is at the head of Q next, leading to the route to A being learnt by node F. Next, node A comes up at the head of Q and provides a route to node C, and node F updates its routing table accordingly. The next choice from Q, that of E, ensures that the previously created entry for C is updated with a shorter one. The last round, with node C making a second appearance at the head of Q, makes no difference to the routing table as the table is complete by this point. For each step, the rightmost field shows the content of S after the step. Let us move on to a difference scheme after figuring out the message complexity of the current one.

13.4.1 Performance and message complexity

Our current way of generating routing tables require three separate phases: one to generate the spanning tree, another for each node to broadcast its local knowledge along the spanning tree, and a final computational round or phase where each node builds its complete routing table based on information collected from every other node. We've already seen the cost of building a spanning tree and know that each broadcast along the spanning tree would have a message complexity of *O(n)*. Since each node does a broadcast, we do end up with a message cost of O(n^2).

How about the time cost of the algorithm as executed at each node? It is readily seen that an outer loop wraps an inner loop, and each loop depends on the number of nodes in the network, i.e. each loop has *O(n)* iterations. This implies a time cost given by O(n^2).

Our current approach is rather laborious: an initial round that is *CPU*-intensive as well as network-intensive, an intermediate one that is network-intensive, and a final phase that is *CPU*-intensive. Further, the routing algorithm as such is not exactly distributed: we collect all the data first, at every location, and then process the data in one shot to generate our routing tables. Let us next consider an approach that is much leaner, distributed, and one that uses the concept of *sink trees*. This algorithm, published in 1980 by Sam Toueg, is a distributed version of the floyd-warshall algorithm. We have already seen how node A cannot make use of routing information from node B unless node A has a path to node B. This is hardly surprising; to benefit from a person's knowledge of how to reach a certain destination (from where he or she is located), one has to know how to reach that person in the first place. Toueg's algorithm makes sure that useless information is never handed over to any node in the network.

13.5 Toueg's algorithm

First of all: we mentioned sink trees earlier, so what exactly is one? We came across the concept of convergecast in section *12.2.2.2.2*; a sink tree is very similar. If we focus on an arbitrary node in a connected network, we can visualise a set of optimal routes leading from every other node to our node of interest, which we label as the *sink node*. We can immediately state that the neighbours of any node are automatically part of its sink tree. Toueg's algorithm proceeds in synchronous rounds, uses the concept of a transit node, and makes sure that information from a transit node (each round has a different transit node) is passed along only to members of the transit node's sink tree. Once again, note that we are talking about a synchronous affair of choreographed events that assume global awareness of the predetermined sequence; all nodes make their way through the rounds in lock-step fashion, each node always knows which round it is, and each node knows the transit node associated with any given round. During each round, if a given node knows a path to the transit node, it is free to request local routing information from the transit node. Indeed, the chief purpose of each round of the algorithm is to propagate routing information possessed by a selected transit node to anyone else in the network who can make use of it, i.e. anyone else in the network who has a path to the transit node. It follows immediately that the algorithm consists of *n* rounds, for a network consisting of *n* nodes.

During each round, the transit node (selected for that round) issues its routing table to its neighbours. Every other node (other than the transit node and its neighbours) will first check if it can use the routing information from the transit node - by checking if the entry corresponding to the transit node in the local routing table has distance marked as ∞. If not, i.e. if the transit node is marked as reachable by a path of finite length, then the transit node is reachable, and its routing information is usable; the local routing entry associated with the transit node will also specify the first hop on the path to the transit node. Each such node (that has a path to the transit node) sends a *request* message to the first hop on the path to the transit node and gets the transit node's routing information forwarded to it in response. Obviously, the first hop in such a case is a node which is either the transit node itself, or a node which knows a path to the transit node. In other words, the transit node's routing information gets dispersed along its sink tree to all members on the sink tree. Once received, each node applies the transit node's routing information to expand and improve the local routing table. Next, let us consider an example to better understand the details described so far.

13.5.1 An example

Consider the 6-node network as depicted in the following diagram:

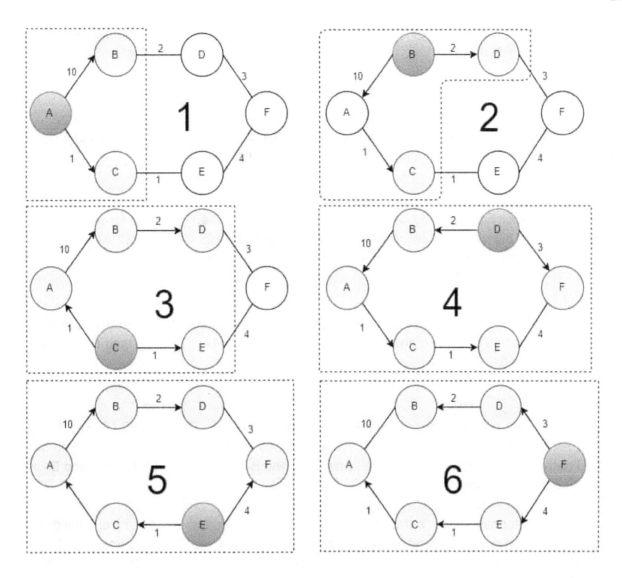

This implies a 6-round execution of the algorithm and let us start with the first one. Note that each round is illustrated in the diagram, with the dotted line indicating the 'coverage' in each round - i.e. the extent to which the transit node's routing information is dispersed - and the directed edges indicate the flow of routing info from the transit node to other nodes.

13.5.1.1 Round 1

During round 1, node A is the transit node. Note that the sequence of transit node selection is predetermined and that all nodes are aware of the same. During the first round, only two nodes have reachable path information to node A - the immediate neighbours B and C. As a result, B and C become aware of a path to reach each other, via the transit node A. This path is of length 11 units. Round 1 has no further consequences.

13.5.1.2 Round 2

Now, it is the turn of node B to play the role of the transit node. There are 3 nodes that know a path to B - the neighbours A and D, and then C (thanks to the previous round). As a result of this round, A and D discover a path of length 12 between them, while C and D note a path of length 13 between them.

13.5.1.3 Round 3

The transit node for the third round is node C. Everyone except node F have a path to C by now. As a consequence of this round, the paths between the pairs [E, D], [E, B], and [E, A] are discovered, and marked to be of lengths 14, 12, and 2, respectively.

13.5.1.4 Round 4

Node D is the transit node, and by now all nodes have a path marked out to the transit node. The availability of the routing information from node D helps connect node F to C, A, and B. The corresponding paths are marked to be of lengths 16, 15, and 5, respectively.

13.5.1.5 Round 5

The penultimate round has node E as the transit node. This brings about a few corrections in the local routing tables of some of the nodes: the pairs [C, F] and [A, F] modify their respective distances to 5 and 6.

13.5.1.6 Round 6

The last round sees a flurry of changes. The transit node is node F. The pairs [E, D], and [E, B] reduce their path distances to 7 and 9, respectively. Nodes C and D discover a shorter path of length 8 between them, while the distance between C and B is reduced to 10. Even A and D modify their distance from 12 to 9.

Note that route information from a transit node is provided on-demand. For example, consider round 3. The transit node is D, whose route information reaches E via B, A, and finally C. Why does E ask C (and not F) for the transit node's route information? Because, E learnt about a path to D, via C, during the previous round when C was the transit node. How did C come to know of a path to D? From B, during the previous (2nd) round, when B was the transit node. And of course, C and B discovered a path between them during round 1. The following table shows how the routing table entries of the various nodes evolve across the rounds just described. Predictably, some entries remain constant throughout - the entries corresponding to the local node and those corresponding to immediate neighbours. Certain others represent unreachability for a few rounds before being updated to reflect paths of finite length. In some other cases, a path is found almost immediately, only to be updated to a shortest one in a later round.

Node Ids	A	B	C	D	E	F
A	[0, A]	[10, B]	[1, C]	[∞, -] → [12, B] →	[∞, -] → [∞, -] →	[∞, -] → [∞, -] →

251

				[12, B] → [12, B] → [12, B] → [9, C]	[C, 2]	[∞, -] → [B, 15]
B	[10, A]	[0, B]	[∞, -] → [A, 11] → [A, 11] → [A, 11] → [A, 11] → [D, 10]	[2, D]	[∞, -] → [∞, -] → [A, 12] → [A, 12] → [A, 12] → [D, 9]	[∞, -] → [∞, -] → [∞, -] → [D, 5]
C	[1, A]	[∞, -] → [A, 11] → [A, 11] → [A, 11] → [A, 11] → [E, 10]	[0, C]	[∞, -] → [13, A] → [13, A] → [13, A] → [13, A] → [8, E]	[E, 1]	[∞, -] → [∞, -] → [∞, -] → [A, 16]
D	[∞, -] → [12, B]	[2, B]	[∞, -] → [13, B] → [13, B] → [13, B] → [13, B] → [8, F]	[0, D]	[∞, -] → [∞, -] → [B, 14] → [B, 14] → [B, 14] → [7, F]	[3, F]
E	[∞, -] → [∞, -] → [C, 2]	[∞, -] → [∞, -] → [C, 12] → [C, 12] → [C, 12] → [F, 9]	[1, C]	[∞, -] → [∞, -] → [C, 14] → [C, 14] → [C, 14] → [7, F]	[0, E]	[4, F]
F	[∞, -] → [∞, -] →	[∞, -] → [∞, -] →	[∞, -] → [∞, -] →	[3, D]	[4, E]	[0, F]

	[∞, -] → [D, 15]	[∞, -] → [D, 5]	[∞, -] → [D, 16]			

For example, the cell in row A and column C has a single entry [1, C], which represents the routing table entry for C, at node A. This entry remains unchanged - because C is an immediate neighbour of A, and there is no shorter route to be found (we do not consider negative edge weights, after all). Contrast this with the contents of the cell at row A and column D: [∞, -] → [12, B] → [12, B] → [12, B] →[12, B] →[9, C] which indicates the progression of the entry for D in the routing table maintained by A. There is no route identified to D in the first round, while the second round picks up a route of length 12 with B as the first hop. Over the subsequent rounds, this entry is modified to a final one of length 9 with C as the first hop.

13.5.2 Message complexity

Message cost can be calculated trivially, since we know that the algorithm runs for n rounds, and each round sees a maximum of 2 messages sent across each edge in the network. As a result, we arrive at a message cost $O(nm)$ for a network of n nodes and m edges.

13.6 Conclusion

In many ways, this relatively short chapter was an extension of the previous one - where we discussed generic concepts like traversals, shortest paths, and spanning trees, and also their algorithms. Here, we took a further step and looked at a couple of algorithms that solve a practical, real life problem in computer networks. After looking at a centralised algorithm, of a somewhat tedious nature, we considered a 'proper' distributed variant which essentially uses the same underlying principles.

13.7 What's next

From our current preoccupation with space and distances, we will make a not-so-subtle switch to the concept of *time* in distributed networks. This move also lays the foundation for understanding certain problem contexts and algorithms that we will take up in subsequent chapters.

Chapter 14. Time and order

14.1 Introduction: a village in Southern Europe

Let us start with a simple story as a warmup to the topic of this chapter. The story only vaguely hints at the context and mechanisms that we will address in this chapter, but that will suffice.

Some say it really happened - many many years back, in a southern european village. The villagers had a huge clock tower of their own, situated in the village square. Of course, each household had their own little clock, but they were all notoriously inaccurate mechanical devices prone to unpredictable fluctuations. Only one thing was predictable with these moody little clocks which every village residence seemed to own: these clocks suffered from drift-ahead, in an unpredictable fashion. In other words, these clocks never ran slow, but instead, were prone to errors by time moving ahead. The big clock tower, situated imposingly in the village square as mentioned earlier, was a different class of machinery altogether - highly accurate, and naturally the entire village depended on the hourly chimes of the clock tower to time and plan their activities, while largely ignoring their house clocks (or by regularly correcting them based on the clock towers chimes).

Disaster stuck one day, sometime in the early 1940s when the 2nd world war had been raging on. An errant bomber aircraft, flying quite out of control, had one of its wings clip the clock tower. Severe mechanical damage was the result to both parties involved: the massive clock failed after years and years of reliable operation, and it is also safe to say that the aircraft never flew another day. As far as the villagers were concerned, the incident left them with no option but to rely on their house clocks. A terrible period of confusion ensued, with each house clock drifting out of sync, leading to bad coordination and attendance among the villagers for various critical group activities in the village. For instance, half the village would turn up for sunday morning mass just when it was about to wind up. As such a scheme of events was unacceptable, the villagers put their heads together and came up with a solution. The alarm on each house clock was set to ring loudly - loud enough for all neighbours to hear - at every hour. Let us say that Graziano's clock is prone to the odd heavy bit of clock drift and races ahead to 10 AM, a few minutes ahead of his neighbours (their clocks, i.e.). Hearing Graziano's alarm ring out, what does his neighbours do? Of course, one or some or all of them can tell Graziano: *'Hey your clock has jumped ahead, why don't you wind it back by a few minutes? None of our clocks are at 10 AM yet!'*

That may work, but wind back by how many minutes exactly? Maybe Graziano's neighbour Romano has a clock which is at 9:58 AM when Graziano's clock emits its 10 AM alarm. Perhaps Linda's clock is only at 9:55 AM. What reference can be used to correct Graziano's clock? Even if Graziano's clock is (somehow) corrected immediately, what about the others? Maybe Lucio's clock is only a few seconds behind Graziano's clock and might sound its alarm any second. Thankfully, the villagers had decided on a much simpler course of remedy. Whenever the first alarm (in a neighbourhood) rings out for a particular hour, all the residents of the neighbourhood move their clocks ahead by the required number of minutes so that all those clocks are synchronised every hour. Since neighbourhoods typically overlap, the entire village had their clocks move ahead in a somewhat synchronised and reliable fashion, with everyone else catching up more or less immediately with the occasional erroneous hard-charging drifter. If the clock tower had kept time, on many days it would have read 9:45 AM or worse when the usual Sunday 10 AM mass convened. But the mass saw a full attendance, and that is all that mattered to the good folks of the village.

The point to this story is very simple: in the absence of a *global clock*, individuals in a system are forced to rely on *local clocks*. One cannot realistically assume local clocks to be 1. completely accurate, or 2. synchronised with each other, so the solution is for all individuals - at least those who interact with each other - to agree to board a common virtual train of logical time, which is maintained and kept on course by frequent corrections (or updates, depending on how you look at the action) by individuals when they interact with each other. If Marco never attends Sunday mass, or any group activity in the village for that matter, maybe has no human contact whatsoever, then Marco is free to leave his little clock undisturbed and to follow its meanderings without a care in the world. As for the others, it is critical that they create a common notion of time - irrespective of how exactly they accomplish that.

Note that none of the villagers ever set their clocks backwards; that was simply not allowed. The hourly alarm system was not the only opportunity which the villagers used to synchronise their notion of time, in fact. Let us say that Graziano had agreed to drop in at the residence of his good pal and neighbour, Pasini, at 2:30 PM sharp. Pasini finishes his lunch around 2:28 PM and is about to wash up when Graziano knocks on his door. What does Pasini do? Of course, he welcomes Graziano - and also moves his clock ahead by 2 minutes to synchronise with Graziano's clock, which is obviously at 2:30 PM already as indicated by Graziano's arrival.

Maybe a bit disappointingly, this story does not have a climax or an ending. No matter really, because this story was all about illustrating the concept of *time* in an environment involving multiple independent entities. Now, let us take a more formal look at not just the concept of time, but that of *order* as well.

14.2 Time and Order

Switching back to our context of interest, i.e. distributed systems and algorithms, what exactly is the relevance of time and order? Let us deal with the concept of order, first. In fact, to make progress, we will start from a seemingly unlikely place - the concept of a *decision*.

14.2.1 Decision

It would be safe to say that a large part of computing is all about making decisions. What exactly does the process of *decision making* involve? In simplified terms: *a decision is all about selecting one from multiple choices or options*. If there was only one option, there simply is no decision making involved. Let us take the next step, then: if we stick with our current definition of what a decision is all about, then it follows that a large part of decision making is all about *comparisons*. We compare one or more aspects of one option with the corresponding ones of another, and we possibly do this multiple times among a set of multiple options. Consider this hypothetical scenario where one is presented with multiple options, but with a devious rule being enforced: *the operation of comparison is not allowed*. Would decision making be possible, then? Obviously, we are talking about calculated decisions, and not impulsive, emotional, or randomised ones. As a more concrete example to back up the hypothetical one, imagine one being asked to write *C* code that is intended to make a particular decision, but an *if* statement (or similar, say *switch*) is not allowed. That piece of code is not very likely to get written.

14.2.2 Comparison and Order

So, starting from the point of view of what a decision is, we have arrived at the concept of comparing options or choices. What exactly is an option or choice? It is nothing but a piece of data. What follows is simple: the pieces of data which form our set of options must be *comparable* quantities. To make a decision, we just might need to compare every element in our data set with every other element. Consider the following (Sci-Fi) example: let us assume that we are working with the data set {John, Fred, Quinn, Selina}, and the following decision is to be made: which one is the tallest among them? Naturally, we will use a trivial comparison algorithm which compares heights (which we will assume to be available) and figure out the result. This worked because all the members of the given data set were comparable with each other. Now, what if the set was something like: {John, Fred, Selina, *Kral-El*} where *Kral-El* is an alien who exists in a dimension which does not align with our concepts of space and time? We would have a problem, because, unlike the earlier set, all pairs from this set are not comparable to each other, since the idea is that the *Kral-El* is from a dimension where the concept of length or height does not exist. The former is a *totally ordered* set, while the latter is a *partially ordered* one. As another example, consider a list or prices, all in euros. We have a totally ordered set, since each item can be compared with every other item. How about a price list where some are in euros, while the others are in yen? Assuming that our software does not have access to a reliable (and dynamic) euro-to-yen conversion table, we have a partially ordered set. What we are arriving at, then, is the simple requirement that we need data items from a totally ordered set if we have to make sensible decisions - because decisions involve comparisons. Now, where does the concept of time get involved in all of this?

14.2.3 About Time?

Let us imagine an algorithm being executed in a distributed environment. Naturally, the correct execution of the algorithm relies on correct decision making at every step. As we arrived at earlier, decisions involve comparisons. For example, consider a node receiving multiple requests, one from each other node. The decision to be made is the following: select a single request out of all the incoming ones. Let us assume that the algorithm compares the priority values of the source nodes and selects the request which was generated by the node with the highest priority (let us assume that each node is assigned a unique priority number, and that the node/priority mapping table is available to all nodes). As long as the priority values are from a totally ordered set, the comparisons and subsequent decision making will work out just fine. The concept of time has no role to play here.

Next, let us ponder the meaning of an *event*. Of course, an event is something that takes place. As an example, *Alex has a blue car* is not an event. However, *Dennis woke up* is an event. We can extend that last statement to something such as *Dennis woke up at 6AM*. Obviously, events happen *in time* and each event can be associated with a *timestamp*. We face a similar situation while dealing with distributed environments. Each node or process in a distributed system can be thought of as dealing with a series of events. A request arriving at a node is an event. A node performing a calculation is an event. A database transaction is an event. The point that arises is: quite often, decision making involves comparisons between events - more specifically, comparison between timestamps associated with events.

To get a better grip on this concept, let us transform the earlier example where a node has to compare between multiple incoming requests; now each request has an associated timestamp, which forms the basis for comparison (rather than source priority). The timestamp associated with a request, of course, is originally inserted by the source node (the node that generated the request) and represents the time of request generation. Imagine node A to be the one who receives all these requests. Let us say that node A has to compare between request B (issued by node B) and request C (source node is node C). As we mentioned earlier, this involves a comparison between the timestamp of request B and the timestamp associated with request C. How do we assume that we are dealing with two comparable quantities?

To elaborate further, timestamp B represents the notion of time from the perspective of node B, while timestamp C corresponds to node C's idea of time. Of course, we have two choices here:

1. Assume that all nodes have access to a global clock
2. Assume that all nodes have a local clock, and that all local clocks are perfectly synchronised

If we go with either of the above assumptions, we find ourselves with no worries. Unfortunately, both are ideal conditions. In a real world, clocks inevitably drift out of sync. A global clock is (usually) impractical for distributed systems. Consider the following implication, for instance: the request from node B is generated earlier than the one from C, yet request C arrives at node A earlier than request B, carrying an earlier timestamp to boot. Naturally, node A gives priority to request C over request B, potentially subverting the subsequent decision making.

As another example, imagine a 10km road race. There is a single starting point, from which all runners start off as the gun fires. To avoid congestion, runners diverge into two different routes after the first 500m. Runners with a blue *BIB* take to the left and follow route A, while those with a red *BIB* branch to the right and take route B. Each route has its own finishing point. At the finishing point, each runner's *BIB* triggers a timing beam which records his or her finishing time based on a local clock fixed near the finishing line. The race start is 7AM, so if Sam crosses the line at 7:52AM, her 10K timing is 52 minutes. Finally, once the last runner crosses the line, the data from both finishing points are merged and sorted to produce the final result table. Now, everything works fine if the local clocks at both finishing points are perfectly synchronised. However, imagine the confusion and potential chaos if these two clocks were out of synch by say, a couple of minutes - particularly if we also imagine both finishing points being covered, simultaneously, on live TV. If we imagine a list of 10K finishing times, some of which are from route A while some are from route B, what we have is indeed a partially ordered set - precisely because a time value from route A cannot be compared reliably with one from route B, thanks to each route having its own local clock.

Coming back to a distributed environment, the following requirement makes itself evident: in the absence of a global clock as well as synchronised local clocks, we need a mechanism by which timestamps generated by different nodes in a distributed system still belong to a totally ordered set. In other words, we need the nodes in a distributed system to generate timestamps that can be reliable compared, even when the pair of timestamps (being compared) are generated by different nodes. The key idea is that we would like the capability to assign an order to events; we are far more interested in the exact order in which things happened, than about what happened just exactly when. Going back to the road race example, the organisers will not worry so much about whether Sam finished at 6:52 or 6:53 (though Sam might), as about whether Sam finished before Gerard or after.

Before we move on to some solutions to our current requirement, let us note: our predicament arises only because nodes interact with each other. If each node was happily doing its own work always, with no interaction with any other node, then every node is free to follow its own notion of time - however out of sync it is with anyone or everyone else. When nodes interact, we are immediately faced with the requirement of a common notion of logical time which will then provide us with the ability to treat events in the system as totally ordered items. To jump ahead a bit, in the solutions which we will soon see, such interactions themselves will play a key role in maintaining a train of logical time for the system as a whole. On that note, let us quickly visit a few fundamental rules around which any solution to this problem will be designed around.

- As we briefly saw earlier, any individual node in the network can be thought of as producing or experiencing a series of events. If the idea is that each of these events should be assigned a timestamp, a logical time value, then it follows that a later event should have a logical time value which is strictly greater than that of an earlier event.

- Consider the interaction between two nodes. This would be in the form of a message being sent from one node to the other. Now, the event of message receipt will happen *after* the event of message dispatch; so, the logical time associated with the former must be strictly greater than the logical time associated with the latter.

- Since we use these timestamps or logical time values for comparisons, we would not want two separate events to have the same timestamp; or at least, we need a tie-breaker mechanism in such situations. Note that the whole idea is to order events in time, so we want each event to have a unique position in the 'stream' of events in the system.

These are the absolute basic necessities, and any solution we consider will have to guarantee these. Now, let us go ahead and see how *Lamport clocks* can help us build a notion of logical time in a distributed environment.

14.3 Lamport clocks

The whole idea behind Lamport clocks is to build a notion of logical time in a distributed system so that we can temporally order events that happen in the system, with the corresponding timestamps forming a totally ordered set. Leslie Lamport, in his landmark paper "*Time, Clocks, and the ordering of Events in a Distributed System*", introduced the concept of *logical clocks* using the following abstract view as a starting point: *a clock is just a way of assigning a number to an event*. The implication of such an outlook is that each node in a distributed system can be thought to have exclusive access to a simple counter, which then works as the logical clock for that node. Note that these counters have no timing mechanism; they are simple counters which can be incremented by the software running on each node. Before we see how these counters or logical clocks are used, let us go through a basic, and useful, notation first:

14.3.1 The 'happened-before' notation

Since the key idea is to order events in time, the key comparison operation between two events is to determine which happened before the other. If A and B are two events, the idea that A happened before B is represented by the following notation:

$$A \to B$$

In such a situation, the logical time associated with A will be strictly less than the logical time associated with B. The challenge is to ensure such a relation between the logical times of any two events in a distributed system. The first step in this direction is to ensure that the *clock condition* is always satisfied. What exactly is the clock condition?

14.3.2 Clock condition

Let us use the notation $L(A)$ to represent the logical time associated with event A. Then, the clock condition is as follows:

For any pair of events A, B in the system:

> if $A \rightarrow B$, then $L(A) < L(B)$

In other words, if event A happened before event B, the logical time associated with event A will be strictly smaller than the one associated with event B. Let us next see how we can achieve this condition using counters that function as logical clocks, and what exactly that entails.

14.3.3 Using counters as logical clocks

How do we use the aforementioned local counters to generate and associate logical times with each event happening in the system? Rather simple: whenever an event happens at a node, increment the node's local counter and associate the new value of the counter with the event. For example, consider the first event happening at a particular node in the system. The counter starts off at 0; once the first event happens, the counter is incremented (to 1) and the logical time of 1 becomes the timestamp of that first event.

How about messages sent from one node to the other? The sending of a message is an event, so the same rule applies. If the first event at a node is that node sending a message to another node, then that send event is assigned a logical time of 1. Additionally, the message carries the logical time associated with the event that is the dispatch of the message (1 in the previous example). How does the recipient make use of this logical time carried by each incoming message? The receipt of a message is an event and must be alloted a logical time which is strictly larger than the logical time associated with the sending of the message. At the same time, the receipt of the message is an event that happens at the recipient node and must have a logical time that is strictly greater than the last event that happened on that node. Hence, the recipient picks the larger of two logical times - the current value of its local counter, and the logical time carried by the incoming message - increments it by one and assigns the resultant value as the logical time associated with the event that is the receipt of the message. Refer the next diagram (Figure 1):

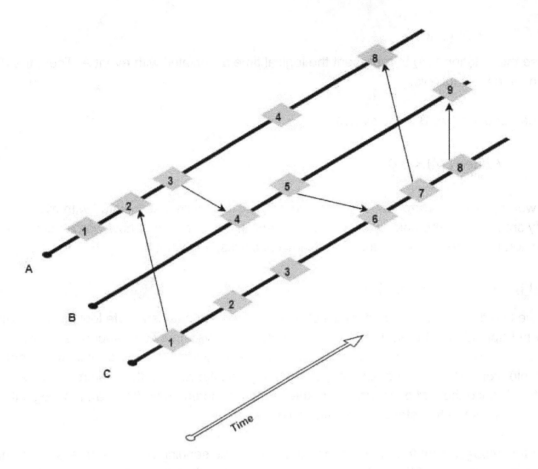

Figure 1

The three black lines indicate the flow of execution on three different nodes in the system: A, B, and C. The numbered squares represent events, while the arrowed lines represent messages sent from one node to another.

Using $L(X)$ as the notation which represents the logical time associated with event X, let us summarise:

- If A and B are events in the same node and A happened before B, then A → B and $L(A) < L(B)$
- If R represents the event of a message receipt, the corresponding logical time is calculated as $L(R) = min(C, L(S)) + 1$ where C is the current value of the recipient node's local counter, and S is the logical time associated with the event that is the dispatch of the message (S is specified in the message)

Note how this approach ensures that interacting nodes will keep catching up their logical times with each other.

So far, we have dealt with events happening in the same node, and events happening across interacting nodes. Does this cover all types of events that happen in the system? Not exactly.

For example, consider two nodes in the system, say node A and node B. Let us assume that 3 events happen on both nodes before any interaction happening between them. On each node, these events will be assigned the logical times 1, 2, and 3. How do we proceed if we have to compare the 2nd event on node A with the 2nd event on node B? Or say, the 1st event on node B and the 2nd event on node A? There is no way to determine which happened before which. If the 4th event on node A is the sending of a message to node B, that event will receive a logical time of 4, and the corresponding receipt event at node B will receive a logical time of 5. This is expected, because when node B receives the message, it compares the logical time carried by the message (4) with the current value of its counter (3), selects the larger value (4), increments it (to 5), and assigns that value as the logical time associated with the receive event. So now we have 4 events on either node, and the only events which we can compare between are the last (4th) event on either node. Any other pair of events, one from node A and one from node B, must be treated as concurrent events because it really does not matter which way we order them - since there is no interaction between the two nodes during that time, there is no dependency either. Maybe events 1,2,3 happened at node A before any events happening on node B - who knows? Maybe it is the other way, or maybe those events happened in an interleaved sequence - it really does not matter which way we order these events. So, if we consider event 2 on A and event 1 or B, we might just as well order them based on their logical times and assume that event 2 on A happened after event 1 on B. That works just fine because we are effectively dealing with concurrent events. The real question is, how do we order event 1 on A and event 1 on B, or event 2 on A and event 2 on B, or event 3 on A and event 3 on B?

To break ties like these, Lamport provides a solution: assign unique identity numbers to nodes and use them to break ties. If the id of node A is 1, and the id of node B is 2, then event 1 on A is considered to have happened before event 1 on B, and the same applies for events 2 and 3 on either node.

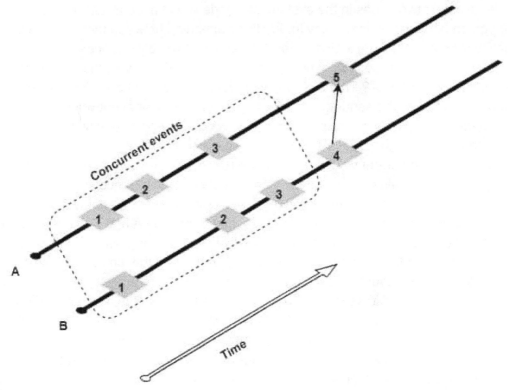

Figure 2

The above diagram (Figure 2) is a pictorial representation of the scenario that was just discussed. If we arrange these events in order, we end up with the following sequence: *A1, B1, A2, B2, A3, B3, B4, A5*. Switching to the diagram previous to the last one (Figure 1), and assigning 1, 2, and 3 as the ids for A, B, and C, we obtain this sequence once we put all events in the system in order: *A1, C1, A2, C2, A3, C3, B4, A4, B5, C6, C7, A8, C8, B9*. This is exactly what we required in the first place: arrange all events in the system as a totally ordered set, thus facilitating reliable comparison between any pair of events, which in turn ensures correct decision making at every step of our distributed algorithm that is executing in the system.

14.3.4 What is missing?

So far so good, but there is indeed a slight deficiency with Lamport clocks. To get a clearer picture, refer back to Figure 1 - for instance, event 4 at node A and event 5 at node B are actually concurrent events; there is no way to determine which one happened earlier, and yet: $L(A) < L(B)$. That specifically is what Lamport clocks lack - the logical time of one event being lesser than that of another event does not necessarily mean that the former event happened earlier. In other words, $L(A) < L(B)$ does not imply that A → B. In fact, if $L(A) < L(B)$, there are *two* possibilities:

1. A → B
2. A and B are concurrent events

What we really need, then, is a mechanism to identify concurrent events decisively. If the logical timestamps associated with two events *can* be compared, we should be able to state with certainty that we can order those two events in time. If the logical timestamps associated with two events *cannot* be compared, we should be able to state with certainty that those two events are concurrent. In other words, we want a system which guarantees that if $L(A) < L(B)$, then $A \rightarrow B$. Let us next see how *Vector clocks* can help us in this regard.

14.4 Vector clocks

So, what is a vector? Of course, a vector is a one dimensional array. While Lamport clocks use a single value to represent a piece of logical time, vector clocks, as the name suggests, use an array of values. Each node not only maintains a local counter (and uses it in the exact same way as Lamport clocks), but also 'remembers' the logical time associated with each other node - based on what it heard last from each node. So, a vector or array of values that represent a logical time value has as many entries as there are nodes in the system. One entry in the vector is the logical time associated with the local node, while each other entry correspond to the logical time of another node in the system.

For example, assume a distributed system which consists of only two nodes - node A and B. Initially, the local counters of both nodes are at zero. Neither node has heard anything from the other. As a result, the logical time vector at either node is [0, 0]. Now, let the first event on node A be the act of node A sending a message to node B. The logical time vector carried by the message in this case would be [1, 0] where 1 is the current value of the local counter node A, and 0 is the perception of node A regarding the last event in node B which A has heard about (it is 0 because node A is yet to hear anything from B). Once node B receives this message, it assigns the logical time vector [1, 2] to the receive event - 1 is the logical time associated with the last event in A which node B has heard about (the send event which resulted in node B receiving the current message), and 2 is the logical time which node B has assigned to the event that is the receipt of the current message. Now, one event has happened on either node - a send event at node A and a receive event at node B. Let us assume the second event at node B to be the act of node B sending a message to node A. This message will carry the logical time vector [1, 3] where 1 is the logical time associated with the last event at node A which node B has heard about, and 3 is the logical time which node B has associated with the current send event. Upon receiving the message, node A will assign the logical time vector [4, 3] to the receive event - 4 representing the logical time associated with the receive event, and 3 being the logical time associated with the last event at node B that node A has heard about (the sending of the current message). Note how the overall mechanism is implemented using two different actions:

1. Each node maintains and uses a local counter just as in the case of Lamport clocks
2. Each node remembers the logical time associated with every other node, based on the last event at the corresponding node which it heard about

Note that each node will use a time vector in an incoming message to update, if needed, its perception of the logical times associated with other nodes. For example, assume that node A has assigned a logical time vector [4, 1, 0] to its last event. The value [4, 1, 0] indicates that the local counter of node A currently reads 4, node A has heard about the first event at node B, and also that node A is yet to hear from node C at all - directly or indirectly. Now, node A receives a second message from node B, carrying the logical time vector [0, 5, 3]. The 0 indicates that node B is yet to hear from node A (hence, as far as node B is concerned, the local counter of node A currently reads 0). The second entry, 5, is the logical time which B has assigned to the dispatch event (of the message which A has currently received). The third entry, 3, indicates that node B did hear from node C, and node C had assigned the logical time of 3 to the event which was the dispatch of that message (to node B). Upon receiving such a message from node B, node A immediately updates its perception of the logical times at node B and node C to 5 and 3 respectively and also assigns the logical time vector [6, 5, 3] to the event representing the receipt of the message. If the next event at node A is the act of sending a message to say, node C, the message will carry the logical time vector [7, 5, 3]. Refer the next diagram (Figure 3):

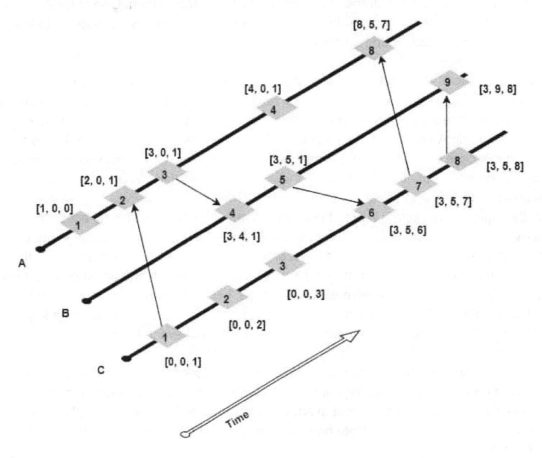

Figure 3

Figure 3 is nothing but Figure 2 that is converted from using Lamport clocks to using Vector clocks. Let us now move on to the next section to understand how exactly vector clocks help us avoid the ambiguity that we discussed in section *14.3.4* by helping us identify concurrent events conclusively. We will be referring back to Figure 3.

14.4.1 Comparing time vectors

Two logical time vectors can either be compared or not. For a logical time vector A to be less than a logical time vector B, the following two conditions must be satisfied:

1. There must be at least one element in A that is less than the corresponding element in B
2. No element in B must be greater than the corresponding element in A

A similar logic applies to the greater-than condition. Here are some examples:

*   [1, 0, 0] is greater than [0, 0, 0]
*   [1, 2, 3] is lesser than [1, 3, 3]
*   [9, 4, 0] is greater than [8, 4, 0]
*   [5, 4, 3] is lesser than [6, 4, 4]

So far so good, but how exactly do we identify concurrent events? For an answer, let us consider some of the concurrent events in Figure 3. We instantly see that concurrent events have associated logical time vectors that are not comparable. Here are some examples:

*   [1, 0, 0] and [0, 0, 1]
*   [2, 0, 1] and [0, 0, 3]
*   [3, 4, 1] and [0, 0, 3]
*   [8, 5, 7] and [3, 5, 8]

This is exactly what we required in the first place - a system which will help us weed out the possibility of concurrent events from comparable logical times so that:

*   If $A \rightarrow B$ then $T(A) < T(B)$

*   If $T(A) < T(B)$ then $A \rightarrow B$

In brief: with the Vector clocks algorithm, we can order two events if we can compare their logical timestamps. With Lamport clocks, even if we could compare the logical timestamps of two events, there was always the possibility that they were concurrent events. What exactly do we give up as result, with Vector clocks? Thanks to certain pairs of events being incomparable, the resultant ordering of all events in the system is indeed a partial ordering.

14.5 Conclusion

After an introductory story, we delved into the concepts of time and order as applicable to distributed systems and ended up with a clear requirement: how to reliably order all the events that happen in a distributed system (where a global clock or synchronised local clocks are not practical), thus enabling proper comparisons and subsequent accurate decision making. We looked at two solutions, the first one being Lamport clocks. The second solution, Vector clocks, addresses a specific deficiency that we observed with Lamport clocks.

14.6 What's next

The current chapter was somewhat of a deviation, dealing with a bunch of abstract concepts and associated techniques that 'higher' algorithms can make use of. We get back on course in the next chapter and continue analysing investigative and control algorithms for distributed systems. While doing so, we will also get to apply some of the learnings from this chapter.

Chapter 15. Mutual Exclusion (part 1)

15.1 Introduction

To start with, let us ponder the meaning of the phrase 'Mutual Exclusion'. In simplified terms, two events are said to be *mutually exclusive* if they are disjoint events; i.e. if those two events cannot happen at the same time. In a much similar vein, we imagine a set of n nodes interested in a 'shared' resource, which is in fact non-shareable - meaning, only one node can access or use that resource at any given time. In other words, mutual exclusion refers to an arrangement where the set of n resource-access events, one for each node accessing said resource, is a set of mutually exclusive events. This means that we use the technique of mutual exclusion to provide an illusion; the illusion that a non-shareable resource is shareable. A node or process who has obtained privileges to a shared resource is said to have entered the *critical section*. A critical section broadly refers to a segment of activity by a process that involves access to one or more shared resources. The problem of mutual exclusion was examined deeply for the first time by Dijkstra in his paper titled "*Solution of a Problem in Concurrent Programming Control*" (1965). In this chapter, we start our analysis of mutual exclusion with two (related) algorithms that employ the concepts (of logical time) that we analysed in the previous chapter. Afterwards, we move on to other algorithms in the same context before examining the more general case of mutual exclusion (resource allocation). In fact, before any of that, let us formally define the basic properties that a mutual exclusion algorithm must provide.

15.2 Properties expected from a mutual exclusion solution

As we mentioned earlier, we want any such solution to make an un-shareable resource *appear* to be a shared one. However, the bottom line is that our resource of interest is fundamentally of an unshareable nature; this immediately leads to an obvious expectation:

- *Only one node or entity must have access to the resource at any given time*

Assuming 'proper' behavior, we will expect any resource-holding node to release the resource sooner or later. This implies that every interested party will get a chance to access the resource, and thus leads to the second property or expectation:

- *Eventually, every interested node must succeed in gaining access to the resource*

This is another way of saying that the algorithm must be *deadlock-free*. In short, we state that a mutual exclusion implementation must provide both *safety* and *liveness* characteristics.

15.2.1 The concept of a critical section

In general, each node in our scenario of interest is assumed to be running or executing a 'program' that can be broadly divided into two segments: a *critical section* and a *non-critical section*. Each node spends an arbitrary amount of time in the non-critical section, executes a mutual exclusion algorithm to gain access to (and leave) the critical section (where it performs a certain number of tasks), with the whole process repeating any number of times.

15.3 Mutual Exclusion using Logical time (Lamport's version)

In his paper "*Time, Clocks, and the ordering of Events in a Distributed System*", Leslie Lamport provides a neat and succinct explanation of an algorithm which uses the tool of logical time to implement mutual exclusion. That said, an example just might present a clearer picture of this simple and elegant algorithm.

15.3.1 An example to illustrate the algorithm

The characters in this story are 4 students. Let us call them Andy, Bob, Chad, and Dan. To kick off the story, we shall present a few facts about these students. Being non-working students, money is not in abundance for them, so penny pinching is usually the way to go in many aspects of their life. They are all of different ages, with Andy being the youngest and Dan being the oldest. They stay in different states of their country and communicate with each other only by email. Last but not the least, they are hardcore fans of online gaming. To play their favorite game online, they pooled in money and bought a single online account - which they share. Only one user can be logged into the account at one time, and hence a routine problem for them is to figure out who gets to play when - something which they have to solve solely by email communication.

As is often the case, their approached their problem initially in a rather haphazard manner. For example, when Andy got a breather from his course work and decided to play the game, he would send an email with everyone else in CC: '*hey I'm gonna login and play the game.*' Sometimes that just worked; if nobody else was using, or planning to use, the game account at that moment (perhaps all three were busy with studies), in which case all the other three would respond with: '*fine, go ahead.*'

Sometimes there would be conflicts, though. For example, Bob and Chad might send out simultaneous emails to everyone, expressing an urgent interest to use the game account. Sometimes even that worked, if one of the two people backed off: 'ok fine, you go ahead, and I will play once you are done.'

As time went by, the process became more and more difficult to handle, particularly once egos start flaring - with none of the interested parties backing down, resulting in a stalemate. They really needed a methodical and clean process to regulate and distribute their access to the online game account. This is when Chad happens to read Lamport's paper on the subject. Soon enough, Chad briefs everyone on a new process which the other three wholeheartedly accept. So, what exactly is their new methodology?

15.3.1.1 Assumptions

Before delving into the new strategy employed by the quartet, let us examine the assumptions they made about their sole means of communication, i.e. email:

1. Emails send from one person to another always arrive in the same order as they were dispatched
2. Emails may get delayed, but never get lost

Additionally, each of the four students maintain a counter of his own, which is initially set to zero, and put to use as explained in section *14.3.3*. In brief, these counters generate the logical time for each person.

15.3.1.2 Message formats

Since email is the only possible means of communication, all four debate and decide on the specific message format to be rigidly followed. The agreed-upon message format allows a finite set of messages:
1. An email with subject "I request access (*XYZ*)"
2. An email with subject "I release access (*XYZ*)"
3. An email with subject "ACK (*XYZ*)"

The pattern *XYZ* represents an integer quantity which is the logical time inserted by the sender of the email in each case. Next, let us go through these individual messages in more detail.

15.3.1.2.1 Request access

This email (subject) format is used when someone needs access to the game account. The person increments his 'local' counter and adds the updated value to the subject line. For example, assume that Andy is the first person to have an 'itch' to play the game after the new process being in place. Andy will increase his counter to 1, and send out an email with the following subject line: "I request access (1)"

15.3.1.2.2 Release access

This format is used once someone has finished using the game account and would like to let others know of the fact - so that someone else can have a go, if needed. Similar to the previous case, the person updates his counter and appends the updated value to the email's subject line. Continuing the previous example, Andy would send an email with the following subject once he has finished using the game account: "I release access (2)". Note how this subject line carries a logical time which reflects the fact that Andy updated his local counter (from 1) before sending out this email.

15.3.1.2.3 ACK

This format represents an acknowledgment, which is sent by someone who receives a request-access email from someone else. For example, if Andy sends out a request-access mail to Ben, Chad, and Dan, all three recipients will send an ACK email to Andy. As in the previous two cases, the updated value of the local counter is mentioned in the subject line. In continuation to the example in *15.3.1.2.1*, upon receiving Andy's request-access email, all the other three would send the following ACK email to Andy: "ACK (2)". Note how this subject line carries a logical time which is obtained by incrementing the logical time specified in the original email sent by Andy.

15.3.1.3 Counter management

Note that logical times are generated in the exact same manner as described in the previous chapter, using local counters. In this case, there are exactly two types of events for each person involved:

1. Sending out an email (to either one person, or to everyone else)
2. Receipt of an email from someone else

In the first case, the local counter is incremented by one. Additionally, the updated counter value is included in the subject line. In the second case, the local counter of the recipient is set to the value obtained by incrementing the larger of the following two quantities - the logical time specified in the incoming email, and the current value of the local counter.

15.3.1.4 The rules of the game

Having defined the communication formats as well as the basics of handling logical time, let us now look at the mechanism that defines the algorithm. The rules are rather simple, and let us look at them in two parts:

1. Any of the four who wishes to access the game account will send out a request-access email to all the other three
2. The recipient of a request-access email will respond immediately with an ACK email
3. Once someone is done using the game account, he sends out a release-access email to all the other three

4. Once a release-access email is sent, the sender will clean up his inbox - by removing all emails which he has read (acknowledgements from others for his last request-access email and possibly request-access emails from others - which he would have already acknowledged)
5. Once a release-access email is received, the recipient will also clean up his inbox - by removing the corresponding request-access email

So far, so good. But how exactly does someone know that he has gained access privileges to the game account? Let us assume that Andy has just sent out a request-access email. What are the rules that Andy will follow to confirm that he can indeed go ahead and access the game account? There are two, actually:

a. Andy's inbox must contain at least one email from the other three, such that, the logical time associated with the email must be higher than the one specified in Andy's request-access email. As a simple example, we shall assume that Andy is the sole person interested in the game at the moment; so, there is only one request-access email seen by all the other three - which is the one sent out by Andy. Now, each recipient of said email will send out an ACK response which will obviously carry a logical time which is an incremented version of the value specified in Andy's request-access email. This leads to Andy seeing an email from each other person, with each such email carrying a higher logical time - which allows him to move on and evaluate the second condition

b. If there are no other request-access emails, there is nothing more to worry about. However, if there are concurrent request-access emails from others, the rule to be followed is simple: the one with the lowest logical time gets priority. What if there are request-access emails with identical logical times? As a simple example, what if all four people send out request access emails right at the start when the new process is first introduced? Obviously, everyone starts off with their local counters at 0, so each request-access email will carry a logical timestamp of 1. How do they resolve the conflict? Simple: since none among the four is of the same age, they decide that, in event of conflict, the youngest person will be given priority. In other words, age acts as a tiebreaker, much as how section *14.3.3* describes the use of node identifiers to achieve the same purpose.

Let us try to understand exactly when and how these conditions are evaluated by senders of request-access emails. Assume that Ben and Dan send out request-access emails, with the one from Ben carrying a lower timestamp. Obviously, the first step is to wait for condition (a) to be satisfied. Once that is done, both Ben and Dan scan their inbox for request-access emails from others, with a lower logical timestamp. In this case, Ben finds none while Dan finds the request-email from Ben - causing Dan to back off. Ben goes ahead and accesses the game account, and in time, sends out a release-access email. Any sender of a request-access email, waiting for the game account to be released (as is the case of Dan in this example) will immediately re-evaluate rule (b). To conclude, Dan receives the release-access email from Ben, finds no more request-access emails that supersedes his own, and takes over access privileges from Ben.

15.3.1.5 Does this actually work?

To start with, something obvious: we assume that someone who has grabbed access to the game account will release it, sooner or later. The primary concern otherwise is *atomicity* - nobody wants a situation where more than one person decides to access the game account, simultaneously. Is this scenario feasible?

Let us assume that Chad and Dan send out request-access emails more or less at the same time, carrying identical logical timestamps. Note that Chad is younger than Dan, and thus will receive priority in situations of conflict (such as this one). As per rules, both Chad and Dan will receive 3 ACK emails each for their respective request-access emails. The expectation as per rules is that Chad decides that he has gained access privileges to the game account. Is it possible that Dan (also) goes ahead and decides that he has gained access privileges?

If we assume that Dan received Chad's request-access email, it cannot happen - thanks to rule (b) mentioned earlier. The reason is simple - Dan will notice Chad's request access-email with an identical logical timestamp, use the age-based tiebreaker, and accept that Chad's request-access email must be given priority.

Is it possible that Dan did not receive Chad's request access email? That is not possible either, since Dan did receive Chad's ACK email - which would imply that Dan has also received Chad's request-access email (in section *15.3.1.1*, we assumed that emails sent from one person to another will arrive in the same order as dispatch).

What if Chad had sent his request-access email *after* acknowledging Dan's request-access email? This would imply that Chad's request-access email will carry a logical timestamp higher than that of the one specified in Dan's request-access email, in which case only Dan will end up with access privileges. Chad will gain access only after receiving a release-access email from Dan.

Let us try to generalise this aspect. We consider the possibility of A and B gaining access to the shared resource simultaneously, in a scenario where mutual exclusion is implemented via Lamport's algorithm. This can happen only if the following two conditions are both met:

1. A finds his/her access request having a logical timestamp lower than that of B, and vice versa
2. A has to see a message from B that specifies a logical timestamp higher than that specified in the access request from A, and vice versa

(1) is clearly impossible if logical times are correctly used, along with a mechanism to break ties. What about (2), then?

Let us analyse the second possibility from the point of view of A. The message which A sees from B, carrying a higher timestamp than the access request from A, can only be one of these two:

- an ACK (to the access request from A)
- an access request from B

Consider the former scenario, to start with. If the ACK from B has a higher timestamp, then the access request from B will have an even higher timestamp - ergo, access goes to A. The latter scenario is even simpler - the access request from B is of a higher timestamp, so again, access goes to A. Simultaneously, a reverse situation will play out at the side of B, resulting in B backing off. It follows that (2) is not viable, either.

15.3.1.6 An optimisation (by Glenn Ricart and Ashok Agrawala)

If you think about it, what purpose does a release-access message serve? Such a message simply lets the next-in-line entity, assuming there is one, know that the shared resource is now available for exclusive access. Going back to our earlier story, let us assume that Andy has acquired privileges to the game account and is using the same. At this point, assume that Ben is next-in-line. The point is, Ben knows the fact that he is next-in-line. This is because Ben has found only the request-access email from Andy to have a logical timestamp less than the one in his own request-access email, and further, he has received acknowledgements from everyone. All Ben is waiting for is...a release-access email from Andy. What if Andy had simply held back his acknowledgement to the request-access email from Ben, rather than send an explicit acknowledgement?

To understand this better, let us assume that Andy has acquired privileges to the game account and is busy playing the game. He has no time for email. Meanwhile Ben sends out his request-access email, notes a similar one from Andy with a lower logical timestamp, and also notes that he has received acknowledgements from everyone else but Andy. In this optimised version of the algorithm, Ben will never wait for an explicit release-access email from Andy. Once Andy finishes using the game, he has now time for email and hence sends an acknowledgement to Ben (for the request-access email from Ben). The moment Ben sees the acknowledgement from Andy, he realises that he has the required full set of acknowledgements and goes on to inherit access to the game account.

In fact, Andy and Ben could send out request-access emails simultaneously; Andy will compare the logical timestamp of his email with that of Ben's email and will send an acknowledgement only if his own email has a higher timestamp (in which case, Ben sees a full set of acknowledgements and gets access privileges). Ben adopts the same process and will acknowledge the request-access email from Andy only if his own email has a higher timestamp. If not, Andy takes over access while Ben will wait for an acknowledgement from Andy. We can summarise the optimisation in these points:

- One would generate an acknowledgement immediately and unconditionally only if one is not interested in the game account (shared resource) currently
- If one is currently using the game account, an acknowledgement will be sent only after finishing using the game account, and no explicit release-access email (message) would be sent
- If one is currently vying for access to the game account, an acknowledgement may be sent on a conditional basis (will be sent for those cases where logical timestamps are lower than that of the one in own request-access email)

15.3.1.7 A note on Acknowledgements

Let us ponder a bit on the utility of these acknowledgement messages (or emails, as in the example). If there is one person or node who does not generate any request-access activity, but still do acknowledge received request-access messages, those acknowledgement messages help other nodes (or persons) understand the 'state' of said person or node and take decisions accordingly. For example, let us consider a simple scenario that consists of only two individuals, whom we will call A and B. if A has sent out a request-access message, and B has no plans to send out one (something which A has no way of knowing or guessing), the only way for A to know for sure that a more-qualified (i.e. carrying a lower logical timestamp) request-access message from B is *not* on its way is for B to generate an acknowledgement message to the request-access message from A. In other words, this acknowledgement mechanism would have been quite unnecessary if B had a request-access message to send at that point in time. These are the possibilities, then:

- If A sees a request-access message from B with a lower logical timestamp, A defers
- If A sees a request-access message from B with a higher timestamp, A assumes privileges
- If A does not see a request-access message from B, but does see an acknowledgement from B for own request-access message, A assumes privileges because A knows that there is no lower-logical-timestamp request-access message arriving from B (due to the assumption that messages from one to another arrive in the same order of dispatch)
- If A sees neither a request-access message nor an acknowledgement from B, then A is definitely in a quandary

Going back to our original story, assume that Andy, Ben, Chad, and Danny generate request-access emails simultaneously. In other words, each person sees 3 request-access emails from others. This is absolutely sufficient for each person to identify the email carrying the lowest logical timestamp (using the age-based tiebreaker if needed), and accordingly, to gain access or backoff. However, assume that only three of them generated a request-access email. Let Chad be the 'silent' person - maybe he is away on vacation, maybe not. We will assume that their new process does not use acknowledgements. Now, each of the other three are left in the dark on whether Chad is a contender for access to the game account or not. Maybe Chad is indeed away on vacation, but perhaps he has a fancy to access the game account and his subsequent request-access email is delayed - who knows? The point to note is this: if each node keeps up a constant stream of request activity, acknowledgements are not needed. Unless such a condition (constant stream of activity from each participating node) is not satisfied, explicit acknowledgements are needed for access requests. The next algorithm expands further in this direction (of eliminating acknowledgements).

15.4 State Machine Replication using Mutual Exclusion

We looked at *SMR* or State Machine Replication in section *11.5.4*, noting the requirement for state to be maintained consistently across multiple nodes in a distributed system. For our current purpose, we will use a simplified representation of state - a single variable *V* maintained by each node in the system. For further simplicity, we will assume V to be an integer variable, the value of which is subject to changes as a result of operations demanded by users external to the system. For example, a user *u1* might send the command "Add 10" to node *n1*. At this point, the job of *n1* is to add 10 to the value of its local copy of V, and further, to get every other node to do the same. We can think of each node in the system having access to a local message queue, into which command messages (such as "Add 10") arrive. The trick is to get all nodes to execute commands in the *same order,* in the presence of multiple concurrent command messages. Obviously, we do not want *n1* executing "Add 10" followed by "Multiply by 2", while *n2* decides to go with "Multiply by 2" followed by "Add 10", resulting in inconsistent state (i.e. value of *V*) between *n1* and *n2*.

The idea is for each node to pick up command messages from its local message queue, execute the commands obtained thus, and to ensure that all nodes follow the same order of command execution. As hinted in section *15.3.1.6*, this algorithm does not employ the use of acknowledgements. Also, each command message carries an associated logical timestamp. The following two rules are used by each node to pick a command message from its local message queue:

1. The command message must have the lowest logical timestamp among all such messages in the queue
2. The last-received message from each other node must have a logical timestamp that is at least as large (as the one in the command message to be picked)

So, what if one or more nodes remain idle - without generating any command messages? To work around this, each node is committed to generating 'dummy' messages constantly and frequently enough, in the absence of demands from external users. This ensures that each node keeps 'hearing' from everyone else, and everyone involved is always in a position to evaluate both rules mentioned above.

Note how rule (2) differs with the corresponding rule in the scenario where acknowledgements are involved. Here, "*the last received message from each...*" must be "*at least as large*" is the criteria; with acknowledgements being used, "*at least one message from each...*" must be "*greater than*". This is to be expected, since acknowledgements will always have a logical timestamp which is higher than the corresponding request-access message (i.e. the message being acknowledged).

In general, we can consider state machine replication to be a 'higher layer' algorithm implemented using the foundation of mutual exclusion. If we consider the access privilege to a critical resource as a *privileged role* - one if you obtain, gives you the authority to tell every other node to do a single specific action on their local copies of the variable - then we can imagine everyone (who has been assigned a command to execute, by an external user) contending for exclusive access to that role, which is in turn regulated using a mutual exclusion algorithm. In fact, tying together *SMR* with our earlier examples on mutual exclusion, we can imagine a node broadcasting a command message immediately upon noting that its request-access message has qualified for exclusive privileges (say, for the role of 'command broadcaster') - which every other node receives, respects, and executes.

15.5 Resource Allocation

When we talk about mutual exclusion, we imply the existence of a single shared resource which multiple parties contend for. In a more general sense, we can imagine a 'resource set' consisting of multiple shared resources, with different interested parties contending for various subsets of the same. Let us look at a classic example.

15.5.1 The Dining Philosophers problem

The *Dining Philosophers Problem* is one where each party (philosopher) involved requires two resources (two forks, one to the left and one to the right) to perform a critical action (eating). The critical action can be performed once the required resources are obtained and said resources will be released once the action is done. The next diagram depicts the situation, with 8 philosophers around a table, with a fork between each of them.

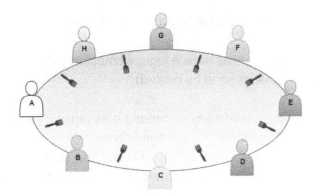

Each philosopher occupies himself with contemplation for an arbitrary amount of time, and then decides to eat. This requires procuring two forks, one on each side. "Procuring a fork" is essentially a blocking operation - if the fork is being used by the adjacent philosopher, one has to wait till that fork is released by the user.

15.5.1.1 Warmup

Obviously, a solution where each philosopher executes the same strategy - a symmetric solution - such as "1. *Procure left fork*, 2. *Procure right fork*, 3. *Eat*, 4. *Release forks*" will not work. For example, imagine the simple case of two philosophers sitting at the table, facing each other. There are two forks on the table; the left fork of one philosopher is the other philosophers right fork, and vice versa. Each person grabs his or her left fork, effectively blocking the other person's right fork; the subsequent attempt from either party to procure the right fork will end in a deadlock.

From the previous diagram, consider any philosopher - A, for example. Let us assume that A reaches out for the fork on his or her left, only to find it unavailable - because it has been picked up by H, of course. The interesting question is, what exactly is the state of H at that point? If H is already eating (which means that H has procured the fork on his or her left as well), there is certainty of progress - sooner or later, H will finish eating and release the forks. However, what if H, at that point in time, is waiting to procure the fork on the left side? Progress is no longer a certainty, and the possibility of deadlock creeps in. Of course, whoever H is waiting on, might be in the process of eating (in which case progress will happen), or in turn is waiting on someone who is eating, and so on - but if it ends up in a cycle that loops back to A, then we have a deadlock problem. One way to prevent deadlocks for sure is to ensure that anyone who has already procured one fork, and is waiting to procure the second one, is waiting on someone who is currently using both both forks (i.e. he or she is eating and will soon release both forks). This would just imply a slightly different behavior for odd and even numbered positions (counting from any arbitrary starting position) at the table. For example:

1. Philosophers at odd numbered slots will try to procure the left-side fork first
2. Philosophers at even numbered slots will try to procure the right-side fork first

In simpler terms, the person you compete with for your second fork must be someone just like you - who already has procured one fork. This simple right-left strategy ensures progress and avoids deadlocks.

15.5.1.2 The Chandy-Misra algorithm

The basic idea is simple - first of all, adopt a perspective which transforms the scenario into a directed graph which we commit to keep acyclic, where the philosophers form nodes, and the edges exist between nodes (philosophers) who share a resource (fork). A representation follows, which does not need more than a glance for an obvious flaw to be revealed:

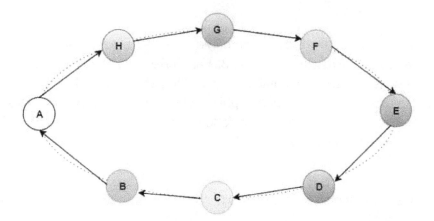

Indeed, what we have is a cyclic graph. This would be a good opportunity to present the reason why a cyclic graph is a strict no-no as per the algorithm. As mentioned earlier, each node (philosopher) has two neighbours with which one fork each is shared. This implies that each node has two incident edges (remember, an edge between two nodes represent the resource which they share). Each node keeps track of the edge directions using two flags: let us call them *left-flag* and *right-flag*. If the edge to the left is incoming, *left-flag* is set to *true*, else *false*. If the edge to the right is incoming, *right-flag* is set to *true*, else *false*. This is a representation of fork availability, in fact. If *left-flag* is true, the fork on the left is available; else unavailable. If *right-flag* is *true*, the fork on the right is available; else unavailable. Here are the key rules of the algorithm, then:

1. A node that has both *left-flag* and *right-flag* is *true*, is free to perform the critical operation
2. Once the operation is performed, a node must 'give up' privileges; this is done by switching both *left-flag* and *right-flag* to false, and informing each of the two neighbours by a message so that they can flip their corresponding flags accordingly

Now, the issue with the cyclic graph becomes apparent; everyone has their *right-flag* set to true and *left-flag* set to false. This is a deadlock since everyone pointlessly keep waiting for the *left-flag* to come true - which will never happen. So, the idea is that we start off with an acyclic digraph. Consider the following configuration next:

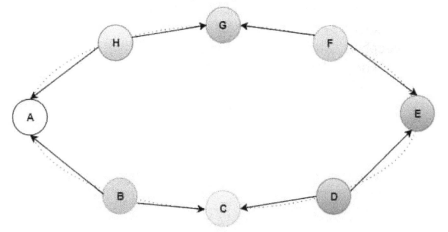

Here, the following nodes are free to perform the critical operation: A, G, E, and C. Once A and G are both done and free their resources, H will be in a position to access the two required resources:

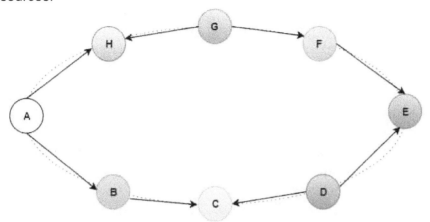

Similarly, once E frees the two resources that it has been using, F gets a chance - and so on. We can easily see that progress is possible, and deadlocks will never happen. In other words, the graph always remains acyclic; this is because, change in edge directions is always about a node *simultaneously* reversing the directions of *both* its incoming edges. Of course, we must assume that the starting configuration is that of an acyclic digraph.

15.5.2 Adapting Ricart/Agrawala algorithm for Resource Allocation

Finally, let us note that the optimised version of Lamport's mutual exclusion algorithm can be trivially adapted to the general case of resource allocation. Since we assume each node to be interested in multiple resources - the *resource set* for each node - we can identify a *quorum* for each node in the system; the group of nodes with resource sets that have at least one element common with the node's resource set. For example, consider the following set of dependencies:

-   A requires resources {r1, r2, r3}
-   B requires resources {r2, r3, r4}
-   C requires resources {r3, r4, r5}
-   D requires resources {r4, r5, r6}
-   E requires resources {r5, r6, r7}

In this case:

-   Quorum of A is {B, C}
-   Quorum of B is {A, C, D}
-   Quorum of C is {A, B, D, E}
-   Quorum of D is {B, C, E}
-   Quorum of E is {C, D}

The essence of the algorithm remains unchanged: a sender of request-access messages will proceed with the critical operation once it receives acknowledgements from everyone in the quorum. A recipient of a request-access message would send an immediate acknowledgement if it is not interested in the shared resource(s) at the moment; if not, there are two further possibilities: it is currently using the shared resources, or it plans to do so (has generated request-access messages to the its quorum). In the former case, acknowledgements are deferred until the shared resources are released (i.e. the critical operation is done with). In the latter case, acknowledgements are sent only for qualified request-access messages (i.e. those carrying a lower logical timestamp). In brief, nodes who have issued request-access messages might ending up waiting for acknowledgements in the following two cases:

- There are members in the node's quorum who are currently using the shared resources
- There are members in the node's quorum who have currently issued request-access messages with a lower logical timestamp

15.6 Conclusion

We started off this chapter with a brief definition of mutual exclusion, following by the formal properties required of any implementation for the same. Leveraging on our learnings from the last chapter, we analysed a mutual exclusion algorithm created by Leslie Lamport, and then we looked at how we can optimise it further. We moved on to state machine replication and identified an interesting relationship between *SMR* and mutual exclusion. We looked at a couple of solutions for the classic dining philosophers problem, before analysing the more general concept of resource allocation.

15.7 What's next?

Next, we move on to the last chapter in the second part of this book before switching to the subject of shared memory algorithms. In the next chapter, our interest and focus will continue to remain on control and monitoring algorithms, and we will come across a few interesting specimens that are of great practical utility when it comes to debugging and analysing distributed systems. Note: we will see much more of mutual exclusion in the final part of the book that deals with shared memory architectures.

Chapter 16. Debug algorithms

16.1 Introduction

Consider a standalone application running on a computer which may or may not be part of a bigger network. We are interested only in the behavior of the application process, which in fact seems to be rather out of the ordinary at the moment - perhaps the process is hung; maybe deadlocked; or maybe it is leaking memory, and thus bloating in size; maybe it does not even seem to be hung, because it does 'other' things correctly while its main service loop seems to have terminated...and so on and so forth. Basically, we would like to collect more information. How do we proceed? In normal conditions, we use some system tool to obtain a 'dump' of the process, which is essentially the memory image of the process that is written out to a disk file. Once this is accomplished, we are free to carefully analyse the dump file, looking for memory leaks, analysing stack traces, probing for hints of memory corruption, inspecting the status of various variables - the list goes on. Suffice to say that we have a clear and traditional *modus operandi* when it comes to debugging a standalone process running inside a host computer. In this chapter, we keep the problem unchanged while shifting the context from a standalone process to an algorithm that is being executed by a distributed network of computers. Let us begin, then, with the memory dump equivalent of a distributed network.

16.2 Snapshots

Since a distributed network obviously is made up of its constituent nodes and their interconnecting channels, at any instant we are interested broadly in two aspects: the state of individual nodes, as well as the contents of individual channels (i.e. messages in transit). These two components together form what we call a *snapshot* of the system. It is indeed reasonable to assume that each node has the capability to take a snapshot of itself; this is followed up by asking neighbours to do the same. All that is left is to ensure that any messages in transit are accounted for. To get a feel for what exactly is involved, let us look at a trivial example.

16.2.1 Warming up with a simple example

Let us assume a very simple banking scenario - so simple that, we will assume a bank that has only two accounts. We shall call them account A and account B. Let account A contain 200$ while B holds 150$. The bank's chief technician is tasked with taking weekly snapshots of this financial 'ecosystem' which consists of all of two accounts. He inspects account A, and notes down its balance as 200$. Immediately afterwards, the technician goes for his morning coffee. Meanwhile, the owner of account A transfers 50$ to account B. Not much later, the technician returns and notes down the balance of account B - as 200$. So, the snapshot which he created looks like the following:

- Account A: 200$
- Account B: 200$

This is obviously inaccurate. The second component of the snapshot (corresponding to account B) includes a transfer (from account A) which the first component (corresponding to account A) does not include or register. In other words - the snapshot of account A has this money transfer in the future while the snapshot of account B has it in the past. This is a simple example of an *inconsistent snapshot*. For a *consistent snapshot*, the following holds true:

- if *e1* is a post-snapshot event, and *e2* happens causally after *e1*, then *e2* must be post-snapshot, too
- If *e1* is a pre-snapshot event, and *e2* happens causally before *e1*, then *e2* must be pre-snapshot, too

Next, let us look at an algorithm designed to obtain consistent snapshots in a distributed network.

16.2.2 The Chandy-Lamport algorithm

We can imagine a snapshot algorithm as a custom module with which an existing, arbitrary, algorithm implementation is augmented. An admin triggers the snapshot functionality on any given node, after which the trigger spreads across the other nodes in the network, eventually causing each and every node to collect a snapshot. Of course, we assume a connected network and that the trigger is propagated using appropriate token messages, not to mention a final 'collection' mechanism (of some description) which obtains the individual snapshots from across the network to construct the cumulative snapshot of the whole system.

The Chandy-Lamport algorithm uses an external trigger to launch the snapshot mechanism, and then uses token messages to achieve coverage across the network. This implies that there are two ways to trigger snapshot functionality in a node:

1. An external trigger, say a message or a signal (invoked by a network admin, perhaps)
2. A token message issued by a neighbouring node

Let us consider the external trigger first, even though the two scenarios are rather close in terms of functionality. The recipient node (the 'source' node, which is 'ground zero' for the whole mechanism) first takes a snapshot of itself (maybe saves its current state into a file), and then issues marker messages along all its channels.

As for the second case, i.e. of a node receiving a token message from a neighbouring node, there are two sub-cases:

    a.   This is the first time the node is seeing a token message
    b.   The node had seen a token message earlier (i.e. it has already taken its snapshot and issued token messages)

In the first case, it behaves as earlier: takes own snapshot and sends out token messages to all its neighbours. In the second case, no action is needed.

So far so good - due to the connected nature of the graph, we are guaranteed that the token is propagated to every node, and hence, that every node takes its snapshot. However, what about the state of channels, i.e. what about any in-flight messages that might exist at the time of snapshot?

As mentioned earlier, apart from the 'ground zero' node (who is prodded by an external trigger), the first appearance of a token message causes a node to take its snapshot and to issue token messages along all its channels. The state of the channel which produced that *first* token message is marked as *null*. As for each of the rest of the channels, the node keeps recording incoming messages until a token message is seen. The output of each channel that precedes a token message forms the state of that channel. For example, if channel $c1$ produces messages $m1, m2, m3,$ and $m4$ before a token message appears, the state of $c1$ is $\{m1, m2, m3, m4\}$. Finally, the snapshot algorithm ends for a node once a token message is produced by each incident channel. A flowchart representation follows:

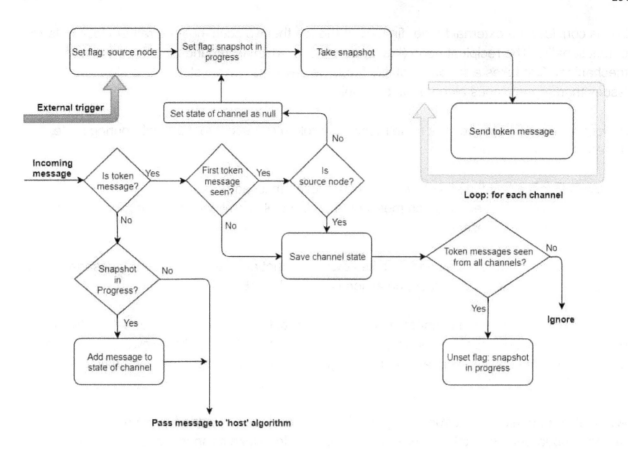

The 'ground zero' or 'source' node which initiates the snapshot algorithm in the system, as seen above, follows a slightly different logic to other nodes. Since such a node is the initiator, the first token message seen does not kick off the snapshot algorithm - because that job has already been completed when the external trigger came in. Such a node can possibly end up with non-null states for *all* of its channels; other nodes will have at least one channel (the one which produced the first token message) with a null state.

16.2.2.1 Application: an example

Let us pick up the example from section *15.5.1.1* to try and understand how a snapshot can help debug the functionality of a distributed algorithm. Specifically, we will be using the first approach mentioned in *15.5.1.1* - where each node or philosopher runs the the symmetric algorithm - yes, the one that produces a deadlock. We assume that the algorithm implementation has been enhanced with a capability to generate snapshots, and that a snapshot is available for inspection at the moment.

What would a snapshot look like? While we can loosely assume a snapshot to be a bunch of data dumped into a file, the exact contents would indeed be implementation-dependent. For this specific problem context, we will assume the snapshot to contain, broadly, the state of a node, which can be one of the following:

1. Thinking

2. Eating
3. Waiting

Clearly, the first two parameters need no further elaboration while the last one would require a sub-parameter which will indicate whether the node or philosopher is waiting for the left fork or the right fork. As we sift through the snapshots of various nodes in the system, we will ignore those in states (1) and (2) - assuming there are any (there will not be any, in the case of a deadlock).

The idea is to construct a graph as we go along. Each time we come across the snapshot of a node in state (3), we update the graph as follows:

- Add a vertex to the graph, corresponding to the waiting node
- Add a vertex to the graph, corresponding to the neighbouring node that is being waited upon
- Add a directed edge from the waiting node to the waited-upon node

Note that a vertex is added to the graph only if it does not exist already. Once the graph is complete, it is trivial to do a static analysis that detects cycles. For example, a simple *DFT* (Depth First Search) will get the job done:

- Traverse the graph in a depth-first fashion, marking each node on the way as 'visited'
- While visiting each node, check if the node is already marked as 'visited'
- If we find ourselves visiting an already-visited node, we have detected a cycle

Note that we have clearly adopted a simplistic approach while analysing node statuses in the earlier example. For example, a node can have a status "Acquired left fork", implying that it is yet to check the availability of the right fork. It follows that multiple snapshot runs might be needed before a deadlock becomes evident.

In the next section, we will look at deadlock detection in a more formal and comprehensive manner.

16.3 Deadlock detection: the bracha-toueg algorithm

The Bracha-Toueg algorithm depends upon the concept of wait-for graphs (*WFG*). Now, a *WFG* is exactly the same dependency graph that we discussed in the previous section. We assume an initiator node (set off, perhaps, by an external trigger) which launches the execution of the deadlock detection algorithm. The basic message used in the algorithm is a *NOTIFY* message. The initiator node, upon receiving an external trigger, as well as any other node that receives a *NOTIFY* message, does the following:

1. Send a *NOTIFY* message along all outgoing channels
2. If the node is *active*, send a *GRANT* message to all incoming channels

3. Receive *DONE* messages from all outgoing channels

Several questions arise immediately, so we will go over them one by one.

16.3.1 What is a *NOTIFY* message?

A *NOTIFY* message is a simple notification to a node that the deadlock detection algorithm must be executed. Upon receiving one (or an external trigger, in the case of the initiator node), the recipient immediately takes a snapshot of itself and identifies its outgoing and incoming channels. A node that has one or more outgoing channels (described next) has a corresponding number of dependencies, and hence is not considered to be an active node (described soon). Note that a node can possibly receive *NOTIFY* messages multiple times (from different incoming channels), in which case only the first one is acted upon (see next paragraph) while the rest are ignored. However, all of them are acknowledged using *DONE* messages.

The first step by the recipient node of a first-time *NOTIFY* is to propagate the *NOTIFY* along all outgoing channels. Once all those *NOTIFY* messages dispatched along the node's outgoing channels receive their corresponding *DONE* (see *16.3.6*) acknowledgements, the received *NOTIFY* is acknowledged by a *DONE* message. Now, if there are no outgoing channels, i.e. if the node has no dependencies, a *GRANT* (see *16.3.5*) message is issued along all incoming channels, i.e. to each node with a dependency on this node. Once all those *GRANT* messages dispatched along the node's incoming channels receive their corresponding *DONE* replies, a *DONE* message is sent to acknowledge the received *NOTIFY*. As mentioned earlier, all subsequent *NOTIFY* message generate the sole reaction of producing an immediate *DONE* reply.

16.3.2 What is an outgoing channel?

In a *WFG*, an outgoing channel represents an external dependency. For example, if node *n1* has an outgoing channel to *n2*, it implies that *n1* is waiting for an event (a 'grant' event) to happen at *n2*. Maybe *n2* is currently holding a resource which *n1* is interested in; perhaps *n2* is a lock provider, and *n1* requires a lock before writing to a log file, and so on.

16.3.3 What is an incoming channel?

The exact opposite. If node *n1* has an incoming channel to *n2*, it implies that *n2* is waiting for an event to happen at *n1*.

16.3.4 What is an active node?

An active node is one that has no dependencies; such a node is not waiting on anyone. In other words, such a node has no outgoing channels in its *WFG*.

16.3.5 What is a *GRANT* message?

Issuing a *GRANT* message to some node simulates the event that the recipient node is waiting for. The recipient, upon seeing a *GRANT* message, reduces its dependency count by one. If the dependency count is found to have dropped to zero, the recipient node marks itself as active and also generates *GRANT* messages along all its incoming channels. Once this much is done, the recipient also acknowledges the *GRANT* message using an *ACK* message. Similarly, the sender of a *GRANT* message waits for *ACK* messages for each *GRANT* message that was sent. Once all the *ACK*s are received, depending upon the context, the next action is taken - which is the dispatch of either a *DONE* message or an *ACK* message. The former happens when an active node receives a *NOTIFY* message (see rule (2) mentioned earlier), and the latter happens when the receipt of a *GRANT* message finds its dependencies dropped to zero, which in turn leads the recipient node to issue its own *GRANT* messages (after which, the incoming *GRANT* is acknowledged).

16.3.6 What is a *DONE* message?

A *NOTIFY* message is acknowledged using a *DONE* message. From the sender's perspective, the algorithm winds down once all *NOTIFY* messages have been acknowledged. Note: if the sender is not deadlocked, it will receive *GRANT* messages from all its outgoing channels - before the last *DONE* message is received.

16.3.7 Termination

The initiator, once it receives all expected *DONE* messages, will find itself marked as active (i.e. it received all required *GRANT* messages) if it is not deadlocked.

16.3.8 Strategy

If the dependencies of a node can be finally converged to a set of one or more active nodes, then the node is not deadlocked and will eventually receive *GRANT* messages from all its outgoing channels. For example, consider the following configuration:

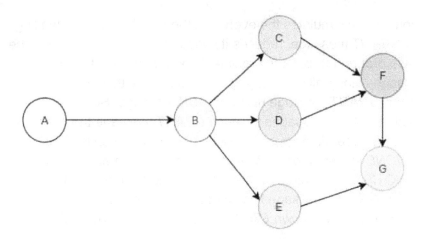

The initiator node in this case is node A. We will assume, then, that node A receives an external trigger which in turn causes it to kickstart the deadlock detection algorithm. As the first step, node A sends a *NOTIFY* message to B. This *NOTIFY* message gets 'propagated' to everyone, all the way to G - who, incidentally, is the only node with no outgoing channels. In other words, node G is the only active node around, and hence, is the only node that can immediately generate *GRANT* messages along its incoming channels.

So, as soon as node G receives a *NOTIFY*, it notices that it is an active node and hence generates *GRANT* message along its incoming channels - i.e. it sends GRANT messages to node E and F. Both E and F have a single outgoing channel, i.e. a single dependency, each; hence the arrival of a single *GRANT* message is enough to switch their statuses to active, causing both to generate *GRANT* messages of their own (after which both acknowledge node G with *ACK* messages). This results in C, D, and B receiving a *GRANT* message each. For B, one *GRANT* message is not quite enough since it has three outgoing channels, i.e. three dependencies. However, this is not a problem - one *GRANT* message is all that C and D require, and the *GRANT* messages they generate in turn go out to B, thus satisfying B's dependencies. At this point, all nodes except A are marked as active. Finally, B sends out a *GRANT* message to A, switching A to active, after which it acknowledges the *NOTIFY* from A with a *DONE* message. At this point, the algorithm is complete, and every node is marked as active.

What if the earlier diagram was modified to add a dependency from G to F? Now we have a deadlock because G and F depend on each other, forming a dependency cycle. In other words, now there is no node in the system without dependencies. Let us assume that F receives a *NOTIFY* from C, which in turn received one from B, who in turn was the recipient of a *NOTIFY* from A. Now, F will send a *NOTIFY* to G, who will identify a single outgoing channel (which is to F) and issue a *NOTIFY* along that. So, F receives a second NOTIFY, which it acknowledges immediately using a *DONE* reply. Note that neither F not G can issue *GRANT* messages due to an unresolved dependency (on each other). Once G receives a *DONE* from F, it acknowledges the *NOTIFY* that it received (from F) using a *DONE* message, which in turn leads F to issue a

DONE to C, leading C to issue a *DONE* acknowledgement to B. The *NOTIFY* messages which B sends to D and E also receive *DONE* acknowledgements quickly, since F and G extend the same behavior to the *NOTIFY* messages received from D and E, respectively (because F and G have seen *NOTIFY* messages already). This allows B to notice that all its *NOTIFY* messages are acknowledged, and allows it to send a *DONE* back to A. Now, it is the turn of A to notice that all its *NOTIFY* messages have been acknowledged and yet - it has not received a *GRANT* message. The conclusion? Deadlock.

16.3.9 A flowchart representation

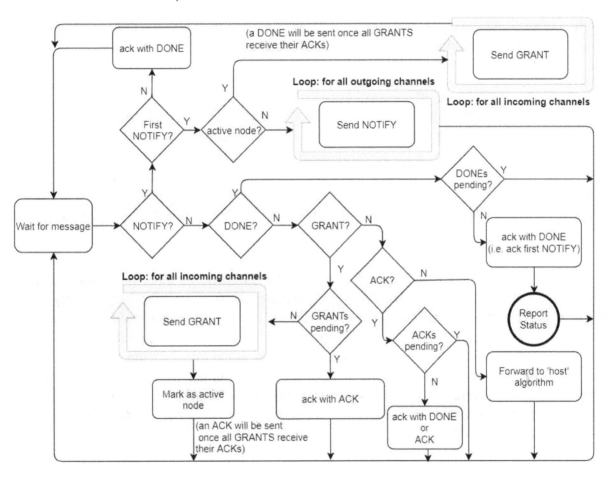

The above diagram is a flowchart representation of the deadlock detection mechanism as specified by the bracha-toueg algorithm. Incoming messages are classified into *NOTIFY*, *DONE*, *GRANT*, and *ACK* types, and the appropriate action taken in each case. The status of the node is either active to start with (i.e. the node has no dependencies) or switched to active once enough *GRANT* messages are received. Note that, for an active node (i.e. one with no outgoing channels) receiving a *NOTIFY* for the first time, the corresponding *DONE* is sent only after receiving *ACKs* along all its incoming channels. For a non-active node (i.e. the node has one or more outgoing channels) -receiving a *NOTIFY* for the first time, a *NOTIFY* is issued along all outgoing channels. The original *NOTIFY* is acknowledged with a *DONE* once all dispatched *NOTIFY* messages receive their *DONE* acknowledgements.

16.4 Termination detection

Let us first define formally the steady state condition of *termination*. Obviously, we would expect each node in the system to be in a *quiescent* or *passive* state - that much is certain. However, is this sufficient? Even if we find all nodes to be in a passive state at a given instant, that could be a transient situation if there are in-flight messages (which could wake up one or more nodes). In other words, termination involves not only a passive state for all nodes, but also a complete absence of messages in any channel in the network. Let us look at how the Dijkstra-Sholten algorithm provides termination detection is a distributed network.

16.4.1 The Dijkstra-Sholten algorithm

This algorithm is peculiar in that an existing 'host' algorithm can be trivially modified to pick up the capability for termination detection; in fact, the Dijkstra-Sholten algorithm introduces no new messages of its own, but only adds acknowledgements for each standard message used by the host algorithm. In other words, once an existing algorithm is augmented with this capability to detect termination, each node will start acknowledging each message it receives (well, almost - as we will see soon). Next, let us list and describe some of the key traits of this algorithm.

16.4.1.1 Source or initiator node

As we've seen with previous algorithms discussed in this chapter, the Dijkstra-Sholten algorithm marks one node as the source or initiator node. Such a node always acknowledges every message it receives. Naturally, this implies that 'regular' nodes will not acknowledge all received messages - and for good reason, as we will see soon. The fundamental approach behind this algorithm is to build a spanning tree with the source node as the root. Starting off, the source node is the sole component of the spanning tree, which then starts growing as messages are exchanged in the system, and then starts shrinking right back towards the root node as termination approaches, and finally the root node also signs off the tree - at which point, termination has happened.

16.4.1.2 'Regular' nodes

All except one are considered regular nodes, and they have the following interesting property: the first message that a regular node receives (from a neighbour) is not acknowledged. For example, let us assume that the distributed application has started up, and node F receives a message from node B. This goes unacknowledged. Next, node C sends a message to node F. This does get acknowledged.

16.4.1.3 Building the spanning tree

Whenever a node sends a message to another node which is not currently part of the spanning tree, the sender marks the recipient as its child (in the tree). If an acknowledgement comes back immediately, that action is reversed - because, the acknowledgement is a way of saying that *"hey, I'm already part of the tree"*. In other words, when a (non-source) node receives its first message (which is not acknowledged), it becomes a child of the sender. Obviously, this is not applicable to the source node because the source node is at the root of the tree and always acknowledges every message that it receives. As for non-source nodes that do not acknowledge the first message, note that the acknowledgement is only delayed; it will eventually be sent, when the node switches to a passive state (more on this in the next section).

16.4.1.4 Status of a node

From the perspective of the Dijkstra-Sholten algorithm, a node is either active or passive. A passive node will switch to active upon receipt of a message but will not spontaneously switch to an active mode. The idea is that only two types of nodes will remain in the spanning tree:

1. Active nodes
2. Nodes with active children

This means that a passive node continues to remain in the tree as long as it has active children.

16.4.1.5 Shrinking the spanning tree

Once a node switches to a passive mode, *and* has no active children left, it sends an acknowledgement to its parent - the acknowledgement it held back when it receives that first message. How does a node know that it has no children left? A node who has received acknowledgements for every message it has sent, knows that it has no active children. Once this condition is satisfied, such a node sends an acknowledgement to its parent, and so on. Every time a node receives an acknowledgement from another node that is marked as a child, the sender of the acknowledgement is unmarked as a child and removed from the tree. This is exactly how the spanning tree shrinks, as more and more nodes switch to passive mode. Let us consider an example, next.

16.4.1.6 An example

Imagine a node, say D, that receives its first message from a node, say C. This message remains unacknowledged, while C marks D as a child. Now, let us assume that C is marked as a child by B , and in turn B is marked as a child of the source node, A. Next, assume that C switches to a passive state because it has reached termination. However, it has to remain a part of the tree (i.e. as child of B) for now, because it has an active child, D (because D is yet to acknowledge that first message). At some point, D turns passive, and sends the held-back acknowledgement to C before doing so. This leaves C with all the conditions required for extraction from the tree - C is in a passive state, and knows that no active children exist, because all messages have been acknowledged - and thus, sends an acknowledgement to its parent, B. Upon receipt of the missing acknowledgement, B promptly unmarks C as a child. At this point, the tree consists of only A and B. Now, once B turns passive, it is free to send an acknowledgement to A, and thus get itself removed from the tree. Once this happens, A remains as the sole member of the tree. If A is already in a passive state, it will immediately perform an 'announcement' that termination has happened - or will do so whenever it switches to a passive state. Of course, if A continues to be active, it can generate further messages which will cause one or more nodes to wake up and thus grow the tree right back, maybe shrink back again, the process possibly repeating multiple times until termination actually happens. Note that once a node goes passive and is taken off the tree, the next message it receives is considered again to be the 'first' message (all records of previous messages are wiped out, as far as the termination detection algorithm is concerned) - which, as usual, will go unacknowledged (for a while, at least).

16.4.2 Detecting termination using traversal

A traversal algorithm can be tweaked to perform the task of termination detection; an example would be Tarry's traversal algorithm, which we studied in section *12.2.3*. This is the strategy:

- A source or initiator node propagates a token through the network
- The token visits every node, before ending up back at the source node
- The token is 'signed' by each passive node on the way
- Termination is declared if the source node finds the returning token to be signed by all nodes in the network

Now, we just described the broad strategy while leaving out some critical details. Those follow:

- Each node maintains logical time for each of its events
- The 'current' logical time t of the source node is specified in the token
- The token is signed by a visited node only if the node has been passive since t or earlier

The above constraint is used to prevent a race condition: a yet-to-be-visited node A, that is active, can switch an already-visited node B to an active state, and switch itself to a passive state by the time the token reaches it (i.e. A). The source node will still see a fully-signed token and declare termination - quite incorrectly.

16.5 Conclusion

In this chapter, we covered a variety of techniques useful for debugging algorithms running in a distributed framework. As a primary aid to debugging, we looked at how snapshots can be collected in such an environment, and how a snapshot can reveal crucial information regarding the health of the system. Afterwards, we switched our focus to the topic of identifying steady state conditions such a termination and deadlocks. In each case, we outlined and analysed a popular and useful algorithm.

16.6. What's next?

We finally come to the end of the last chapter in the second part of this book - one which focused exclusively on network algorithms. We now move to the next and final part of this book that is dedicated to algorithms specific to the shared memory model. In the next few chapters, we will revisit several problem contexts; the differentiator being, they will now be addressed from the perspective of a shared memory environment rather than that of a message-passing network.

PART 3: THE SHARED MEMORY MODEL

Chapter 17. Introduction

So far, we assumed our distributed algorithms to run on a message passing network. From now on, we switch our focus to shared memory systems. Broadly, we will assume the 'system' to consist of a set of processes that execute some distributed algorithm; the processes communicate with each other, asynchronously, through a set of one or more *shared variables*. Note that there is no message passing involved. A shared variable can be thought of as an entity that can hold a certain value; it also allows the value to be read, as well as written to. More technically, we can think of a shared variable as a register, or an address location in shared memory. The next question is, how exactly do we manipulate, operate, or use a shared variable? Exactly what sort of facilities can an algorithm implementor expect from a shared memory system?

17.1 Read and Write operations

In simple terms: if x is a shared variable and y is a local variable at any process in the system, the following actions are assumed to be possible:

1. $y = x$
2. $x = y$

These are the absolute minimum facilities that we assume. In certain cases, we have to assume more complicated operations of an atomic nature.

17.2 Atomic increment/decrement

For example, consider how the value of a shared variable might be incremented:

1. $y = x$
2. $y = (y + 1)$
3. $x = y$

This gets the job done, indeed. First, we read the value of x into a local variable, increment the locally stored value, and then copy it back to the shared variable. However, the operation lacks atomicity and is ripe for race conditions. Let us consider an example to clarify this subtle point.

We shall assume that process *P1* is doing an increment operation - basically *P1* wants to increment the value stored in x. Let the value stored in x be 17. Assume further that *P1* has finished step 2 and is about to write the locally incremented value (18) to the shared memory variable. At this moment, *P2* steps into the picture with the following intention - increment the value of x, not once but twice. *P2* follows the same sequence as *P1*, but twice, except that it gets long enough of an 'execution slice' from the system scheduler to finish all six steps. Now, x holds the value 19.

Next, *P1* resumes its execution from where it left off last; i.e. it executes step (3), overwriting (with 18) the value which *P2* had stored in x barely a moment ago (19). x now holds the value 18; effectively, two increments are lost. The system 'sees' three increments - one by *P1* and two by *P2* - but the value of x (18) reflects only one increment from its initial value (17). To preclude such race conditions, we choose to use atomic increment / decrement utilities that accept the shared variable name (technically, its address) as input, atomically increment its value, and return the result. For example:

```
incremented_value = atomic_increment(value);

decremented_value = atomic_decrement(value);
```

Note: readers familiar with high level programming languages, in particular C or C++, might notice the *pass-by-value* semantics used above. To avoid details that does not concern us too much, we will stick to this simple approach and refrain from using pointer syntax or including function declarations that specify reference arguments.

17.3 Test and Set

The requirement is that you want to set (i.e. assign 1 to) a variable only if the variable currently holds a value of 0. The code representation would be:

1. If x == 0 then x = 1

The above is not an atomic operation, so what we need is a test-and-set (*TAS*) routine:

```
if test_and_set(x) == 0
then
....
else
....
```

Such a *TAS* routine checks the value held by the variable, modifies it to 1 *only* if it held the value 0, atomically, and returns the previous value. Obviously, the return value would be 0 if it managed to set the variable. In fact, a more accurate code representation of a TAS routine would be the following:

1. If x == 0
2. then
3. x = 1
4. return 0
5. else
6. return x

17.4 Compare and Swap

Sometimes we find ourselves with a slightly more complicated requirement: write a value to the shared variable, only if the existing value matches a specified one. For example, here is a flawed approach:

1. y = x
2. If y == 17 then x = 21

The idea is to set *x = 21* only if the existing value is 17. This approach is not atomic, because another process can very well change the value of *x* while the 2nd statement/operation is in progress - in particular, utilising the window between the comparison and assignment operations. As a possible solution, let us contract the logic as follows:

1. If x == 17 then x = 21

This will not help either, since the single statement above breaks down to multiple instructions, and we have done nothing to 'close' the 'window' between the comparison and assignment operations where another process can modify the contents of *x*.

What we really need, then, is a compare-and-swap (*CAS*) routine. Such a routine takes three arguments:

1. The shared variable name (technically, address of the shared variable)
2. The new value meant for the shared variable
3. The value which must be found in the shared variable for the assignment of the new value to be done

It is standard practice for such a routine to return the value found in the shared variable before the assignment is attempted. For example:

If compare_and_swap(x, newvalue, oldvalue) == oldvalue

Then

...   /* *Success - the shared variable now contains newvalue* */

Else

...   /* *Failed - shared variable has been modified by someone else* */

17.4.1 Atomic increment/decrement using *CAS*

Note that a *CAS* routine can be used as a primitive to implement an atomic increment or decrement operation:

1. y = x
2. compare_and_swap(x, y + 1, y)
3. y = x
4. compare_and_swap(x, y - 1, y)

17.4.2 Test-And-Set using *CAS*

Yet another useful operation is a *test-and-set* routine:

compare_and_swap(x, 1, 0)

Such an operation sets the target flag only if the flag is found to be unset in the first place. If the operation succeeded, the *CAS* utility will return 0. This brings us to an interesting conclusion: a *CAS* routine along with a single shared variable is sufficient to implement mutual exclusion. For example:

1. y = compare_and_swap(x, 1, 0) /* attempt to obtain lock */
2. If y != 0 then goto (1)   /* go back to step 1 if we failed to obtain lock */
3. ...   /* have obtained lock: enter critical section */
4. x = 0   /* unlock */

Such kind of a lock is known as a *spinlock*.

17.5 Shared variable types

Let us note a formal classification when it comes to the types of shared variables:

1. *read-write*
2. *read-modify-write*

As far as capabilities go, the first one is weaker. The second type of shared variable, a read-modify-write one, offers the powerful capability where the contents of the variable can be read, inspected or modified, and written back in one indivisible/uninterruptible operation. The formal representation of a read-modify-write() operation would be the following routine, executed in an atomic fashion:

```
value read_modify_write(register, function)
{
    // Remember current value
    temporary = register

    // Apply modification
    register = function(register)

    // Return old value
    return temporary
}
```

Examples are the operations seen in previous sections: *CAS* and atomic increments/decrements. In comparison, a read-write shared variable will allow such operations only if divided into discrete steps, thus losing atomicity in the process. For example, using a read-write variable where a *CAS* is required will certainly lead to race conditions.

17.6 Synchronisation model

In the discussions and algorithms to follow in the section, we will assume that processes take steps in an asynchronous fashion, while communicating with each other using shared memory.

17.7 What's next

Having had a quick familiarisation with the shared memory environment and having looked at some of the primitive operations as well as higher level facilities available, we start off with a familiar problem: mutual exclusion.

Chapter 18. Mutual Exclusion (part 2)

18.1 Introduction

In chapter *15*, section *15.1*, we defined and elaborated on the concept of mutual exclusion; in section *15.2*, we stated the safety and liveness characteristics expected of a mutual exclusion implementation. While chapter *15* analysed mutual exclusion algorithms for a message-passing model, we will now look at algorithms that provide mutual exclusion for a shared memory platform. We will start with simple scenarios before moving on to more complex ones. In fact, we will begin with a couple of algorithms that allow two processes to 'share' a resource which is, in fact, indivisible/unshareable. In each case, we go through a brief explanation of the strategy involved, pseudocode for program initialisation, pseudocode for the resource-access attempt (the various operations involved in the attempt to gain entry to the critical section), followed by an analysis of the properties satisfied (or not satisfied) by the algorithm.

18.2 Mutual exclusion via Strict Alternation

18.2.1 Introduction

In this approach that provides mutual exclusion for a set of two processes which compete for a shared resource, the strategy is simple: there is a shared variable, a flag, which holds either 0 or 1. We assume the initial value to be 1. Let us call the two processes as p0 and p1. Whenever the flag holds 0, p0 is free to enter the critical section. Once done, p0 sets the flag to 1. Now, p1 is free to enter the critical section, after which it will set the flag to 0, and so on. In other words, the two processes take turns in a strict manner - ergo, strict alternation. Let us now look at the pseudocode, starting with program initialisation:

18.2.2 Program initialisation

```
whose_turn_next = 0 /* starting off, p0 gets the chance to access the resource */
```

18.2.3 Pseudocode

	Process 0
1.	while whose_turn_next != 0
2.	{
3.	/* Spin */
4.	}
5.	
6.	/* Critical section */
7.	
8.	whose_turn_next = 1
9.	

	Process 1
1.	while whose_turn_next != 1
2.	{
3.	/* Spin */
4.	}
5.	
6.	/* Critical section */
7.	
8.	whose_turn_next = 0
9.	

18.2.4 Strategy

Each process, while trying to enter the critical section, spins in a tight loop till its turn arrives in the form of a flag being set accordingly - an event that will happen only when the other process accesses and releases the resource. Clearly, deadlock is not a possibility; simply because whose_turn_next can be either 0 or 1, implying that both threads cannot be spinning simultaneously. If whose_turn_next is 0, p1 will spin upon attempt to enter the critical section; if whose_turn_next is 1, p0 will spin upon attempt to enter the critical section.

18.2.5 Safety

As we saw in the previous section, deadlocks are not a possibility - because the while loops of the two processes are controlled based on different values of the same variable. Along the same lines, mutual exclusion is guaranteed because, for example, p0 being in the critical section implies that whose_turn_next is 0, which precludes p1 being in the critical section - because p1 can break out of the while loop only when whose_turn_next holds the value of 1.

18.2.6 Liveness and Fairness

While this method guarantees mutual exclusion (safety), liveness is compromised; for example, consider p1 relinquishing the shared resource. Now, if p1 needs to access the resource again, it has to wait its turn - it cannot access the resource again until p0 accesses it once (because p0 alone is responsible for setting the turn flag to 1, which it does while releasing the resource). Or, as another example, consider the early stages of program execution; the turn flag initialises to 0, so p1 will have to wait as long as p0 is not interested in accessing the resource.

Interestingly, fairness is guaranteed as a direct consequence of loss of liveness. It is the strict adherence to fairness which causes the potential loss of liveness in the first place. It is indeed natural and expected: if strict alternation is enforced, it immediately raises the possibility of an interested party being blocked by a lack of interest from the other party.

18.3 Dekker's algorithm

18.3.1 Introduction

Interestingly, Dekker's algorithm is said to be the first known algorithm that solved the problem of mutual exclusion. Once again, we are dealing with an algorithm that is designed to provide mutual exclusion to a set of two competing processes. Unlike the strict alternation scheme that we analysed previously, Dekker's algorithm does provide liveness. However, fairness is not guaranteed - as we will see shortly.

18.3.2 Strategy

Let us address the two processes involved as p0 and p1. Corresponding to each, the algorithm employs a flag that expresses the intention (or lack of it) of the process to access the shared resource. Whenever a process is interested in entering the critical section, it sets the corresponding flag (*p0_wants_resource* or *p1_wants_resource*) to 1, first. The first hurdle to cross is simple: the corresponding flag of the other process must be set to 0. There is also a 'global' flag *whose_turn_next* to specify whose turn it is (to access the resource) next; each process, while relinquishing the shared resource, sets the *whose_turn_next* flag to point to the other process. In short, here is the overall strategy adopted by a process who wants to enter the critical section:

1. Announce intention by setting own flag to 1
2. Enter the critical section if the other process is not interested in the critical section at the moment
3. Otherwise, wait (i.e. spin) until the turn flag is set in own favour
4. Enter critical section and do whatever that has to be done
5. Clear own flag to show loss of interest in the critical section
6. Set turn flag to indicate that it is the turn of the other process, next

18.3.3 Program initialisation

Here is how the program initialisation would look like:

```
p0_wants_resource = 0   /* set to 1 when process 0 wants to access the resource */
p1_wants_resource = 0   /* set to 1 when process 1 wants to access the resource */
whose_turn_next = 0     /* set to 0 or 1, to indicate whose turn it is next */
```

Next, look us look at the implementation of the algorithm - as executed by each process.

18.3.4 Pseudocode

Process 0	Process 1

```
Process 0

1.   p0_wants_resource = 1
2.   while p1_wants_resource == 1
3.   {
4.       If whose_turn_next != 0
5.       {
6.           p0_wants_resource = 0
7.           while whose_turn_next != 0
8.           {
9.               /* Spin */
10.          }
11.          /* whose_turn_next is now 0 */
12.          p0_wants_resource = 1
13.      }
14.  }
15.
16.  /* p0 has the resource now */
17.
18.  /* now p0 is about to release it */
19.
20.  whose_turn_next = 1 /* p1 next */
21.  p0_wants_resource = 0
22.
23.  /* p0 no longer has the resource */
```

```
Process 1

1.   p1_wants_resource = 1
2.   while p0_wants_resource == 1
3.   {
4.       If whose_turn_next != 1
5.       {
6.           p1_wants_resource = 0
7.           while whose_turn_next != 1
8.           {
9.               /* Spin */
10.          }
11.          /* whose_turn_next is now 1 */
12.          p1_wants_resource = 1
13.      }
14.  }
15.
16.  /* p1 has the resource now */
17.
18.  /* now p1 is about to release it */
19.
20.  whose_turn_next = 0 /* p0 next */
21.  p1_wants_resource = 0
22.
23.  /* p1 no longer has the resource */
```

18.3.5 Safety

As far as deadlocks are concerned, an argument similar to the previous section prevails: the variable *whose_turn_next* can be either 0 or 1, implying that only one process can block (spin) at any point in time.

We can easily see that mutual exclusion is a satisfied condition. For example, if p0 is in the critical section, then *p0_wants_resource* must be 1. In which case, p1 cannot get out of the outer while loop (lines 2 - 14).

18.3.6 Liveness

What about liveness? Obviously, there is no strict alternation involved - and a process can enter the critical section as many times as needed even when the other process is completely uninterested in the shared resource. Progress always happens, and we say that dekker's algorithm satisfies the liveness requirement.

18.3.7 Fairness and Bounded fairness

What about fairness? We can easily show that a quirk of scheduling is all it takes for one process to possibly enter the critical section, multiple times, in a sequential manner. Let us try to understand how this can happen. For the following analysis, we assume a single-*CPU* machine.

To begin with, suppose that p1 is inside the critical section. It finishes the job and is on its way out - when it executes line 20, setting *whose_turn_next* to 0. At this point, p1 gets scheduled out and p0 starts executing - p0 is spinning in the while loop (lines 7-10), and it gets a chance to evaluate the loop condition (line 7), which evaluates to false and thus breaks the loop, before p0 gets scheduled out. Note that p0 does not get a chance to execute line 12 and thus announce its renewed interest in the shared resource. Now, p1 starts running and we assume that it gets a slightly extended time slice on the *CPU*. This allows p1 to resume from line 21, exit the critical section, perform a few operations in its non-critical section, and try to enter the critical section again. p1 finds *p0_wants_resource* to be 0 (since p0 is yet to execute line 12), and immediately finds its path clear to enter the critical section (again). Theoretically, depending upon the length of the current time slice extended to p1, it can do this multiple times. However, once p0 gets a chance to run, it needs to execute a single operation (line 12) to secure the next access to the shared resource (since *whose_turn_next* is set to 0). As a result, we state that dekker's algorithm provides fairness but not *bounded fairness*. We define bounded fairness as follows: a stronger notion of fairness which guarantees that a process will gain access to the shared resource, within a fixed number of access provisions to the other process(es).

18.4 Dijkstra's Mutual Exclusion algorithm

18.4.1 Introduction

In 1965, Dijkstra updated and extended Dekker's algorithm, removing the 2-process limit to come up with his own version that supports an arbitrary number of processes. While the essential strategy has not changed a lot, the supporting data types have to be expanded to support a higher number of processes. While *whose_turn_next* remains unchanged, the pair of *p0_wants_resource* and *p1_wants_resource* is replaced by a single integer array that must be large enough to support the process contingent. Let us first look at program initialisation, and we will assume a set of 8 processes competing for a single shared resource.

18.4.2 Program initialisation

```
const numprocs = 8
p_wants_resource[numprocs + 1] = {0, 0, 0, 0, 0, 0, 0, 0, 0} /* initialise array to all zeroes */
whose_turn_next = 0
```

18.4.3 Strategy

The algorithm is not very complicated. Each process has a corresponding slot in a global integer array which it uses to advertise its current state (interested in critical section, not interested, made progress, etc). The first step is to set own state to 'interested in critical section'. Next, the global turn variable (*whose_turn_next*) comes into play. The idea is to set the value of *whose_turn_next* to own id. Now, this can be done only if the slot in the global array which corresponds to the current id in *whose_turn_next* is set to zero (which happens when the current user of the shared resource releases it). The moment this condition is identified, *whose_turn_next* is set to own id, and the status in the global slot is changed to reflect this particular progress. The next step is to ensure that no other process has progressed to a similar state; if this check yields a positive result, the shared resource is considered to be available for the taking. If not, go all the way back and try again. The pseudocode follows, where the variable *myid* indicates the identification number (1 - 8) assigned to the process. Note that 0 is considered special, and hence is not a process id. For the same reason, the *p_wants_resource[0]* remains unused.

18.4.4 Pseudocode

```
1.    /* Announce interest in the shared resource */
2.    p_wants_resource[myid] = 1
3.
4.    /* Loop till you manage to wrestle the next turn to yourself */
5.    while whose_turn_next != myid
6.    {
7.      /* Check if the current user of the shared resource released it */
8.      If p_wants_resource[whose_turn_next] == 0
9.      {
10.       /* Try to assign next turn to yourself */
11.       whose_turn_next = myid
12.     }
13.   }
14.
15.   /* Announce that you are just one step away */
16.   p_wants_resource[myid] = 2
17.
18.   /* A temporary counter */
19.   i = 1
20.
21.   /* Now check if anyone else has also reached the same state ('one step away') */
22.   while (i <= numprocs)
```

```
23.  {
24.      If (i != myid)    /* check status of other processes */
25.      {
26.          If (p_wants_resource[i] == 2)    /* is this process 'one step away' too? */
27.          {
28.              goto line (2)    /* if so, conflict; go back and try again */
29.          }
30.      }
31.      i = i + 1   /* increment counter */
32.  }
33.
34.  /* Enter critical section and access the shared resource */
35.
36.  p_wants_resource[myid] = 0 /* release access to the shared resource */
37.
```

18.4.5 Safety

The second while loop (lines 22 - 32), in particular, ensures that only one process can end up in the critical section. Any assumption otherwise will end in a contradiction. If process 0 is in the critical section, we know for sure that the corresponding global slot holds the value 2. If process 1 is also in the critical section simultaneously, and let us assume without loss of generality that process 0 entered the critical section first, process 1 must have scanned through the global slots and found none (except own) with a value of 2 - which is a contradiction, because process 0 being in the critical section, as stated earlier, implies that its global slot holds the value of 2.

18.4.6 Liveness

Is it possible that one or more processes keep spinning to gain access to the critical section without anyone succeeding, ever? Because of the increased complexity of the algorithm and higher number of 'consumer' threads, this question warrants an analysis that is slightly more detailed that what we have been used to so far in this chapter. We will consider both scenarios in this section: that of one process, and that of more than one process.

18.4.6.1 Single contender process

Let us start with the simpler one of the two cases. A single process, B, is in the critical section, while another process A is spinning to gain access. The value of *whose_turn_next* at this point is the id of the process occupying the critical section, i.e. process B, and it is this very fact that keeps process A spinning - thanks to the while loop's condition (line 5) remaining true, in turn because *p_wants_resource[whose_turn_next]* is not zero. Once process B leaves the critical section, all this changes. Process A notices that *p_wants_resource[whose_turn_next]* has switched to zero and sets *whose_turn_next* to its own id, thus breaking out of the while loop spanning lines 5 - 13. Since there are no other processes to compete with A, it is all easy going at the moment; process A sets p_wants_resource[myid] to 2, notices that no other global slot has the value 2, and proceeds to the critical section. A similar argument applies for a process trying to enter the critical section that is unoccupied at the moment. One way or the other (either due to program initialisation or due to the last process which left the critical section), *p_wants_resource[whose_turn_next]* is found to be zero, and the lone process finds a smooth passage to the critical section. What we have seen so far, then, is that a lone contender will sooner or later succeed in setting *whose_turn_next* to own id, and inevitably gain access to the shared resource. So, what if there are multiple contenders vying for access to the critical section?

18.4.6.2 Multiple contender processes

Let us consider that all 8 processes, more or less simultaneously, enter the while loop (spanning lines 5 - 13). We know that *p_wants_resource[whose_turn_next]* is 0 at this point, either due to program initialisation or due to the last process which left the critical section. Let us consider an extreme possibility, next. In fact, to help us further in this regard, let us assume only a single *CPU* to be available. Let every process execute line 8, find the condition to be true, and get scheduled out immediately. At this point, every process is now set to execute line 11 next - the assignment of *myid* to *whose_turn_next*. As program execution continues, each process will execute line 11 and assign its own id to *whose_turn_next*, only for the next scheduled process to overwrite the same. Finally, *whose_turn_next* will retain the id of the process that executed line 11 last (in this particular scenario).

We will also assume that each process which got scheduled in and executed line 11 retained the *CPU* time slice just long enough to evaluate the while loop condition on line 5 to false, break out of the while loop, and execute the assignment on line 16. Once the last process has finished doing so, we see that all processes have set the value in their global slots to 2. Note that one of these processes will have its id assigned as the value of *whose_turn_next*. Once execution proceeds from this point, each process will see another process slot with a value of 2, and thus execute the goto statement on line 28 to go back (to line 2) and try again. However, as mentioned earlier, one process among the lot will still have its id set as the value of *whose_turn_next*, and this process will not enter the while loop (lines 5 - 13) thanks to the loop condition (on line 5) evaluating to false, and thus (sooner or later) enter the critical section. Note the reference to the potential delay though; such a process might have to execute the goto statement on line 28 a few times before every other process has modified its global slot to a value of 1.

18.4.6.3 Conclusion?

Finally, in both scenarios we see that a contender process makes progress and arrives at the critical section. Based on the strength of these results, we therefore conclude that Dijkstra's algorithm for mutual exclusion guarantees liveness or progress.

18.5 Peterson's algorithm

Here, we go back to a 2-process scenario which uses 2 flag variables, one for each process. We will start with a naive version, expose it for what it is, and then move to the actual algorithm designed by Gary Peterson in the early 1980s.

18.5. 1 A naive version

The idea is that each process uses a flag of its own to signal its intent to the other process. The procedure is simplicity itself:

- Set own flag
- Make sure the 'other' flag is not set
- Enter the critical section
- Unset own flag when leaving the critical section

Let us look at program initialisation, followed by the pseudocode.

18.5.1.1 Program initialisation

```
/* initialise both global flags to 0 */
flag[2] = {0, 0}
```

18.5.1.2 Pseudocode

Process 0	Process 1
1. flag[0] = 1	1. flag[1] = 1
2. while flag[1] == 1	2. while flag[0] == 1
3. {	3. {
4. /* Spin */	4. /* Spin */
5. }	5. }
6.	6.
7. /* Enter critical section */	7. /* Enter critical section */
8.	8.
9. flag[0] = 0 /* Exit critical section */	9. flag[1] = 0 /* Exit critical section */
10.	10.

18.5.1.3 The flaw

At first glance, this looks good enough. If p1 does not have its flag set, p0 is free to enter the critical section and vice versa. However, we need to factor in the possibility that both flags may get set more or less simultaneously, resulting in neither process making any progress. In other words, *flag[1]* is set by the time p0 executes line (2), and *flag[0]* is set by the time p1 executes the same. This results in both processes spinning endlessly.

18.5.2 The original version

To correct the potential problem mentioned in section *18.5.1.3*, Peterson's algorithm uses a global flag which the two processes use for signalling each other. The strategy follows:

- Set own flag
- Update global flag to give turn to the other process
- Spin as long as: other flag is set *and* turn belongs to the other process
- Enter critical section
- Unset own flag while leaving the critical section

18.5.2.1 Program initialisation

```
/* initialise both global flags to zero */
flag[2] = {0, 0}
/* initialise global turn flag to zero */
turn = 0
```

18.5.2.2 Pseudocode

Process 0	Process 1
1. flag[0] = 1	1. flag[1] = 1
2. turn = 1	2. turn = 0
3. while flag[1] == 1 and turn == 1	3. while flag[0] == 1 and turn == 0
4. {	4. {
5. /* Spin */	5. /* Spin */
6. }	6. }
7.	7.
8. /* Enter critical section */	8. /* Enter critical section */
9.	9.
10. flag[0] = 0 /* Exit critical section */	10. flag[1] = 0 /* Exit critical section */
11.	

18.5.2.3 Immediate re-entry

What is immediately obvious is that a process cannot re-enter the critical section immediately after leaving it. Either the execution of line 10 will unblock (i.e. halt spinning) the other process, thus allowing it to enter the critical section, or, even if the process (the one that just left the critical section) reaches line 3 before the other process gets scheduled, the while loop condition will remain true, and force the (greedy) process to spin. Sooner or later, the other process gets a *CPU* time slice and enters the critical section.

18.5.2.4 Safety

Let us first inspect the guarantee of mutual exclusion. We will consider two cases, of which the simpler one is our first candidate. We assume that p1 is inside the critical section. At this point, we know for sure that *flag[1]* is set to 1 and turn is set to 0. Assume that p0 decides to try and enter the critical section and executes lines (1) and (2), setting *flag[0]* to 1 and *turn* to 1. This ensures that p0 evaluates the while loop condition (line 3) to true and keeps spinning until p1 exits the critical section (and sets flag[1] to 0).

As for the second scenario, suppose that p0 and p1 attack the critical section simultaneously, i.e. they execute lines (1) and (2) more or less concurrently. Still, one of the two processes will be the last to update the *turn* variable - which will carry the value 0 if p1 was the last to update it, or 1 otherwise. Depending upon the value of *turn*, the while loop condition of one process will evaluate to false, while for the other, the condition evaluates to true. This implies that one process will proceed to the critical section, while the other will block (i.e. keep spinning) till the shared resource is released.

As for the possibility of a deadlock, it is clear that both processes cannot be blocked in the while loop simultaneously. For example, if p0 is spinning in the while loop, it implies that *turn* is 1. This, in turn, means that p1 cannot be blocked in the while loop simultaneously - because, that can happen only if *turn* is 0.

In the next section, we will see how this algorithm can be extended to cope with more than 2 processes.

18.6 Peterson's algorithm - extended version

18.6.1 Introduction

The idea here is to cope with the limitation that your mutual exclusion algorithm is designed to work with only two processes, while your process set is larger than two. The solution resembles a tennis tournament, with each round consisting of singles matches (pairs of players competing with each other), with only the winners progressing to the next round, the process progressing through the initial rounds, leading to quarter finals, then two semi final matches, and lastly the final match where the two remaining players face each other to produce a single winner for the whole tournament.

18.6.2 The PetersonLock class (and a quick C++ introduction)

We have already seen the data type requirements for a single instance of peterson's algorithm: an array of size two, and a turn variable. Let us first build an object around this set of variables. Rather than use pseudocode, we opt for C++ this time to deal with the increased complexity of the algorithm. Besides, C++ is a very expressive language which even beginners to computer programming should find easy to read and follow. The following *class* describes the object which we have in mind:

```cpp
class PetersonLock {
  public:
    PetersonLock() : turn(false)
    {
        flags[0] = flags[1] = false;
    }

    void lock(bool index)
    {
        flags[index] = true;
        turn = !index;
        while (flags[!index] && turn == !index) {
          // Spin
          ;
        }
        // Have lock
    }

    void unlock(bool index)
    {
        flags[index] = false;
    }

  private:
    bool turn;
    bool flags[2];
};
```

The idea is to package the whole locking functionality (a set of functions or subroutines), along with the associated data, into a single object. We can create multiple instances of this object - as we will need to, while extending peterson's algorithm to work with more than two processes. In fact, to implement mutual exclusion for *N* processes, we will need *N - 1* lock instances of the above type.

A brief explanatory note to those who are new to C++ :

C++ supports the traditional approach of procedural programming (as supported by C, from which C++ is meticulously derived), while also facilitating more expressive programming styles - data abstraction in particular. While traditional programming languages of the procedural style, C again being an example, supports 'lower level' data types that closely resemble the underlying hardware memory units (integers, bytes, etc), C++ allows data types of a higher and more expressive style. A C++ *class* can be thought of as a 'user defined' data type that holds both subroutines (functions) and the data they operate on. Referring to the *PetersonLock* example, the class has the *constructor* (of the same name) and the *lock() / unlock()* subroutines that operate on data that consists of the *turn* and *flags* member variables. Note the *private* nature of *turn* and *flags* - implying that they can be modified or accessed via the class subroutines. This provides the author (of the class) with strict control over the 'state' of a class object, for example by preventing a user of the class from assigning meaningless or erroneous values directly to *turn* or *flags*.

18.6.3 The tournament mechanism

Let us imagine the system at startup time. We have N processes; nobody has the lock yet; the first move by everyone is to acquire the lock, say. As we mentioned earlier, a tournament format has to be followed. To get past the first round, p0 has to compete with p1 to acquire a lock, p2 has to compete with p3 to acquire another lock, and so on. This implies that round one alone requires $N/2$ locks. If p0 wins the lock (while p1 blocks), p0 moves to round 2 where it will have to compete with either p2 or p3 for access to a second round lock, and so on. It follows that round 2 requires $N/4$ locks. At this point, it should be becoming clear that the locks can be thought of as the nodes of a binary tree. In the end, two 'survivors' compete for the lock at the root node, and the winner gets to enter the critical section; every other process is blocking (spinning) on a lock. The following diagram represents the locks represented as the nodes of a binary tree for a process set of size 8.

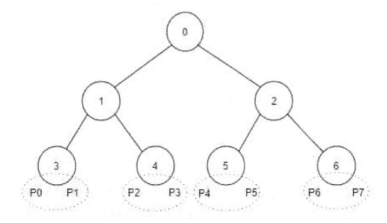

As seen above, p0/p1 compete for l3 (lock representing node 3), p2/p3 compete for l4, p4/p5 compete for l5, while p6/p7 compete for l6. The winners from this round, four in number, will progress to round 2 where l1 awaits the two winners from p0/p1 and p2/p3, and l2 awaits the two winners from p4/p5 and p6/p7. The two survivors of round 2 move up and compete for the root lock at node 0, and the winner enters the critical section. As seen from above, 8 processes require 8 - 1 = 7 locks. If the height of the tree is k, the number of locks (nodes) is given by $2^k - 1$ and the number of processes is 2^k.

18.6.3.1 Nuts and bolts

Let us focus on p0 and p1 competing for the lock at node 3. As mentioned earlier, each node represents a single instance of a peterson lock implementation. As we have also seen before, the basic algorithm works with two competitors, assigning them the indices of 0 and 1. In this particular case, p0 uses the index 0 while p1 works with the index 1. This is another way of saying that p0 approaches the lock from the left while p1 approaches the lock from the right. In other words, we can translate the basic algorithm's concept of (binary) index to that of a direction while thinking in terms of locks being represented as nodes in a binary tree.

Now, the winner of the two (p0 and p1) will have to figure out two aspects:

1. The next node to target
2. The direction (left or right) from which to target the next node

Let us consider the first problem. The next node is obviously the parent of the current (child) node, and we need to identify its id. The following simple formula provides the answer:

- If the child node id is odd, then parent node id = (child node id - 1) / 2
- If the child node id is even, then parent node id = (child node id - 2) / 2

For example:

- For node 3, the parent id is given by (3 - 1) / 2 = 1
- For node 4, the parent id is given by (4 - 2) / 2 = 1
- For node 5, the parent id is given by (5 - 1) / 2 = 2
- Etc

Let us now move on to the second problem - that of identifying the 'direction of attack'. Two points are immediately obvious:

- The direction is determined by the thread id when it comes to targeting the leaf nodes
- While switching aim to a parent node, the child node determines the direction

The first case should be trivial: if the thread id is odd, then the direction is left; otherwise, the direction is right. For the second one, it boils down to whether the child node is a left child of the parent or a right child. In the former case, the direction to be used while going for the parent lock is left, and for the latter, it is right. Now, having gone through the introduction to the tournament-based strategy, the actual mechanism, as well as some low level details involved, not to mention a quick introduction to our programming language of choice, let us wrap up this section by looking at the actual implementation.

18.6.4. The code

```
/**
 * petersonlock.cpp
 * - Implements peterson's extended mutual exclusion algorithm
 *   which uses a tournament format. Originally written for
 *   Linux platforms
 * Usage:
```

```
 * $ g++ petersonlock.cpp -lpthread -o petersonlock
 * $ ./petersonlock <thread-count>
 */

#include <stdio.h>
#include <stdlib.h>
#include <unistd.h>
#include <pthread.h>

#include <iostream>

// User-specified parameter that determines the number of
// worker threads which we will spawn
int thread_count;

void *thread_function(void *data);

// Class that encapsulates the peterson lock functionality
class PetersonLock {
   public:
     PetersonLock() : turn(false)
     {
        flags[0] = flags[1] = false;
     }

     void lock(bool index)
     {
        flags[index] = true;
        turn = !index;
        while (flags[!index] && turn == !index) {
          // Spin
          ;
        }
        // Have lock
     }

     void unlock(bool index)
     {
        flags[index] = false;
     }

   private:
     bool turn;
     bool flags[2];
};
PetersonLock *plock;

// Class that encapsulates a worker thread which is interested
// in moving through the tournament to acquire the 'final' lock
class ThreadObject {
```

```cpp
public:
  ThreadObject() : threadid(0), nodeid(0)
  {
    // Empty
  }

  bool start(void *data)
  {
    // Pick up our id
    threadid = (int)((long)data);

    // This step is important
    reset();

    // Create the underlying native thread
    if (pthread_create(&nativethread, NULL, thread_function, this)) {
      fprintf(stderr, "failed to create thread (%d)\n", threadid);
      return false;
    }

    // All good, our thread is up and running
    return true;
  }

  void join()
  {
    pthread_join(nativethread, NULL);
  }

  int getThreadId()
  {
    return threadid;
  }

  int getNodeId()
  {
    return nodeid;
  }

  void reset()
  {
    // Calculate our 'starting' lock id. This refers to
    // a specific leaf node on the binary tree - the tree
    // which represents the collection of locks that we work
    // with
    nodeid = (thread_count / 2) - 1 + (threadid / 2);
  }

private:
```

```cpp
      // The actual/native thread
      pthread_t nativethread;
      // Our thread id
      int threadid;
      // Id of the lock which this thread will target first
      int nodeid;
};
ThreadObject *threadobjects;

// The basic lock routine used by each thread.
// id: the calling thread's id
// nodeid: the id of the lock to be targeted
// index: the direction from which the lock is targeted
// (direction is either 0 or 1, for left or right)
void peterson_lock(int id, int nodeid, bool index)
{
   // Secure a lock on this node
   plock[nodeid].lock(index);
   if (nodeid == 0) {
      // We have entered the critical section
      std::cout << id << ": Acquired root lock" << std::endl;
      // We now leave the critical section
   } else {
      std::cout << id << ": Acquired node lock: " << nodeid << std::endl;

      // Calculate the new lock direction
      bool nextindex = (nodeid + 1) % 2;

      // Move up the tree to the parent node.
      // Calculate the parent node's id based on whether we are a left
      // child or a right one.

      int parentnodeid = (nodeid % 2) ? nodeid - 1 : nodeid - 2;
      parentnodeid /= 2;

      // Secure a lock on the parent node, blocking if need to
      peterson_lock(id, parentnodeid, nextindex);
   }

   // Unwind the stack, unlocking locked nodes as we go down the tree
   plock[nodeid].unlock(index);
}

// The 'entry point' for each thread
void *thread_function(void *data)
{
   ThreadObject *obj = (ThreadObject *)data;

   // Grab the thread id
   int id = obj->getThreadId();
```

```
    // Grab the id of the corresponding lock node which
    // will be the starting point
    int nodeid = obj->getNodeId();

    // Grab the lock direction (0 or 1, for left or right)
    int index = id % 2;

    // Go for the lock
    peterson_lock(id, nodeid, index);
}


// Start up our 'worker' threads. Each thread is passed
// its identification number
void initialise_threads()
{
    // Allocate thread objects: as many as a user-provided
    // count
    threadobjects = new ThreadObject[thread_count];
    if (threadobjects == NULL) {
        fprintf(stderr, "failed to allocate thread objects\n");
        exit(3);
    }

    // Start up each thread
    for (int i = 0; i < thread_count; i++) {
        threadobjects[i].start((void *)((long)i));
    }
}

// initialise the set of of PetersonLock objects that
// we need; each of them corresponds to one node of a binary
// tree. In the beginning, each pair of threads will compete
// for a lead node lock, implying N/2 leaf nodes for N threads,
// in turn implying N - 1 total nodes for N threads.
void initialise_peterson()
{
    plock = new PetersonLock[thread_count - 1];
}

// Wait for threads to wind up
void join_threads()
{
    for (int i = 0; i < thread_count; i++) {
        threadobjects[i].join();
    }
}
```

```
// Utility routine to check if provided value is a
// power of 2
int check_log2(int val)
{
    // Force a quick result, if possible
    if (val == 0 || val == 1) {
        // Is a power of 2
        return 0;
    }

    // Do it the hard way
    while (1) {
        int oldval = val;
        val >>= 1;
        if (val * 2 != oldval) {
            // Not a power of 2
            return 1;
        }
        if (val == 1) {
            // Is a power of 2
            return 0;
        }
    }
}

// Program entry point
int main(int argc, char *argv[])
{
    // Sanity-check provided arguments: we need one argument
    if (argc != 2) {
        fprintf(stderr, "Usage; %s <thread-count>\n", argv[0]);
        exit(1);

    }

    thread_count = atol(argv[1]);
    // Sanity-check provided arguments: we need a valid thread count
    if (thread_count <= 0) {
        fprintf(stderr, "%d: invalid thread count\n", thread_count);
        exit(2);
    } else if (check_log2(thread_count)) {
        // Thread count must be a power of 2
        fprintf(stderr, "%d: invalid thread count; must be a power of 2\n",
            thread_count);
        exit(3);
    }

    // Basic initialisation
    initialise_peterson();
```

```
    // Start up the threads and let them do their thing
    initialise_threads();

    // Wait for threads to wind up
    join_threads();
}
```

18.6.4.1 A brief guide to the implementation

As is the case with any C or C++ code, the entry point to the program is the function *main()*. The code expects the user to provide an integer thread count which is a power of 2, failing which the execution is aborted. If the provided integer thread count is good, then we proceed to do some basic initialisation first: since we now know the thread count, we know how many lock instances are needed (one less than the thread count) and we proceed to allocating the same. Once that is done, we bring up our worker threads. We also ensure that each worker thread is aware of its id.

Each worker thread calculates its target leaf node lock based on its id and wastes no time in trying to lock the same. Obviously, the code simulates a situation where the immediate and initial action of each involved party is to procure access to the critical section. Every time a lock attempt succeeds, the worker thread moves up the tree by implementing the calculations mentioned in section *18.6.3.1*. Finally, once a thread realises that it has just succeeded in procuring a lock to the root node, it starts descending the tree, releasing each lock on the way that it obtained on its way up.

The entry point to each worker thread is the function *thread_function()*. The actual peterson locking algorithm is encapsulated inside the *PetersonLock* class, in particular using the *lock()* and *unlock()* member functions. Each lock instance relies on its own private data members, *flags* and *turn*. The binary tree traversal is handled by the function *peterson_lock()*, which uses as tools the *lock* and *unlock* facilities encapsulated by the *PetersonLock* class.

18.7 Bakery algorithm

18.7.1 Introduction

The *bakery algorithm* was first introduced by Lamport in his 1973 paper *"A New Solution of Dijkstra's Concurrent Programming Problem"*. In this section, we will take a different approach to the previous ones and skip code-based analysis in favour of a lighter, example-based approach. Let us first take a look at how Lamport introduces his algorithm:

- *The algorithm is quite simple. It is based upon one commonly used in bakeries, in which a customer receives a number upon entering the store. The holder of the lowest number is the next one served.*

In more detail, and in the context of multiple processes or nodes participating in a distributed algorithm, the following broad steps are involved for a node wishing to enter the critical section:

1. Select a number which is one larger than the largest number selected by any other node
2. Wait on each node that is currently in the process of selecting a number (till it has selected a number)
3. Wait on each node that is found to have selected a lower number (till it exits the critical section)
4. Enter the critical section

Note that two loops are involved - step (1) forms the first loop, while steps (2) and (3) form two parts of each iteration of the second loop. Both loops involve iterating 'over' every other node. The first loop 'visits' each node (except oneself), and simply notes down the number selected by the node, in order to choose the largest one out there. The result of the loop, then, is a number, which is incremented and selected as own number.

The second loop is a bit more involved. The main task of each iteration here is to wait on a node if it has a lower number, but this in turn might involve a pre-wait in case the node is still in the process of selecting a number. In other words: if a node has not selected a number, then wait till it has done so; after which, inspect the number, and if it is found to be a lower one, wait till the node exits the critical section. The simplest case for any iteration of this loop is when the target node for that iteration has neither selected a number nor has any intention of doing so - in other words, that particular node is not interested in the critical section at all.

18.7.2 Further analysis

Looking at the steps mentioned earlier, a couple of requirements should be immediately obvious:

a. Each node should 'advertise' the number it selected (if any)
b. Each node should advertise a 'status'

While the first requirement is rather straightforward from step (1), the second one is a result of step (2) as well as step (3). The status of a node should indicate one of three possibilities:

I. The node is not interested in the critical section
II. The node is currently interested in the critical section (could even be in the critical section)
III. The node is currently in the process of selecting a number (by inspecting the numbers selected by other nodes)

Yet another minor detail should emerge: each node's number defaults to 0, to which it is reset once the critical section is left. In fact, a number selection of 0 (or otherwise) can very well be used to represent the status described above by (I) and (II). This implies that the status just needs to be a 'toggle' that represents the state described above by (III). We will shortly visit an example that will shed more light on this particular approach.

It is also interesting to note that multiple nodes could simultaneously hold the status represented by (III), implying that multiple nodes could select the same number. Imagine every node entering the node-selection stage, i.e. step (1), simultaneously. Every node will find every other node to have a number of 0 and select 1 as own number. This implies that some sort of tie-breaker is required while comparing numbers - which is usually accomplished by assigning unique ids to nodes. Next, rather than rely on pseudo-code, let us use an example to clarify the algorithm further.

18.7.3 An example scenario

We will consider a netmeeting, that is attended remotely by multiple critical stakeholders of an organisation. Let us assume the netmeeting screen, as displayed on the computer monitor of each individual, to consist of two parts: one, a larger presentation screen, and a side panel that lists each attendee, with a corresponding status description alongside for each. The presentation screen does not concern us at all; we are only interested in the list of attendees, as well as the status of each person. Now, the status of an attendee can be any alphanumeric, or even ascii, text, but in this case we will restrict ourselves to some very specific possibilities.

The fundamental idea is that, due to the emergency nature of the discussion at hand, only one person can be allowed to be *AFK* (*Away From Keyboard*) at any time. We will imagine the group to implement the bakery algorithm to accomplish this in a safe and progressive manner. First of all, let us list the various status descriptions allowed:

- 0
- -1
- Any n, where $n > 0$

As aligned with the assumptions derived in the previous section, a status of 0 indicates that the attendee is not interested in being *AFK*. A status description of -1 indicates that the attendee is going through the list of attendees in the side panel, looking at the status of each attendee, to identify the larger number seen as a status. Lastly, any n such that $n > 0$ indicates a number selected by the attendee (who could very well be *AFK* at that point, if that number is the smallest among the lot). Needless to say, the status of each attendee defaults to 0, and is reset to 0 once the person is back at the keyboard (after his or her break for whatever reasons).

Now, let us assume that Alex needs to use the restroom. What does he do? As identified in the previous section, he needs to 'execute' two loops, i.e. he needs to go through the list of attendees on his netmeeting side panel, each time with a different agenda. Let us consider the first loop.

Alex examines each attendee, and selects the largest status seen. If a status is seen as -1, it is considered to be the default of 0 - because such a person has not selected a number yet (which is what he/she is trying to do at the moment, and hence the status of -1). Once Alex finishes scanning the list of attendees, he has a number - which he increments and updates as his own status. The first 'part' of the algorithm is done by this point.

Next, Alex re-scans the list of attendees. This time, he ignores any attendee with a status of 0. That leaves two possibilities:

1. Attendees with a status of -1
2. Attendees with a non-zero positive status

For each instance of the first type, Alex pauses his scan till that particular status changes to that of the second type, i.e. the status changes from -1 to n where $n > 0$. Next, if n is found to be smaller than his own status selection, Alex pauses till that status switches to 0 (which will happen only when that attendee goes *AFK* and come back).

For each instance of the second type, the last part of the previous description applies: for each person with a status n where n is smaller than own status value, Alex pauses till the person returns from AFK. Once this second scan is completed, Alex moves to a status of *AFK*. Upon returning, Alex switches his status back to 0. Lastly, let us recollect the need for a tiebreaker parameter as identified in section *18.7.2*, which in this case is resolved by the simple choice of using unique employee identification numbers as assigned by the organisation.

18.8 Conclusion

We revisited the topic of mutual exclusion in this chapter, albeit in the context of shared memory systems. Armed with an introduction to the shared memory model from the previous chapter, we proceeded to evaluate multiple algorithms, roughly in the order of increasing complexity. For each, we laid out a discussion on general strategy, the pseudo code, as well as an analysis on safety, liveness, and fairness considerations. Towards the end, we looked at a fairly complicated, tournament-based version that extended a 2-process mutual exclusion mechanism to a larger set of processes; we also gave a brief introduction to C++ before presenting a C++ implementation for said algorithm. We concluded by analysing a relatively simple algorithm proposed by Leslie Lamport.

18.9 What's next

Next, we will broaden our horizons and switch to the more generic issue of resource allocation. Apart from revisiting a classic problem in the context of resource allocation, we will also consider a practical problem of restricted resource sharing that is frequently encountered while developing distributed architectures.

Chapter 19. Resource allocation

19.1 Introduction

We briefly defined and discussed the resource allocation problem in section *15.5*, where we also outlined and shortly analysed the classic dining philosophers problem. We have two related aims in this chapter. One is to refresh the problem of resource allocation in general, followed by a close look at a practical development problem where a resource has to be shared (under certain limitations) among multiple processes or nodes; the second is to revisit the dining philosophers problem and consider a solution that uses the technique of randomisation.

19.2 Describing the problem

During our brief fling with resource allocation in section *15.5*, we defined the problem as one where multiple interested parties contend for various subsets of a resource set. A specific example, of course, is mutual exclusion where the resource set is a singleton set. We can state the general problem in multiple ways, actually; that last definition being just one of them. For example, there could be multiple instances (say, 7) of a particular type of resource, and a process or node could be happy with any (say) 2 of them. Here, we consider another variant: there is a single resource, which can be shared - albeit with certain restrictions involved. Let us label this the *restricted resource sharing* problem. Naturally, this means that we will have multiple parties inside the critical section, thanks to the shareable nature of the resources which we will consider. The real challenge lies in handling the multiple constraints associated with entering the critical section, while exiting the critical section is relatively straightforward.

19.3 Restricted resource sharing

To describe the problem, we assume a set of processes communicating with each other using shared memory. It could very well be multiple threads belonging to the same process, but that is a detail which we will remain unconcerned about. Next, we introduce one or more resources which these processes are interested in.

19.3.1 The resource

To start with, we imagine a single resource that each process will require intermittently. This resource could be anything, but we assume it to be in the form of a wrapper object lying in shared memory. Thinking in terms of a programming language, we could imagine a C++ class that provides access to a resource such as:

- *TCP* connection to a remote server
- Printer link
- RDMA channel to a different machine
- UDP link to a local log collection entity
- Etc

With these examples in mind, the next step is to obtain a basic idea of how a corresponding C++ class might look like.

19.3.2 A basic layout for the resource class

We will begin with a basic interface for the class which represents such a resource as exemplified in the previous section; it should provide *open()* and *close()* routines. In other words, a caller first invokes *open()* on the resource object, does an arbitrary amount of I/O or other operations, and finally does a *close()* on the object. This gives us a base layout to start working from:

```
class ResourceWrapper {
    open();   // grab access to the object

    // I/O and control routines
    read();
    write();
    control();

    close();   // release access
};
```

Next, let us introduce some restrictions.

19.3.3 Introducing restrictions to resource access

The first one should be obvious: we want this resource to be shareable, i.e. multiple processes should be able to use it concurrently. This in itself does not present much of a challenge, but it is not trivial either. For example, consider two processes calling *open()* concurrently; assume also that these are the first two calls on the object. Let us assume that we are working with an object that represents a *TCP* connection. So, maybe we have a *TCPResourceWrapper* implementation; we don't want each *open()* invoked on such an object to create a new (underlying) *TCP* connection. This obviously leads to the simple conclusion that *open()* must internally use a locking mechanism, so that the critical section inside - one which creates an actual *TCP* connection - allows only one party at a time. The process which enters the critical section after the first one will notice an active connection in place and refrain from creating another one. Or we could avoid all this complication by simply assuming that the class constructor takes care of resource initialisation - in which case,. even the very first invocation of *open()* would find the *TCP* connection already in place. Note that member functions of the class which handle I/O would still need their lock mechanisms to prevent data from being mixed up across different streams. All that said, we will not concern ourselves any further with the implementation strategies associated with this particular restriction - we certainly will find our hands full dealing with the next two ones.

Next, we introduce the second restriction: there should be a limit on the maximum number of processes that can simultaneously use a single resource object. For example: if we assume the limit to be 16, and if we also assume that 16 processes are currently using the object, a 17th process calling an *open()* on the resource object should see a failure.

The final restriction: the resource class should provide a *shutdown()* call. If any process calls *shutdown()* on the object, all further *open()* calls should fail. Note that such a *shutdown()* invocation must not interrupt ongoing sessions. While this condition might look trivial, it introduces an additional complication: a *shutdown()* call must not trigger any immediate implications if there are other processes currently using the resource object. In such a case, when does the *shutdown()* actually take effect, then? The answer is simple: the *close()* invoked by the last process releasing the resource object should trigger the 'actual' shutdown (for example: close the underlying TCP connection). Note that no new processes will acquire the resource object once a *shutdown()* is invoked; so, the number of processes using the resource object can only decrease over time.

19.3.4 Modifying the resource class layout to accommodate restrictions

So, we have a total of three restrictions (we won't worry about the first one, though). The third restriction immediately points out one modification that is needed to the class layout: add a *shutdown()* member. We also noted that *shutdown()* may not have immediate consequences; yet it should still note down the fact (that the object is marked for shutdown) somewhere or somehow. This implies the requirement for a *shutdown flag*.

The second one enforces an access limit on the resource object, so it is evident that the class needs a reference count. Let us update the class layout based on what we have so far:

```
// Maximum concurrent usage of resource object
#define REFERENCE_MAX 16

class ResourceWrapper {
public:

    open();    // grab access to the object

    // I/O and control routines
    read();
    write();
    control();

    close();   // release access
```

```
    shutdown();  // destroy the underlying resource

private:

    int reference_count; // initialised to 0, cannot exceed REFERENCE_MAX
    int shutdown_flag;    // initialised to 0, can be set to 1
};
```

Next, let us see how we can use these newly added members. Obviously, *open()* now will use *reference_count* as a basis to decide its course of action. If *reference_count* is already at *REFERENCE_MAX*, the *open()* call fails. Otherwise, *reference_count* is incremented, and the call succeeds. Correspondingly, *close()* decrements *reference_count*.

At this point, we are forgetting something - the *shutdown_flag*. Indeed, *open()* should fail if it finds *shutdown_flag* to be set. Similarly, *shutdown()* should set the *shutdown_flag* and trigger the actual shutdown if no processes are currently using the resource object. We will assume that only a privileged process, one not part of the regular process set, will invoke the shutdown mechanism. The shutdown feature also requires that *close()* perform the actual shutdown if the caller process is the last one to release the resource object. Let us next see why the mentioned approach is (obviously) a naive one.

19.3.5 Analysing the naive approach

The immediate problems are clear: an abundance of race conditions. For example, let us consider an admin or privileged process invoking *shutdown()* while a single process is currently using the resource object. The *shutdown()* call first sets the *shutdown_flag*, but not before the lone active process has invoked a *close()*, which in turn checks *shutdown_flag* and finds it to be false. The next step for the *shutdown()* call is to check *reference_count*. At this point, the *close()* invoked by the remaining active process has not decremented *reference_count* (to 0) yet; this causes *shutdown()* to wrap up without taking any further action (i.e. all it did was to set *shutdown_flag*). On the other side, that one last process releases the resource object without triggering any shutdown measures either because the *close()* that it invoked found *shutdown_flag* to be disabled. In the end, we are left with a resource object that has been incompletely cleaned up, i.e. one with a dangling resource.

Similarly, we can easily see how the *REFERENCE_MAX* limit can be easily exceeded in the absence of proper locking. Imagine reference_count to be at 15, at which point 10 processes concurrently call *open()* which in turn inspects the value of *reference_count*. The *open()* invoked by each process finds *reference_count* to be below the *REFERENCE_MAX* limit and proceeds ahead with granting access to the resource object. As a side effect, *reference_count* gets bumped up to 25.

19.3.6 Fixing the naive approach

The obvious fix is to preclude race conditions by proper locking in all three functions that access *reference_count* and *shutdown_flag*. Let us look at some rough implementations, starting with that of *open()* :

```
int open()
{
   lock();

   if (shutdown_flag) {
      unlock();
      // Error: shutting down
      return 1;
   }

   if (reference_count == REFERENCE_MAX) {
      unlock();
      // Error: too many concurrent accesses
      return 1;
   }

   reference_count++;

   unlock();

   ...
   ...
   ...

   return 0;
}
```

Here, the *lock()* and *unlock()* routines are assumed to be member functions of the resource class that implement (some algorithm for) mutual exclusion. As seen above, *open()* declares failure in two cases: if the *shutdown_flag* is set, or if the concurrent access limit has been reached. If all is good, *reference_count* is incremented. The implementation of *close()* is next:

```
void close()
{
   lock();

   reference_count--;

   // Check for the last process to release the resource
   if (shutdown_flag && reference_count == 0) {
```

```
        // Initiate shutdown mechanism
        ...
        ...
        ...
    }

    unlock();
}
```

Along similar lines, close() makes sure to honour commitments set by *shutdown_flag* and *reference_count*. We look at the implementation of shutdown() next:

```
void shutdown()
{
    lock();

    shutdown_flag = 1;

    // If nobody is currently using this resource
    if (reference_count == 0) {
        // Initiate shutdown mechanism
        ...
        ...
        ...
    }

    unlock();
}
```

19.3.7 A critique of the updated implementation

While we might have solved our problems functionality-wise, our current approach leaves much to be desired performance-wise. What stands out is our coarse-grained approach to locking; the question being, can we adopt a strategy that will effectively reduce the amount of code that occupies each critical section? The idea would be to let multiple lines (threads or processes) of execution to 'interweave' in a better fashion, rather than ending up serialised completely. In fact, if we rethink and hone our class layout - the way critical class data is stored and handled, in particular - and adopt a spin-based strategy, we just might come up with an optimised version of what we have currently. This is another way of saying that, with the planned approach, we will say goodbye to clearly-marked critical sections. The following side-to-side comparison best illustrates the point at hand, where both versions perform the simple act of atomically incrementing a shared variable:

Solution 1	Solution 2

lock();
 	
c++;
 	
unlock();
	while (true)
	{
	  // Grab a copy of the current value
	  int o = c;
	  if (compare_and_swap(c, o + 1, o) == o)
	  {
	    // Success
	    goto done;
	  }
	  // No luck yet; keep spinning and trying
	}
	done:

The spin-based strategy has potential for considerable performance improvements, albeit predicated on the *lock()/unlock()* implementations, the actual context of use, as well as the underlying system/hardware architecture. Either way, it would be instructive to go ahead and optimise our current resource sharing implementation along similar lines.

19.3.8 An optimised version

Our plan of action will consist of the following sequence: recruit a bunch of utility functions that will make our life easier, re-model the resource class in terms of its data members, and finally work on each of our target functions.

19.3.8.1 Utility functions

As hinted at by the previous example, our new strategy hinges on adopting a couple of techniques which we introduced in sections *17.2* and *17.3*. We will assume the availability of the following routines:

- *atomic_increment(target)*
- *atomic_decrement(target)*
- *compare_and_swap(target, newvalue, oldvalue)*

Additionally, we will assume the following bit-manipulation routines to be available:

- *bit_set_val(val, bitindex)*
- *bit_unset_val(val, bitindex)*
- *bit_get_val(val, bitindex)*

bit_set_val(val, bitindex) returns a value that is equal to that of *val* with the bit at *bitindex* set. For example, *bit_set_val(0, 0)* would return 1 while *bit_set_val(0, 3)* would return 8.

bit_unset_val() does the opposite: it returns a value that is equal to that of *val* with the bit at *bitindex* unset. For example, *bit_unset_val(12, 3)* would return 4 while *bit_unset_val(255, 7)* would return 127.

bit_get_val(val, bitindex) returns the value (0 or 1) of the bit in *val* at the specified *bitindex*. For example, *bit_get_val(8, 0)* returns 0 while *bit_get_val(16, 4)* returns 1.

Finally, we assume that our atomic utility functions work with unsigned arguments.

19.3.8.2 Redesign class data storage

A critical task, as previewed earlier in the previous section, is to optimise the data layout of the resource class. Currently, the two data members - *reference_count* and *shutdown_flag* - are stored in separate memory locations. How exactly does that affect us? To understand this further, consider what *open()* does and what it does not - *open()* modifies *reference_count* but only reads *shutdown_flag*. In fact, the primary concern of *open()* is to increment *reference_count* while ensuring that *shutdown_flag* remains at 0. Obviously, *open()* needs to honor *REFERENCE_MAX* as well, but we will deal with this at a later step. This leads to a simple conclusion: we need both pieces of information in a single memory location, which can then be operated upon by our *compare_and_swap()* routine.

The plan, then, is to use a single 32 bit variable such that bits 0 - 30 hold the *reference_count* value while the *MSB*, bit 31, represents the *shutdown_flag* boolean. What follows is the new data layout of the reference class:

```
private:

    int state; // Holds reference count and shutdown flag
};
```

In *open()*, we will read the value at the location, make sure that the *MSB* is unset (fail, otherwise), and try to increment only the reference count value held in bits 0 - 30 in an atomic fashion - using *compare_and_swap()*, which of course will fail if either component at the location has been updated. In failure situations, we continue to spin and retry only if the *MSB* remains unchanged at 0 (which indicates that another process updated the reference count, but the shutdown flag remains unset). Without further ado, let us take a look at the optimised version of *open()*.

19.3.8.3 Optimising open()

```
void open()
{
```

```
    // Fail immediately if the shutdown flag is set
    if (bit_get_val(state, 31))
    {
        return 1;
    }

    while (true)
    {
        // Strip out the reference count component from state
        int ref = bit_unset_val(state, 31);

        // Try to increment the reference count component, while
        // ensuring that the shutdown flag stays unset
        int res = compare_and_swap(state, ref + 1, ref);
        if (res == ref)
        {
            // Managed to increment reference count
            // while the shutdown flag stayed unset
            goto open_success;
        }

        if (bit_get_val(res, 31))
        {
            // Another process set the shutdown flag
            return 1;
        }

        // Another process updated the reference count. Spin
        // and try again. The shutdown flag remains unset as of now
    }

open_success:

    ...
    ...
    ...

    return 0;
}
```

We still need to get *open()* to honour *REFERENCE_MAX*, though. This can be accomplished by the following minor modification:

```
    int res = compare_and_swap(state, ref + 1, ref);
    if (res == ref)
    {
        // Fail if we have exceeded the concurrent access limit
        If (ref + 1 > REFERENCE_MAX)
        {
```

```
        atomic_decrement(state);
        return 1;
    }
    // Managed to increment reference count
    // while the shutdown flag stayed unset
    goto open_success;
}
```

Note that we are still left with a race condition; the newly added if() condition would evaluate to true only if the reference count is large enough, but there is always a chance that every other process released the resource object before atomic_decrement() is executed. In other words, we could have a situation where the last release of the object happens without shutdown procedures being triggered. This issue can be addressed by the following update:

```
    // Fail if we have exceeded the concurrent access limit
    If (ref + 1 > REFERENCE_MAX)
    {
        // Decrement reference count
        int s = atomic_decrement(state);
        // If every other process released the object and we are
        // the last to do so, then initiate shutdown procedures
        If (bit_unset_val(s, 31) == 0)
        {
            // Initiate shutdown mechanism
            ...
            ...
            ...
        }
        return 1;
    }
```

19.3.8.4 Optimising close()

Having fixed *open()* in iterative steps, *close()* presents much less of a challenge while the essential technique remains quite similar:

```
void close()
{
    // Decrement reference count
    s = atomic_decrement(state);

    // Check if the shutdown flag is set and whether
    // we are the last process to release the resource
    if (s == bit_set_val(0, 31))
```

```
    {
        // Initiate shutdown mechanism
        ...
        ...
        ...
    }
}
```

In fact, *open()* calls the same sequence of code to tackle a race condition. That alone should describe the gap in complexity between the two functions. The reasons are twofold. For one, close() does not have to worry about the shutdown flag *while* updating the reference count - it can afford to decrement the reference count first and consider the shutdown flag next. As for the second, *close()* has fewer decisions to make, in comparison. On the other hand, *open()* must worry about multiple conditions involving the reference count and shutdown flag. One way to look at it is that *close()* does not have to worry about returning a value to its caller. Lastly, let us switch our attention to *shutdown()*.

19.3.8.4 Optimising shutdown()

shutdown() does not have it quite as easy as close(), essentially because it has to update the *MSB* of *status*. In comparison, *close()* can rely on a simple *atomic_decrement()* since the reference count is what *close()* needs to update. The code follows:

```
void shutdown()
{
    while (true)
    {
        // Copy of current state
        int o = state;
        // Intended new state, with shutdown flag set
        int n = bit_set_val(state, 31);
        // Try to swap in the new state in an atomic fashion
        int res = compare_and_swap(state, n, o);
        // Success?
        if (res == o)
        {
            // If the resource object is currently unused
            if (bit_unset_val(o, 31) == 0)
            {
                // Initiate shutdown mechanism
                ...
                ...
                ...
            }
            goto shutdown_done;
        }
        // Someone updated the reference count meanwhile.
        // Spin and try again.
```

    }
shutdown_done:
}
```

Having optimised the last of the functions we had in mind, let us quickly consider the problem of managing multiple resources in a similar fashion before switching focus back to resource allocation in general, and to a classic problem in particular.

### 19.3.9 Sharing multiple resources

So far we worked with a single resource, but it should be clear that the same design and implementation will work unchanged with multiple resources of the type as described by section *19.3.1*. Each resource will have a specified limit on the number of concurrent accesses; a node can simultaneously hold references to multiple resources as long as said limit is honoured for each of them.

## 19.4 Revisiting the dining philosophers problem

In section *15.5.1*, we described the basic problem and noted subsequently in *15.5.1.1* that a symmetric solution will not work for the same. The odd/even solution which we analysed afterwards does indeed solve the problem - while requiring differing strategies from odd and even members in the system. Such a solution would normally imply that adjacent members run (slightly) different programs, or at least that adjacent members require different configurations. From an administrative or maintenance point of view, such a situation is not particularly optimal.

### 19.4.1 A randomised solution

Another technique to break symmetry is randomisation. This approach ensures identical code and configuration being run on all members in the system. Let us first try to arrive at an intuitive understanding of the randomised approach before looking at a formal solution. Our starting point, perhaps surprisingly, will be the unfeasible symmetric strategy.

#### 19.4.1.1 An intuitive understanding

Let us consider a symmetric solution where each philosopher selects the left fork first, and the right fork next. We will assume that everyone simultaneously launches into the algorithm, which obviously results in a deadlock - with everyone holding on to their left forks but being stranded with no chance of ever obtaining the right fork. What if we tweak the algorithm a bit at this point? The idea is to not wait for that right fork (which will never come). Upon seeing that the right fork is unavailable, take a step back - drop the left fork which you are holding on to - and start again.

So, all philosophers were holding on to their left forks, found their right forks unavailable, released their left forks, and decided to 'start again'. What exactly does 'start again' mean? Do they repeat the same strategy? If they all decide to go for the left fork again, the same result is
```

guaranteed. What if they first go for the right fork, instead? Again, same result. What if 'some' go for the right fork, while 'others' go for the left fork? Now we have some chance of progress. This is exactly where we bring in randomisation. Note that the odd/even solution described in section *15.5.1.1* is clearly one of the 'configurations' produced by a randomised solution. Next, let us look at a formal solution to the dining philosophers problem that uses randomisation.

19.4.1.2 The Lehmann-Rabin algorithm

These are the steps involved:

1. Choose a fork randomly (left or right one)
2. Wait till the chosen fork is available
3. Grab the chosen fork
4. Check if the other fork is available
5. If not, drop the grabbed fork and go back to step (1)

19.4.1.2.1 Implementation

Let us first look at the code which represents the basic 'lifecycle' for a philosopher:

```
void dining_philosopher()
{
   while (true)
   {
      contemplate();

      eat();
   }
}
```

Clearly, a halcyon existence. Before we switch focus to the internals of *eat()*, let us see how a fork is represented as an object:

```
class Fork {
   public:

      // Constructor
      Fork()
      {
         // initialise to an unused state
         busy = 0;
      }

      // Grab the fork, waiting as long as it takes
      void get()
      {
         while (true)
         {
```

```
        if (compare_and_swap(busy, 1, 0) == 0)
        {
            // Success; got fork
            return;
        }
        // No luck yet; continue to spin and try
    }
}

// Check if the fork is busy
int is_busy()
{
    return busy;
}

// Release the fork
// (invoked only by a party who holds this fork)
void put()
{
    busy = 0;
}

private:

// The shared variable associated with this resource
int busy;
};

// initialise two fork objects
Fork forks[2];
```

As it should be clear from above, each resource - i.e. fork - has an associated shared variable that can be read/modified/written by either party that shares it.

We move on to inspect the implementation of *eat()*:

```
void eat()
{
    while (true)
    {
        // Randomly choose a fork
        int fork = get_random_zero_or_one();

        // Wait till the chosen fork is available
        forks[fork].get();

        // Have obtained the chosen fork; check if the
        // other one is available. If not, drop the fork
```

```
        // that we just picked up, and try again
        if (forks[!fork].is_busy()) {
            // Release the fork that we grabbed
            forks[fork].put();

            // Go back and try again with another random
            // selection
            continue;
        }

        // Grab the second fork();
        forks[!fork].get();

        // Time to eat
        goto eat_now;
    }

eat_now:
    ...
    ...
    ...
}
```

Note that we assume the availability of a function *get_random_zero_or_one()* which returns 0 or 1 on a random basis.

19.4.1.2.2 Analysis

Even if, by pure chance, everyone decides to go for the same (say, left) fork first, they will drop that fork upon realising that the other fork is unavailable - and start again. What if this repeats, or worst case, keeps on repeating? That would obviously mean zero progress. But what are the odds? Assuming *n* philosophers, the probability of all of them picking the same fork during step (1) is obviously $1/2^n$. If that has to happen in succession, forever, we are talking about an infinite series given by $1/2^n \times 1/2^n \times 1/2^n$....an endless one, the value of which keeps approaching zero the further it goes on.

Importantly, we have not considered the scheduling aspect that is actively involved for a zero-progress situation to happen. Assuming that each 'philosopher' is executing on a different *CPU*, we will need all of them to be in exact sync; when philosopher A checks the availability of the right fork after obtaining the left fork, the neighbour on the right must be in the exact same state. If the neighbour has already found the right fork to be unavailable and has replaced the left one, philosopher A will find the right one to be available and thus make progress. Another way of looking at the requirement (for zero-progress) is that the philosophers much execute individual steps in a strict round-robin fashion. This is easier to visualise if we imagine all philosopher programs or processes being run on a single *CPU*, with each individual process being scheduled out after being allowed to execute a single step, and the operating system's scheduler following a strict round-robin scheduling policy.

19.5 Conclusion

In this chapter on resource allocation, we handled two related yet different matters. We started off with resource sharing and analysed a practical programming problem that posed the challenge of sharing an individual resource, with certain restrictions in place, by multiple parties. Having immediately arrived at a naive solution, we fixed it, and further, optimised it. Moving on to resource allocation in general, we revisited the dining philosophers problem and analysed a randomised algorithm for the same. Lastly, we presented the code for the key functions involved and finished with a brief analysis of the algorithm's characteristics.

19.6 What's next

We will revisit the problem of consensus - this time, in the context of a shared memory environment. We have already given a fair amount of attention to the *FLP* impossibility result elsewhere; we will visit a variation of the same and conclude by analysing a set of consensus algorithms where the participants communicate using shared memory.

Chapter 20. Consensus in shared memory architectures

20.1 Introduction

Having covered the topic of consensus across multiple chapters of this book, where we analysed algorithms, protocols, and related topics for asynchronous and synchronous environments, we dedicate the last chapter of the book to study the consensus problem in the context of shared memory architectures. Broadly, we will be interested in revisiting a variant of the impossibility proof which we rather exhaustively handled in chapter *10*, along with a brief look at implementing consensus algorithms for multiple shared memory models, each with a different level of capability.

20.2 Revisiting the FLP impossibility proof

Recall from section *17.6* that we deal with asynchronous algorithms for shared memory architectures in the third and final part of this book. This would imply that the *FLP* impossibility result is applicable here, just as it was when we considered asynchronous algorithms for message passing infrastructures. In fact, we will now consider a related impossibility result and attempt to present our proof in such a way that it takes into account the inter-process communication using shared memory.

Chapter *10* focused on proving that consensus is not possible if even a single failure must be tolerated - in other words, that particular discussion was all about proving the impossibility of *single-failure consensus*. In this chapter, we will focus on the impossibility of *wait-free consensus or wait-free termination*. This impossibility was proven by Hosame Hassan Abu-Amara and Michael C. Loui, and independently by Maurice Herlihy.

20.3 Impossibility of wait-free consensus

Let us formally state what we are trying to prove here:

- *For n ≥ 2, there is no algorithm in the read/write shared memory model that solves the consensus problem and guarantees wait-free termination.*

Apparently, we need to formally define 'wait-free termination' as well, so that is next:

- *Every non-failing process eventually decides.*

This is a rather loaded statement, in fact. If there are *n* processes, technically this definition allows all of them to fail. In a more realistic sense: even *n - 1* processes can fail and yet the sole survivor will output a decision. Note the parallel to Brewer's theorem (*CAP* theorem) which we visited in chapter 2. The consistency condition requires that all responses be correct irrespective of internal network outages. Similarly, the availability condition requires that each request receive a response, even if every message generated as part of the corresponding execution goes undelivered.

As far as the reference to 'read/write shared memory model' is concerned, section *17.4* has a brief introduction to the various types of shared memory models.

Now that we have the definitions in place, let us first take a broad look at how we plan to go about proving this impossibility. What follows is in many ways similar to what we have already seen in chapter *10*.

20.3.1 Plan of action

We assume to be analysing a consensus algorithm, one that is supposed to be correct (i.e. it delivers wait-free termination). The system in which the algorithm runs is an asynchronous one consisting on n nodes. The following will be the three broad steps during our attempt to prove that such an algorithm cannot exist:

1. Establish that the *initial* configuration of the system is bivalent
2. Establish that the existence of a *final* bivalent configuration is required for termination
3. Establish that a bivalent configuration can always lead to another one, thus establishing that a final bivalent configuration does not exist

Some clarifications are in order:

- Refer sections *10.4.1.1* and *10.4.1.2* for definitions of univalent and bivalent configurations
- A final bivalent configuration is one from which any step - by any process - will move the system into a univalent configuration
- Step (3) establishes a possibility where a result never happens, with the system moving from one bivalent state to another, perpetually
- Finally, the proof does not establish that the algorithm will fail always; the proof only points out that the algorithm cannot be correct always

We shall move on to the first step, then.

20.3.1.1 Initial bivalent configuration

The proof is similar to what we have seen in section *10.4.1.2*, but for the sake of completeness perhaps a different example is in order. We will consider a scenario involving coffee-loving Jane and beer-loving John. The basic story is about them going out and deciding on whether to go out for coffee or for beer. Two situations are immediately apparent:

Case 1. Jane prefers coffee, and John, for a change, prefers coffee on the day
Case 2. Jane, for a change, prefers beer on the day, and John prefers beer

The decision in the first case should be obvious: both end up going out for coffee.
The decision in the second case should be obvious, too: both end up going out for beer.

Now, let us consider a slight variation of Case 2:

Case 3: the situation is exactly the same as case 2, but the moment they are about to get out of the front door, Jane gets an urgent call from office and has to stay back home and finish some work. John alone steps out as a result and goes to have a beer or two.

Next, we consider Case 4.

Case 4: Jane wants her usual, which is coffee. However, today John wants his beer. They arrive at a decision: John defers to Jane, and they go out to have coffee.

Case 5 is minor variation of Case 4: the situation is exactly the same as Case 4, but the moment they are about to step out of the front door, Jane gets a call - just like in Case 3 - and has to stay back. John steps out alone and goes to have beer - which is expected, since that is his preference on that day, as well as most days. Further, this matches the result of Case 3, where John went out alone and had beer.

The essential idea here is to compare Case 4 with Case 5. The initial configuration was the same in both cases - both situations started off with Jane preferring coffee and John opting for beer - but the sudden 'failure' or 'disappearance' or 'non-involvement' of an entity (in case 5) ended up changing the result or decision. Case 4 ended in coffee while case 5 resulted in beer. This proves that the initial configuration was of a bivalent nature, one that contained the potential or possibility for both results. The following is to be noted carefully:

- The failure, or perceived failure, of an entity is what that produces the bivalent nature.

    - Example: perhaps Jane stayed on the phone for too long, giving John the perception that she will not be joining him, causing him to leave by the time she finished the call and came out ready to leave (we can extend this story to prevent a result, in fact: just like a couple of examples from chapter *10*)

- The very potential for a bivalent configuration is what, in turn, produces the possibility for a result-less execution.

Having established that the initial configuration is a bivalent one, we now move on to confirm or refute the possibility of a final bivalent configuration.

20.3.1.2 Final bivalent configuration

If there is no final bivalent configuration, we can let the algorithm hop from one bivalent configuration to another - in an endless fashion. Considering such a configuration, which we shall label $C1$, we can identify at least one process that takes an infinite number of steps. Let P be that process. We can also identify a set of processes that take only a finite number of steps in that execution, and let F denote the set of such processes. Now, such an execution is no different from another one, call it $C2$, where P takes an infinite number of steps while every process in F fails. In such a configuration, as per the definition of wait-free termination, P must decide. This implies that P must decide in $C1$, as well - because $C1$ and $C2$ are indistinguishable for all practical purposes - which implies that $C1$ must have a final bivalent configuration that leads to a decision.

Another approach would be to start from the end and work backwards, step by step - i.e. start from the ending configuration where a decision has happened, and go back one step at a time, each time meeting an older configuration. At some point, we have to encounter a bivalent configuration (if nothing else, the initial configuration is a bivalent one), implying the presence of a final bivalent configuration from which a univalent path or route opens, leading to a decision.

Our next step is to show that a final bivalent configuration does not exist, because any bivalent configuration *can* always lead to another bivalent configuration.

20.3.1.3 Proving the impossibility

Consider a bivalent configuration B which we assume to be the final one. If process $P0$ takes a step, assume that B goes to $B0$ which is a 0-valent state. If process $P1$ takes a step, B goes to $B1$ which is a 1-valent state.

The overall strategy for the proof is as follows:

- We allow the step by $P0$ to be immediately followed by the step from $P1$.
- In other words, $P0$ takes a step and we reach configuration $B0$; from $B0$, $P1$ takes a step, and let us call the resultant configuration $B01$.
- We assume that $P0$ takes no further steps after $B0$. We do not need to state that $P0$ fails, but just that it would appear so to every other process.
- We show that $B01$ is indistinguishable from $B0$, as far as anyone except $P0$ is concerned.
- However, the route leading in the direction of $B0$ is supposed to be 0-valent.
- At the same time, the direction of the step taken by $P1$ is supposed to be 1-valent.
- Hence we have a contradiction.
- Either the step by $P0$ leads us to a bivalent configuration, or the step by $P1$ leads us to a bivalent configuration.
- In other words, either $B0$ or $B1$ is bivalent.
- The Implication is that B is not a final bivalent configuration.

Next, let us define the concept of a 'step' in the context of a shared memory architecture. There are two possibilities:

1. Reading from a register
2. Writing to a register

If consider the step by *P0* to be a read, then obviously the step does not affect anything else except the internal configuration of *P0*. This implies that *B01* is equivalent to *B0* to everyone except *P0*. The possibility of the step by *P1* being a read is a symmetric one - we assume the step by *P0* to follow the one by *P1* and use the same argument.

What if we consider the steps by *P0* and *P1* to be write operations? There are two possibilities:

1. *P0* and *P1* write to different registers. Let *P0* write 0 to register *R0*, and *P1* write 1 to register *R1*. Consider the two possibilities where in one, *P0* takes a step first and *P1* next, and in the second, *P1* takes a step first and *P0* next. Both possibilities arrive at configurations that are indistinguishable from each other - in either case, *R0* holds 0 and *R1* holds 1. This is a contradiction because the step by *P0* was supposed to bring a 0-valent configuration while the step by *P1* was supposed to produce a 1-valent configuration.
2. *P0* and *P1* write to the same register. In this case, we consider the value written by one to be overwritten by the other. If the step by *P0* is followed by the step by *P1*, then *P1* overwrites the 0 written by *P0* with its own value, which is 1. This again implies that the step by *P0* has had no effect on anyone but itself, and that the configuration produced (from *B*) by the step from *P0* being followed by the step from *P1* is equivalent to the configuration produced (from B) by a step from *P1*. Once again, there is a contradiction.

Since we have generated contradictions for all the scenarios which we considered, we conclude that the final bivalent configuration - whose existence is required to guarantee termination - does not exist, because any bivalent configuration can be shown to lead to another bivalent configuration.

20.4 Implementing a consensus algorithm

In this section, we try and implement a consensus algorithm using different levels of capabilities available in a shared memory environment. We start off with a 2-process consensus algorithm that uses the weakest model - the *read/write* one - followed by a 2-process/*test-and-set* scenario, a 3-process/*test-and-set*, and lastly, the most capable one of the lot, the n-process/*compare-and-swap* model. In all cases, the processes communicate with each other using a single shared variable.

20.4.1 read-write model with 2 processes

So, we have two processes - *P0* and *P1* - sharing a single variable, which we will call *x*. The strategy is as follows: *x* is initialised to -1, and whoever manages to set *x* first to 1 has the final say in the decision. If *P0* sets *x*, then the decision is 0; if *P1* sets *x*, then the decision is 1.

The (obviously flawed) code follows:

```
// If x has not been modified yet
if (x == -1)
{
    // myid is 0 for process P0 and 1 for P1
    x = myid;
}

decide(x);
```

The problem is obvious: both *P0* and *P1* could find the *if()* condition to evaluate to true, and both would end up writing to *x*, and possibly arrive at different decisions.

How about a different approach, then? We will let *P0* be the one with priority, and *P1* will agree with whatever *P0* decides. The code follows:

```
// P0 gets to make the decision
if (myid == 0) {
    x = myid;
} else {
    // P1 waits for P0 to decide
    while (x == -1) {
        ; // wait till P0 updates x
    }
}

decide(x);
```

This might appear to be a viable option - till we consider what will happen if *P0* fails before it gets a chance to update *x*. A wait-free termination will not happen, because *P1* will forever be stuck waiting for *x* to be updated.

20.4.2 test-and-set model with 2 processes

So, we have two processes trying to modify a single shared variable using a *test_and_set()* utility. The idea is that who succeeds (to set the variable) gets to make the decision while the other simply agrees to the same. The code follows:

```
if (test_and_set(x) == 0)
```

```
{
    // Decision is own value
    decide(myid);
} else {
    // Decision is other value
    decide(!myid);
}
```

We shall next attempt to achieve the same result using *test_and_set()* for a set of 3 processes.

20.4.3 test-and-set model with 3 processes

Obviously, we cannot reuse the code from the previous section - because the following statement makes no sense once we have 3 processes:

```
decide(!myid);
```

The test_and_set() routine allows one process to clearly take command by setting the variable exclusively, and thus force a decision. However, the problem is with the other two processes: either process has no way of determining just who (of the other two processes) set the shared variable. For example, assume that *P0* sets *x*. Both *P1* and *P2* can detect *x* being set, but *P1* has no way of figuring out whether *P0* set *x* or if it was *P2*. Similarly, *P2* can never confirm if it was *P0* or *P1*. As a solution, we could perhaps consider the following:

```
// An array of flags that is supposed to reveal
// the decision maker's identity
int r[3] = {0, 0, 0};
...
...

...
if (test_and_set(x) == 0)
{
    // Advertise decision maker's identity
    r[myid] = 1;
    // Decision is own value
    decide(myid);
} else {
    // Iterate through the array, looking for a slot that is set
    for (int i = 0; i < 3; i++)
    {
        if (r[i])
        {
            // Found out the decision value
            decide(i);
            goto done;
        }
    }
```

```
    }
    // One could reach here, if the decision maker has not yet got
    // around to setting the corresponding slot in the array
}
```

The process that manages to set the shared variable *x* also advertises own identity by setting a corresponding variable, a corresponding slot in an array. Anyone failing to set *x* just needs to iterate through the array, looking for a slot that is set - and the index of the slot provides the identity of the decision maker, and thus the decision as well. There is a subtle race condition present above: a process failing to set the shared variable *x*, can still find no entry set in the array - because the decision maker has not yet got around to updating the array. This can be solved trivially by looping till a slot in the array is found to be set. But what if the decision maker crashes immediately after setting *x*?

20.4.4 compare-and-swap model with n processes

Compared to the previous scenarios, the *compare-and-swap* model allows us to easily solve the consensus problem with the guarantee of wait-free termination - for any number of processes. Indeed, the size of the code below reflects the same:

```
int x = -1;
...
...
...
if (compare_and_swap(x, myid, -1) == -1)
{
    // The decision maker
    decide(myid);
}
else
{
    // Someone else already made the decision
    decide(x);
}
```

Any number of failures will not disturb the wait-free termination condition because the first process that manages a *compare-and-swap* gets to force a decision.

20.4.5 Summary

To summarise, we define the *consensus number* for each of the various models which we experimented with. The consensus number for an object defines the maximum number of processes for which the consensus problem can be solved using said object. Obviously, the consensus number of the read-write model is 1, since it fails to solve the consensus problem for anything more than that. For the *test-and-set* model, the consensus number is 2, while *compare-and-swap* has no limit.

20.5 Conclusion

In the final chapter of this book, we looked at a variation of the *FLP* impossibility in the context of shared memory architectures. We formally stated the impossibility for wait-free consensus, produced the relevant and associated definitions, and proceeded to prove the impossibility through multiple steps while using an example or two. Subsequently, we switched focus to implementing consensus algorithms for different shared memory models and varying number of processes. Finally, we defined the concept of a consensus number and assigned a consensus number to each of the shared memory models that we worked with.

Bibliography

1. T. D. Chandra and S. Toueg. *Unreliable failure detectors for reliable distributed systems*, 1996.

2. M. J. Fischer, N. A. Lynch, and M. S. Paterson. *Impossibility of distributed consensus with one faulty processor*, Apr 1985

3. Marcos K. Aguilera, Sam Toueg. *The correctness proof of Ben-Or's randomised consensus algorithm*, Oct 2010

4. Maurice Herlihy. *Impossibility and Universality Results for Wait-Free synchronisation*, Jan 1988

5. T.D. Chandra and S. Toueg. *Unreliable failure detectors for asynchronous Systems*, Aug 1991

6. E. Dijkstra and C. Scholten. *Termination detection for diffusing computations*, Aug 1980

7. K. Chandy and L. Lamport. *Distributed snapshots determining global states of distributed systems*, Feb 1985

8. M. Fischer, N. Grieth and N. Lynch. *Global states of a distributed system*, May 1982

9. K. Chandy J. Misra and L. Haas. *Distributed deadlock detection*, May 1983

10. G. Bracha and S. Toueg. *A distributed algorithm for generalised deadlock detection*, 1987

11. Tushar D. Chandra Vassos, Hadzilacos and Sam Toueg. *The weakest failure detector for solving consensus*, Aug 1992

12. N. Lynch and N. Shavit. *Timing-based mutual exclusion*, Dec 1992

13. Leslie Lamport and P. M. Melliar-Smith. *synchronising clocks in the presence of faults*, Jan 1985

14. M. Fischer, N. Lynch and M. Merritt. *Easy impossibility proofs for distributed consensus problems*, 1986

15. Barbara Liskov. *Practical uses of synchronised clocks in distributed systems*, Aug 1991

16. Miguel Correia, Giuliana Santos Veronese, Nuno Ferreira Neves and Paulo Verissimo. *Byzantine consensus in asynchronous message-passing systems: a survey*, 2011

17. Leslie Lamport. *A New Solution of Dijkstra's Concurrent Programming Problem*, Jul 1973

18. Michael Ben-Or, *Another Advantage of Free Choice: Completely Asynchronous Agreement Protocols*, 1983

19. Nachum Dershowitz, D. N. Jayasimha, and Seungjoon Park. *Bounded fairness*

20. Gabriel Bracha and Sam Toueg. *Asynchronous Consensus and Broadcast Protocols*, 1985

21. Seth Gilbert and Nancy A. Lynch. *Perspectives on the CAP Theorem*, 2011

22. Leslie Lamport and P. M. Melliar-Smith. *Byzantine Clock synchronisation*, 1984

23. KIM POTTER KIHLSTROM, LOUISE E. MOSER AND P. M. MELLIAR-SMITH. *Byzantine Fault Detectors for Solving Consensus*, 2001

24. K. M. CHANDY and J. MISRA. *The Drinking Philosophers Problem*, 1984

25. Nancy A. Lynch. *A Hundred Impossibility Proofs for Distributed Computing*, 1989

26. Leslie Lamport. *Time, Clocks, and the Ordering of Events in a Distributed System*, 1978

27. Mohsen Ghaffari. *An Improved Distributed Algorithm for Maximal Independent Set*,

28. Michael Luby. *A Simple Parallel Algorithm for the Maximal Independent Set Problem*, 1985

29. R. G. GALLAGER, P. A. HUMBLET, and P.M. SPIRA. *A Distributed Algorithm for Spanning Trees*, 1983

30. Leslie Lamport. *The Part-Time Parliament*, 1998

31. ROBBERT VAN RENESSE and DENIZ ALTINBUKE. *Paxos Made Moderately Complex*, 2016

32. Jonathan Kirsch and Yair Amir. *Paxos for System Builders*, Mar 2008

33. Tushar Chandra, Robert Griesemer, Joshua Redstone. *Paxos Made Live - An Engineering Perspective*, Jun 2007

34. Leslie Lamport. *Paxos Made Simple*, Nov 2001

35. Diego Ongaro and John Ousterhout. *In Search of an Understandable Consensus Algorithm*, 2014

36. Diego Ongaro. *CONSENSUS: BRIDGING THEORY AND PRACTICE*, Aug 2014

37. Alysson Neves Bessani and Eduardo Alchieri. *A Guided Tour on the Theory and Practice of State Machine Replication*

38. Vassos Hadzilacos and Sam Toueg. *A modular approach to fault-tolerant broadcast and related problems*

39. Brian Masao Oki. *Viewstamped replication for highly available distributed systems, Aug 1988*

40. Barbara Liskov and James Cowling. *Viewstamped Replication Revisited*

41. L. Lamport, R. Shostak, and M. Pease. *The Byzantine Generals Problem*, Jul 1982

42. Jean Dollimore, Tim Kindberg, George F. Coulouris, *Distributed systems : concepts and design* (Third Edition), 2003

43. Nancy A. Lynch, *Distributed Algorithms*, 2003

44. Nicola Santoro, *Design and Analysis of Distributed Algorithms*, 2007

45. Leslie Lamport. *A Fast Mutual Exclusion Algorithm*, 1985

46. Glenn Ricart and Ashok K. Agrawala. *An Optimal Algorithm for Mutual Exclusion in Computer Networks*, 1981

47. Gary L. Peterson. *Myths about the Mutual Exclusion problem*, 1981

48. G. Tarry, *Le probl`eme des labyrinthes, Nouvelles Annales de Math´ematiques*, 1895

49. S. Toueg. *An all-pairs shortest-path distributed algorithm*, 1980

50. Kruskal, J.B. *On the shortest spanning subtree of a graph and the traveling salesman problem*, 1956

51. Danny Dolev , Maria Klawe , Michael Rodeh. *An O(n log n) Unidirectional Distributed Algorithm for Extrema Finding in a Circle*, 1982

52. Ernest Chang; Rosemary Roberts. *An improved algorithm for decentralised extrema-finding in circular configurations of processes*, 1979

53. Hirschberg, D. S.; Sinclair, J. B. *Decentralised extrema-finding in circular configurations of processors*, Nov 1980

54. Wan Fokkink. *Distributed Algorithms, an intuitive approach*, 2013

55. Andrew S. Tanenbaum and Maarten Van Steen. Distributed Systems, Principles and Paradigms, 2007

56. E. A. Akkoyunlu K. Ekanadham R. V. Huber. *SOME CONSTRAINTS AND TRADEOFFS IN THE DESIGN OF NETWORK COMMUNICATIONS*, 1975

57. Piotr Berman, Juan A. Garay, Kenneth J. Perry. *TOWARDS OPTIMAL DISTRIBUTED CONSENSUS*, 1989

Index

www.ingramcontent.com/pod-product-compliance
Lightning Source LLC
Chambersburg PA
CBHW062054050326
40690CB00016B/3092